THE OFFICIAL
HISTORY OF THE

FIFA
WORLD
CUP™

Published in 2021 by Welbeck

An Imprint of Welbeck Non-Fiction Limited, part of Welbeck Publishing Group.

20 Mortimer Street London W1T 3JW

First published by 2017 in Carlton Books

Copyright © FIFA World Football Museum 2017, 2019, 2021

A CIP catalogue record for this book is available from the British Library

ISBN 978-1-80279-088-7

Created by: FIFA World Football Museum
Translated from French to English by: First Edition Translations
Publisher: Welbeck Publishing

Printed in the United Kingdom

10 9 8 7 6 5 4 3 2 1

MIX
Paper from
responsible sources
FSC
www.fsc.org   FSC® C007785

THE OFFICIAL HISTORY OF THE

FIFA WORLD CUP™

SECOND EDITION

FIFA WORLD™
FOOTBALL MUSEUM

WELBECK

Contents

Foreword

There is simply nothing like the FIFA World Cup. There is certainly no other sporting competition – and arguably no single event in any area of society – with the power to trigger the passion of so many different people around the whole planet.

I am not referring only to those few weeks during which the tournament is staged, when the convergence of passion and excitement overflows at once. The magic lies in how the outcome of that handful of matches somehow determines what millions of human beings will feel for years to come. It is a tournament that creates archetypes and hones characters. It defines images and, eventually, writes true history.

Football would not be what it is today if it was not for the FIFA World Cup. There would be no Lionel Messi and no Diego Armando Maradona without Guillermo Stábile. No Neymar and no Pelé without Leônidas da Silva. No Philipp Lahm and no Franz Beckenbauer without Fritz Walter. I could go on forever; we all could. This is exactly what this competition triggers in us, football fans.

In 2018, the unforgettable FIFA World Cup in Russia kicked off only a few days after the 90th anniversary of what appeared to be a rather ordinary day for football: 28 May 1928. This was when the 29 member associations that composed FIFA at the time gathered in Amsterdam for the 18th FIFA Congress and decided that it would be a good idea to organize the maiden edition of the FIFA World Cup two years later. Little did they know that they were discreetly sowing the seeds of what would go on to evolve into the greatest show on earth.

This is how every work of art starts: with a single brushstroke. As the governing body of football, we are the custodians of the FIFA World Cup's aura, and it is our duty to preserve the memories of each step that resulted in football's masterpiece as we know it. This is what this book is about. I hope you enjoy it.

Yours in football,

Gianni Infantino
FIFA President

◀ **The First World Cup Final**
Montevideo's Estadio Centenario, venue for the first World Cup Final.

Introduction

▲ Champions of the World
Before 1930, the winners of the Olympic Football Tournament were the world champions. This trophy, presented to the winners in 1908, 1912, and 1920, was commissioned by The Football Association in 1906 at a cost of £100. At 59.5 centimetres tall, it was more than double the height of the Jules Rimet Cup. The use of Nike, the winged Greek goddess of victory, and the globe on which she stands, gives the trophy a resonance with the two World Cup trophies that followed.

The 2018 FIFA World Cup in Russia marked the 88th anniversary of this famous sporting event. And yet association football – the code of football of which FIFA is the world governing body – has been around for over 150 years. Since 1863 to be precise. So why did it take so long for the world's most popular sport to have a world championship?

The answer is that it didn't! 1930 may mark the birth of the World Cup, but the origins of the tournament go back to the start of the 20th century and the creation of FIFA in 1904, because association football's first world championship took place just four years later in 1908…

FIFA is founded and claims the right to organize an international championship

On 21 May 1904, three delegates – C.A.W. Hirschman from the Netherlands, Switzerland's Victor Schneider and Denmark's Ludvig Sylow – joined the French trio of Alphonse Fringnet, André Espir, and Robert Guérin in a modest room at the headquarters of the USFSA in Paris to witness the creation of FIFA. These were humble beginnings compared to the IOC, when ten years earlier 78 delegates and an audience of 2,000 had gathered in the amphitheatre of the Sorbonne to witness the rebirth of the Olympics. But FIFA's future power lay in article 9 of its new statutes:

"Only the International Union has the right to organize an international championship."

For the first year FIFA existed on paper only. The event that ensured its early development and success was a conference organized in 1905 by The Football Association in England. It was staged at the Crystal Palace ground in Sydenham, South London to coincide with the England – Scotland match of April that year. FIFA sent a delegation that included Hirschman, Guérin and most importantly the Belgian aristocrat Baron Edouard de Lavelaye. A sporting colossus on the continent, Lavelaye used his renowned diplomacy to persuade the English that the future lay in the body created 11 months earlier in Paris. He had been asked by FIFA in 1904 to approach Frederick Wall and Dan Woolfall, two key figures at The FA with a view to getting the English on board. And it worked.

At the 1905 conference, Lavelaye received the good news in one of the grand staterooms at the Crystal Palace ground, as he later recalled: "Mr. Woolfall, who should have been the first president of the real FIFA, informed us, to our great pleasure, that our proposals had been taken up. Within 36 hours the embryo FIFA had assumed shape and was destined to become, within a very short time the powerful organization over which the President can truly say, the sun never sets…"

The failed world championship of 1906

Two months later FIFA held a second congress in Paris, and it was here that the first plans were laid for an international championship. Four groups were chosen, the winners of which would travel to Switzerland during Easter 1906 to play for a cup donated by Victor Schneider of the Swiss association. They were:

1. The British International Championship.
2. Spain, France, Belgium, and the Netherlands.
3. Switzerland, Italy, Austria, and Hungary.
4. Germany, Denmark, and Sweden.

The intentions were noble, but the practicalities of playing the games proved insurmountable. At the time of the 1905 Paris Congress just 11 international matches had been played on mainland Europe – six of those between Austria and Hungary. Germany, Denmark, Italy and Sweden had yet to field an international team and it would be 15 years before Spain took to the field. So it was perhaps unsurprising that when Dan Woolfall became FIFA President at the FIFA Congress in Berne in June 1906, he observed "FIFA was not yet founded on sufficiently stable bases. One had not the assurance that there existed in each country only one Association governing football, and that in order to establish an international championship, one must be assured that all the Associations play in accordance with the same Laws of the Game."

However, a ready-made solution was to soon emerge…

The Football Association organizes the first world championship

Following the withdrawal of Rome as the host city of the 1908 Olympic Games, London was asked to step in and The FA was tasked with organizing a football tournament by the British Olympic Committee. Woolfall, in his joint position as treasurer of The FA and President of FIFA, took control – and the pattern of international competition was set. For the next two decades, the Football Tournament of the Olympic Games would be football's world championship.

London was not the first Olympic Games to feature association football, but it was the first to have a properly organized competition involving national teams. The regulations allowed each country to enter four teams in order that the four British nations could send separate sides – as happened in the hockey tournament. But the Scots, Irish and Welsh declined the offer. And so it was the England amateur team that entered the 1908 Olympic football tournament as perhaps the hottest favourites of any football tournament ever.

The England amateurs had been created in the aftermath of the 1906 Berne FIFA Congress. Anxious to play against the English, delegates at the Congress asked The FA to send the national team to play matches on the continent. Fearing a gulf in standards, The FA instead created the England amateur team to tour abroad. Over the two years before the Olympics, matches were played against France, the Netherlands, Belgium, Germany and Sweden, all resulting in big wins for England. It was not expected to be any different in the tournament itself, and the England amateurs comfortably took the gold medal.

The most extraordinary story of the tournament, however, was the performance of Denmark, who marked their first ever international with a 9-0 victory over a France 'B' team. In the semi-final they then beat the France 'A' team 17-1, with Sofus Nielsen scoring an extraordinary 10 goals, before losing 2-0 to England in the Final.

The age of the amateur

The winners of the 1908 Olympic football tournament successfully defended their title four years later, but this was a team with an identity crisis. The 1908 report referred to it as the United Kingdom, while the 1912 report calls it Great Britain. The reality was that it was neither. At the meeting of the International Football Association Board at Bundoran in Ireland in 1909, the Scottish

▲ The First World Championship Final
Played at the White City Stadium in London, the 1908 Olympic Football Final saw England Amateurs beat Denmark 2-0 to become the first World Champions of association football. The extract above, from *the Illustrated Sporting and Dramatic News*, appeared a week after the game.

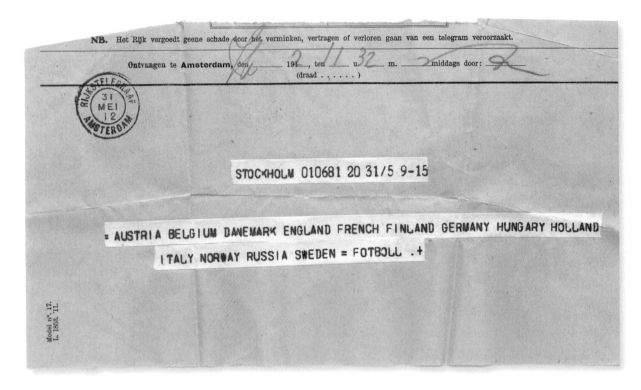

NB. Het Rijk vergoedt geene schade door het verminken, vertragen of verloren gaan van een telegram veroorzaakt.

Ontvangen te **Amsterdam**, den _____ 19__, ten ____ u. ____ m. ____ middags door: ____
(draad . . . . . .)

STOCKHOLM 010681 20 31/5 9-15

= AUSTRIA BELGIUM DANEMARK ENGLAND FRENCH FINLAND GERMANY HUNGARY HOLLAND
ITALY NORWAY RUSSIA SWEDEN = FOTBOLL .+

1912 Telegram
Telegram sent by FIFA's
C.A.W. Hirschman
confirming the list
of teams taking part
in the 1912 Olympic
Football Tournament.

▶ **FIFA World Football
Museum collection.**

representatives let it be known in no uncertain terms that they resented the team using the name United Kingdom. As such, the following resolution was passed:

"… we wish to point out that such a title was a misnomer, Scotland being without representation. We desire to protest one National body in the British Isles being termed the United Kingdom, or playing as such without the consent of the other three National Associations."

And so, without this consent forthcoming in 1912, it was again the England amateurs who travelled to Stockholm to play in the second Olympic football tournament. The Stockholm Olympics of 1912 can be regarded as the first major gathering of football nations. Eleven teams were present, compared to just five four years earlier in London, among them an Italian team coached by Vittorio Pozzo and an Austrian team managed by Hugo Meisl. The two met in the semi-final of a consolation tournament organized for teams knocked out before the semi-finals. Meisl won on this occasion but Pozzo would get his revenge in a World Cup semi-final 22 years later.

England were not as overwhelming favourites as four years earlier (in 1910 the Danes had become the first team to beat the English amateurs) – but they still retained the title, after beating Denmark 4-2 in the Final. Indeed, the gold, silver, and bronze medals all ended up in the same hands with the Dutch beating Finland to once again take third place. The Final of the consolation tournament was won 3-0 by Hungary over neighbours Austria.

Two years after the Stockholm Games, the Olympic football tournament was given the stamp of approval at the 1914 FIFA Congress in Christiana when it was recognized as the official amateur world championship. But it would be six years before the next tournament was played…

FIFA in crisis
The immediate postwar years were deeply troubled times for FIFA. Two weeks before the armistice of November 1918, Dan Woolfall

was taken ill and died, leaving FIFA without a president for nearly two and a half years. Sweden's Ludvig Kornerup stepped in as acting president but was immediately faced with a serious challenge from Belgium, the four British associations, Luxembourg and France, who wanted to ban all contact with Germany and its allies and who all threatened to set up a rival federation. Kornerup and Hirschman resisted these calls, and not for the first or last time, the quiet diplomacy of Hirschman, FIFA's secretary-treasurer, was to prove crucial and a damaging split was avoided.

It was against this background that fourteen nations gathered in Antwerp for the 1920 Olympic football tournament, with Czechoslovakia and Yugoslavia playing their first games as newly created nations. There were also international debuts for three other countries: Spain, Greece, and Egypt, the first non-European participants. Hosts Belgium became the first non-British world champions after a controversial Final against Czechoslovakia which they won 2–0. Unhappy with the referee and an intimidating crowd, the Czechs walked off just before half-time and the match had to be abandoned.

The tournament used the peculiar Bergvall knockout system, where the losing finalists would have to play-off against teams knocked out in previous rounds in a separate tournament for the silver medal. Czechoslovakia were barred from taking part while France had left for home, so Spain took silver by beating the Netherlands, who finished with bronze for the third tournament running.

The age of the shamateur
Five months after the 1920 Antwerp Games, Frenchman Jules Rimet was elected as the new president of FIFA. At the first FIFA Congress for nine years (Geneva 1923), the number of affiliated nations leapt from 20 to 32. The landscape of world football was evolving and with that came fresh challenges, the most significant being the changing status of players in Continental Europe and South America. Until the early 1920s, players had been overwhelmingly

◄ **More than just a game**
The post first world
war era saw a surge
in interest in association
football around the world.
Between 1920
and 1930, membership
of FIFA jumped from
20 to 47 member associa-
tions and games often
aroused fierce passion.
The 1920 Olympic Final
between Belgium
and Czechoslovakia in
Antwerp, left, was
abandoned after the
Czechoslovaks walked off
just before half-time,
complaining about the
intimidating crowd and
the referee. Belgium were
winning the game 2–0.
The result stood.

amateur, with professionals restricted to the British Isles, where the practice had been accepted since 1885. This worked in Great Britain, but the conditions for a professional league were just not in place in much of the rest of the world, with a major problem being the distances players had to travel to play matches. For wealthy players of private means this was not an issue, but working-class footballers, who were beginning to take up the sport in numbers, were often faced with the prospect of losing wages by playing football.

The strict amateur regulations were also encouraging the practice of illegal inducements to players by clubs wanting to attract the best talent. So the 1920s ushered in the era of a third unregulated class of player – the 'shamateur' – and the related debate about whether players should receive 'broken time' payments to compensate for lost wages.

Some saw this as a good thing. At the 1924 FIFA Congress in Paris, held just before the Olympic Games, Belgium's Rodolphe Seeldrayers spoke out. "If a workman receiving money for broken time could be under severe control of a good amateur, it would not be right to let his wife and family suffer because he lost money through playing football." Others, like Austria's Hugo Meisl, viewed the idea as dangerous. He argued that there would not be a level playing field between the different types of player, and noted that the England amateur team had withdrawn from the 1924 Olympic football tournament in Paris, unhappy at the prospect of playing against players who were professional in all but name.

Uruguay dazzle the world

Thankfully, the absence of the English amateurs, along with the still uninvited Germans and Austrians, did little to diminish the status of the tournament in Paris. It turned out to be an extravaganza, accounting for over a third of the revenue for the whole games and much of the entertainment. It was the first Olympic football tournament organized entirely by FIFA, and 22 countries took part

– the largest gathering of football nations until the 1982 FIFA World Cup in Spain – many of them taking their first steps in international football. It was also the first Olympic football tournament with teams from the Americas, especially Uruguay, who dazzled the Parisian crowds on their way to Olympic gold. They beat Yugoslavia 7–0, the USA 3–0, hosts France 5–1, the Netherlands 2–1, and Switzerland 3–0 in the Final – the first part of a unique hat-trick of world titles.

The professionals

At its 1924 Congress on the eve of the Olympic Games in Paris, FIFA had recognized professionalism, but the definition of what constituted an amateur footballer was proving far more problematic. As a result the four years before the 1928 Olympics in Amsterdam was marked by a fierce dispute with the IOC which almost led to the withdrawal of football from the Olympic programme. It was a dispute that would ultimately shape the football world of today.

In the aftermath of the Paris Games, the Vienna-based league in Austria was the first outside the UK to turn professional. It was soon followed by Hungary and Czechoslovakia, both of whom were fearful of losing their best players to Austria if they didn't. But it wasn't just the rise of professionalism which threatened Olympic football as the sport's world championship, it was the question of broken-time payments which became a major issue in the summer of 1925 as the sporting world gathered in Prague, first for the FIFA Congress, and then the IOC Congress.

In Prague, FIFA took a decision to allow broken time payments to players. Congress also voted to accept a resolution which proved to be the basis for the idea of a World Cup open to all players:

"In international matches and competitions the teams of clubs or national associations may meet each other, whatever might be the status of their players (amateurs, non-amateurs

◄ **Cornelius August Wilhelm Hirschman**
C.A.W. Hirschman can be considered as the 'father' of the World Cup. He was the first to come up with the idea of an international championship, in 1902, and was the key figure in the creation of the World Cup 28 years later.

or professionals) provided authorization from the respective national associations be obtained."

This was revolutionary. Amateurs and professionals were used to playing among themselves. By breaking down these barriers, FIFA was challenging the ideology of the IOC. The decision wasn't universally accepted and feelings ran high. The Swiss and Swedish delegates even walked out, complaining about the way the discussion was being handled!

After the FIFA delegates had returned home, the IOC delegates arrived in Prague and promptly fell into line behind the hardline amateur definition promoted by their new president, Henri Baillet-Latour. The IOC Congress voted that players who had been professional at any time in any sport would not be allowed to compete in the Olympics and nor would those who had received compensation for lost salaries. In other words, only pure amateurs would be invited to the Olympic Games.

Rimet vs Baillet-Latour – the match of the century
The decisions of FIFA and the IOC in Prague would set Rimet and Baillet-Latour on a collision course which would lead to the first World Cup five years later. But in the meantime, the Dutch organizers of the 1928 Games, fearing a financial disaster, appealed to Baillet-Latour to come up with a solution that would allow football to be played at the Games.

Swedish IOC member Sigfrid Edström summed up the feelings of many in the Olympic movement when he wrote to Baillet-Latour in June 1927: "If we should give in to the football people, we must give in to everybody else and in that case we might as well open up the Olympic Games for the best man whether he be professional or not."

Heaven forbid! But Rimet held all the cards and he was quite prepared for football to be excluded from the Olympics and may even have wanted it. That was because during the course of 1926, he and Hirschman discussed reviving Hirschman's plans for an international championship, originally put forward in 1902 when the Dutchman had written to The FA about creating an international federation.

At a meeting of the FIFA Executive Committee on 10 December 1926, Hirschman was tasked with gauging opinion amongst the national associations about whether they would support an international championship and what form it should take. He set up an Advisory Committee under the chairmanship of Switzerland's Gabriel Bonnet, and discussions about creating a World Cup were launched in Zurich on 25 February 1927.

On 8 August that year, Baillet-Latour caved in to pressure from the Dutch organizers of the 1928 Olympics, and allowed broken-time payments for football only, with the proviso that the money would be paid not to the players but to their employers. This was a sticking-plaster solution and was hugely unpopular amongst the members of the IOC like Edstrom. Baillet-Latour indicated that the 1930 IOC Congress would make a final decision on broken-time – and the general view was that there would be no football at the 1932 Olympics in Los Angeles.

Jules Rimet understood the times he lived in perhaps better than anyone else and he had a clear vision of how he wanted FIFA and world football to progress. Also, he was a pragmatist, insisting that along with amateurs and professionals that there was a third way. "There is an intermediate class," he stated, "that of the athlete who, without receiving remuneration for his efforts, needs to receive compensation in terms of the time that he invests into practising sport…"

Rimet also noted that it wasn't just the issue of broken time that prompted his desire to create a World Cup run by FIFA, stating, "It is a little odd that our sport should be subject, for its only worldwide competition, to the definitions, the principles, formulas and the beliefs imposed by another body. It is illogical that football, knowing that it constitutes a major element of the financial appeal of the Olympics, should not derive even the merest benefit from it."

The creation of the World Cup
Two days before the football tournament at the 1928 Olympic Games, the FIFA Congress taking place in Amsterdam held an historic vote on the following resolution:

"The Congress decides to organize in 1930 a competition open to the representative teams of all affiliated National Associations."

Denmark, Estonia, Finland, Norway and Sweden voted against, but 23 countries voted for it and the World Cup was born.

FIFA had gone against the prevailing sporting ethos by creating a tournament open to everyone and not just a privileged few. It would be another 60 years before the IOC followed suit.

In the event, the football tournament at Amsterdam more than lived up to expectations. The Uruguayans were joined by an American contingent including neighbours Argentina, Chile, Mexico and the USA in what was almost certainly a truer test of international strength than the World Cup that followed two years later. But the outcome was the same – a Final between Uruguay and Argentina, won by Uruguay.

The World Cup takes shape

For world football, the Amsterdam Olympics signalled the end of a significant chapter in the history of the game. Football was the first major sport to break away from the Olympics and organize its own world championship. Swimming didn't follow suit until 1973, with athletics a decade later in 1983, and many would still regard the Olympics as the more important for both. Not so in football.

Instead, FIFA put its whole weight behind organizing its first open world championship. The World Cup Advisory Committee which had met in February 1927, morphed into the first World Cup Organizing Committee, chaired by Switzerland's Gabriel Bonnet with Henri Delaunay from France, Felix Linnemann from Germany, and Austria's Hugo Meisl.

That 1927 meeting, also attended by Rimet, Hirschman and Italy's Zanetti, had discussed a number of ideas before submitting three proposals to the FIFA Executive Committee. Firstly, a European Cup played every two years in groups, the top teams from which would qualify for a World Cup every four years. Secondly, a similar organization to the first but with a knock-out format instead of a group system. And thirdly, two World Championships, one for amateurs and one for professionals, with the professional World Cup taking place every two years.

At the next meeting in September 1928, also in Zurich, those ideas were dropped in favour of a single knock-out competition – with a second division if there were more than 16 entries – proposed by Hirschman and backed by Rimet and Bonnet. The committee also came to the conclusion that the whole tournament should be played in just one country.

Destination Uruguay

This was the proposal which was put to the 1929 FIFA Congress in Barcelona, where Hungary, the Netherlands, Sweden, Italy and Uruguay put themselves forward as hosts. Having been presented with the financial requirements and obligations, the Netherlands withdrew. The Swedes then retired in favour of Italy before the Argentinian delegate Dr Adrián Beccar Varela made an impassioned plea for Uruguay based on their two Olympic successes; the fact that the tournament would coincide with the centenary of Uruguay's constitution; the enormous development of football in the country; and that the whole of South America would share the honour of hosting the inaugural World Cup.

It worked. Hungary withdrew, as did the Italians "in order to demonstrate its feelings of sympathy for Uruguay where so many Italians worked and played football." The Uruguayan delegate Dr Enrique Buero thanked Congress for their support, especially the Italians and the Spanish, and set the dates for the tournament: 15 July to 15 August 1930.

However, when push came to shove twelve months later, that support quickly evaporated. In particular, Spain and Italy were conspicuous by their absence when the Conte Verde set sail from Barcelona to Montevideo with the FIFA President on board. Of the 16 European nations who had voted for Uruguay at the Barcelona Congress, just two – France and Belgium – bothered to take part.

▲ **Destination Europe**
Uruguay dominated the 1924 and 1928 Olympic Football Tournaments, winning gold in both. Here they were photographed travelling to Europe in 1928. Scandalously, most European teams failed to make the reverse journey two years later for the first World Cup.

1930

FIFA's plans for a world championship outside the confines of the Olympic Games came to fruition in 1930. Uruguay was chosen as the host nation in honour of its centenary celebrations and the Olympic gold medals of 1924 and 1928, but only four European nations made the journey by ship to South America. In the newly built Estadio Centenario in Montevideo, Uruguay won the first World Cup by beating Argentina 4–2 in the final.

Uruguay embarks on an adventure

ORGANIZING the first-ever football World Cup required a spirit of adventure and, in view of the scale of the task, Uruguay got the nod ahead of its few European competitors. The small South American nation had put itself on the global map through football, having won the 1924 and 1928 Olympic tournaments in Paris and Amsterdam respectively. The impact of those triumphs was resounding and even helped unite the fledgling nation. The Uruguayan government, its diplomats (led by Enrique Buero), the City of Montevideo and the country's football association joined forces to convince FIFA of their project's soundness. They made the World Cup the showpiece event of the centenary celebrations commemorating the country's first constitution (18 July 1830). Moreover, the stadium which they constructed for the occasion symbolized both the young nation's history and its recent sporting successes, with the stands of the Estadio Centenario named Colombes and Amsterdam in homage to their Olympic victories. All that was lacking now was a World Cup triumph to cap what would be regarded as an entire nation's work.

◄ Uruguayan players Fernandez, Cea and Scarone celebrate their team's victory in the first World Cup Final.

► View of the Estadio Centenario, built for this first World Cup.

URUGUAY 1930

The great crossing

▼ FIFA President, Jules Rimet, waves to the crowds as he disembarks the Conte Verde.

O N 19 JUNE 1930, the *SS Conte Verde* sailed into the bay of Villefranche-sur-Mer in southern France. Owned by Italian shipping company Lloyd Sabaudo, the transatlantic liner welcomed aboard a band of young men with a sporty air. They were the members of the French delegation en route to the inaugural football World Cup, which was due to kick off 24 days later in Uruguay. With them travelled an elegant, white-haired gentleman – none other than FIFA President Jules Rimet. In his luggage was an object that would soon set the entire world dreaming, the lovely winged trophy dreamt up by the sculptor Abel Lafleur. While on board, the French passengers met the players of the Romanian national team, who had come aboard in Genoa. Romania's commitment to the World Cup had been one of the first acts of the new king, Carol II. The *SS Conte Verde* then headed for Barcelona, where it picked up the Belgium team. Yugoslavia, meanwhile, the fourth European nation that travelled to Uruguay, departed from Marseilles aboard the *Florida*. Described in depth by Jules Rimet in his memoirs, the voyage resembled a pleasure cruise, with parties, balls and… training sessions all on the programme. After stopovers in Lisbon, the Canaries, Rio and Buenos Aires, the ship finally docked in Montevideo on 5 July. Eight days later, the World Cup got underway.

The cover of an unofficial set of postcards from the finals. Note the Bulgarian flag, bottom left!

▲ FIFA World Football Museum collection.

Group stage

GROUP 1	
FRA	4–1	MEX
ARG	1–0	FRA
CHI	3–0	MEX
CHI	1–0	FRA
ARG	6–3	MEX
ARG	3–1	CHI

	W	D	L	+	–	PTS
ARG	3	0	0	10	4	**6**
CHI	2	0	1	5	3	**4**
FRA	1	0	2	4	3	**2**
MEX	0	0	3	4	13	**0**

GROUP 2	
YUG	2–1	BRA
YUG	4–0	BOL
BRA	4–0	BOL

	W	D	L	+	–	PTS
YUG	2	0	0	6	1	**4**
BRA	1	0	1	5	2	**2**
BOL	0	0	2	0	8	**0**

GROUP 3	
ROU	3–1	PER
URU	1–0	PER
URU	4–0	ROU

	W	D	L	+	–	PTS
URU	2	0	0	5	0	**4**
ROU	1	0	1	3	5	**2**
PER	0	0	2	1	4	**0**

GROUP 4	
USA	3–0	BEL
USA	3–0	PAR
PAR	1–0	BEL

	W	D	L	+	–	PTS
USA	2	0	0	6	0	**4**
PAR	1	0	1	1	3	**2**
BEL	0	0	2	0	4	**0**

Knockout stages

SEMI-FINAL	
URU	6–1	YUG

SEMI-FINAL	
ARG	6–1	USA

FINAL	
URU	4–2	ARG

ARG BEL BOL BRA
CHI FRA MEX PAR
PER ROU URU USA
YUG

13 TEAMS

18
MATCHES PLAYED

1
CARDS

590 549
SPECTATORS

OFFICIAL POSTER

URUGUAY
WINNERS

×8

GUILLERMO STABILE
LEADING GOALSCORER

3.9
AVERAGE GOALS
PER MATCH

T-MODEL
OFFICIAL MATCH BALL

One city, three stadiums

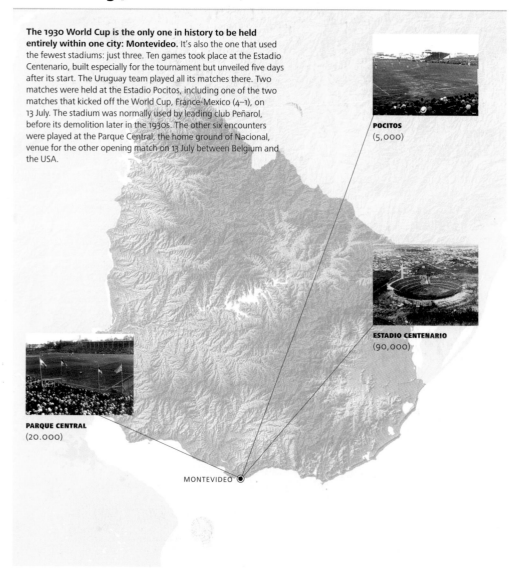

The **1930 World Cup is the only one in history to be held entirely within one city: Montevideo.** It's also the one that used the fewest stadiums: just three. Ten games took place at the Estadio Centenario, built especially for the tournament but unveiled five days after its start. The Uruguay team played all its matches there. Two matches were held at the Estadio Pocitos, including one of the two matches that kicked off the World Cup, France-Mexico (4–1), on 13 July. The stadium was normally used by leading club Peñarol, before its demolition later in the 1930s. The other six encounters were played at the Parque Central, the home ground of Nacional, venue for the other opening match on 13 July between Belgium and the USA.

POCITOS
(5,000)

ESTADIO CENTENARIO
(90,000)

PARQUE CENTRAL
(20.000)

MONTEVIDEO

Europe's big boys stay away

Uruguay was selected to host the first FIFA World Cup at the 1929 FIFA Congress in Barcelona. Italy and Spain, also candidates at one point, had withdrawn their own bids and had got behind the Uruguayan bid. But when the time came to register their national teams, the majority of European countries opted out, citing excessive distance, cost and risk. So Europe's leading football nations did not make the voyage to South America. The most notable absentees were Austria and its *Wunderteam,* the British teams, Spain and their star goalkeeper Ricardo Zamora, Hungary, Czechoslovakia and Italy – the best-performing European team at the 1928 Olympics. Jules Rimet, FIFA's French president, personally went to great pains to convince his compatriots to take part. The South American nations, who had backed Uruguay's bid, were in attendance, but not with all of their star players. Brazil, for instance, sent a team with no players from São Paulo state, due to a dispute between the associations from Sao Paulo and those from Rio. The legendary striker Arthur Friedenreich – the man who netted 1,239 goals – did not make the trip and the Brazil team did not fully reflect the country's genuine footballing strength at the time. Finally, Uruguay's supporters were disappointed by the absence of their renowned goalkeeper Andrés Mazali, a double Olympic champion in 1924 and 1928. During their World Cup preparations, Mazali had disobeyed team orders by leaving the hotel at night and scaling the wall to go and hug his wife and child. The coach Alberto Suppici suspended him and replaced him with Enrique Ballestrero. Mazali would not become a world champion.

◀ The French team before their match against Mexico at the Estadio Pocitos.

Deşu's lightning opener

14 JULY 1930

ROMANIA 3–1 **PERU**

DEŞU 1	SOUZA 75
STANCIU 79	
KOVACS 89	

ON 14 JULY at the Estadio Pocitos, Romania and Peru faced each other in their opening World Cup games. In just the 50th second, Romanian forward Adalbert Deşu opened the scoring on what was his fifth international appearance. Before the tournament, he had already scored twice for his country, the first against Bulgaria on his debut in 1929. The Peruvian keeper whom he beat in the first minute was winning his first cap. Juan Valdivieso, the 20-year-old shot-stopper from Alianza Lima, would pick the ball out of the net twice more during the match (1–3), which also saw the first player to be sent off in a World Cup, Peru's captain Plácido Galindo receiving his marching orders 20 minutes before the end. Replaced by Jorge Pardón for the second match, Valdivieso never made another World Cup appearance, although he did appear at the 1936 Olympic tournament.

"It'll be great fun with all the lads!"

13 JULY 1930

FRANCE 4–1 **MEXICO**

LAURENT 19	CARRENO 70
LANGILLER 40	
MASCHINOT 43, 87	

DURING ONE of the World Cup's two opening matches on 13 July, French striker Lucien Laurent, who at the time played semi-professionally for FC Sochaux while holding down a day job, scored the first goal in the fledgling tournament's history. In 2001, he shared his memories of that day with the magazine *France Football*, recalling the move that led to his goal as though it were yesterday: "Ernest Libérati broke free down the wing and then cut back a cross to me about 16 metres out. I hit it first time and bang! It nestled in the top corner!" But Laurent said he never felt as though he'd made history, especially at the time, as he and his teammates had no inkling of just how big the football World Cup was going to become. "We gave each other a bit of a high five on our way back to the centre circle, but that was it," he explained. In those days, we weren't in the habit of putting our shirts over our heads after

scoring a goal. Just as well, as it would have been tricky; our shirts were so tight! All of us just saw it as a big international tournament that had been organized by invitation. When I got my call-up, I said to myself: nice, it will be great fun with all the lads. I was mainly thinking about the journey, being on the boat and discovering distant lands."

In 1990, as the first-ever goal scorer at a football World Cup, Lucien Laurent was invited to Rome for the FIFA World Cup draw in Italy. "I was surrounded by world champions such as Pelé, Beckenbauer and Rossi, along with several famous English and Argentine players. There I was, little old Lulu, wondering what I was doing among all these legends. It was only then that it became widely known in France that the first goal scorer in World Cup history lived in Besançon in the Doubs region!" Lucien Laurent died there on 11 April 2005, aged 97.

A festival of penalties

On 19 July, the Estadio Centenario hosted two Group 1 ties, Chile-France (1–0) and then Argentina-Mexico (6–3). A total of four penalties were awarded during these two encounters, with the French No.1 Alex Thépot becoming the first goalkeeper to save a penalty in a World Cup match when he kept out the unfortunate Carlos Vidal's effort. In the second match, Mexico's Manuel Rosas (18 years and 93 days old) scored one spot-kick but missed another (although he did score from the rebound), while Argentina's Fernando Paternóster saw his penalty saved by Mexico's keeper Oscar Bonfiglio.

▼ Mexican keeper Óscar Bonfiglio dives for a shot from Argentina's Guillermo Stábile.

◄ The two captains, Manuel Ferreira (left, Argentina) and Guillermo Subiabre (right, Chile), swap pennants before the match.

► Peruvian goalkeeper Jorge Pardon catches the ball in front of Uruguay's Pedro Cea.

Monti sparks a brawl

22 JULY 1930		
ARGENTINA 3–1 CHILE		
STABILE 12, 13, EVARISTO 51	SUBIABRE 15	

DURING THE Argentina-Chile match (3–1), Argentine Luis Monti made a crunching challenge on the Chilean Casimiro Torres. The Belgian match referee, John Langenus, recalled what happened next in his memoirs (*En sifflant par le monde*): "The whistle was blown for the foul and everything seemed to be under control. I saw the Chilean player whom Monti had clattered walk calmly towards his opponent, touch his head and give him a stroke! It seemed as if there were no hard feelings, but in a flash, the Chilean grabbed hold of Monti's head with one hand and, with the other, delivered a vicious uppercut. Then all hell broke loose! All at once, every Argentine player seemed to throw themselves upon the nearest Chilean and engage in 11 separate boxing matches, but it was definitely not Queensbury rules as there was quite a bit of kicking! There were bloody noses everywhere and some of the players were injured. The police intervened and, all the while, the photographers kept snapping away at the combatants. It was outrageous. What a way to behave on such an occasion. Eventually, order was restored, cuts were bandaged and a truce was agreed. Going by the book, all of the players should have been sent off and the match cancelled, but other countries have other ways of doing things! Such an appalling incident had taken place, but a team was still needed to contest the semi-final. So play eventually resumed and the players on both sides played out the rest of the match as calmly and sportingly as if nothing at all had happened. Argentina won it 3–1 and the Chileans even went to congratulate their opponents!"

On 17 July 1930, American forward Bert Patenaude bagged a hat-trick against Paraguay, the first registered by any player at a World Cup. He also became the first player (of five) to score all three goals in a 3–0 victory.

Referees who were coaches

Bolivia's coach Ulises Saucedo actually doubled as a referee at the tournament. He took charge in the Argentina-Mexico match (6–3) and was also a linesman at the Uruguay-Argentina final (4–2). In the first of those two games, Saucedo was assisted by Costel Rădulescu… the Romanian coach. In 1936, the latter was involved in the Olympic Games at Garmisch-Partenkirchen… as a competitor in the bobsleigh event!

Castro gives Uruguay reason to cheer

18 JULY 1930		
URUGUAY 1–0 PERU		
CASTRO 60		

ON 18 JULY 1930, the Republic of Uruguay marked the official celebration of its centenary by unveiling the vast stadium that would serve as the majestic setting for the first football World Cup final. To mark the event, the 13 participating delegations paraded with their flags raised. But for the party to be complete, the host nation needed to win their opening match. Against a dogged Peru, the *Celeste* and their 60,000 supporters had to wait for an hour before, in the 60th minute, Nacional's inside-right, Héctor Castro, scored his side's opening goal. The goal was historic in more ways than one: it was the first scored at the Estadio Centenario and it was Uruguay's first at a World Cup. Nicknamed *El Manco* (*the one-armed man*) – he had lost his right hand aged 13 while using an electric saw, Castro was no newcomer to football's global stage. An international since 1923, he had played a key role in his country's South American Championship triumph in 1926 (he scored six goals). He had also tasted victory at the 1928 Olympic Games, where he found the back of the net against Germany (4–1) and played in the first of the two finals against Argentina (1–1). In 1930, he also scored another iconic goal, the fourth of the final, that helped secure the world title for Uruguay. In 1935, his international career ended on yet another high with a second South American Championship. In all, he had netted 18 goals in just 25 appearances for the Uruguay national team.

▲ The Yugoslav keeper, Milovan Jakšić, saves the ball under pressure from Uruguay's Santos Iriarte.

▶ The Uruguayans, gathered around a radio set to listen to the match report during the competition's group stage.

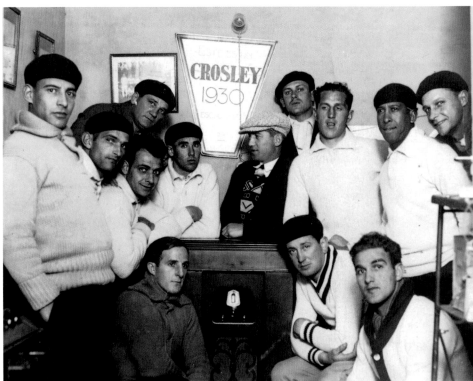

Cea, Uruguay's "Basque" striker

27 JULY 1930

URUGUAY 🏴 6–1 🏴 **YUGOSLAVIA**

CEA 18, 67, 72	VUJADINOVIC 4
ANSELMO 20, 31	
IRIARTE 61	

WHEN PEDRO CEA netted Uruguay's sixth and final goal in the 72nd minute against Yugoslavia, he became the first player to score three times in a World Cup semi-final. Known as "the Basque" due to having been born in Spain, Cea was the talisman of the Uruguay team and one of the keys to their international success. Not only was he the sole Uruguayan player to feature in every match of their trio of tournament triumphs, in 1924 (Paris Olympic Games), 1928 (Amsterdam Olympic Games) and the 1930 World Cup, but he was also one of only two players to score at least once in all three competitions.

When he netted the second goal in the World Cup Final, Cea became the first player to have scored in both an Olympic final (in 1924) and a World Cup Final. Hungary's Ferenc Puskás and Zoltán Czibor (1952 Olympics and 1954 World Cup) would go on to emulate him.

The feuding brothers from the River Plate

FROM THE MOMENT the first World Cup began, a Final between Uruguay and Argentina had seemed inevitable. The flood of opt-outs from Europe's leading footballing nations had left the two neighbouring countries, separated only by the broad estuary of the River Plate, as the two main contenders for the inaugural World Cup title. The pair had been dominating South American football since the start of the century, winning ten out of 12 South American Championships between them: six for Uruguay, and four for Argentina. They had also both been finalists at the last Olympic tournament in 1928, when Uruguay had prevailed after two extremely tight matches (1–1 and 2–1).

Supporters on both sides of the river were cautiously optimistic, each aware that the result could go either way. The two countries felt a mix of contradictory feelings for each other, expressed daily by the papers in Montevideo and Buenos Aires. While attesting to their shared sense of brotherhood, they also expressed the strong rivalry between the two countries; rivalries that were not just limited to sport. At each of their games, the Argen-

tinian media focused at length on the treatment meted out to their team by the Uruguayan public, pronouncing shock at how France had been roared on against Argentina. This was despite Argentinian captain Manuel Ferreira's assertion that it was "logical for the crowd to cheer on the French, as we're Uruguay's most dangerous opponent, so our elimination would help them more than anyone."

After Argentina's victory in the semi-final, Montevideo's *El Dia* newspaper declared: "The great victory achieved yesterday by our brothers from across the River Plate is a success that really resonates with us, because their triumph is also a triumph for the vibrancy and youthful dynamism of the River Plate nations."

The near-identical paths of both teams through the tournament and the strikingly equal score of 6–1 by which they both went through to the Final served only to strengthen the animosity between the two countries. The referee for the final, John Langenus, observed in his memoirs that: "Argentines were not liked in Montevideo, despite journalists constantly referring to their Argentine 'brothers'." And now the "clash of the titans" was awaited more feverishly than ever.

▲ Guillermo Stabile deceives American keeper Jimmy Douglas to score his team's sixth goal.

Suspense-free semi-finals

26 JULY 1930
ARGENTINA 🇦🇷 6–1 🇺🇸 USA
MONTI 20, SCOPELLI 56   BROWN 89
STABILE 69, 87
PEUCELLE 80, 85

OR THE ONLY time in the annals of World Cup history, the 1930 semi-finals, Uruguay-Yugoslavia and Argentina-United States, were both won by a five-goal margin (6–1). It was a testament to the South American pair's clear superiority. The only doubt concerning the outcome of either of these games was limited to the first 20 minutes of the Uruguay-Yugoslavia match, after the Yugoslav forward Ðorđe Vujadinović had opened the scoring in the 4th minute. But following Pedro Cea's 18th-minute equalizer, followed by another goal from Peregrino Anselmo two minutes later, any misgivings were quickly dispelled. Leading 3–1 at half-time, Uruguay

got their sixth goal with 20 minutes to spare. The previous day, Argentina were never in trouble against the United States, who nonetheless restricted the damage to a single first-half goal, only to cave in after the break. Midway through the second half, Alejandro Scopelli and Guillermo Stábile increased the lead to three, before three further goals were added late on. For the Americans, a solitary last-minute consolation from Jim Brown restored a modicum of honour.

It would not be until the 1954 semi-final between West Germany and Austria that another 6–1 scoreline would grace this stage of the event. Then, in 2014, Germany went one better against Brazil (7–1).

The chloroformed protestor

During the Argentina-United States semi-final (6–1), the Americans took umbrage with several of Belgian referee John Langenus's decisions. Just after half-time, when the American team was pulled up for yet another foul, Jack Coll, assistant to their coach Robert Millar and also the side's first-aid man, ran onto the field to berate the referee. Langenus recalled what happened next: "He headed straight for me at full pelt and started to question me really aggressively. When he'd done arguing, he furiously hurled his first-aid case on the ground. It burst open amid a mess of broken bottles and vials, including a bottle of chloroform, which promptly anesthetized both Mr Coll and the player Andy Auld." In his long career as a referee, Langenus never saw calm restored to the field as effectively.

Petrone's watch

Silver-and-enamel pocket watch presented to Uruguay's Pedro Petrone.

▲ **FIFA World Football Museum collection.**

The Tartan Americans

The United States team that reached the semi-finals at the first-ever World Cup consisted of several players born in the UK. In fact, they were recruited and freshly naturalized specifically to reinforce an American football scene that was still in its infancy. Six of them were born in Great Britain – five in Scotland and one in England. But only one of them, George Moorhouse, had been a professional player in England (with Tranmere) before emigrating, initially to Canada. The others, like so many migrants, had arrived in the United States in their youth. Bart McGhee, a scorer against Belgium, had been born in Scotland. At the age of 12, he had joined his father Jimmy – a genuine Scottish international – who had left for the USA two years earlier.

Jim Brown, scorer in the semi-final, was born in Kilmarnock. He joined his father Stateside, aged just 19, having never even played for a team in Europe. Two more Scots, Jimmy Gallagher and Alec Wood, had emigrated to the United States aged 12 and 14 respectively. The latter finally became a professional player, with Leicester City and then Nottingham Forest, after the World Cup. Finally, Andy Auld had impressed for amateur club Parkhead FC in Glasgow, before heading across the Atlantic in 1923.

Even the USA's coach, Robert Millar, was a Scot who had himself emigrated years before after playing for St Mirren. From as early as 1912, he had plied his trade as a player and then coach in various North American leagues.

▲ Juan Botasso, the Argentine keeper, reaches for the sky. Uruguay forward Héctor Castro scores his team's fourth goal of the final.

Uruguay on top of the world

30 JULY 1930

URUGUAY 4–2 ARGENTINA

DORADO 12, CEA 57, IRIARTE 68, CASTRO 89   PEUCELLE 20, STABILE 37

ALTHOUGH URUGUAY opened the scoring in the 12th minute through Pablo Dorado, it was Argentina who dominated the first half of the final, reducing the Uruguayan crowd to silence on several occasions. As such, Carlos Peucelle's 20th-minute equalizer came as no great surprise and, before long, Argentina's wiry inside-forward from the Huracán club, Guillermo Stábile, put his side ahead thanks to his eighth goal of the competition. Uruguay were on the ropes and must have been relieved to reach the interval without suffering any further damage. But in the second half the hosts came out firing and finally calmed their nerves in the 57th minute thanks to Pedro Cea's equalizer. From then on, the momentum swung from one side to the other. Argentina seemed to sense that their opportunity had passed. They defended resolutely until the 68th minute, when Uruguayan defender Ernesto Mascheroni set off on the counter, ran 30 metres, evaded a challenge from Luis Monti and fed Héctor Scarone. Aged 31, *El Mago* (The Magician) was in his swansong with the

Celeste. He had represented them for 13 years and was due to retire after the final, having won 52 caps. He'd already won every honour in South America, as well as the Olympic Games, so there was space for just one more medal on his mantelpiece. A master strategist and an expert in the art of attack (he had scored 31 international goals), Scarone sensed – as surely he couldn't have heard it over the frenzied noise inside the stadium – the call of his left winger, Santos Iriarte. With an impeccable half-volley, Scarone moved the ball on. Travelling at full pelt, Iriarte executed an incredible shot that sailed into the net. The match had now swung full circle and, in the final minute, the one-armed Héctor Castro gave the scoreline a dash of added gloss for the *Celeste*. Uruguayans inside the great stadium and throughout the land celebrated. After the Olympic victories, Uruguay now had its global hat-trick. On the other side of the River Plate, meanwhile, despondency reigned. Two years on from the Amsterdam Games, Argentina had again been outsmarted by their smaller neighbour.

To each his own ball

As each team wanted to play the final with a ball manufactured in their own country, referee John Langenus came out onto the pitch with a ball under each arm, one made in Uruguay and the other brought from **Argentina.** A drawing of lots resulted in the Argentinian ball being chosen for the first half, with the Uruguayan ball used in the second half.

Nasazzi: captain every time

JOSÉ NASAZZI etched his name into the pantheon of world football on several occasions, but a single event is sufficient to secure his eternal legendary status: on 30 July 1930, he became the first captain to lift the World Cup aloft. An imposing figure at 1.8 metres tall, he also stood out due to his strong personality and long list of international honours. Aged 29 at the time of the 1930 final, Nasazzi was at his peak, having already experienced numerous successes prior to this ultimate triumph. An international since 1923, he was the *Celeste*'s permanent captain and had led their side to Olympic glory in 1924 and again in 1928. He also led his team to success in the South American Championships in 1923, 1924 and 1926, and would still be rallying the troops for their next continental success in 1935. In footballing terms, Nasazzi was considered to be one of the greatest defenders of the inter-war period. In the playing systems of the day, the full-back position was broadly comparable to the role of modern-day central defenders. It mattered little that his technique was not exactly flawless, as his chief qualities, namely strength, speed, bravery and a good command of tactics, made him the automatic and universally respected boss of the triple Olympic & World Champions' backline. He was captain in every one of his 41 matches for Uruguay.

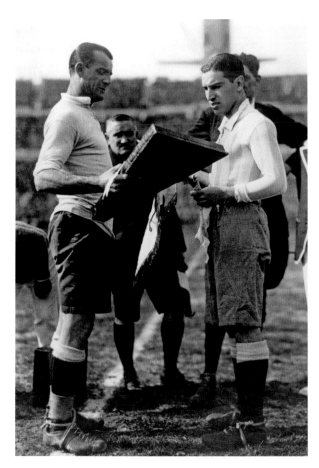

◄ Uruguayan captain José Nasazzi, greets his Argentine counterpart, Manuel Ferreira, before the final.

An historic shirt

Shirt worn by a Uruguayan player during the finals.

◄ FIFA World Football Museum collection.

Andrade, the "Black Marvel"

Together with captain José Nasazzi and the attacking trio of Pedro Cea, Pedro Petrone and Héctor Scarone, José Leandro Andrade was one of the five key players behind Uruguay's triple world crown, consisting of their two Olympic victories (1924 and 1928) and the 1930 World Cup. Regarded as the first great black player in football history, the wing half (the term midfielder had not yet been coined) from Nacional had been one of the revelations of the Olympic Games in Paris, where his skin colour had been the focus of considerable curiosity and enhanced the "exotic" appearance of the Uruguayan team. It was after the 1924 Olympic tournament that he had been dubbed "the Black Marvel". His international career, which had begun in 1923, ended after the 1930 World Cup final. To this day, a plaque at the Estadio Centenario celebrates his memory.

100

The Uruguay-Argentina final was the 100th encounter between the two teams from the banks of the River Plate. Their first meeting had taken place in Montevideo on 16 May 1901 (a 3–2 victory for Argentina).

After Uruguay's World Cup triumph, the balance of results between the two sides stood as follows: 35 wins for Uruguay, 40 successes for Argentina, and 25 draws.

The ref departs in a side-car

Legend has it that the final's Belgian referee, John Langenus, had to exit the Estadio Centenario in a hurry after the game, flanked by a police escort to ensure his safety. The man himself though offers a quite different version of events. In fact, he and the other Belgian official on World Cup duty, Henry Christophe, were in a rush to get back to their ship before it departed for Europe. A pair of side-cars driven by policemen were laid on for this purpose, while the officers conducting traffic were instructed to keep the route as clear as possible so that the convoy could pass. Despite the post-match bottlenecks and Uruguay's victory celebrations, the two referees made it to the boat on time.

1934

Against a backdrop of Mussolini's Fascist propaganda, Italy staged and won the second World Cup. With defending champions Uruguay absent, this was a tournament dominated by Europe. Italy beat Austria's "Wunderteam" in the semi-final and Czechoslovakia 2-1 in the Final. An extra-time goal by Angelo Schiavio gave the Italians the World Cup and an extra trophy: the Coppa del Duce.

The World Cup *and* the Coppa del Duce

◀ Coach Vittorio Pozzo is held aloft by the Italian team after victory in the Final over Czechoslovakia.

▼ Benito Mussolini in the VIP box during the Czechoslovakia-Germany semi-final.

THE HOST COUNTRY for the second World Cup was decided at the 1932 FIFA Congress in Stockholm. There were two declared bids, from Italy and Sweden, so when the latter withdrew, the honour was naturally awarded to Italy. Its delegate, Giovanni Mauro, nonetheless requested a delay before the confirmation of his country as hosts, so Italy's staging of the 1934 World Cup wasn't officially announced until several months later. For the Fascist regime that had been in power in Italy since 1922, the organization of what would be the first World Cup to be held in Europe was an opportunity for a massive display of propaganda. The tournament was divided between eight cities, where the recently constructed stadia drew effusive praise from foreign visitors. Their architecture was characteristic of the style imposed by the regime, namely symbolizing the return of Roman grandeur. Rome's main stadium, the venue for the final, bore the name of the National Fascist Party, while the largest and newest arena – in Turin – was called the Stadio Benito Mussolini. The Fascist salute was omnipresent, from the tournament posters to the presentation of the Italian side before each match, accompanied, of course, by images of the dictator, who presided over the matches held in Rome from the balcony of the official stand. Although Italians only seemed interested in the tournament when their team was playing, they had no doubt that it would be their country's captain who, after the final on 10 June, would hold both the World Cup and the Coppa de Duce aloft. Italy's youth were fully expecting their champions to triumph.

ITALY 1934

WORLD'S CUP ITALY 1934

Story of the qualifiers

Africa and Asia enter the fray

TWO CONTINENTS that had been absent from the inaugural World Cup were on board for the 1934 tournament: Africa and Asia. The pair of "pioneers" bidding to represent them were Egypt and Palestine. Since 1920 and the San Remo Conference, Palestine had been under a British mandate. Egypt, meanwhile, had been granted independence in 1922. Initially, the two teams had been drawn in a qualifying group that also contained Turkey, before the latter withdrew its entry. So Egypt and Palestine were left to fight it out for qualification. Egypt won both matches, which had British Army referees, in Cairo on 16 March (7–1) and in Jerusalem on 6 April (4–1). Egypt thus became the first nation from outside Europe and the Americas to participate in the final tournament. Africa would have to wait another 36 years before being represented again, at the 1970 World Cup, by Morocco. Like Europe in 1930, the Americas largely snubbed the first European edition. Uniquely in the entire history of the competition, reigning world champions Uruguay didn't travel to defend their crown. Argentina, beset by a serious domestic crisis, only sent an amateur team, while Brazil selected a second-string squad. But Europe's big hitters were all present and correct, apart from England, who instead played friendlies against Czechoslovakia and Hungary just before the finals. They lost both matches.

▲ Egypt's players salute the crowd before their match against Hungary.

Regulations

Group format gives way to knockout

The low number of teams taking part in the first World Cup (13) had meant a format combining a group phase with semi-finals and a Final. The 1934 World Cup, on the other hand, was able to comply with a principle laid down at the 1931 FIFA Congress in Berlin: to have a final phase involving 16 teams. A cup system was chosen, which meant half the teams only got to play a single game. The draw for the first round had taken place on 3 May three weeks before the tournament kicked off. Fixtures were predetermined, so Italy knew that if they beat the USA their quarter-final opponents would be the winners of the Spain-Brazil match. This cup system would be used only one more time, in 1938.

Results

FIRST ROUND		
ITA	7–1	USA
ESP	3–1	BRA

FIRST ROUND		
AUT	3–2 A.E.T.	FRA
HUN	4–2	EGY

FIRST ROUND		
TCH	2–1	ROU
SUI	3–2	NED

FIRST ROUND		
GER	5–2	BEL
SWE	3–2	ARG

QUARTER-FINAL		
ITA	1–1 A.E.T.	ESP
ITA	1–0	ESP

QUARTER-FINAL		
AUT	2–1	HUN

QUARTER-FINAL		
TCH	3–2	SUI

QUARTER-FINAL		
GER	2–1	SWE

SEMI-FINAL		
ITA	1–0	AUT

SEMI-FINAL		
TCH	3–1	GER

PLAY-OFF FOR THIRD PLACE		
GER	3–2	AUT

FINAL		
ITA	2–1 A.E.T.	TCH

ARG AUT BEL BRA
EGY ESP FRA GER
HUN ITA NED ROU
SUI SWE TCH USA

16 TEAMS

17
MATCHES PLAYED

1
CARDS

363 000
SPECTATORS

CAMPIONATO MONDIALE DI CALCIO
OFFICIAL POSTER

ITALY
WINNERS

×5
OLDŘICH NEJEDLÝ
LEADING GOALSCORER

4.1
AVERAGE GOALS PER GAME

FEDERALE 102
OFFICIAL MATCH BALL

Host cities and stadiums

The stadiums were not completely full

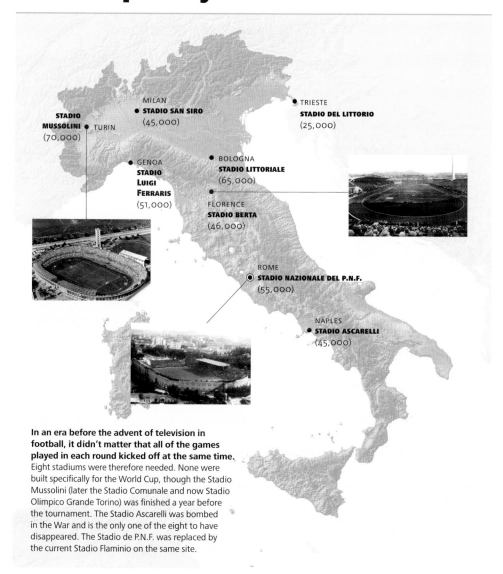

STADIO MUSSOLINI (70,000) — TURIN

MILAN
STADIO SAN SIRO (45,000)

GENOA
STADIO LUIGI FERRARIS (51,000)

BOLOGNA
STADIO LITTORIALE (65,000)

FLORENCE
STADIO BERTA (46,000)

TRIESTE
STADIO DEL LITTORIO (25,000)

ROME
STADIO NAZIONALE DEL P.N.F. (55,000)

NAPLES
STADIO ASCARELLI (45,000)

In an era before the advent of television in football, it didn't matter that all of the games played in each round kicked off at the same time. Eight stadiums were therefore needed. None were built specifically for the World Cup, though the Stadio Mussolini (later the Stadio Comunale and now Stadio Olimpico Grande Torino) was finished a year before the tournament. The Stadio Ascarelli was bombed in the War and is the only one of the eight to have disappeared. The Stadio de P.N.F. was replaced by the current Stadio Flaminio on the same site.

Mexico fail to qualify... in Italy

THE QUALIFIERS for the 1934 World Cup gave rise to two unique events in World Cup history. For the only time, the host nation was required to get through the preliminary round and, on 25 March 1934 in Milan, Italy duly obliged by beating Greece 4–0. Another first was a qualifying match in the country where the tournament was taking place. In the North and Central America preliminary group, a dispute had flared up between the four teams involved (United States, Cuba, Mexico and Haiti) over where the games should be played – New York or Mexico City. It was decided that the United States would play the winner from among the other three competitors in a single match to be held in Rome. And so Mexico, who had prevailed over Cuba after winning three matches held in Mexico City (3–2, 5–0 and 4–1), crossed the Atlantic to take on the United States. On 24 May, three days before the start of the tournament proper, the United States beat them 4–2, courtesy of four goals from Aldo Donelli. So the Mexican team made a return journey across the Atlantic without even playing in a World Cup finals match.

▲ The Hungarian team before their match against Egypt.

▲ Empty seats in the Stadio Mussolini for the match between Austria and France.

Egypt give Hungary a scare

27 MAY 1934

HUNGARY 4–2 EGYPT

TELEKI 11   FAWZI 35, 39
TOLDI 31, 61
VINCZE 53

ALTHOUGH WIDELY expected to win their first round clash in Naples, the Hungarians were wary of their Egyptian adversaries. After all, they were still nursing painful memories of the 3–0 mauling that Egypt had inflicted on them at the 1924 Olympics. Moreover, the Hungarians went into this opening match without their star striker György Sárosi, who had stayed at home to play an important match for his club, Ferencváros. After half an hour, Hungary thought they had dispelled any chance of another surprise result by easing into a 2–0 lead thanks to strikes from Pál Teleki and then, more controversially, Géza Toldi, who appeared to foul Egypt's inexperienced 19-year-old goalkeeper Mustapha Kamel Mansour. But then, in a four-minute period approaching half-time, an Abdel Rahman Fawzy brace levelled the tie at 2–2. After the interval, the Hungarians' greater maturity and superior technique began to tell, allowing Jenő Vincze and Toldi to secure their place in the next round. However, the Egyptians had been admirable first ambassadors for African football.

8

The eight ties that made up the first round were all played at the same time on the same day, 4pm on 27 May, producing eight European winners. It's the only time in the entire history of the World Cup that only one continent has been represented in the quarter-finals.

249

That's the number of special correspondents from the Italian and international press given accreditation for the 1934 World Cup. The global football gathering was clearly becoming a top-level media event. Most numerous was the Italian contingent, comprising 65 journalists, but the French (27) and German (23) papers were also well represented. There was even a special correspondent from Britain, despite the absence of all four UK nations.

WM fails to stop Sindelar & Co.

27 MAY 1934

AUSTRIA 3-2 A.E.T. FRANCE

SINDELAR 44, SCHALL 93, BICAN 109   NICOLAS 18, VERRIEST 115 (PEN)

A CHANGE to the offside rule, introduced by the International Board in 1925, led to the emergence of a new playing system, invented in the UK and perfected by the Arsenal manager, Herbert Chapman. It was known as the "WM", as these were the letters spelled out by the players' positions on the field. Arsenal's subsequent success made the new method well-known. Few countries adopted it, however, but it was introduced in France by a British coach, George Kimpton, who took charge of the French team for the 1934 World Cup. In their opening game, *Les Bleus* came up against the celebrated Austria side, loyal proponents of the traditional attacking centre-half system. Kimpton instructed his players to man-mark Austria's outstanding forwards, with Georges Verriest detailed to stick closely to the skilful Matthias Sindelar. To get across what was expected of him, Kimpton told the Roubaix player: "If Sindy goes to the toilet, you go with him!" The tactics very nearly paid off. Austria, who one year earlier had crushed France 4–0 in Paris, found the French to be much more stubborn opposition on this occasion. After France had opened the scoring early in the match, an Austrian equalizer took the tie to extra time – the first time this had happened in World Cup history. Austria scored twice more in extra time, with France scoring once, to secure their progression to the quarter-finals.

Belgians see the sights

27 MAY 1934

GERMANY 5–2 **BELGIUM**

KOBIERSKI 25, SIFFLING 49, CONEN 66, 70, 87   VOORHOOF 29, 43

HAVING had little preparation for the tournament, Belgium were downbeat about their chances against Germany in Florence. Their players from the club Union Saint-Gilloise – of which there were four in the team – arrived straight from Algeria, where their club was on tour. The Belgian Football Association had already scheduled their return home, allowing three days for sightseeing in Rome. And when they left Brussels, the team had been accompanied by just one supporter. After arriving in Florence, they spent the eve of the match touring the city and, just a few hours before the game, a reception was given in their honour at the Palazzo Vecchio! But the Belgians didn't appear to suffer as a result of this casual approach to their preparations and even went into the break 2–1 in front after a Bernard Voorhoof brace. In the second half, however, the Germans took the game by the scruff of the neck, running out 5–2 victors thanks to a hat-trick by the young Saarbrücken striker, Edmund Conen (aged 19).

Kielholz,
the bespectacled striker

27 MAY 1934

SWITZERLAND 3–2 **NETHERLANDS**

KIELHOLZ 7, 43, ABEGGLEN 66   SMIT 29, VENTE 69

BEFORE THE WORLD CUP had even kicked off, the group of Dutch supporters that had made the trip to Italy were singing "We're on our way to Rome!", but instead their trip ended at the first hurdle, in Milan. Defeated by Switzerland (3–2), the Netherlands went straight out, the victims of a formidable centre-forward named Poldi Kielholz, from the Geneva club Servette. His two first-half goals gave Switzerland a lead that the Dutch were unable to cancel out. Unusually, Kielholz, who had vision problems, liked to keep his glasses on during matches. And it obviously didn't hinder him, as he scored 12 times in 17 appearances for the Swiss national team.

▲ The Belgian team before playing Germany.

◀ Swedish keeper Anders Rydberg gets the better of Argentine captain Alfredo De Vincenzi.

◀ Poldi Kielholz and his famous glasses during the first round match between Switzerland and the Netherlands.

South America's disappearing act

Whereas the South American sides had largely dominated the first World Cup, they were nowhere to be seen by the end of the first round in 1934. Brazil – who had qualified for the final phase without playing after Peru had pulled out – soon found themselves trailing heavily against Spain. In the match's first half-hour, the Spanish scored three goals, courtesy of the Basque forwards José Iraragorri from Oviedo (two goals, including a penalty) and Bilbao's Isidro Lángara. In the 52nd minute, Leônidas, earning his second Brazilian cap, reduced the deficit, and then with 20 minutes left on the clock, Brazil won a penalty for a foul by Quincoces on Waldemar de Brito. One Spanish observer had noticed that, in training, de Brito always put his penalties to the left. The great Spanish keeper Ricardo Zamora had been given this information and dived the right way. Just like four years earlier, Brazil had lost their opening match, something that hasn't happened to them at a World Cup since.

Argentina, meanwhile, with its team of amateur players, put on a dogged display against Sweden. They even led 2–1 in the second half, before the Swedes turned things around in the final 25 minutes, courtesy of goals from Sven Jonasson (67th minute) and Knut Kroon (79th).

Mercet, friend of Italy?

After the first Italy-Spain match, the Belgian referee Louis Baert had been replaced, possibly due to nervous fatigue caused by refereeing such a fraught encounter. However, what really set tongues wagging was the appointment for the replay of Swiss official René Mercet. In the 11th minute of the encounter, he appeared to give Italy a helping hand by allowing what proved to be the only goal of the game, despite a foul on the Spanish goalkeeper. After the match, he was suspended by the Swiss football association.

Italian idols

Postcards featuring the Italian champions Luis Monti (left) and Luigi Bertolini (right).

◀ **FIFA World Football Museum collection.**

MONTI

BERTOLINI

Austria and Hungary take no prisoners

31 MAY 1934

AUSTRIA	2-1	HUNGARY
HORVATH 8, ZISCHEK 51		SAROSI 60 (PEN)

T HE QUARTER-FINAL in Bologna promised a flamboyant footballing spectacle. After all, the two sides facing each other were among central Europe's finest exponents of the game. However, sometimes, when two giants meet, the sparks can really fly... Austria and Hungary were old and familiar foes, having first played each other back in 1902, even before FIFA was created. And when the 22 players came out onto the pitch, they were meeting for no less than the 75th time. Their previous encounter had taken place just one month earlier, with Austria prevailing 5–2 in Vienna. Although the Austrian *Wunderteam* were unbeaten in their last seven matches against their old rival, their manager, Hugo Meisl, was wary. He knew that his side was not on top form, as in the previous round they had needed extra time to see off the French, a team they were accustomed to beating comfortably. Nonetheless, they had the better of the opening exchanges and, in the eighth minute, outside-right Karl Zischek was freed by "Pepi" Bican and sent in a low cross. Hans Horvath ghosted into the penalty area and knocked it home from close range. This first period saw some splendid play from both teams, despite the pressure-cooker atmosphere. With half-time beckoning, Zischek had a chance to net a second, only to see his shot saved by Antal Szabó.

After the interval, the artists were transformed into warriors. The Italian referee Francesco Mattea found himself constantly fire-fighting, as one bad tackle followed another. Amid this venomous atmosphere, Zischek, found by Bican, increased the *Wunderteam*'s lead to 2–0 and was flattened unceremoniously by Szabó for his trouble. From then on to the end, it was virtually non-stop brawling, especially after a György Sárosi penalty really ratcheted up the Austrians' stress levels. Even the aesthete Matthias Sindelar got involved in the argy-bargy. After the referee sent off Hungary's Imre Markos (even though other bad fouls had deserved the same punishment), the Bologna crowd got behind the ten-man *Magyars*, but amid the stifling atmosphere, Austria held out for the win which their superior football had merited... Yes, there had been at least some football in amongst all the fighting.

The legendary Ricardo Zamora

Ricardo Zamora's only World Cup appearance came near the end of his glittering career. When he captained the Spanish side on the global stage in 1934, he was already 33 years of age, having first kept goal for Spain at the 1920 Olympic Games. During that time, he had imposed his immense frame on all the fields of Europe – except in England, where he had suffered a humiliating defeat (7–1) in 1931. At home, in the colours of Español, Barcelona and Real Madrid, he was the country's leading football figure. When the World Cup began, he had already gained 42 caps, and he hit the ground running in the first round against Brazil, saving a penalty from Waldemar de Brito. Against Italy, he was a key part of the heroic Spanish rearguard action, but having suffered an eye injury, he was unable to resume his post the following day. Despite his fleeting presence in football's top competition, Zamora remains an iconic figure from the international game's inter-war pantheon of greats.

▶ Spain captain and goalkeeper Ricardo Zamora, pictured here in 1931.

210 minutes of fierce combat

▲ Ricardo Zamora saves a shot in front of Angelo Schiavo, Giuseppe Meazza and Jacinto Quincoces during the first match of Spain and Italy's quarter-final tie.

	31 MAY 1934	
ITALY	1-1 A.E.T.	SPAIN
FERRARI 44		REGUEIRO 30

	1 JUNE 1934	
ITALY	1-0	SPAIN
MEAZZA 11		

AT THE STADIO BERTA in Florence, a sort of Latin football final was played out between Italy and Spain. Under the gaze of Benito Mussolini's two sons, the *Azzurri* set about using sheer strength to weaken the Spanish resistance. Their eagerness and enthusiasm was excessive at times, as if the process of winning had nothing at all to do with skill. In the stifling Tuscan heat, it was the Spanish side which, initially, opted to slow things down a bit and play possession football. And they were rewarded with the opening goal, when a Lángara free-kick was met by Regueiro. But the Spanish goal only served to spark even more frenetic Italian attacks and, just before the break, their key strategist, Giovanni Ferrari, restored parity, also from a free-kick. From then on, the Spanish defended heroically. In front of the legendary keeper Ricardo Zamora, a seemingly impenetrable protective shield was formed by Real Madrid defenders Ciriaco and Quincoces, whose headband marked him out on the pitch. The more heightened the tension in the stadium and on the field, the more valiant became their resistance. They wore out the Italian forwards, whose attacks became more frenzied. The Spanish defence, as intuitive as it was courageous, held out until the end of 30 minutes' extra time, which meant a replay the next day. All witnesses to this heavyweight bout couldn't help but wonder what kind of state the two teams would be in.

In both camps, fresh legs were now of the essence. The Italians changed four players, including the striker Schiavio and scorer Ferrari. The Spaniards, meanwhile, rested seven players, among them the two heroes Ciriaco and Zamora. One of Spain's newcomers, winger Crisant Bosch, was injured in the fifth minute, another victim of the infamous Luis Monti. In the 11th minute, Giuseppe Meazza gave the *Azzurri* the lead from a Raimundo Orsi corner, while Zamora's replacement in goal, Juan José Nogués, was being impeded by Italian players. It was too much for Spain. Exhausted and subjected to pressure and aggression from a hyped-up Italy, they were unable to get back into the game.

▲ An Italian attack in Austria's penalty area during the semi-final.

▲ Three of Italy's *oriundi* at the 1934 World Cup: Anfilogino Guarisi, Raimundo Orsi and Enrique Guaita.

◀ The Argentine passport of Italy's Luis Monti.

FIFA World Football Museum collection.

Faith triumphs over science

3 JUNE 1934

ITALY 1–0 **AUSTRIA**

GUAITA 19

Italy grateful to the *Oriundi*!

Two of the main architects behind Italy reaching the 1934 World Cup final were in fact born in Argentina: fearsome defender Luis Monti and winger Enrique Guaita. What's more, three further members of the Italian side also originated from Latin America: Amphilóquio Guarisi, the Lazio forward who played in the first match of the tournament, had previously played for Brazil (four caps); Atilio Demaría, the Inter player, had appeared at the first World Cup in Argentina's colours, as had Monti, the only player in World Cup history to have played in two finals for two different countries. And Raimundo Orsi, who scored in the 1934 final, had previously played in another global final, at the 1928 Olympic Games with Argentina. These naturalized players were referred to in Italy as "Oriundi", a word meaning "originally from".

In those days, and up until 1962, the rules regarding the naturalization of athletes were very flexible. When Italy's coach Vittorio Pozzo was asked about whether it was right to select players of foreign origin, he had this to say: "They need to have completed their Italian national service. If they have the right to die for Italy, then they have the right to play for Italy!"

TALY HAD TO PLAY their semi-final against Austria just 48 hours after their no-holds-barred replay with Spain, so the supporters in Milan's San Siro stadium were wondering if their players had recovered from that gruelling encounter. In previous clashes between the pair, Austria had come off considerably better, with the Italians having tasted victory just once in 13 encounters, back in 1931. In their most recent meeting the previous February, the Austrians had prevailed 4–2 in Turin, despite the absence of their star player Matthias Sindelar. But the *Wunderteam* had since lost some of their sparkle and while they remained a side with great technical know-how, their strikers were struggling to deliver in the toughest games.

On the morning of the semi-final, a severe downpour had left the pitch badly waterlogged and scarcely conducive to free-flowing football. But the game still offered a splendid contrast of styles, with Italy adopting a much more technical approach than they had done in previous games. Due to the influence of the two coaches, Italy's Vittorio Pozzo and Austria's Hugo Meisl, the emphasis was firmly on tactics. Faced with Austria's highly intricate game, Italy drew upon their high energy and spirit. And at the forefront, as always, was Luis Monti, unsettling Viertl and Sindelar, usually with his elbows or studs, whenever they got near him. The breakthrough came in the 19th minute, when Giuseppe Meazza, the Milanese idol, challenged Austria's keeper Peter Platzer, leading to a scramble in the penalty box that ended with Guaita converting. When the Italians remembered to play, they showed themselves to be on a par with the Austrian maestros and, at times, the game reached a very high technical level. However, when the Austrian forwards tried to attack, they were muscled out of it, and several times, Sindelar, Zischek and Schall implored Swedish referee Ivan Eklind to intervene. Despite being under pressure from the Italian crowd, the referee managed to maintain control. Despite their fatigue, the two sides showed admirable effort and commitment throughout. In the end, the Italians deserved their narrow victory, their will to win having ultimately prevailed over Austria's skill.

◄ Germany's Fritz Szepan and Czechoslovakia's František Plánička shake hands before the semi-final.

Nejedlý gets the Golden Boot, 72 years on!

It wasn't until 2006 that Czech forward Oldřich Nejedlý officially became the top scorer at the 1934 World Cup. This delay resulted from some doubt that existed regarding the Czechoslovakia-Germany semi-final, as certain sources cited Rudolf Krčil as scorer of the second goal. Nejedlý's belated confirmation as the scorer gave him five goals overall, one more than both Italy's Angelo Schiavio and Germany's Edmund Conen. Before his semi-final hat-trick, he had netted the winning goal in each game, against Romania (2–1) and Switzerland (3–2). The Sparta Prague striker would also go on to score twice at the 1938 World Cup. Over his international career, he clocked up 28 goals in 43 appearances.

Czechoslovakia in command

	3 JUNE 1934	
CZECHOSLOVAKIA	3–1	**GERMANY**
NEJEDLY 21, 69, 80		NOACK 62

THE ITALIAN PUBLIC were clearly much more interested in the World Cup when their own team was playing. While Italy were reaching the final amid the fever and passion of Milan, the other semi-final in Rome was being played out in front of a crowd of just 13,000 fans, one of them Benito Mussolini, who was cheered enthusiastically when the good news came in from Milan. The teams from Germany and Czechoslovakia took to the field amid relative indifference, but having been preceded by three flags instead of two (the Czechoslovakian and German flags… plus one swastika), the subdued welcome was somewhat understandable.

Contested without much passion, the match unfolded fairly predictably amid an atmosphere of calm and correctness that contrasted with the frenzied nature of the tournament's other encounters. The Czechoslovaks' football was methodical, but also defensive. Germany had a younger, more vibrant team, but their individual sharpness did not necessarily translate into a fast-flowing team style. In the first quarter of an hour, neither goalkeeper had to make a save, but then in the 19th minute, Oldřich Nejedlý opened the scoring from a penalty box melee, a lead that, on the balance of play, was just about deserved. With half an hour remaining, the Czechoslovaks maintained their one-goal lead. The Germans were creating several chances through the likes of Kobierski, Siffling and Conen, but Czechoslovakia's keeper František Plánička was in defiant mood.

Nejedlý had a chance to secure victory for the Czechoslovaks, but his shot came back off the crossbar. Then, in the 62nd minute, Rudolf Noack evaded two defensive challenges before levelling the score. For a moment, the balance seemed to have swung Germany's way, but their opportunity had passed. In the 69th minute, from a free-kick struck by Puč, Nejedlý headed home to restore Czechoslovakia's lead. Eleven minutes later, he completed his hat-trick to put the tie beyond doubt. Late on, Siffling managed to come close for the Germans, but the Czechoslovak defence stood firm.

24

It took just 24 seconds for Germany's striker from Augsburg, Ernst Lehner, to score the first goal of the third-place playoff match.

PLAY-OFF FOR THIRD PLACE

▲ Germany, in white, and Austria play for third place.

Too late for the *Wunderteam*

	7 JUNE 1954	
GERMANY	3–2	**AUSTRIA**
LEHNER 1, 42		HORVATH 28
CONEN 27		SESTA 54

Anyone during the 1920s and '30s who had been fortunate enough to witness the exploits of the Austrian team, retained warm memories of them. As in several other Central European nations, Austrian football had made rapid progress by employing British coaches who implemented a high-quality technical style. But the man who had put together this great Austrian side was Hugo Meisl, who managed the national side from 1912 until his death in 1937. A master tactician, he also promoted professionalism in his country, aided by the emergence of an extraordinary generation of football virtuosos. Under his stewardship (he was assisted by the British coach Jimmy Hogan), Austria went from strength to strength, recording an impressive run of 17 matches from 1931 to 1933, which earned the team the moniker *Wunderteam*. They achieved some striking victories in their run: 5–0 against Scotland, 6–0 and 5–0 against Germany, 8–1 against Switzerland, 8–2 against Hungary, 6–1 against Belgium, and 4–0 against France. Only England were able to resist their powers, beating them 4–3 in a famous match at Stamford Bridge on a foggy afternoon in 1932. Their players were all among the best of their era, but the finest of all was the forward Matthias Sindelar, nicknamed "the paper man" on account of his frail appearance, which somehow served to accentuate the magic of his play. They went into the 1934 World Cup on another great run of 12 games without defeat, but Hugo Meisl himself knew that his side was no longer at its peak. So the World Cup came a little too late for the *Wunderteam*, even though they had etched their names indelibly into footballing folklore.

▲ Italy's Angelo Schiavo (not in picture) scores the winning goal in the 1934 World Cup Final.

Champions, Italian style

O N 10 JUNE 1934, a few minutes before the kick-off of the World Cup final, several planes flew over Rome. As they passed over the north of the Eternal City just before 5pm, they spied the stadium of the National Fascist Party, packed to the rafters and overflowing with excitement, as it had been for hours. The people of Rome were restless, yet firmly expecting the last match to be an apotheosis for the Italy team. Italy had never lost on home soil against Czechoslovakia, but in reaching the final, they had expended much more energy than their central European rivals. The Czechslovak style of play was well-known. Thoughtful and meticulous, they were capable of dampening the passions of the most enthusiastic opponents. All of Italy and its leader Benito Mussolini, who was of course present in the stand, knew that their players would have to dig deep in order to prevail.

Vittorio Pozzo's players began the encounter with uncharacteristic circumspection. The first half finished goalless, but after the restart, the Italians began to wrestle control, speeding up the pace of a game the Czechoslovaks were attempting to stifle. And whenever Czechoslovakia did try to launch an attack, Luis Monti was as vigilant as ever. Midway through the second half, however, it was not him who clattered into Antonín Puč, but his team-mate Attilio Ferraris. The incident took place in the penalty area, but the referee chose not to award a penalty. Puč had to leave the field to get treatment for a head injury, but on returning to the fray, he appeared none the worse for wear as he got involved in a string of dangerous Czech moves. Then, in the 71st minute, he was fed by Stefan Čambal, left Eraldo Monzeglio for dead and buried a cross-shot into the corner of the net.

An ominous hush enveloped the stadium, as the Italian side threatened to collapse. František Svoboda struck a post, and then Oldřich Nejedlý missed a chance to clinch the world title for his team. There were still ten minutes left to play though, and the Italians duly galvanized themselves to launch a frenzied wave of attacks. In an 81st-minute assault led by two of their *Oriundi*, Enrique Guaita and Raimundo Orsi, the latter dribbled past Ladislav Ženíšek, dummied with his left foot and promptly buried it with his right.

All of Italy released a deep sigh of relief. Master tactician Pozzo, meanwhile, got Guaita to switch positions with Schiavio, their exhausted centre-forward. This change caused problems for Czechoslovakia's system, stymieing the attacking moves that had been flowing through their midfield schemer Čambal. As the end of normal time approached, Guaita missed a gilt-edged chance to win it for Italy, so the game went into extra time with the score at 1–1.

Then, five minutes into extra time, Italy took the lead. Monzeglio intercepted Puč's pass and played it to Giuseppe Meazza, who was in space out on the left wing after just having received some treatment. He fed the ball through to Guaita, who immediately squared it for Schiavio. The latter's cross-shot wrong-footed Plánička – and the whole team, the whole stadium and the whole nation were engulfed by an immense wave of relief.

Instead of crumbling, however, Czechoslovakia responded in impressive style. Their forwards Puč, Svoboda and Junek all looked menacing, but the Italian defence held out, with keeper Combi pulling off a save after save. In the second period of extra time, the Czechoslovak assaults lost their verve and the game descended into a scrappy affair. Amid a frantic atmosphere, Italy hung on to their slender advantage. As he presented team captain Gianpiero Combi with the elegant trophy that confirmed Italy's place as the best team in the world, Mussolini was finally able to bask in the ultimate triumph. And Vittorio Pozzo, the consummate strategist and architect of Italy's triumph, was carried aloft on his players' shoulders.

95

Italy's winning goal, scored by Bologna striker Angelo Schiavio, came in the 95th minute. It was the first World Cup final in which 30 minutes of extra time was needed to decide the new world champions.

Two great keepers and captains

BEFORE THE 1934 WORLD CUP FINAL, the two captains who shook hands in front of the Swedish referee were the goal-keepers who, along with Spain's legendary shot-stopper Ricardo Zamora, were among the most famous exponents of their art during the inter-war period. Italy's captain, Gianpiero Combi (aged 31), was earning his 47th and final cap for the *Azzurri*, having graced their goal for ten years. This was a record for the day, as was the number of appearances he made for Juventus.

Facing Combi was František Plánička, a year younger than his opposite number and equally loyal to his only club, Slavia Prague. But unlike Combi, this was far from Plánička's international swan-song, as he would continue through to the 1938 World Cup, accumulating 73 caps in all, a world record at the time. In Italy, he played a key role on his country's path to the final and was later named as goalkeeper of the tournament.

▶ Italy's coach Vittorio Pozzo would often leave the dugout during matches. In the 1934 World Cup Final he was photographed next to the Czechoslovak goal.

Pozzo behind Plánička's goal

Italy's manager Vittorio Pozzo was not only a master tactician, he was also an early proponent of psychological mindgames. During the final, he spent several minutes crouched down behind the Czech goal. Perhaps his aim was to draw his team towards František Plánička's goal… but also perhaps to unsettle Czechoslovakia's captain.

The Coppa del Duce

The head of the Italian state, Benito Mussolini, was determined to leave his own imprint on this World Cup. He did so by holding court at the matches played in Rome, and by introducing his own trophy, the Coppa del Duce, a huge and heavy cup with bronze embroidery that dwarfed the real World Cup trophy by the French sculptor Abel Lafleur.

COPPA DEL DVCE

◀ Two keepers, two captains: Giampiero Combi and František Plánička shake hands before the Final in front of referee Ivan Eklind.

Eklind, the baby-faced referee

At the age of 28, Swedish referee Ivan Eklind is the youngest to have taken charge of a World Cup Final. After the match, he gave this assessment of the world champions' playing style: "It was a very physical game, and that was down to the Italians. That was the wrong choice on their part, as we saw from the point when Monti started playing the ball rather than the man. From then on, the *Squadra Azzurra* seemed transformed and, in technical terms, were able to fully match their opponents."

Prior to the final, Eklind had officiated in two other World Cup matches: Switzerland-Netherlands (3–2) in the first round and the Italy-Austria semi-final (1–0). He would also referee games at the 1938 and 1950 World Cups.

1938

With dictators on the march and the map of Europe being redrawn, the 1938 World Cup in France was played in uncertain times. Austria qualified, but played as part of the Germany team knocked out by Switzerland in the first round. France were beaten in the quarter-finals by Italy, who were provocatively kitted out in Fascist black. The Italians went on to retain their title with a 4–2 victory over Hungary in the Final.

The last days of peace

THE THIRD World Cup, held in France from 4 to 19 June 1938, was the first to suffer the consequences of the era's tumultuous political events. The Spanish Civil War that had been raging since July 1936 prevented Spain from assembling a team and so their entry was withdrawn before the tournament began. Austria, meanwhile, had qualified at the expense of Latvia (2–1) and were drawn to play Sweden. The Austrians were then scheduled to play a warm-up game against France in Paris on 24 March, but the French instead ended up playing Bulgaria on that day. Austria's absence was due to the *Anschluss* that had occurred on 12 March, when the invading German army had annexed the country and promptly scrapped the Austrian national team. On 3 April, the Nazis even held a parody football match in which the Austrian team had to play under

the name of *Ostmark*, meaning "Eastern Territory". The Austrian *Wunderteam* was now nothing more than a memory.

This World Cup would, therefore, only have 15 participants. Sweden progressed to the quarter-finals by default, while some of the Austrian players were added to the German team. On the eve of the tournament proper, FIFA held their annual congress in Paris to discuss the organization of the next World Cup in 1942, which Brazil were hoping to host. But the German delegate strongly emphasized that his country had submitted their bid in 1936… The congress, therefore, opted to delay their decision on this issue. The general feeling at the time was summed up by the French sports daily *L'Auto*: "It's important to remember that an event like the World Cup should be a demonstration of universal understanding".

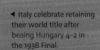

◄ Italy celebrate retaining their world title after beaing Hungary 4–2 in the 1938 Final.

▼ After the annexation of Austria, the Austrian "A" is replaced by the German "D" on cars.

FRANCE 1938

Story of the qualifiers

Welcome, Asia!

▲ Achmad Nawir, captain of the Dutch East Indies team (holding the ball), alongside his teammates during the finals in France.

AFTER THE AMERICAS AND EUROPE in 1930 and Africa in 1934, in 1938 it was the turn of Asia to make its debut at the final phase of the World Cup. Japan had initially been due to take part, but withdrew, leaving the Dutch East Indies (in what is now Indonesia) as the sole representatives of their continent, despite having not played a single qualifying match.

Apart from Austria and Spain, the most notable absentees included Uruguay and Argentina, along with the UK teams, who once again had opted not to take part. Just four countries were playing in their third World Cup: Brazil, Belgium, France and Romania. And in the last three of those teams, several players were appearing in their third World Cup tournament: the Belgian Bernard Voorhoof, French pair Edmond Delfour and Étienne Mattler, and Romania's Nicolae Kovács, brother of the future coaching legend Stefan Kovács.

Joint champions?

THE 1938 WORLD CUP used the same format as in 1934 – a purely knockout system. The teams needed to get through three rounds to reach the final, but the organizing committee did make a change concerning the final and how the winner would be decided in the event of a draw: a second match would be held to settle matters. And if at the end of this replay, the score remained level, both teams would be pronounced joint winners and each would get to keep the trophy for two years.

Results

FIRST ROUND		
ITA	2–1 A.E.T.	NOR
FRA	3–1	BEL

FIRST ROUND		
BRA	6–5 A.E.T.	POL
TCH	3–0 A.E.T.	NED

FIRST ROUND		
HUN	6–0	INH
SUI	4–2	GER
SUI	1–1 A.E.T.	GER

FIRST ROUND		
SWE	-	AUT
CUB	2–1	ROU
CUB	3–3 A.E.T.	ROU

QUARTER-FINAL		
ITA	3–1	FRA

QUARTER-FINAL		
BRA	1–1 A.E.T.	TCH
BRA	2–1 A.E.T.	TCH

QUARTER-FINAL		
HUN	2–0	SUI

QUARTER-FINAL		
SWE	8–0	CUB

SEMI-FINAL		
ITA	2–1	BRA

SEMI-FINAL		
HUN	5–1	SWE

PLAY-OFF FOR THIRD PLACE		
BRA	4–2	SWE

FINAL		
ITA	4–2	HUN

16 TEAMS

18
MATCHES PLAYED

4
CARDS

375 700
SPECTATORS

OFFICIAL POSTER

×7

4.7
AVERAGE GOALS
PER MATCH

ITALY
WINNERS

LEONIDAS DA SILVA
LEADING GOALSCORER

THE ALLEN
OFFICIAL MATCH BALL

Host towns and stadiums

A mix of old and new

The 1938 World Cup was the first for which the cost of building stadiums for the tournament became a big political issue. When France was named as host, many of the country's existing stadia were deemed to be inadequate. Prior to the 1924 Olympic Games, the idea of building a 100,000-seater stadium had been the subject of lengthy political debate in France, culminating in the adaptation of the Stade Colombes. In 1938, due to a lack of support from the state, the French football association managed to secure only the enlargement of Colombes, raising its capacity to 65,000. And so it was at the old stadium, where Uruguay had clinched their first Olympic title in 1924, that the third world champions would go on to be crowned. Of the ten arenas used for the competition, only one was new: Parc Lescure in Bordeaux, unveiled on 12 June for the quarter-final between Brazil and Czechoslovakia. The average attendance at the tournament came to 20,872 per match, the lowest recorded of any World Cup.

▲ The draw for the first round, performed by five-year-old Yves, Jules Rimet's grandson.

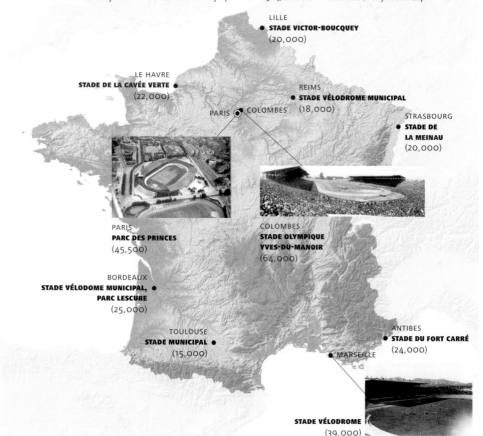

LILLE
● **STADE VICTOR-BOUCQUEY**
(20,000)

LE HAVRE
STADE DE LA CAVÉE VERTE ●
(22,000)

REIMS
● **STADE VÉLODROME MUNICIPAL**
(18,000)

PARIS ○ COLOMBES

STRASBOURG
● **STADE DE LA MEINAU**
(20,000)

PARIS
PARC DES PRINCES
(45,500)

COLOMBES
STADE OLYMPIQUE YVES-DU-MANOIR
(64,000)

BORDEAUX
STADE VÉLODOME MUNICIPAL, ●
PARC LESCURE
(25,000)

TOULOUSE
STADE MUNICIPAL ●
(15,000)

ANTIBES
● **STADE DU FORT CARRÉ**
(24,000)

● MARSEILLE

STADE VÉLODROME
(39,000)

Regulations

Rimet's original idea

When France was awarded the World Cup at the 1936 FIFA Congress in Berlin, doubts were raised as to whether the country would be able to stage a successful tournament. FIFA's French president Jules Rimet was himself scarcely convinced of France's commitment to holding the tournament, so he dreamed up an original solution that he explained in his memoirs, *The marvellous history of the World Cup*: "I first believed I'd found the solution by planning to split the risk which was causing concern: three associations, the French, the Belgian and the Dutch, would be jointly responsible for the organization. My motion was politely rejected, both by the executive committee and by the associations I'd wished to involve." It would be 64 years before Rimet's novel idea would be realized (Japan and South Korea in 2002).

▲ Jakob Streitle leaves the pitch with a bloodied face following Germany's first round exit at the hands of Switzerland.

▲ Italian keeper Aldo Olivieri repels another Norwegian attack.

The champions get a fright

5 JUNE 1938

ITALY 2–1 **NORWAY**
A.E.T.

FERRARIS 2, PIOLA 94   BRUSTAD 83

Switzerland beat Germany

4 JUNE 1938

SWITZERLAND 1–1 **GERMANY**
A.E.T.

ABEGGLEN 43   GAUCHEL 29

9 JUNE 1938

SWITZERLAND 4–2 **GERMANY**

WALASCHEK 42, BICKEL 64, ABEGGLEN 75, 78   HAHNEMANN 8, LOERTSCHER 22 (O.G.)

THE 1938 WORLD CUP got underway on 4 June at the Parc des Princes in Paris, with Switzerland against Germany. In the wake of Austria's recent annexation by Germany and the integration into the German team of some of Austria's players (five for this first match), many wondered if the differing football styles and the "political" obligation to combine them would adversely affect the team's cohesion. The Parisian public got firmly behind the Swiss in what was a fiercely contested affair. Germany opened the scoring through Jupp Gauchel (29th minute), only for Switzerland to equalize before half-time courtesy of Trello Abegglen. There was no further scoring, so a replay was held five days later.

The start of the second encounter saw the Germans take the upper hand and, by the 22nd minute, they were 2–0 ahead. The tension and public animosity towards Germany went up a notch when Switzerland's Georges Aeby and Germany's Ludwig Goldbrunner clashed violently. The Swiss player was removed on a stretcher, but Eugène Walaschek halved the deficit just before the break. Then, in the 64th minute, the stadium erupted when Alfred Bickel, the Grasshoppers striker, drew his side level. And when Abegglen struck twice more for the Swiss in quick succession (in the 75th and 78th minutes), it was sheer pandemonium. The Swiss had started as favourites, but a French newspaper summed up the result as follows: "Little Switzerland fell mighty Germany…"

AMID A SOMEWHAT hostile atmosphere in Marseilles, the Italian world champions began their title defence. Among the few thousand spectators at the Stade Vélodrome were some who had fled the Fascist regime in Italy and who did not take kindly to the salute with outstretched arm given by the Italian players during the presentation of the teams. Even those without a political axe to grind opted to support Norway, who were making their World Cup debut. When Pietro Ferraris scored after just two minutes, the Italians' progression seemed almost a *fait accompli*, but the defending champions were taking nothing for granted. Vittorio Pozzo, their manager, had not forgotten how the Norwegians had stood up to Italy in the semi-finals of the 1936 Olympic Games in Berlin, only bowing out 2–1 after extra time. Eight of those same Norwegian players were on the field in Marseilles, and Italy were again forced to repel numerous Viking assaults in order to retain their slender advantage. Aldo Olivieri, the Lucchese keeper, pulled off one save after another but, in the 83rd minute, he was powerless to prevent an equalizer by Arne Brustad, who had also scored against Italy in Berlin. Early in extra time, the distinguished Lazio striker Silvio Piola saved face for the champions, but Pozzo knew changes would have to be made…

▲ Brazil, in dark shirts, attack the goal of Poland keeper Edward Madejski.

Raining goals in Strasbourg

5 JUNE 1938

BRAZIL 🇧🇷 **6–5** A.E.T. 🇵🇱 **POLAND**

LEONIDAS 18, 93, 104   SZERFKE 23 (PEN)
ROMEU 25   WILIMOWSKI 53, 59, 89, 118
PERACIO 44, 71

A RADICAL CONTRAST of styles was on offer in Strasbourg. Up against each other for the first-ever time were the Brazilian artists and the Polish athletes, an original encounter that served up spectacular end-to-end fare from the outset. First blood went to Brazil's Leônidas, only for Fritz Scherfke to cancel his goal out with a penalty. By the end of the first period, Romeu and then Perácio had given Brazil a substantial cushion, but then the storm that had been looming unleashed torrential rain upon Strasbourg's Stade de la Meinau. The fans who had positioned themselves by the pitch-side hoardings received a thorough drenching, but the legendary match they witnessed more than made up for it. Amid apocalyptic conditions, Poland clawed their

way back to level the score at 3–3 thanks to two goals from their centre-forward Ernest Wilimowski. Brazil promptly restored their advantage, but the irrepressible Wilimowski levelled the tie again in the 89th minute. Caked in mud, Leônidas discarded his boots and played for a while with bare feet, before Swedish referee Ivan Eklind ordered him to put them back on. Then came extra time. The deluge had stopped, but the goals continued to pour down. Leônidas added two more to take his personal tally to three. Wilimowski managed to bag another, but it was too late. The Polish striker was unsurprisingly devastated: he had produced the Herculean effort of scoring four goals and yet still ending up on the losing side.

Cuba surprise Romania

5 JUNE 1938

CUBA 🇨🇺 **3–3** A.E.T. 🇷🇴 **ROMANIA**

SOCORRO 44, 103, MAGRINA 69   BINDEA 35, BARATKY 88, DOBAY 105

9 JUNE 1938

CUBA 🇨🇺 **2–1** 🇷🇴 **ROMANIA**

SOCORRO 51, FERNANDEZ 57   DOBAY 35

THE CUBAN SIDE were the sole representatives of North and Central America at the 1938 World Cup. They hadn't needed to play any qualifiers; after all, the other teams from the region declined to take part. But in Toulouse, the Cubans set about representing their continent with aplomb. To general surprise, they first forced Romania to extra time, even taking the lead twice and eventually forcing a replay (3–3). For the second game, four days later, the Cubans changed their keeper, with the highly acrobatic Juan Ayra coming in for the plucky Benito Carvajales. Early on, Ayra saved a powerful shot from Iuliu Prassler and kept his side in the game with a string of fine first-half saves. Romania did, however, finally take a 1–0 lead in the 35th minute thanks to a volley from Ştefan Dobay, who also spurned several other chances. Shortly after the interval, however, the Cubans turned the tie on its head with two goals in six minutes. Iuliu Baratky then missed a gilt-edged chance to restore parity, after which the Cubans defended manfully, leaving the Romanians to rue their profligacy in front of goal. In the following round, Cuba paid the price for their tremendous exertions when they conceded eight goals against Sweden.

The Blackshirts

When France and Italy play each other, one of them has to play in a colour other than their usual blue and, at the Parc des Princes in December 1937, it was France who had sported bright red shirts as they played host to the Italians in a friendly match. But at Colombes in the World Cup quarter-final, France donned their traditional blue jerseys, whereas Italy were clad in black from head to toe. In this era of international tension, it echoed the black shirts worn by the Fascist militia, and the choice did not go down well with many French supporters.

▶ Action from the quarter-final between Italy and France at Colombes.

▲ Italy's infamous black shirts: From left to right: Pietro Rava, Amedeo Biavati, Giovanni Ferrari, Silvio Piola and Giuseppe Meazza, in their black shirts before kick-off.

French illusions shattered

12 JUNE 1938

ITALY 🇮🇹 3–1 🇫🇷 **FRANCE**

COLAUSSI 9, PIOLA 51, 72   HEISSERER 10

HAVING progressed to the quarter-finals at the expense of Belgium (3–1), the French allowed themselves to dream ahead of their last-eight encounter. But their opponents, Italy, were very much their "bogey team": the last time they had beaten them was way back in 1920. But France derived a modicum of hope from a recent memory, as on 5 December 1937, a team built around a solid defence made up of Sochaux players (Laurent Di Lorto in goal, behind Étienne Mattler and Héctor Cazenave) had withstood all that the world champions could throw at them (0–0), with Di Lorto in particular performing miracles. The hope was that, in Colombes, he could repeat those heroics. Moreover, Italy manager Vittorio Pozzo's repeated claim that his team was not at the same level as in 1934 offered a further source of optimism for France.

When it came to it, the Italian side were indeed not at their best, but the French lacked the resources to exploit this. Early in the game, both teams scored in quick succession, Italy through Gino Colaussi (in the 9th minute), and France through Oscar Heisserer a minute later. There was no further scoring before the interval, but in the 51st minute, Silvio Piola netted after his captain Giuseppe Meazza had robbed Mattler of the ball. France then dominated as Italy sat back, but France seemed to lack any real belief that they could actually win the game. Italy were defending with their customary canniness, while their counter-attacks made them a constant threat. When Piola increased their lead, any remaining French illusions were well and truly shattered. For the first time, the World Cup was not going to be won by the host nation.

The Uruguayan presence

▲ Héctor Cazenave and Michele Andreolo.

Although Uruguay, the first World Cup winners, opted not to travel to France in 1938, there were still two Uruguayans on the field in Colombes for the France-Italy quarter-final. Each team had a player who originated from the South American republic: for France, it was defender Héctor Cazenave, born in Montevideo in 1914, who had joined FC Sochaux in 1936 along with some other South American players. And slightly earlier, in 1935, Michele Andreolo, another native of Montevideo, had arrived in Italy to boost Bologna's ranks. Against Italy, Cazenave was making his eighth and final appearance for France, whereas Andreolo would go on to win 26 caps, the last of them in 1942.

"Knockout matches never produce great football"

Gaston Barreau, coach of the French team eliminated by Italy.

Gaston Barreau had been part of the selection committee for the France team since 1920.
Since 1936, he had been solely responsible for the team's selection and, after the quarter-final defeat at the hands of Italy, he felt that he had not seen a great match. He also thought he knew the reason why: "Basically, because the competition's format is not conducive to it. Whether in the French Cup or the World Cup, a match where the loser goes straight out cannot produce great football. The players are too nervous and their usual ability deserts them."

▲ The Czechoslovak keeper, Karel Burkert, saves a Brazilian shot.

An echo of the French Championship

12 JUNE 1938		
HUNGARY	2–0	SWITZERLAND
SAROSI 40 ZSENGELLER 89		

O N 12 JUNE in Lille, Hungary defeated Switzerland (2–0). Each team featured a player who had plied his trade in the French top flight. Trello Abegglen, FC Sochaux's Swiss striker and three-goal hero in the previous round against Germany, had been both a title-winner and the league's top scorer in France in 1935. He then won the French Cup in 1937 before returning to his homeland in 1938 to join Geneva's Servette. For the Hungarians, their left winger Willy Kohut had just won the French Cup with Marseilles, one year after helping them win the French league title.

The "Battle of Bordeaux"

12 JUNE 1938		
BRAZIL	1–1 A.E.T.	CZECHOSLOVAKIA
LEONIDAS 30	NEJEDLY 65 (PEN)	

14 JUNE 1938		
BRAZIL	2-1	CZECHOSLOVAKIA
LEONIDAS 57, ROBERTO 63	KOPECKY 25	

T HE QUARTER-FINAL at Bordeaux's brand-new Parc Lescure stadium between Brazil and 1934 runners-up Czechoslovakia promised to be a tremendous spectacle. However, the contrasting styles of the South American artists and the methodical Central Europeans resulted in a horribly violent brawl. The outcome of this fracas was three players sent off (Machado and Procópio for Brazil, Říha for Czechoslovakia), two Czechoslovak players left with fractures, a leg in the case of striker Nejedlý and an arm for their legendary keeper Plánička (making his 73rd and final international appearance), together with various other injuries. But they did find time to play a little bit of football, and the score finished 1–1, Leônidas – from an offside position? – had opened the scoring in the first half, before Nejedlý equalized from the penalty spot.

Two days later, the pair met again but with barely recognizable teams. The Brazilians made nine changes and the Czechoslovaks five. Czechoslovakia adopted a more attacking approach, which was rewarded by Vlastimil Kopecký's first-half goal. But their offensive endeavours seemed to exhaust them and the South Americans gradually made their superior skill count. Leônidas in the 57th minute and Roberto in the 62nd both scored to turn the tie on its head and send Brazil through. Incredibly, their technical staff had been so confident that they had already opted to send the players not needed for the game down to Marseilles, where the semi-final was to take place two days later.

◀ The Italian centre-forward, Silvio Piola, gets the better of Brazilians Arthur Machado and Domingos da Guia.

Radio Brazil

The first radio broadcast of a football match had been in 1924 in Uruguay. Radios, like the Cruzeiro 100, allowed Brazilian fans to follow the World Cup in France.

▲ **FIFA World Football Museum Collection.**

Italy banish Brazil

16 JUNE 1938

ITALY 🇮🇹 2-1 🇧🇷 **BRAZIL**

COLAUSSI 51, MEAZZA 60   ROMEU 87 (PEN)

THE SEMI-FINAL in Marseilles promised to be the final in all but name. It pitted Italy, reigning champions and conquerors of hosts France, against Brazil, mercurial and at times mesmerizing so far in the tournament. The Stade Vélodrome was swamped by spectators in a rush to get through the turnstiles and secure their place in the stand. Many were shut outside, but when the teams were announced, those inside were disappointed to learn that they wouldn't be seeing Brazil's star player Leônidas. Rumour had it that the striker and his attacking partner Tim were being rested with a view to the final. It was also reported that the Brazilians were so confidant they had already reserved their train tickets for the trip up to Paris. But the truth was less interesting: the reason Leônidas and Tim were absent was that they were both still carrying knocks from their double-header against Czechoslovakia.

Italy's coach, meanwhile, had picked the same team that had seen off France. Wary of the unpredictable Brazilians and their attacking flair, the Italians adopted a cautious approach to the game, strictly maintaining their defensive line. Their two midfield schemers, Giuseppe Meazza and Giovanni Ferrari, stayed very deep, while their wing-backs, Pietro Serantoni and Ugo Locatelli, shadowed the Brazilian wide men closely in a bid to prevent their trademark darting runs into the box. But Italy still found time to force Brazil's goalkeeper to make some extraordinary saves before half-time.

And the Brazilians were not their usual selves either. Had they been affected by the media criticism of what was seen as their overly individualistic play? Whatever the reason, they attempted to play a short passing game that lacked a cutting edge, and the first half passed off without score. After the break, Brazil let the tempo drop and Italy promptly filled the void, sensing they had the beating of their opponents. In the first 15 minutes of the second half, Italy took the tie by the scruff of the neck, opening the scoring through Gino Colaussi and then doubling their lead through a Meazza penalty. In the second period, the duel between Silvio Piola and Domingos da Guia had become increasingly tetchy and it was another foul by the Brazilian that gave away the spot kick, the third conceded by Domingos in the tournament. For Meazza, it was his 33rd goal for his country, a record that would remain in place until the advent of Gigi Riva in the 1970s. Brazil managed a consolation goal in the 87th minute through Romeu, but for the Marseilles public who left the ground disappointed, the match's outcome had been clear for some time.

35

That's the number of seconds it took for Sweden to open the scoring in their match against Hungary. The scorer was the Gothenburg inside-right, Arne Nyberg, who had already netted against Cuba and went on to bag his third goal of the tournament in the third-place playoff match against Brazil.

Hungarians much too strong

16 JUNE 1938

HUNGARY 5–1 **SWEDEN**

JACOBSSON 19 (o.g.), TITKOS 37   NYBERG 1
ZSENGELLER 39, 85, SAROSI 65

◀ Hungary and Sweden before their semi-final match at the Parc des Princes in Paris.

"Oh if only we'd drawn Sweden!"

Gusti Jordan, the French defender.

At the Parc des Princes to watch the Hungary-Sweden semi-final, the French centre-half found himself wishing his team had been drawn against Sweden: "This semi-final was much too easy a game for the Hungarians. They're in another class from the Swedes. It's a shame France didn't meet Sweden instead of Italy!"

IN THE other semi-final between Hungary and Sweden, the gap in levels was too great for the crowd at the Parc des Princes to be gripped by even the slightest suspense. Even the goal scored by Arne Nyberg from the Swedes' first attack failed to unsettle this fine Hungarian team. They simply proceeded to lay siege to the Swedish goal, calmly and without any fear. Their superiority in all areas was striking, leaving the Swedes to rely on only their big hearts as they fought to repel the Hungarians. Others would have used any means to try to mask their deficiencies, but the Scandinavians did not resort to any chicanery. Man-mark their opponents? It was not in their nature. Cover their defenders when they came forward for set-pieces? They didn't think of it. Against such likeable and naive opponents, the Hungarians easily imposed their authority, without having to exert themselves. A Sven Jacobsson own goal levelled the score in the 19th minute. Then, in the space of two minutes (37th and 39th), outside-left Pál Titkos and Zsengellér gave Hungary a two-goal advantage. A further two goals then followed (from Gyula Zsengellér and the captain György Sárosi). And at the final whistle, the Parisian crowd left the stadium mindful that the margin of victory could easily have been higher…

Swedes on a wing and a prayer

◀ Sweden made history by becoming the first team to travel to a World Cup by aeroplane. They were pictured here prior to their departure home.

Sweden's fast track to the semi-final had been nothing if not unconventional. First, their players had made history by being the first-ever team to arrive in the host country by plane. Then, having been initially drawn to play Austria in Lyon in the opening round, they instead passed straight into the quarter-finals without playing a game when the Austrian team were unable to take part due to their country's annexation by Germany. In Antibes, their Cuban opponents, exhausted from their exertions in their two first-round games against Romania, proved no match for the Scandinavians, who ran out 8–0 winners. This unexpectedly easy route having opened for them, they progressed to the semi-final stage, as they had done at the 1924 Olympic Games in Colombes, where they ended up with the bronze medal.

PLAY-OFF FOR THIRD PLACE

▲ The *Black Diamond*, Leônidas Da Silva, scored twice in this match.

Leônidas back again

19 JUNE 1938

BRAZIL 4–2 **SWEDEN**

ROMEU 44   JONASSON 28
LEÔNIDAS 63, 74   NYBERG 38
PERACIO 80

Brazil returned to Bordeaux for the third-place play-off. The game was to be played in the same stadium where they had faced Czechoslovakia in the quarter-finals and where Leônidas had scored two goals in two games. Against Sweden, the Brazilian striker scored twice more, which secured the bronze medal for Brazil and left him as the tournament's leading goalscorer, with eight goals in four matches. Both prizes were small consolation for a player who many viewed as being the best in the world at the time.

▲ Italy's Silvio Piola takes on Hungarian defenders Sándor Biró and György Szűcs. Piola scored twice in the Final.

A well-deserved double for Italy

19 JUNE 1938

ITALY 🇮🇹 4–2 **HUNGARY**

COLAUSSI 6, 35, PIOLA 16, 82   TITKOS 8, SAROSI 70

Capdeville, the French presence

Although the France team had failed to reach the final of the 1938 World Cup, a French presence was assured in the shape of referee, Georges Capdeville. His appointment was perhaps a reward for the fine job he had done in the replay of the potentially tricky Brazil -Czechoslovakia quarter-final (2–1) in Bordeaux, which had passed off without incident, in contrast to the two teams' first encounter. In the final, the quality of his refereeing was once again hailed. Capdeville would go on to become an administrator and in the 1960s and '70s, he served as president of the South-West League, his home region.

FOUR YEARS previously, Czechoslovakia had represented Central European football against Italy in the World Cup Final; this time it was the turn of Hungary. En route, the Hungarian team enjoyed an easier path to the final than their opponents, including comfortable wins against the Dutch East Indies (6–0) in the opening round and Sweden (5–1) in the semi-finals. Hungarian football had, for many years, drawn plaudits for its finesse and technique, but their players were sometimes criticized for a half-hearted approach and poor athletic conditioning. These same virtues and defects were epitomized by their most iconic player, György Sárosi, scorer of four goals in the tournament so far. Well aware of both the passing and scoring ability of the Hungarian captain, Italy's manager Vittorio Pozzo came up with a plan. He assigned Miguel Andreolo to man-mark Sárosi, effectively blocking all of the Hungarian's attempted moves and further highlighting the Hungarian captain's somewhat lethargic style. Deprived of their usual supply line, the two wingers, Pál Titkos and Ferenc Sas, were unable to wreak their usual havoc. Hungary was not exactly solid at the back either, especially in the absence of their most experienced defender, Lajos Korányi.

The early exchanges suggested that the match might be evenly balanced. In the sixth minute, Hungary's defensive frailties were exposed when a Piola cross found Gino Colaussi unmarked at the far post, but less than two minutes later, Titkos equalized with a fierce shot.

From that moment on, though, it was the Italians who seized the initiative, led by the imperious Meazza-Ferrari duo. In the 16th minute, a one-two between the pair allowed Piola to bypass the defence and blast the ball into the top corner. Twenty minutes later, the lightning-fast Colaussi latched on to a long searching ball from Meazza and promptly buried the third. But Hungary weren't quite finished yet and, in the 70th minute, Sárosi for once evaded his marker to register his fifth strike of the tournament to revive Hungary's faint hopes. Italy promptly dropped deep to rely on the counter. In the 85th minute, Rava burst away on one such forward foray, before feeding Ferrari. The move continued with Piola, whose speed took him clear of the flailing defenders. He then played in Biavati on the right, before adopting a central position from which to bury the return pass. It had been a smooth move and a comfortable victory. Italy were worthy champions.

Piola, key striker

With his five goals, Silvio Piola may not have been the top scorer at the 1938 World Cup, but he was the tournament's most influential player. In the first round, it was he who scored in extra time to secure Italy's win over Norway. In the quarters, he was on target twice to bring France to their knees, while in the final, he first restored his side's advantage against Hungary (2–1), before grabbing the killer goal that ensured a second title for the Italians. The rangy Piola was 24 at the time. In 1935, he had taken over from the centre-forward of the victorious 1934 side, Angelo Schiavio, hitting the ground running with two goals in a prestigious win over Austria (2–0). The interruption to international competitions caused by the Second World War temporarily prevented him from adding to an already sizeable list of honours, but he continued to represent his country up until 1952 and became the most prolific Italian striker of all time (scoring 364 goals in all competitions, including 274 in Serie A and 30 in just 34 internationals).

▶ The World Cup trophy on display before the Final between Italy and Hungary.

Meazza and Ferrari, the great schemers

Two Italian players were involved in both of their country's World Cup Final triumphs in 1934 and 1938: Giuseppe Meazza and Giovanni Ferrari. The pair were old pals, having played together for Inter since 1935, and had been making the national team tick for many years. Meazza was first capped at the tender age of 19 and, aged 27 at the time of this tournament, he was one of Europe's most experienced players. The balding 30-year-old Giovanni Ferrari had the look of the veteran. Although lacking the speed of his younger years, his experience was invaluable when it came to guiding the side's young strikers. Lucien Gamblin, France's former international defender and a journalist in 1938, had this to say the day after Italy's second World Cup success: "Italy's play would not have reached such heights if Meazza and Ferrari had not put in such incredible performances."

Everyone gets a medal

Participation medal given to Leonidas da Silva. Every player at the World Cup received such a medal.

◀ FIFA World Football Museum collection.

◀ Giuseppe Meazza and Giovanni Ferrari visiting Marseille's Stade Vélodrome, prior to the start of the World Cup.

Pozzo's triumph

THE IMAGE is a famous one. In the midst of the blue-shirted Italian players, a white-haired gentleman with a beaming smile is clutching the World Cup trophy that he and his charges have just won for the second time. Vittorio Pozzo, aged 52, is experiencing the ultimate achievement. His career as Italy manager did not end on this day of 19 June 1938 at Colombes, but it was at its pinnacle. He was the undisputed "old master" of Italian football, so immense had been his technical and strategic influence over the years: he had also been at the helm of Italy's Olympic team in both 1912 and 1924, a period when he played a leading role in developing national football and the domestic championship. In 1929, he was named sole selector of the national team, seemingly an open-ended post as he continued to occupy it until 1948. During those 19 years, he won 60 matches out of 87, losing just 11. When the World Cup drew to a close in 1938, his side was on a run of 22 consecutive games without defeat.

1950

In a world still feeling the effects of war, Brazil hosted a tournament whose trophy had been renamed the Jules Rimet Cup in honour of the competition's founder. The only World Cup without a knockout system produced Italy's first World Cup defeat, the USA's shock win over England, and a winning goal by Alcides Ghiggia in Uruguay's sensational 2–1 victory over Brazil in the final match.

In the shadow of the *Maracanazo*

◄ Uruguay before their match against Spain.

▼ View of the Maracanã Stadium, still under construction a few days before the tournament kicked off.

AFTER two successive World Cups held in Europe, the competition logically returned to a South American continent that had been largely spared the turmoil of the Second World War, even though Brazil had joined the Allies' side in 1942. Since the overthrow of dictator Getúlio Vargas in 1945, the country had been enjoying a period of both democracy and economic prosperity. In view of the large distances between the cities, the teams travelled about by plane. Built at the heart of Rio de Janeiro, which was still at that time the country's capital, the Maracanã stadium was designed to be a symbol of the "order and progress" from Brazil's national motto. But the construction work on the Estádio Municipal overran and its unveiling took place before all the cement

had fully dried… Still, across the nation the enthusiasm was at fever pitch. Far from the low-key atmosphere experienced at the 1930 World Cup in Uruguay, Brazil launched itself into three weeks of festivities which could surely only lead to the triumph of the national team, whose exploits were followed closely in every neighbourhood by huddles of people clustered around radios. There was a strong sense of nationalism too, with the Brazilian dailies orchestrating campaigns against their opponents before each of their team's games. In this context, Uruguay's victory in the deciding game over the hosts was seen as a national humiliation. Referred to as the *Maracanazo* (Maracana disaster) the game cast a shadow over Brazilian football that has never entirely disappeared.

BRAZIL 1950

JULES RIMET CUP (WORLD'S CUP) 1950 IN BRAZIL

Story of the qualifiers

The British finally join in

FIVE YEARS after the end of the war, football was still being affected by the global upheaval. Both Germany and Japan were barred from the tournament by FIFA. The communist bloc countries, apart from Yugoslavia, refused to take part in the qualifiers, while Argentina also declined to participate. But the British nations, the game's founders who had ignored the first three World Cups, finally came on board. England, Scotland, Wales and Northern Ireland locked horns in a group of four, with two World Cup places up for grabs. England finished top ahead of Scotland, who refused to travel to Brazil; believing that second place did not entitle them to do so. Despite having qualified, Turkey and India also failed to take up their places, so Portugal and France, eliminated by Spain and Yugoslavia respectively, were reinstated, only to themselves withdraw at the 11th hour. Consequently, as in 1930, only 13 teams ended up taking part in the final phase, with two of the groups truncated.

▶ The England team made its World Cup debut at the 1950 finals in Brazil.

Regulations

A cup with no final

◀ Italy's Giovanni Mauro (standing), presents the newly named Jules Rimet Cup after bringing the trophy with him to Brazil. During the war it had been stored safely in a bank vault in Rome.

To prevent European nations from crossing the Atlantic to face the possibility of only playing in one game (if they lost), the knockout system used in 1934 and 1938 was scrapped in favour of a group format, as used in 1930. The four group winners then had to fight it out within a single final group. As luck would have it, the draw determined that the title was contested in the last match, between Brazil and Uruguay, a final in all but name.

GROUP 1

BRA	4–0	MEX
YUG	3–0	SUI
BRA	2–2	SUI
MEX	1–4	YUG
BRA	2–0	YUG
MEX	1–2	SUI

	W	D	L	+	–	PTS
BRA	2	1	0	8	2	5
YUG	2	0	1	7	3	4
SUI	1	1	1	4	6	3
MEX	0	0	3	2	10	0

GROUP 2

ENG	2–0	CHI
ESP	3–1	USA
ESP	2–0	CHI
USA	1–0	ENG
ESP	1–0	ENG
CHI	5–2	USA

	W	D	L	+	–	PTS
ESP	3	0	0	6	1	6
ENG	1	0	2	2	2	2
CHI	1	0	2	5	6	2
USA	1	0	2	4	8	2

GROUP 3

SWE	3–2	ITA
SWE	2–2	PAR
ITA	2–0	PAR

	W	D	L	+	–	PTS
SWE	1	1	0	5	4	3
ITA	1	0	1	4	3	2
PAR	0	1	1	2	4	1

GROUP 4

URU	8–0	BOL

	W	D	L	+	–	PTS
URU	1	0	0	8	0	2
BOL	0	0	1	0	8	0

Final group stage

FINAL GROUP STAGE

BRA	7–1	SWE
URU	2–2	ESP
BRA	6–1	ESP
URU	3–2	SWE
SWE	3–1	ESP

	W	D	L	+	–	PTS
URU	2	1	0	7	5	5
BRA	2	0	1	14	4	4
SWE	1	0	2	6	11	2
ESP	0	1	2	4	11	1

"THE FINAL"

URU	2–1	BRA

BOL BRA CHI ENG
ESP ITA MEX PAR
SUI SWE URU USA
YUG

13 TEAMS

22
MATCHES PLAYED

0
CARDS

1 045 246
SPECTATORS

OFFICIAL POSTER

URUGUAY
WINNERS

×8

ADEMIR
LEADING GOALSCORER

4
AVERAGE GOALS
PER MATCH

SUPERBALL DUPLO T
OFFICIAL MATCH BALL

Host cities and stadiums

Considerable distances

The 1950 World Cup was the first to attract more than a million spectators, helped by the construction of the Maracanã. Four of Brazil's games played at the venue attracted crowds of more than 138,000. Six stadiums were chosen for the tournament, with nearly 3,000 kilometres separating Recife in the north, where Chile played the United States (5–2), and Porto Alegre in the far south. The weather played its part too. This was a winter World Cup, but the conditions varied across the venues. Before taking on Brazil on 1 July in the heat of Rio, the formidable Yugoslavs had played Mexico just three days earlier in the cool southern air of Porto Alegre… Away from the huge population centres of Rio and São Paulo, there was limited public enthusiasm for matches not involving the national team: in Curitiba, for instance, a crowd of fewer than 8,000 fans watched the draw between Paraguay and Sweden (2–2), while in Belo Horizonte scarcely 5,000 spectators attended Uruguay's stroll against Bolivia (8–0). The smallest crowd of them all, however, was at the Switzerland-Mexico encounter (2–1) in Porto Alegre, where just 3,580 turned up to watch, despite the fixture being played in Brazil's own group.

RECIFE
**ESTADIO DO RECIFE
ILHA DO RETIRO**
(10,000)

**ESTADIO MUNCIPAL
DO PACAEMBU**
(55,000)

BELO HORIZONTE
ESTADIO INDEPENDENCIA
(12,000)

RIO DE JANEIRO
**ESTADIO MUNICIPAL
DO MARACANÃ**
(200,000)

SÃO PAULO

CURITIBA
**ESTÁDIO DURIVAL
DE BRITTO**
(15,000)

STADE ILDO MENEGHETTI
(12,000)

PORTO ALEGRE

Commemorative medal

From the first World Cup in Uruguay, it has been customary for the host country to produce medals to commemorate the tournament. These souvenirs were given to the CBD, who organized the tournament.

▲ **FIFA World Football Museum collection.**

A Maracanã and a Brazil under construction

24 JUNE 1950
BRAZIL 🇧🇷 4–0 🇲🇽 **MEXICO**
ADEMIR 30, 79
JAIR 65
BALTAZAR 71

THE CONSTRUCTION of Rio's Estádio Municipal, in the Maracanã district, didn't start until August 1948. When the global football feast got under way, the ground was not completely finished. Eventually, it would supersede Hampden Park in Glasgow as the largest stadium on the planet, but on 24 June 1950, a "mere" 81,649 supporters were in attendance, amid scenes of complete disarray: they had to step over sacks of cement and cross muddy pools to find their places on the terraces. The referee, meanwhile, only arrived in the changing rooms 20 minutes before kick-off. Half an hour earlier, violent winds had torn loose a metal panel, fortunately with no injuries. But the atmosphere was electric, complete with firecrackers, fanfares, a cacophony of cries and the release of balloons and then five thousand pigeons. At 3pm precisely, 21 cannon shots marked the start of the World Cup… as the public were still dusting off the shower of plaster and fresh concrete that the explosions had sent tumbling from the roof.

On the field of play too, in their white jerseys with blue collars, Brazil seemed to be a work in progress. Mexico had only come to defend, and against clearly inferior opponents, it took the *Seleçao* half an hour to open the scoring through their strong and incisive inside-forward Ademir (1–0), whose understanding with the elusive and clinical Jair (who made it 2–0 in the 65th minute), masked the Brazilians' own shortcomings as a team. After a 71st-minute third goal from Baltazar, Ademir took up Jair's invitation to notch his second (4-0, 79th). For the moment, everything was shaping up nicely for the hosts.

▲ Brazil take to the field to face Mexico in the opening match. Left is Maneca while Baltazar is pictured holding the ball.

▶ Swedish goalkeeper Kalle Svensson fails to block a shot from Italian Ermes Muccinelli, who brings the score to 3–2.

A first defeat for Italy

25 JUNE 1950	
SWEDEN 🇸🇪 3–2 🇮🇹 **ITALY**	
JEPPSSON 25, 69, ANDERSSON 34	CARAPELLESE 7, MUCCINELLI 78

ABSENT FROM the 1930 World Cup but tournament winners in both 1934 and 1938, Italy arrived in Brazil undefeated in the competition (eight wins and one draw). But in their very first game, against Sweden in São Paulo, Italy's air of invincibility was shattered. At the origin of this surprise defeat lay the Superga disaster, named after the hillside overlooking Turin where, on 4 May 1949, the plane transporting the great Torino football team, champions of Italy in 1946, 1947 and 1948, crashed, killing everyone on board. The death toll included 18 players, many of them internationals: Aldo Ballarin, Romeo Menti, Guglielmo Gabetto, Valentino Mazzola… Not only was the Italan team decimated, but the trauma was so deep that, one year later, Italy travelled to Brazil by sea. The crossing from Naples to Santos lasted two weeks and it was impossible for the players to train properly on board or to work properly on their physical condition.

Facing them were Sweden who, despite having claimed the Olympic crown at the 1948 Games in London, were not widely expected to do well at the tournament. The Swedish football association had decided to dispense with the services of Gunnar Gren, Gunnar Nordahl and Nils Liedholm, their attacking trio known as "Gre-No-Li", as the three players had just agreed to move abroad, to Milan, and as professionals, they were left behind. With the crowd firmly behind the Italians courtesy of the significant numbers of Italian migrants who had made Brazil their home, the world champions were quick to seize the initiative through a seventh-minute volley from their captain Riccardo Carapellese. But Sweden proceeded to turn the match round with their dynamic and attack-minded brand of play. Winger Nacka Skoglund was a thorn in Italy's side, while Hans Jeppson, dubbed "an exterminating angel" by the Italian press, netted twice (1–1, 25th; 3–1, 69th). In between Jeppson's two goals, Sune Andersson registered with a long-range strike (2–1, 34th). Despite the deficit being reduced by Muccinelli (3–2, 78th), Sweden successfully repelled most Italian assaults on their goal, where keeper Kalle Svensson was working wonders. With only seconds remaining on the clock, Carapellese at last had a chance to equalize. His shot struck the post and rebounded to Muccinelli, unmarked with the goal gaping… but he sent it wide.

Italy had been outfought for the first time at a World Cup. Back home, the shock was considerable. What conclusions should be drawn about Italian football? A very simple one, as it turned out: over the coming weeks, six of the 11 Swedish players from the match in São Paulo were snapped up by Serie A clubs…

◀ Joe Gaetjens is carried aloft by fans after scoring the game's decisive goal against England.

The miracle of Belo Horizonte

29 JUNE 1950

USA 🇺🇸 1–0 ✚ ENGLAND

GAETJENS 38

FOR WHAT was the first World Cup match in their history, England were greeted by a sparsely populated Maracanã stadium when they emerged from the tunnel on 25 June. Watched by fewer than 30,000 spectators, they beat Chile 2–0. That same day, the USA had lost 3–1 to Spain, so the English no doubt saw their upcoming encounter with the semi-professional Americans as a *fait accompli*. However, the warning signs were there for all to see, with a plucky US team having led the Spanish 1–0 until the 80th minute… But over in the States, football was only played by students and some immigrant groups… England, on the other hand, were the inventors of the game. In 1950, they had only ever lost nine times against non-UK nations, so the match was regarded by many as a formality and the England manager Walter Winterbottom even left his biggest star, outside-right Stanley Matthews, on the bench.

The early exchanges in the match, played on 29 June 1950 in Belo Horizonte, appeared to justify Winterbottom's thinking. During the first 12 minutes, the American keeper Frank Borghi, a hearse driver by trade, kept out several clear-cut chances. "At that stage, I was just hoping to stop them scoring five or six," he later recalled. But despite the one-way traffic from England, the breakthrough came at the other end: in the 37th minute, a mishit shot from the American Walter Bahr, a Philadelphia primary school teacher, ended up being more of a cross. England's goalkeeper Bert Williams started out to claim it, but the ball instead hit the head of USA player Joe Gaetjens and went in. So who was this Joe Gaetjens? A Haitian student studying accountancy in New York, who earned his living washing dishes in a Brooklyn restaurant…

The second half saw wave upon wave of English attacks continually break up against the rock-solid American defence and their heroic keeper Borghi. Tom Finney was guilty of over-dribbling at times, and Stan Mortensen had a shot cleared off the line. In the 82nd minute, Mortensen ran through on goal, but was taken out American football-style by US defender Charlie Colombo. After a few final skirmishes, time was up and it was a historic job done for the Americans. Gaetjens, Borghi and half the team were chaired off the ground in triumph. The English, meanwhile, were at an all-time low: "I think at some point we decided it just wasn't our day and we stopped playing," lamented Tom Finney. "If we played them a hundred times, we'd win 99 of them easily."

To make the loss even harder to stomach, it emerged that three of the "American" players should never have been on the field that day: the goalscorer Joe Gaetjens, as he was Haitian; Joe Maca, born in Belgium; and the captain Ed McIlvenny, who was Scottish. None of the trio were American citizens when the match was played on 29 June 1950. After this "Miracle of Belo Horizonte", FIFA tightened the nationality criteria whereby a player could not play for a country other than that of his birth.

Yugoslavia come a cropper

1 JULY 1950

BRAZIL 🇧🇷 2–0 YUGOSLAVIA

ADEMIR 4, ZIZINHO 69

▶ The Brazilian keeper, Moacir Barbosa, saves a Yugoslav shot.

IN THEIR EARLIER Group 1 games, Yugoslavia and their "magic square" (Zlatko Čajkovski, Predrag Đajić, Rajko Mitić and Stjepan Bobek) had blasted away first Switzerland (3–0) and then Mexico (4–1). Brazil, meanwhile, had been frustrated by the Swiss, who held the hosts to a 2–2 draw in a fiercely contested encounter. But even before the kick-off of their match with Yugoslavia, the balance swung in Brazil's favour when Mitić, returning to the changing rooms after the warm-up, gashed his head badly on a section of concrete. The resulting deep cut required two stitches and a bandaged skull. The stunned Yugoslavs had no replacement and so were forced to start with ten men. When Mitić re-joined his team mates five minutes after kick-off, Brazil were already 1–0 in front: in the fourth minute, Bauer had taken advantage of a muddle in the penalty area to feed Ademir, who promptly netted his second goal of the tournament from close range. Thereafter, the Yugoslavs were kept at bay by Brazil, before Zizinho doubled the score in the 69th minute and Brazil emerged as clear favourites to win the trophy.

▲ Goalkeeper Antoni Ramallets and defender Gabriel Aristiaguirre under pressure as Spain lose 6–1 to hosts Brazil.

"There's no other attacking trio on Earth as good as Zizinho-Ademir-Jair."

Kalle Svensson, Sweden goalkeeper

Brazil in exhibition mode

13 JULY 1950

BRAZIL 6–1 **SPAIN**

PARRA 15 (o.g.), JAIR 21   IGOA 71
CHICO 31, 55, ADEMIR 57
ZIZINHO 67

Ademir makes it eight

Powerful thighs, a prominent chin which earned him the nickname "Queixada" (jawbone in Portuguese), and a head that bobbed to the right when he ran… Ademir, the Brazilian team's goal machine, perhaps wasn't the most elegant player to watch, but he was undeniably clinical. A national star from the moment he scored a hat-trick in the 1949 Copa América playoff against Paraguay (7–0), the Vasco de Gama player had begun his World Cup with two goals against Mexico, followed by a third against Yugoslavia. The final round saw him overtake Uruguay's Míguez in the scorers' rankings courtesy of four goals against Sweden and another goal against Spain. This made Ademir the joint record-holder for the most goals in World Cup finals matches, along with the Argentinian Guillermo Stabile, from the 1930 tournament.

I N THE FIRST MATCH of the final group, the Brazilian wizards ran rings round Sweden, winning 7–1, with Ademir netting four. "There's no other attacking trio on Earth as good as Zizinho-Ademir-Jair," marvelled as fine a player as the Swedish goalkeeper Kalle Svensson. But how would they fare against Spain? The Spanish had previously seen off shell-shocked England (1–0), before again upsetting the odds in the final group's other opening match against Uruguay (2–2). The only European side remaining thought to have any realistic chance of winning the tournament, Spain were proving to be the competition's surprise package. After the first round, four of their players were named in the "team of the tournament" by the international press: goalkeeper Antoni Ramallets, midfielder Antonio Puchades, forward Zarra and winger Estanislau Basora, who had just scored twice against Uruguay. Spain were drawing praise for their excellent organization and combative spirit, while their playmaker José Luis Panizo seemed capable of exploiting the slightest flaw that might appear in the Brazilian defence.

But when it came down to it in the Maracanã, Spain were torn to pieces just as badly as Sweden had been four days earlier. One factor in their capitulation was the stadium, officially filled with 155,572 spectators, all of them shouting, singing and dancing in expression of their love for the Brazilian team. Having been tucked away in a hotel on the slopes of Corcovado to escape the muggy winter heat and the frenzy gripping Rio, the Spanish were simply not prepared for this atmosphere. Then – and above all – there were the Brazilian virtuosos. Able to escape their markers with derisory ease, their dribbles wreaked havoc among the opponents. On the quarter-hour mark, an Ademir shot was turned into his own net by Spain's central defender José Parra. Six minutes later, Jair seized possession on the halfway line, made a beeline for the Spanish goal, brushing off all resistance, and left Barcelona keeper Ramallets stranded by a firm low shot (2–0). When Chico buried a poor Spanish clearance into the back of the net (3–0), the outpouring of joy was such that the Brazilian forward was struck by a firecracker thrown from the stands. This third goal was a cue for dummies, feints and stepovers galore from Chico and Jair, along with killer passes from Ademir and Zizinho, as the goals continued to rain down. First Chico got another, then Ademir bagged his eighth goal of the competition to make it 5–0, before Zizinho finally volleyed home to make it six. Despite a consolation goal for Silvestre Igoa, Spain's best performer on the day was their goalkeeper Ramallets, who pulled off numerous saves. Brazil was bouncing with delight and satisfaction. The maestros had given a recital. Now all that remained was their *finale*.

The leading goalscorer's boots: Ademir

By the end of the tournament, Ademir's boots were in a sorry state. At the time players did not have spare pairs and boots were worn for both training and matches.

◄ FIFA World Football Museum collection.

Uruguay's mental strength

13 JULY 1950

URUGUAY ☰ 3–2 🇸🇪 **SWEDEN**

GHIGGIA 39, MIGUEZ 77, 85   PALMER 5, SUNDQVIST 40

AFTER AN EASY first round (they played just one match, an 8–0 win over Bolivia), Uruguay struggled against Spain in the final round, trailing 2–1 for a long period and only snatching a draw courtesy of a 73rd-minute strike from their captain Obdulio Varela. In their next match, at São Paulo's Pacæmbu stadium, the Uruguayans were initially put to the sword by a fully committed Swedish side. Having already come back from 0–1 to 1–1 in the first half, Uruguay found themselves chasing the game again after a 41st-minute Sundqvist goal (1–2), before finally turning the tie around in the last quarter of an hour. Their breakthrough came when they started to use the full width of the pitch. First, in the 77th minute, Alcides Ghiggia, crossed for Omar Míguez to shoot home (2–2), then Míguez scored his fifth goal of the tournament in the 85th minute (3-2). On the final whistle, the Swedes acknowledged the physical superiority of their opponents. Uruguay, meanwhile, were concerned by their own errors, knowing that if they gave the Brazilians a one- or two-goal head start, their task might be insurmountable.

◄ Karl Svensson leaps to catch the ball, but fails to stop his team from being knocked out.

▲ The players in action during the match between Sweden and Spain.

Sweden, Kings of Europe

16 JULY 1950

SWEDEN 🇸🇪 3–1 🇪🇸 **SPAIN**

SUNDQVIST 15   ZARRA 82
MELLBERG 33
PALMER 80

Not only did the 1950 World Cup have no official final, there was no play-off for third place either. But just as the Brazil-Uruguay game was effectively a final, the Sweden-Spain match, played at the same time in São Paolo, determined who would finish third in the gorup. Like Brazil, Spain only needed a draw to finish ahead of their Scandinavian opponents, but like the Brazilians, they were also destined to lose. However, Spain were fielding several replacements against a Swedish side that showed greater focus and commitment, despite the strange atmosphere resulting from the live radio broadcast of the Brazil-Uruguay game over the stadium loudspeakers. Man of the match, Swedish striker Bror Mellberg, led his side to an easy 3–1 win, ensuring Sweden left Brazil with the unexpected title – as Italy and England had both been present – of Kings of Europe.

▲ Brazil's keeper Moacir Barbosa is powerless to stop the Uruguayans' winning goal.

▲ Uruguay goalkeeper Roque Máspoli makes a save by deflecting the ball over the crossbar.

The Maracanã is silenced

16 JULY 1950

URUGUAY 2–1 **BRAZIL**

SCHIAFFINO 66, GHIGGIA 79   FRIACA 47

AT 3PM PRECISELY, 52 million Brazilians had no doubt that their team were at last going to become football champions of the world. Their date with destiny was at the Maracanã, the vast arena constructed without a single post supporting its circular roof, against their greatest South American rivals, Uruguay. All had gone smoothly so far in the tournament, and having scheduled the clash with the Uruguayans for the end of the final round, the organizers were clearly expecting the match to effectively serve as the final. Uruguay had not yet played at the Maracanã, having been stationed in Belo Horizonte for the first round and then São Paulo for their first two matches of the final round, while hosts Brazil had enjoyed the luxury of spending the previous two weeks in Rio de Janeiro. The game also set a new attendance record: 173,850 spectators officially, but the real figure was probably more like 200,000. Every Brazilian fan knew that their team only needed a draw to be crowned world champions, but the possibility of them failing to win was unthinkable.

"Before this match, I had to sign nearly 2,000 autographs with the words 'Brazil, champions of the world'," recalled attacking midfielder Zizinho. "The biggest problem was this feeling among the supporters, the media and the directors that our name was already on the trophy," recounted Brazil's coach Flávio Costa. Uruguay, meanwhile, not yet firing on all cylinders at the tournament, were fielding a 19-year-old winger, Rubén Morán, with just two previous caps, in place of their stalwart Ernesto Vidal. They were firmly expected to suffer a similar fate to Mexico (4–0), Sweden (7–1) and Spain (6–1). But their coach, Juan López, had not forgotten the first round, when a highly organized Swiss side had seriously stymied Brazil's attacking panache and emerged with a 2–2 draw.

Almost from the outset, shots from Ademir and then Jair forced Uruguayan keeper Roque Máspoli into decisive saves. Then came a header from Ademir and a strike from Chico... Brazil were monopolizing possession and launching attack after attack, but the strict man-to-man marking system deployed by their opponents was undeniably disrupting their flow. Ademir alone was being marked by both Eusebio Tejera and the captain Obdulio Varela, and in the first half, the closest thing to a goal came from Uruguay, when a long-range effort from Omar Míguez struck the foot of Barbosa's left post in the 38th minute.

But in the 47th minute, Zizinho and Ademir combined to lay on the opener for Friaça, and the only goal that he would ever score for Brazil sent an entire nation into rapture (1-0). "The public were convinced it was the kick-off of the attacking festival to which they were accustomed," recalled Brazil coach Flávio Costa. "That goal should have set us free, but instead we switched off, as the fans started to party." Jair: "We were overcome by a tremendous sense of relief." But on the Uruguayan side, Varela was wasting no time galvanizing his troops. Having been behind against Spain and twice against Sweden, the team had fought back, so why not a third time? According to Míguez: "Obdulio spent a minute or so shouting at everyone: the match officials, the assistants, the Brazilians, and ourselves. We had to win. It was an order."

Brazil, meanwhile, seemed to start playing for time. Varela was thus able to dictate the play more, while on the right flank, the lively and elusive Ghiggia was regularly outfoxing Brazil's defender Bigode. In the 66th minute, on his umpteenth dribbling run, Ghiggia broke free into the penalty area and squared the ball for Juan Schiaffino to level the score (1–1). "Silence descended over the Maracanã, striking fear into my players' hearts", recounted Flávio Costa. "I felt as if all the Brazilians were now fearing defeat", added the Uruguayan keeper Roque Máspoli.

▲ Ghiggia deceives Barbosa to score the winner and secure a second World Cup win for Uruguay.

A tactical readjustment was required to support the beleaguered Bigode, but instead of tracking back, Juvenal was accused of going missing. Brazil only knew how to attack. Jair forced Máspoli into a good save, before Friaça homed in on goal, only to be dispossessed by a last-gasp tackle from Víctor Rodríguez Andrade. But then with 12 minutes left on the clock, Uruguay launched another lethal counter-attack. Ghiggia's deft one-two with Julio Pérez left the hapless Bigode for dead. "I saw Schiaffino call for a ball into the middle, just like for the first goal," recalls Ghiggia. Barbosa was anticipating the cut-back and I sensed an opening. I shot at goal without thinking." Barbosa dived to his left to narrow the angle, but could only touch the ball as it went in. Ghiggia had just scored from his only shot on target (1–2). When Barbosa picked himself up, slowly and sadly, he seemed crushed by the weight of culpability. The stadium was deathly quiet, apart from the sobbing of men, women and children alike. At the other end, Jair attempted one final shot, then Máspoli rushed out to foil Chico, but time was running out. Ademir sent a volley over the bar, and Máspoli spilled a high cross but was relieved to see the loose ball fall to a Uruguayan defender… before the referee, England's George Reader, blew the final whistle.

And so a veil of shadow enveloped the Maracanã, Rio, and Brazil as a whole. The 11 Uruguayan players themselves appeared to be in a state of shock. "I was crying even more than the Brazilians", recalled Juan Schiaffino, "because I felt pain seeing them suffer. I was crying for them… It was a tragedy. A funeral." The prize-giving ceremony for the Jules Rimet Cup, led by Jules Rimet himself, ended up being a rushed affair.

A page of football history had just been turned. Until this match, winning had depended on attacking continually and scoring as many goals as possible. But now Uruguay had demonstrated that you could also win by organizing your back line and maintaining tactical discipline. Over the course of 90 minutes, defensive football had just triumphed.

In 1950, the Uruguayan Alcides Ghiggia became the first player to score in each of his country's matches at a World Cup tournament: one goal in each match, against Bolivia (8–0), Spain (2–2), Sweden (3–2) and Brazil (2–1).

The end of the white shirt

The defeat at the hands of Uruguay would have far-reaching consequences for Brazilian football. In its wake, the team went nearly two years without playing a single match, not even a friendly. And the legendary three-pronged attack formed by Ademir, Jair and Zizinho would never appear together again. But the most dramatic decision made was to abandon the white shirt worn on that fateful day of 16 July 1950, as it was considered cursed. The now-famous yellow jerseys with green edging, blue shorts and white socks would be worn for the first time during a match against Chile in 1954.

▲ FIFA World Football Museum collection.

Barbosa forever blamed

At fault for Ghiggia's goal, Brazil's goalkeeper Moacir Barbosa was made a scapegoat. This was not without an element of racism: he was one of three black players in the team, all of whom were criticized. Barbosa would never reappear in the national team, and spent the rest of his life as a virtual pariah. In 1963, he was given the goalposts from the final and promptly burnt them in his garden in an exorcism ceremony. But his efforts were to no avail. In a 1994 interview, he told how, a few months earlier, he had been refused access by the Brazilian football association to the *Seleção* training centre at Tersepolis. He had also been barred from commentating on a Brazil game on television. "In Brazil, the maximum penalty for criminals is 30 years," he pointed out. "I didn't commit any crime, but I've already served ten years more than that. I think I should have the right to sleep peacefully now." He passed away in 2000.

1954

In a world now divided by the Iron Curtain, Switzerland organized the World Cup that saw the highest number of goals per game. It was the first to be broadcast on television and had overwhelming favourites in Hungary. However, in what became known as the "Miracle of Berne", West Germany came from two goals down in the Final to beat the Hungarians 3–2, with Helmut Rahn scoring a late winner.

Benevolent neutrality

N THE MIDST OF THE COLD WAR, the choice of neutral Switzerland, the only candidate, to host the fifth World Cup encouraged a number of Communist countries to take part. The USSR abstained, but Bulgaria and Romania took part in the qualifiers (unsuccessfully), and Yugoslavia, Czechoslovakia and Hungary were involved in the final stages. The Swiss World Cup was, in fact, one of the least politicized: the encounter between Communist Hungary and South Korea, just emerging from three years of fratricidal warfare with the North, which had been supported by China and the Soviet Union, did not cause any tension. The real difficulties occurred before the competition… within the Swiss federal administration. Up to this time, Switzerland had organized only the Winter Olympic Games (in 1928 and 1948, at St Moritz) and one section of public opinion, and of the country's stolid political and economic establishment, did not see the need for all this upheaval just so people could kick a ball around… But in the end everyone was delighted, even the Hungarians who, the day after their painful defeat in the final, took the opportunity to go on a shopping spree with their wives in the opulent streets of Berne.

◄ The West Germany captain, Fritz Walter, holds the World Cup after his team's surprise victory in the Final.

▶ Post-war reconstruction in West Germany as a new tramway line is laid in West Berlin.

SWITZERLAND 1954

WORLD CHAMPIONSHIP
JULES RIMET CUP 1954 IN SWITZERLAND

Story of the qualifiers

Turkey qualifies by drawing lots

THE TWO BEST European teams that had played in Brazil in 1950 did not make it to Switzerland. Sweden were defeated by Belgium in the qualifying stage, while Spain came up against Turkey: after each nation had won at home, a play-off was organized in Rome. At the end of extra time, after the score had ended 2–2, lots were drawn by a blindfolded young Roman – 14-year-old Luigi Franco Gemma – and Turkey were chosen to compete in the World Cup for the very first time. Other teams making their debut were Scotland, runners-up in the all-British qualifying tournament, and South Korea, who had eliminated Japan. In their group, West Germany had to overcome Norway, and also the Saarland, one of its former provinces, that was still a French protectorate. In South America, Argentina, as they had done in 1938 and 1950, declined to take part, while for the first time Brazil won its place in the final phase on the field of play, a new experience for them.

▶ German captain Fritz Walter and Turkish keeper Turgay Şeren shake hands before the start of their match.

Regulations

Unhelpful complexity in the group phase

Despite devising a format based on a first round group stage followed by knockout rounds, an experiment was tried in the first round: four matches, rather than six, were to be played in each group of four, with no match between the two teams regarded as the strongest and the weakest. To reduce the risk of equal rankings, extra time was decreed in the event of a draw. Despite this unusual arrangement, playoffs had to be organized in groups 2 and 4 to decide between West Germany and Turkey, and between Switzerland and Italy.

FIFA's 50th anniversary

In 1954, the year that FIFA celebrated its jubilee and issued this commemorative medal in a box, FIFA President Jules Rimet left his post after 25 years.

▲ **FIFA World Football Museum collection.**

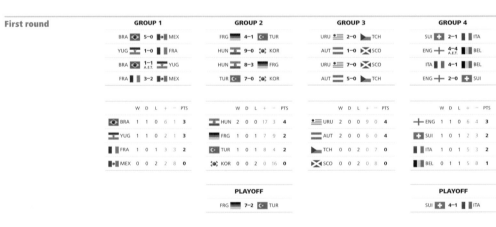

First round

GROUP 1		
BRA	5–0	MEX
YUG	1–0	FRA
BRA	1–1 A.E.T.	YUG
FRA	3–2	MEX

	W	D	L	+	–	PTS
BRA	1	1	0	6	1	3
YUG	1	1	0	2	1	3
FRA	1	0	1	3	3	2
MEX	0	0	2	2	8	0

GROUP 2		
FRG	4–1	TUR
HUN	9–0	KOR
HUN	8–3	FRG
TUR	7–0	KOR

	W	D	L	+	–	PTS
HUN	2	0	0	17	3	4
FRG	1	0	1	7	9	2
TUR	1	0	1	8	4	2
KOR	0	0	2	0	16	0

PLAYOFF

FRG	7–2	TUR

GROUP 3		
URU	2–0	TCH
AUT	1–0	SCO
URU	7–0	SCO
AUT	5–0	TCH

	W	D	L	+	–	PTS
URU	2	0	0	9	0	4
AUT	2	0	0	6	0	4
TCH	0	0	2	0	7	0
SCO	0	0	2	0	8	0

GROUP 4		
SUI	2–1	ITA
ENG	4–4 A.E.T.	BEL
ITA	4–1	BEL
ENG	2–0	SUI

	W	D	L	+	–	PTS
ENG	1	1	0	6	4	3
SUI	1	0	1	2	3	2
ITA	1	0	1	5	3	2
BEL	0	1	1	5	8	1

PLAYOFF

SUI	4–1	ITA

Knockout stage

QUARTER-FINAL		
FRG	2–0	YUG

QUARTER-FINAL		
AUT	7–5	SUI

QUARTER-FINAL		
HUN	4–2	BRA

QUARTER-FINAL		
URU	4–2	ENG

SEMI-FINAL		
FRG	6–1	AUT

SEMI-FINAL		
HUN	4–2 A.E.T.	URU

PLAY-OFF FOR THIRD PLACE

AUT	3–1	URU

FINAL

FRG	3–2	HUN

AUT	BEL	BRA	ENG
FRA	FRG	HUN	ITA
KOR	MEX	SCO	SUI
TCH	TUR	URU	YUG

16 TEAMS

26
MATCHES PLAYED

3
CARDS

768 607
SPECTATORS

OFFICIAL LOGO

WEST GERMANY
WINNERS

×11
SÁNDOR KOCSIS
LEADING GOALSCORER

5.4
AVERAGE GOALS
PER MATCH

SWISS WORLD CHAMPION
OFFICIAL MATCH BALL

Host towns and cities and stadiums

Three purpose-built stadiums

▲ Postcard from May 1954 depicting the La Pontaise Stadium with a commemorative World Cup stamp.

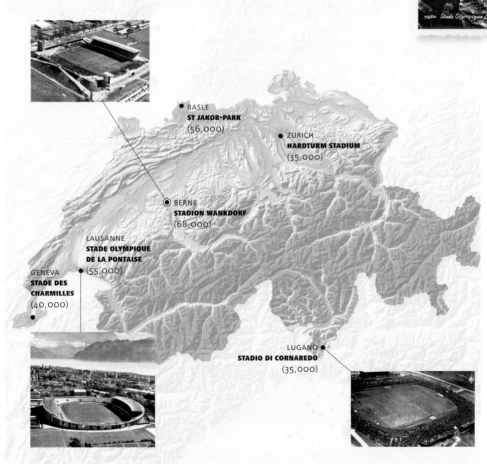

BASLE
ST JAKOB-PARK
(56,000)

ZURICH
HARDTURM STADIUM
(35,000)

BERNE
STADION WANKDORF
(68,000)

LAUSANNE
STADE OLYMPIQUE DE LA PONTAISE
(55,000)

GENEVA
STADE DES CHARMILLES
(40,000)

LUGANO
STADIO DI CORNAREDO
(35,000)

Three venues were specially constructed for the 1954 World Cup in Switzerland: the St Jakob-Park in Basle, the Stade Olympique de la Pontaise in Lausanne and the Stadio di Cornaredo in Lugano (although only one match, between Italy and Belgium in the group phase, was actually played there). Meanwhile, the Stadion Wankdorf in Berne, the Stade de Charmilles in Geneva and the Hardturm-Stadion in Zürich were enlarged for the occasion. Good attendances by the Swiss, and their Austrian and West German neighbours, created a lively atmosphere and made the event a popular success. Unexpectedly, however, the Swiss World Cup was affected by extreme weather conditions: high temperatures very much to the liking of the South Americans during the first part of the competition, followed by heavy rains towards the end. The Hungarians were exhausted by a series of tense struggles on muddy pitches, while the West Germans, led by Fritz Walter, flourished in conditions that called more for physical strength than for technical skill. For years afterwards, Germans would use the expression "Fritz Walter Wetter" (Fritz Walter weather) to describe a day of abundant rain.

▶ Suffering from cramp, a number of Korean players struggled to finish the match against Hungary.

Two bizarre playoffs

The unusual group system devised for the first round (with the highest and lowest seeded teams not matched against each other) bore some strange fruit. It is true that, in Group 1, Brazil and Yugoslavia (who were unseeded) had a clear points advantage over France (who were) and Mexico. Similarly, in Group 3, Uruguay and Austria finished above Scotland and Czechoslovakia. In Groups 2 and 3, however, things did not go according to plan. The unexpected victories of West Germany over Turkey (4–1) and Switzerland over Italy (2–1) were insufficient for these two countries to qualify, as they had not had the opportunity to score points against the weakest teams in their groups, South Korea and Belgium, unlike the rivals they had beaten… Playoffs, therefore, had to be organized. Six days later, West Germany and Turkey, Switzerland and Italy faced up to one another for a second time. Fortunately, for the sake of fairness, the same winners emerged: the German team beat Turkey 7–2, while the Swiss overcame the Italians (4–1). But both of the winners suffered: they were exhausted after having to play three matches in the space of a week.

The sufferings of South Korea

17 JUNE 1954

HUNGARY 📏 9-0 🇰🇷 **SOUTH KOREA**

PUSKAS 12, 89, LANTOS 18
KOCSIS 24, 36, 50
CZIBOR 59, PALOTAS 75, 83-

OR SOUTH KOREA, qualifying for the World Cup was no mean feat, involving a hard tussle with Japan, both legs of which were contested in Tokyo. The South Korean president, Syngman Rhee, refused to let the former invader trample again on Korean soil, even in football boots. A brilliant 5–1 victory, followed by a solid 2–2 draw, ensured South Korea's presence in Switzerland.

The "mystery team", as they became known, were eagerly awaited at Zürich airport on Monday 14 June by a delegation of Turkish players, whom the Koreans were to face in their second match. The men who eventually alighted from the plane were smiling, but totally exhausted. There were only 16 of them. Four others were due to arrive on Wednesday 16 June, the day before their match against Hungary, because there had been no room for them on the plane. The squad therefore consisted of 20 players, rather than 22. To make matters worse, they had been travelling for 55 hours, with changes of plane or stops to refuel in Tokyo (Japan), Saigon (Indochina), Calcutta (India), Karachi (Pakistan), Baghdad (Iraq), Damascus (Syria) and Rome (Italy). To add insult to injury, their beige suits had shrunk by one or two sizes during the course of this epic journey.

This left them with just 72 hours to get over their jet lag and prepare for their match against Hungary. A training session was scheduled to blow away the cobwebs. Their coach, Kim Yong Shik, who had played at the Olympic Games of 1936 (under the Japanese flag) and 1948, opted for a demanding work-out, rather than a more gentle recovery period. It was not a good idea…

From the start of the match at the Hardturm Stadium in Zürich, the Hungarian wizards effectively confiscated the ball from the Koreans, whose game plan was soon abandoned in favour of total defence. Ferenc Puskás drew first blood with a fine shot in the 12th minute and the floodgates opened. The score at half time was 4–0, following two goals from Sándor Kocsis, who completed his hat-trick in the 50th minute (5–0). Exhausted, the Koreans rarely got over the halfway line in either half. In the 77th minute, after Péter Palotás had scored the seventh Hungarian goal, three Koreans were laid out on the grass, suffering from cramp. But an amazingly courteous atmosphere prevailed throughout. The Koreans did not commit a single foul against their superior opponents. An eighth then a ninth goal, again from Puskás in the 88th minute closed the scoring. "After each goal, I sensed that the Koreans were relieved, because they could at least take a breather while waiting for the kick-off," recalled the Hungarian captain. According to the Korean coach, Kim Yong Shik: "We came to Zürich without any pretensions. We have learned an excellent lesson and are looking for opportunities to continue this sort of apprenticeship." His wish was immediately granted in the following match, which they lost 7–0 to Turkey…

The Koreans' 9–0 defeat went straight into the history books as the heaviest defeat ever suffered in the World Cup. It has since been equalled (Yugoslavia beat Zaire 9–0 in 1974 and Hungary defeated El Salvador 10–1 in 1982), but never beaten.

▲ Sándor Kocsis scores his team's eighth and final goal against West Germany.

Kocsis downs West Germany

20 JUNE 1954

HUNGARY ⬛ 8–3 ⬛ WEST GERMANY

KOCSIS 3, 21, 69, 78, PUSKÁS 17   PFAFF 25, RAHN 77, HERRMANN 84
HIDEGKUTI 52, 54, TOTH 75

W AS FOOTBALL EVER PLAYED with greater intelligence, skill, fluidity and subtlety than by the Hungarian team of Ferenc Puskás? Probably not. The Hungarians came to the World Cup with only one defeat in their last 30 matches since May 1950 (24 wins, 5 draws), including two resounding victories over England: 6–3 at Wembley in November 1953 (a first-ever home defeat against a non-British team) and 7–1 in Budapest in May 1954.

After the comedy performance against South Korea (9–0), it was the turn of West Germany to provide the opposition to the Hungarian maestros, in a St Jakob Stadium crammed to the gunnels (56,000 spectators). And yet, emerging from the tunnel, Puskás, Sándor Kocsis, Nándor Hidegkuti and József Zakariás found themselves matched with an experimental German team: of the 11 players who had beaten Turkey in the Germans' first game (4–1), only four had been retained by coach Sepp Herberger: Werner Kohlmeyer in defence, Jupp Posipal and Horst Eckel in midfield, and captain Fritz Walter up front. The West German selectors did not believe they could win, or even draw, and so were keeping their powder dry for a playoff. Predictably, the Germans were a goal down after just three minutes: goalkeeper Heinz Kwiatkowski collided with one of his own defenders at a corner and dropped the ball at the feet of Kocsis, who took full advantage of the opportunity (1–0). Kocsis went on to score three further goals: sweeping one in from close range from a pass laid on by Puskás (3–0) in the 21st minute, in a one-on-one confrontation with the goalkeeper (6–1) in the 69th minute, and with a shot through a forest of German legs (8–2) in the 78th minute. But it was a bitter victory: Puskás sustained an injury to his heel from a heavy tackle by Werner Liebrich in the second half, and his future participation was in doubt. In just two matches, the Hungarian favourites had nevertheless scored 17 goals, seven from the boot of Sándor Kocsis.

England slip up

17 JUNE 1954

ENGLAND ✚ 4–4 ⬛ BELGIUM
A.E.T.

BROADIS 25, 63, LOFTHOUSE 38, 92   ANOUL 6, 73, COPPENS 77, DICKINSON 94 (O.G.)

F OUR YEARS after their humiliating defeat in Brazil by the USA (0–1), the English team featuring the veteran Stanley Matthews, now aged 39, looked poised to win an easy victory over Belgium at the St Jakob Stadium in Basel. Although the Belgians were quick off the mark with a goal by Pol Anoul in the sixth minute (0–1), the English appeared to have gained a decisive advantage when Ivan Broadis shot past Léopold Gernaey to take a two-goal lead in the 63rd minute (3–1). But after Anoul clawed one back in the 71st minute, Belgium drew level six minutes later when a shot from Rik Coppens went in off the post (3–3). An unexpected point for the Belgians? Not yet, because the 1954 World Cup rules decreed that extra-time should be played in the event of a draw, even at the group stage.

Extra-time was just one minute old when the Belgian defence let Nat Lofthouse through to score his second goal of the match (4–3), thinking the England player was offside. It looked as if the Belgian goose was well and truly cooked. Far from it. Three minutes later, the English inside-left Jimmy Dickinson headed a free-kick into his own net (4–4). It was the only goal the Portsmouth player scored in 48 appearances for his country…

Champions in majestic form

19 JUNE 1954

URUGUAY ⬛ 7–0 ✖ SCOTLAND

BORGES 17, 47, 57
MIGUEZ 30, 83
ABBADIE 54, 85

H ARD PRESSED BY CZECHOSLOVAKIA in their opening match (they won 2–0, though the scoreline had been 0–0 until the 72nd minute), the world champions Uruguay produced a technical masterclass against Scotland at the St Jakob Stadium, a game played in tropical heat. Juan Schiaffino, probably the most elegant player in the world, alternated unpredictable long passes with sudden turns of speed which left the Scots standing. Centre-forward Omar Míguez, who had already scored five goals for his team at the 1950 World Cup, and had opened the scoring against the Czechs three days earlier, bagged two further goals. This brought his World Cup tally to eight, an achievement never since equalled by a Uruguay player (Diego Forlán ranks second, with six). But the Uruguayans who really exposed Scotland's weakness were the two wings: the powerful Carlos Borges on the left, who scored a hat-trick, and the stocky Julio César Abbadíe on the right, master of the dummy, who scored twice. Strangely, the Scots refused to change their defensive system, though their full backs were stretched beyond their limits, outclassed by superior opponents… They returned from their first World Cup with two defeats (they were also beaten 1–0 by Austria) and without a goal to their credit.

◤ Swiss goalkeeper, Eugène Parlier, dives on a penalty missed by Austrian Robert Körner.

▲ Swiss forward Josef Hügi (right), scoring one of his three goals during the match.

Avalanche in the Alps!

26 JUNE 1954

AUSTRIA 7–5 **SWITZERLAND**

WAGNER 25, 27, 53   BALLAMAN 16, 39
A. KOERNER 26, 34   HUEGI 17, 19, 60
OCWIRK 32, PROBST 76

▶ Stanley Matthews played in the 1954 World Cup at the age of 39.

N EVER SO MANY BEFORE, never so many since. An avalanche of 12 goals, the highest total in World Cup history, descended on the Stade de la Pontaise in Lausanne on 26 June 1954, during the quarter-final between Alpine cousins Austria and Switzerland.

The explanation? One factor was the amazing success the Swiss had enjoyed to date: no one imagined that the host country would beat high-ranking Italy twice (2–1 and 4–1). And now it was the turn of proud Austria to be hustled by the unlikely Swiss challengers. For a magical period of three first-half minutes, every loose ball found a Swiss foot, every shot was on target and the Austrian defence was in total disarray. Robert Ballaman, with a long shot (1–0), then Seppe Hügi, benefiting first from an Austrian mix-up (2–0) then from an accurate cross by Kiki Antenen (3–0), propelled Switzerland into an unhoped-for lead. In the stands, the spectators looked on in disbelief before raising their famous battle-cry: "Hop Suisse!"

But then the Austrian genius reasserted itself. "Everything seemed lost. Therefore we relaxed. And we began playing football as calmly as you like," commented Austrian captain Ernst Ocwirk after the match. By alternating runs up the wings, long angled passes and shots from a distance, they finally picked the "Swiss lock", which journalists had been praising since the start of the competition. And the door was soon wide open: in the space of just nine minutes, from the 25th to the 34th,

the Austrians scored five goals. The Swiss had their own explanation for this disastrous collapse: their defender and captain, Roger Bocquet, was violently elbowed by Theo Wagner and knocked unconscious, before getting up and playing on in a daze. And the Austrians took full advantage of the situation.

Although Bocquet recovered, the Swiss defence was unable to regain its former impermeability in the second half, partly because of the heat (several players complained of sunburn, or even sunstroke, at half time), and partly because they were tired out: the Swiss were playing their fourth match in nine days, whereas the Austrians had enjoyed seven days' rest since their group-stage victory over Czechoslovakia (5–0).

The Swiss were nevertheless pleased with the final scoreline (7–5), their unexpectedly good performance and the thrilling spectacle they had put on in Lausanne. "Austria deserved to win," acknowledged the Swiss team's (Austrian) coach, Karl Rappan. Seppe Hügi scored the final Swiss goal in the 58th minute (6–5), thus matching the hat-trick scored by the Austrian Wagner and bringing his World Cup tally to six, still the record for a Swiss player. Roger Bocquet, having recovered from his concussion and sunburn, found himself facing another arduous trial: he was diagnosed with a brain tumour shortly after the competition. After a successful operation, however, he lived on until 1994, to the age of 72.

Farewell to two giants of the game

The best player on the pitch at the Uruguay-England quarter-final was undoubtedly Juan Schiaffino, who produced some magical passes, deceptive nutmegs and a masterful solo goal in the 46th minute (3–1). But this game also saw two other legendary players make their last World Cup appearances. For the English team, which, despite its defeat, played its best game of the competition, it was the indefatigable Stanley Matthews who ruled the roost. The oldest player in the tournament, aged 39, who would go on to win the inaugural Ballon d'Or in 1956, ended a complicated relationship with the World Cup. Though he had made his international debut in 1934, like England itself, he was not involved in the competition until 1950. On that occasion, he was on the bench during the victory over Chile (2–0) and the defeat by the United States (0–1), and played in only one match, the 0–1 defeat to Spain. In 1954, after the 4–4 draw with Belgium, manager Walter Winterbottom rested him during the game with Switzerland (2–0). Then he was included against Uruguay… So Matthews was never on the winning side in a World Cup match.

It was quite the opposite for Obdulio Varela. The Uruguayan captain, who had received the Jules Rimet trophy at the Maracanã, made his exit on another high note. However, having sustained a thigh injury at the end of the first half, he spent the second period directing his fellow-players with hand gestures from out on the left wing, and missed the semi-final defeat at the hands of Hungary.

Brazil in the spotlight

Tip, an illustrated magazine in German, celebrates the Brazilian stars.

▲ **FIFA World Football Museum collection.**

◢ An intense battle between the Hungarians and the Brazilians during their quarter-final.

▼ Yugoslav defender Ivan Horvath scores an own goal under pressure from West Germany's Hans Schäfer.

"The Battle of Berne"

27 JUNE 1954

HUNGARY 4–2 **BRAZIL**

HIDEGKUTI 4	DJALMA SANTOS 18 (PEN)
KOCSIS 7, 88	JULINHO 65
LANTOS 60 (PEN)	

EUROPEAN MÆSTROS v. South American artists… The concluding quarter-final, played at the Wankdorf Stadium in Berne, turned out to be one of the most notorious matches in World Cup history. After their disastrous 1–2 defeat to Uruguay at the Maracanã in the final match of the 1950 competition, Brazil had replaced their 1950 white shirts with new yellow jerseys, excluded the guilty players (only the defender Bauer, now captain, played in both matches), and drew with Yugoslavia in the group stage (1–1).

When asked before the match what difference the absence of Puskás (out injured) would make, Zezé Moreira, the Brazilian selector, replied: "I'm not interested in what the other teams are doing."

He was wrong because, in the fourth minute, Nándor Hidegkuti beat the Brazilian goalkeeper Castilho following a series of shots on target (1–0). Three minutes later, following an exquisite pass by Hidegkuti with the outside of his left foot, the Brazilian defence thought a Hungarian player was offside. Not Sándor Kocsis, who headed the ball home (2–0). But the Brazilians were a very good side. It took a block on the goal-line by Kocsis to stop a shot from Indio, while in the 18th minute a clumsy tackle by Jenő Buzánszky brought down Indio again in the area. Djalma Santos hammered in the resulting penalty to make it 2–1.

The match, rich in quality (including an amazing piece of dribbling by Didi at the end of the first half), could then have gone either way. But, 15 minutes into the second half, the English referee, Arthur Ellis, blew for another penalty, this time in favour of Hungary, for an incident that will forever remain controversial: in response to a cross by Zoltán Czibor, Bauer fell in front of Kocsis and seemed to handle the ball as he went down. Mihály Lantos beat Castilho from the spot (3–1).

The Brazilians, feeling they had been robbed, responded with some great play, including a magical goal with the outside of the right foot by Julinho in the 65th minute (3–2), but also with some "anti-play". The fouls came thick and fast: Bauer slapped József Bozsik; Humberto felled and injured Hidegkuti; then Nílton Santos and Bozsik came to blows and were sent off in the 71st minute. First Didi, then Indio, in the same sequence of play, hit the crossbar and one of the uprights. But Brazil had let the game slip through their fingers, especially when Czibor, on the right wing, crossed to Kocsis, who deceived Castilho with a wonderful header in the 88th minute to make it 4–2. The Brazilians were not to be world champions, but could not accept their fate. Humberto committed yet another foul, on the Hungarian defender Gyula Lóránt, and was shown the way to the dressing-room.

When the final whistle blew, the tension was palpable. One Brazilian supporter burst onto the pitch and started fighting with a Swiss policeman. The Brazilian photographers got involved and a general punch-up ensued. In the tunnel, the two teams also came to blows. Players, officials, hangers-on: everyone joined in. A window and two doors were broken. The Hungarian selector Gusztáv Sebes, struck on the cheek-bone, needed four stitches. The young Brazilian defender João Carlos Pinheiro (aged 22), hit by a flying bottle, was streaming with blood.

"The Brazilians are artists… but of the dark arts," commented Puskás in the heat of the moment. Sándor Kocsis restricted himself to a technical analysis: "When the play was more or less normal, we scored four times. We were the better team and, however many times this match was replayed, we would have won every time."

Horvat's only mistake

The quarter-final played by the two outsiders at the Charmilles Stadium in Geneva saw Yugoslavia fall behind to West Germany as early as the ninth minute. Their defence, which had resisted so tenaciously in the group stage against France (1–0) and Brazil (1–1), let in a headed own goal by Ivan Horvat. Rajko Mitić and his team-mates dominated a very physical West German side, calmly led by Fritz Walter, but never managed to find their weak spot. Just before the break, Miloš Milutinović, alone in front of goal, delayed his shot and missed the unmissable. In the second half, the German left back Kohlmeyer saved three times off the goal-line, when keeper Toni Turek was beaten. Helmut Rahn took advantage of the spaces that opened up towards the end of the game to deliver the coup de grace in the 85th minute (2–0). Who would ever have imagined the West Germans reaching the semi-finals of the World Cup?

▶ Hungarian Sándor Kocsis clears the ball with an overhead kick.

A feast of football

30 JUNE 1954

HUNGARY 🏁 4–2 🏁 **URUGUAY**
A.E.T.

CZIBOR 12, HIDEGKUTI 47, KOCSIS 109, 116   HOHBERG 75, 86

"This was the greatest match I have ever witnessed during my 26-year career as player and manager."

The Hungarian selector Gusztáv Sebes.

WHEN THE FINAL WHISTLE blew in a rain-soaked Stade de la Pontaise in Lausanne, the Swiss police escorted the 22 players off the field. They feared further clashes, as had occurred after the quarter-final between Hungary and Brazil in Berne (4–2). But the fears were totally unfounded. After 120 minutes of strenuous effort, the losers congratulated the winners, the winners comforted the losers and there were handshakes and hugs all round. Hungary and Uruguay, two small sister nations, both tucked away at the heart of major continents, both brilliant exponents of football, had put on a wonderful three-act show.

It began, despite the absence of Ferenc Puskás, with 75 minutes of Hungarian domination featuring arabesques, deflections, and unconventional and highly inventive play. The dazzling Czibor, the indefatigable József Zakariás, the devilish Nándor Hidegkuti, the midfield general József Bozsik and that great header of a ball, Sándor Kocsis, demonstrated the infinite variety of the Hungarian game. Czibor volleyed in an early 12th-minute goal, from a headed pass by Kocsis (1–0). The Hungarians added a second in the 47th minute, when Hidegkuti dived to head in a cross from winger László Budai (2–0). The Uruguayans were not playing badly, far from it. It was just that without Obdulio Varela

and Julio César Abbadíe, both injured, and despite the skills and talent of Juan Schiaffino, they were the slightly weaker side. But Uruguay never give up, as they proved in the 1950 World Cup, when they were behind four times but never beaten.

The second act began in the 75th minute when Juan Eduardo Hohberg, in one of Uruguay's rare counter-attacks, came face to face with the Hungarian goalkeeper Gyula Grosics. Everyone was expecting a powerful shot from this almost-unknown player with the lumberjack's shoulders. Instead, Hohberg chose to slide the ball delicately between keeper and post (2–1). So who was this number eight who was now making his debut in the tournament, replacing Omar Míguez? A naturalized Argentinian, whose selection for the Uruguayan squad had been contested by public opinion back home. With only four minutes to play, Hohberg scored another goal which finally silenced his detractors. Schiaffino started a counter-attack and slipped the ball to Hohberg. Surrounded by Hungarians, the attacker saw Grosics come out of his goal and half-block the ball, which Hohberg recovered with a quick turn before driving it into the net (2–2). As Jenő Buzánszky hid his head in his hands, the Uruguayans converged on Hohberg and buried him so thoroughly that he fainted!

Third act: extra-time. After ten unbearable minutes during which both teams mounted attacks, Hohberg, from well outside the area, beat Grosics with a superb angled shot… which ricocheted off the right-hand Hungarian goal-post. But the status of great hero of this semi-final fell to another player, a Hungarian. When Budai made a run and centred in the 109th minute, Kocsis rose higher than José Santamaría to beat Roque Máspoli (3–2). The Uruguayans were powerless against his jumping and heading ability. This was demonstrated a second time seven minutes later when Hidegkuti crossed the ball and Kocsis again had the better of Santamaría and Máspoli (4–2). Hungary were in the final.

"Even when I have a long white beard, I shall still be talking of Sándor Kocsis and his unique heading ability," commented the Uruguayan goalkeeper Roque Máspoli. "I have seen wingers of all shapes and sizes: tall, short, thick-set, slim, but never such a terror as Czibor!," sighed defeated defender Victor Rodríguez Andrade. A little way off, on a massage table, having sustained a shin injury during extra-time, Juan Schiaffino wept in silence. He knew that Uruguay, world champions in 1930 and 1950, absent from the European competitions of 1934 and 1938, had just lost a World Cup match for the first time.

West Germany, a new force to be reckoned with

30 JUNE 1954

WEST GERMANY 6–1 **AUSTRIA**

SCHAEFER 31, MORLOCK 47, F. WALTER 54 (PEN), 64 (PEN), O. WALTER 61, 89 — PROBST 51

UNTIL NOW, West Germany's progress in Switzerland had been viewed with scepticism. Which teams had Sepp Herberger's players in fact beaten? The Turks twice (4–1 and 7–2) and the Yugoslavs (2–0). So what? Germany and Austria, despite similar histories at the World Cup (they were both losing semi-finalists in 1934), were not equally matched. In the run-up to the game at the St Jakob Stadium in Basel, the heirs of the *Wunderteam* and exponents of the *Wiener Schüle* (Vienna School) were more highly favoured than their coarse German cousins.

But had not the Austrian victory over Switzerland in the quarter-finals (7–5) been somewhat deceptive? Foreseeing trouble, their coach Walter Nausch was very conscious of the five goals they had let through. He replaced goalkeeper Kurt Schmied with Walter Zeman and arranged the team in a WM formation, which was something of a novelty for his players. But it was at the back that Austria's delicate technical lacework was to unravel. In the German team, the brothers Fritz and Ottmar Walter, left-wing Hans Schäfer and inside-right Max Morlock roamed free, changed positions, pierced the defensive screen and totally bamboozled the Austrians. At the break, the Germans were only 1–0 up, because the Austrian strategist Ernst Ocwirk was able to fill most of the gaps. But when the second half began, the Austrians really came unstuck, letting in four goals in less than 20 minutes. Zeman dived in vain, wandered around his area, and gave away a penalty with a blatant foul on Ottmar Walter (5–1, 64'). His three defenders were no better: Ernst Happel, in the centre, lacked mobility; Walter Schlegel, on the left, had serious limitations; Gerhard Hanappi, on the right, lost all his duels with Schäfer, eventually unending him clumsily in the area (3–1, 54').

A final headed goal in the 89th minute from Ottmar Walter (6–1) produced a scoreline similar to the two 1930 semi-finals World Cup semi-final (a semi-final record not beaten until 2014, when the Germans were again involved…). The West German team could not boast an elusive Didi, a graceful Juan Schiaffino or an elusive Hidegkuti, but they had proved to the whole world that they could beat the very best opposition by relying on two other qualities: physical prowess and sound organization.

▼ Ottmar Walter, Horst Eckel, Josef Posipal (partially hidden), Helmut Rahn and Werner Kohlmeyer perform a lap of honour with the West German flag, having just eliminated Austria.

A tale of two Walters, from War to World Cup final

Here is a statistic that will surely never be equalled: two brothers – Fritz and Ottmar Walter – were involved in all six goals in West Germany's semi-final. **For the first (1–0), it was older brother and captain Fritz, officially inside-left but roaming on the right wing, who provided the cross for Schäfer.** For the second (2–0), a corner taken by the West German captain was headed in by Morlock. The third goal was a penalty (3–1), converted by Fritz. And what about Ottmar? He scored the fourth goal (4–1) heading in a pass from his older brother. The German centre-forward was then fouled in the area by Zeman, a misdeed punished from the spot by his *brother* (5–1). Finally, Ottmar scored the sixth goal, again with a header, this time assisted by Schäfer (6–1).

Fritz and Ottmar began and ended their careers with the same club: 1. FC Kaiserslautern. Born respectively in 1920 and 1924, they both served in the Second World War. Fritz won his first international caps from 1940 to 1942, before he was called up, then was taken prisoner at the end of the conflict by the Red Army in Romania. During a match between POWs and soldiers, he was recognized by one of his Hungarian guards. His admirer managed to pass him off as an Austrian, press-ganged into the army. Instead of being sent to the gulag in Siberia, Fritz Walter returned home safe and sound in the autumn of 1945. Enrolled in the German navy, Ottmar's souvenir of his wartime service was a knee full of shrapnel. He could still play football but underwent seven operations in the course of his life and ended his days in a wheelchair.

▲ The German and Hungarian captains before kick-off. Fritz Walter and Ferenc Puskás with referee Bill Ling.

▲ Helmut Rahn was named man of the match, after his two goals won the World Cup for West Germany.

The Miracle of Berne

4 JULY 1954

WEST GERMANY 3-2 **HUNGARY**

MORLOCK 10, RAHN 18, 84   PUSKÁS 6, CZIBOR 8

HUNGARY were the best team in the world, having lost just once in their previous 30 matches. Their brilliant captain, Ferenc Puskás, injured on 20 June and said to be still recovering, would in fact play in the second World Cup final contested by the Hungarians, the first having been in 1938. Facing them on the grassy pitch of the Wankdorf Stadium in Berne were the West Germans, whom Hungary had swept aside 8–3 in the group stage. During the singing of the national anthem before the final, they spontaneously held hands to keep their courage up.

But Hungary went 2–0 up after just eight minutes. In the sixth minute, a shot by Sándor Kocsis was blocked by Horst Eckel but rebounded directly to Puskás, who had only to steer the ball wide of Toni Turek to open the scoring. Two minutes later, the German goalkeeper failed to grasp a back pass from his left-back Werner Kohlmeyer (the laws then allowed the goalkeeper to handle the ball in such circumstances) and spilt the ball into the path of Zoltán Czibor, who put it in the back of the net. As expected, the game was all wrapped up… Or was it? In fact, Hungary would go on to lose. And the match would forever after be known as the "Miracle of Berne". Had the Hungarians underestimated the West Germans? To some extent, it seems. In an interview with the French daily newspa-

per *L'Équipe* two days before the final, Kocsis, who had scored 11 goals in four matches to date, made the unfortunate comment: "The hardest thing after winning this title will be to carry on an maintain our present standard." But the team selector, Gusztáv Sebes, was not so sanguine: "I think it will be a very hard match." His assistants, who had watched the Germans' easy victory over Austria (6–1), noted the "relative mediocrity" of the German goalkeeper Turek, their defence (with the exception of Werner Liebrich) and the half-backs, but emphasised the "excellence" of the two inside-forwards and the three attackers.

And these were the five men who quickly recovered the situation for Germany. In the tenth minute, Helmut Rahn crossed the ball into the Hungarian penalty area, where József Zakariás diverted it towards his goalkeeper, Gyula Grosics, only for Max Morlock to slide in and poke the ball into the net (2–1). Less than ten minutes later, Fritz Walter took a corner on the left. Grosics could only just touch the ball as it sailed over his head, and Rahn was on hand at the far post to drive the ball into the net (2–2).

The West Germans had equalized in spectacular fashion, but now they had to hang on for a further 70 minutes. Several factors were in their favour. First, the constant rain, which for more than a week had made the ground

heavy and unsuited to the Hungarians' more subtle style of play. Second, their organization and physical condition: Horst Eckel was constantly on the heels of Nándor Hidegkuti, while Karl Mai never let Kocsis out of his sight. Third, the performance of Turek, who redeemed himself by fending off a fierce shot from Hidegkuti in the 24th minute. Fourth, the Hungarians' lack of precision: Hidegkuti hit the post in the first half; Puskás, with only Turek to beat, drove the ball straight at the German goalkeeper; then, in the second half, a header by Kocsis rebounded off the bar. Finally, the Hungarians were worn out: they were effectively playing their third "final" in eight days, after wins against Brazil and Uruguay, the second after extra-time, whereas the West Germans had had enjoyed relatively easy wins over Yugoslavia (2–0) and Austria (6–1).

It all culminated in the 84th minute. Helmut Rahn, on the edge of the Hungarian penalty area, recovered a ball headed clear by Mihály Lantos. He controlled the ball with his right foot, avoided one defender and shot home with his left. Germany were ahead. Immediately afterwards, the referee denied Puskás a goal on the grounds of offside. Then Turek parried a final shot from Czibor. Hungary may have been the best team in the world, but West Germany were the champions.

0

The number of non-European teams faced by West Germany on the way to the title. In the other 19 World Cups played from 1930 to 2014, the champions met at least one country from another continent.

The record for Kocsis, the glory for Rahn

With 11 goals to his name, Sándor Kocsis established a new World Cup record, comfortably overtaking the eight scored by the Argentinian Guillermo Stábile in 1930 and the Brazilian Ademir in 1950. He also received the nickname "Golden Head", having scored four of his goals with his head. Although only 1.76 m tall, the Hungarian striker possessed a long and powerful neck, which enabled him to impart force and direction to the ball. A prolific goalscorer (76 goals in 69 appearances for his country), his international career was ended by the Soviet invasion of Hungary in 1956, when he was 27 years old. He sought refuge in Switzerland, before a successful conclusion to his career with Barcelona.

But in the days following the final, during which Kocsis did not score, all the praise went to another attacker: the West German Helmut Rahn, who netted twice. As right-wing for his club Rot Weiss Essen, Rahn had already left for a tour of Uruguay when Sepp Herberger called him back for the 1954 World Cup. Before the final, he had not particularly impressed the Hungarians: "They tell us that Rahn is awkward and effective in attack," said one of Gusztáv Sebes's assistants. "But we have noted that he has no stamina. He's a player you need to wear out quickly, even if it means giving him a degree of freedom in the first few minutes. He tires, gradually loses his effectiveness and is then fairly easy to keep tabs on." How wrong they were!

Magic Magyars

Portraits of the Hungarian players in a commemorative booklet.

▲ **FIFA World Football Museum collection.**

PLAY-OFF FOR THIRD PLACE

▲ The Austrian team on the offensive in front of the Uruguayan goal.

Central Europe holds sway

3 JULY 1954		
AUSTRIA 🏳	3–1	🏳 **URUGUAY**
STOJASPAL 16 (PEN)	HOHBERG 22	
CRUZ 59 (O.G.)		
OCWIRK 79		

In the contest for third place, held the day before the West Germany-Hungary final, Austria recorded a convincing win over Uruguay at the Hardturm Stadium in Zurich (3–1). The three best teams in the world, as produced by this tournament, therefore all originated from the same region of just one continent.

Uruguay put up a stiff resistance until half time. Austria opened the scoring with an Ernst Stojaspal penalty in the 16th minute, after William Martínez, the Uruguayan captain replacing Obdulio Varela, had brought down Robert Dienst. But Uruguay equalized with a shot from the now irrepressible Juan Eduardo Hohberg six minutes later (1–1). In the second half, Juan Schiaffino and Víctor Rodríguez Andrade, exhausted by their demanding semi-final which had gone to extra time (much like the Hungarians the following day), let down their guard. It was the unfortunate Luis Cruz, with a headed own goal, who gifted the Austrians a 59th-minute lead (2–1), before a long shot by Austrian captain Ernst Ocwirk 20 minutes later put the game beyond doubt (3–1).

This was the last time Juan Schiaffino played for Uruguay, as the Peñarol player took advantage of the World Cup to sign for AC Milan.

◀ Adi Dassler revolutionized football boots.

An improved football boot

And what if the key to the German success lay with their equipment?
Adidas had designed some revolutionary boots with screw-in studs which enabled the Germans to adapt to all sorts of pitch conditions. On the wet, slippery grass of the Wankdorf, they gave Fritz Walter's men a much better grip throughout the final, which saw the Hungarians ill at ease on the muddy surface. The new boots were also much lighter. When weighed after the match, they tipped the scales at just 700 grams, as compared with 1.5 kilos for the conventional boots worn by the Hungarians.

1958

Sweden's small intimate venues provided a picturesque backdrop to a tournament in which the hosts went all the way to the Final. Just Fontaine scored a record 13 goals, but neither France nor Sweden were a match for the superb Brazilians, who beat them both 5–2. A brilliant 17-year-old Pelé scored three goals in the semi-final against France and two in the Final against Sweden.

A force for unity

◄ Pelé poses in his team suit with the Jules Rimet Cup after Brazil's victory over Sweden.

▼ Brazil's Garrincha and Gilmar, in conversation with Sweden's Gunnar Nordahl (centre).

FOUR YEARS AFTER THE World Cup in Switzerland, the choice of Sweden, another neutral country, to host the competition ensured the widest possible participation. King Gustav VI, aged 75, who had chaired the organizing committee of the 1912 Stockholm Olympic Games, attended the opening match and the Final. The USSR took part in the tournament, its "footballer comrades", who were officially amateurs, receiving a "productivity bonus". Only one diplomatic incident marred this World Cup: the day after the execution of Imre Nagy, on 16 June in Budapest, some Hungarian protesters staged a demonstration in the almost-empty stands of the Råsunda Stadium during the group play-off between Hungary and Wales. Otherwise, the football, followed with enthusiasm, was a force for

unity among nations. A month after the attempted coup d'état in Algiers that brought about the return to power of General De Gaulle in Paris, the French forgot for a time the political crisis that was dividing their country and concentrated on the goal-scoring abilities of Just Fontaine. Thirty kilometres east of Gothenburg, the little town of Hindås was the scene of an amazing event. The day after their defeat by Brazil (2–0), the Soviet players visited the hotel at which the South Americans were staying, 200 metres from their own. They arrived in their best suits and ties, colossal and impassive. The Brazilians wondered what was going on. But smiles were the order of the day: the Soviets had come to congratulate their talented opponents and wish them good luck.

SWEDEN 1958

WORLD CHAMPIONSHIP
JULES RIMET CUP 1958 IN SWEDEN

Story of the qualifiers

A first for the USSR

TWO SURPRISES: Uruguay, double world champions (1930 and 1950), ceded their place to Paraguay, who beat them 5–0; and Italy, also two-time winners (1934 and 1938), were overtaken in their group by Northern Ireland. The four British nations did not play against one another as in the past, with two places reserved for them in the final phase, but were treated in the same way as other European countries. The result was that all four "Home Nations" qualified. The case of Wales was highly unusual: eliminated from their group behind Czechoslovakia, they were drawn by lot to play a decider against Israel, against whom a string of opponents (Turkey, Indonesia and Sudan) had declined to play. The Welsh ran out 2–0 winners (twice) and so made their World Cup debut, along with Northern Ireland and the USSR, the Olympic champions from the 1956 Games in Melbourne having at last decided to mix with the great footballing nations. In the end, four Eastern European, four Western European, four British and four teams from the Americas qualified. FIFA picked one nation from each of these four "pots" to form the groups for the first round of the final phase.

▶ Soviet keeper Lev Yashin signs autographs during a training session.

Regulations

A re-worked mixed system

FIFA CONTINUED with the mixed system adopted in 1954 (a group stage, followed by a knockout contest for the last eight), with two readjustments: on this occasion, each team played the three others in its group, with no extra time in the event of a draw. Instead, a new goal-average rule was applied to decide between teams with the same number of points, but playoffs were held if the teams concerned had finished second and third. West Germany had triumphed after coming through a playoff in 1954, but in 1958 the three playoff winners lost in the quarter-finals.

Group stage

GROUP 1

FRG	3–1	ARG
NIR	1–0	TCH
ARG	3–1	NIR
FRG	2–2	TCH
FRG	2–2	NIR
TCH	6–1	ARG

	W	D	L	+	–	PTS
FRG	1	2	0	7	5	4
NIR	1	1	1	4	5	3
TCH	1	1	1	8	4	3
ARG	1	0	2	5	10	2

GROUP 2

FRA	7–3	PAR
YUG	1–1	SCO
YUG	3–2	FRA
PAR	3–2	SCO
FRA	2–1	SCO
PAR	3–3	YUG

	W	D	L	+	–	PTS
FRA	2	0	1	11	7	4
YUG	1	2	0	7	6	4
PAR	1	1	1	9	12	3
SCO	0	1	2	4	6	1

GROUP 3

SWE	3–0	MEX
HUN	1–1	WAL
MEX	1–1	WAL
SWE	2–1	HUN
SWE	0–0	WAL
HUN	4–0	MEX

	W	D	L	+	–	PTS
SWE	2	1	0	5	1	5
WAL	0	3	0	2	2	3
HUN	1	1	1	6	3	3
MEX	0	1	2	1	8	1

GROUP 4

BRA	3–0	AUT
URS	2–2	ENG
BRA	0–0	ENG
URS	2–0	AUT
ENG	2–2	AUT
BRA	2–0	URS

	W	D	L	+	–	PTS
BRA	2	1	0	5	0	5
URS	1	1	1	4	4	3
ENG	0	3	0	4	4	3
AUT	0	1	2	2	7	1

Knockout stages

PLAYOFF

NIR	2–1 A.E.T.	TCH

PLAYOFF

WAL	2–1	HUN

PLAYOFF

URS	1–0	ENG

QUARTER-FINAL

BRA	1–0	WAL

QUARTER-FINAL

FRA	4–0	NIR

QUARTER-FINAL

SWE	2–0	URS

QUARTER-FINAL

FRG	1–0	YUG

SEMI-FINAL

BRA	5–2	FRA

SEMI-FINAL

SWE	3–1	FRG

PLAY-OFF FOR THIRD PLACE

FRA	6–3	FRG

FINAL

BRA	5–2	SWE

ARG AUT BRA ENG
FRA FRG HUN MEX
NIR PAR SCO SWE
TCH URS WAL YUG

16 TEAMS

35
MATCHES PLAYED

3
CARDS

819810
SPECTATORS

OFFICIAL POSTER

FOOTBALL
FUTBOL
FUSSBALL

BRAZIL
WINNERS

×**13**

JUST FONTAINE
LEADING GOALSCORER

3.6
AVERAGE GOALS
PER MATCH

TOP STAR
OFFICIAL MATCH BALL

Host towns, cities and stadiums

A record twelve host stadiums

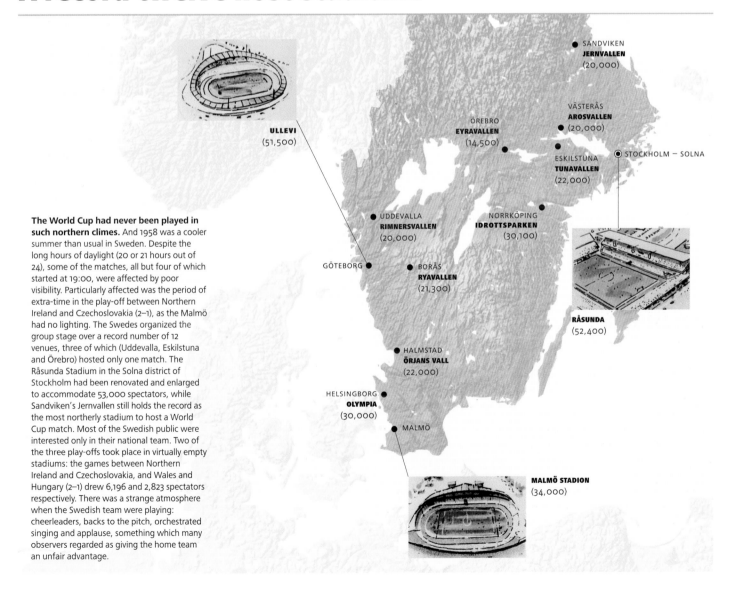

ULLEVI
(51,500)

SANDVIKEN
JERNVALLEN
(20,000)

VÄSTERÅS
AROSVALLEN
(20,000)

ÖREBRO
EYRAVALLEN
(14,500)

ESKILSTUNA
TUNAVALLEN
(22,000)

STOCKHOLM – SOLNA

UDDEVALLA
RIMNERSVALLEN
(20,000)

NORRKÖPING
IDROTTSPARKEN
(30,100)

GÖTEBORG

BORÅS
RYAVALLEN
(21,300)

RÅSUNDA
(52,400)

HALMSTAD
ÖRJANS VALL
(22,000)

HELSINGBORG
OLYMPIA
(30,000)

MALMÖ

MALMÖ STADION
(34,000)

The World Cup had never been played in such northern climes. And 1958 was a cooler summer than usual in Sweden. Despite the long hours of daylight (20 or 21 hours out of 24), some of the matches, all but four of which started at 19:00, were affected by poor visibility. Particularly affected was the period of extra-time in the play-off between Northern Ireland and Czechoslovakia (2–1), as the Malmö had no lighting. The Swedes organized the group stage over a record number of 12 venues, three of which (Uddevalla, Eskilstuna and Örebro) hosted only one match. The Råsunda Stadium in the Solna district of Stockholm had been renovated and enlarged to accommodate 53,000 spectators, while Sandviken's Jernvallen still holds the record as the most northerly stadium to host a World Cup match. Most of the Swedish public were interested only in their national team. Two of the three play-offs took place in virtually empty stadiums: the games between Northern Ireland and Czechoslovakia, and Wales and Hungary (2–1) drew 6,196 and 2,823 spectators respectively. There was a strange atmosphere when the Swedish team were playing: cheerleaders, backs to the pitch, orchestrated singing and applause, something which many observers regarded as giving the home team an unfair advantage.

◄ Uwe Seeler scores West Germany's second goal as Argentine goal-keeper Amadeo Carrizo looks on.

Argentina's failed comeback

8 JUNE 1958

ARGENTINA 1–3 WEST GERMANY

CORBATTA 2   RAHN 32, 79, SEELER 40

ARGENTINA had not participated in the World Cup since 1934, at which they were defeated by Sweden 3–2 in the first round. Victorious in the 1957 *Copa América*, beating Brazil 3–0 in the process, Argentina dominated Bolivia and Chile in the qualifiers. They therefore approached the competition as worthy contenders, with a romantic aura and a reputation for artistry.

But the Argentinians came to Sweden without the attacking trio who had helped them win the *Copa América*. Humberto Maschio (nine goals), Antonio Angelillo (eight) and Omar Sivori, nicknamed the "Angels with Dirty Faces" with reference to a 1938 film starring Humphrey Bogart, had all signed for Italian clubs (Bologna, Inter Milan and Juventus), who refused to release them for the World Cup. The Argentinian coach, Guillermo Stábile, top scorer in the 1930 competition, put on a brave face, detailing the "non-principles" that would inspire their game: "I let my players follow their inspiration where it takes them. I am not opposed to imagination and the joy of playing the game." Even against West Germany, the world champions? "I would shoot myself, rather than spy on another team. A coach and his team must be able to understand their opponents' line-up and organization inside five minutes." While he was delighting the press with these pronouncements, his players broke off their training session to go and chat with some young Swedes on a neighbouring pitch…

In Malmö, playing their first match, the Argentinians could rely for a time on the superiority of their football, all clever play and back-heels, thanks to an early goal by their diminutive right-winger Oreste Corbatta (1.60m)· But the West German machine soon clanked into action, driven by the durable Fritz Walter (now 37 years old) and Hans Schäfer, now the captain. It was efficient, physical, and skilful. Helmut Rahn, four years after his two goals in the final against Hungary, claimed another double with clever shots, the first with his left foot in the 32nd minute, and the second with his right in the 79th. The Argentinians certainly played a skilful game, but their defence was slow, rigid and very much to blame for the second German goal, scored by Uwe Seeler in the 40th minute, who dived in with both feet to claim a ball that had run loose. The South Americans' playmaker, Néstor Rossi, was overwhelmed by the sheer speed of the Germans, the impact of their shoulder charges and the way in which they closed down the space. Argentina may have dominated possession, but the West German goalkeeper, Fritz Herkenrath, was rarely troubled. Rossi, seeking revenge, was guilty of a horrible late tackle on Fritz Walter.

Having failed to bring their alternative strip, the Argentinians were obliged to don the yellow jerseys of IFK Malmö. In their own colours – and with Ángel Labruna, at 39 the oldest player in the tournament – Argentina beat Northern Ireland (3–1). But, in their third match, they went down ignominiously against Czechoslovakia (6–1), contributing to a radical rethink of football in Argentina. The 1960s were to witness a very different ethos. The romantic notion of how the game should be played was replaced by a physical, often brutal approach. It was win at all costs.

The game between Brazil and England, played on 11 June 1958 in Gothenburg, was the first in World Cup history to end in a goalless draw. In all of the previous 109 matches, at least one goal had been scored.

A first point for Mexico

11 JUNE 1958

MEXICO 1–1 WALES

BELMONTE 89   ALLCHURCH 32

FOR MUCH of the game at the Råsunda Stadium in Solna, Mexico seemed to be reliving their recurrent nightmare. Beaten 3–0 by Sweden in the opening match, the Mexicans were playing Wales, who had managed a draw against Hungary (1–1). The Central Americans had changed five of their players and were dominant in possession, but allowed the Welsh to score from a corner through Ivor Allchurch in the 32nd minute). The minutes ticked away and yet another defeat was on the cards. It would be their tenth: Mexico had played their first match in the competition in 1930 (1–4 against France), and lost every one. Then, in the 89th minute, a cross came over and Jaime Belmonte, aged 23, who had not played against Sweden, headed it into the net to make it 1–1. Mexico's run of nine defeats in the World Cup was over. Their unenviable record stands to this day…

▲▲ Garrincha laces his boots, all smiles.

▲ Aged just 17, Pelé became the youngest player to take part in the World Cup.

Garrincha and Pelé make their World Cup debuts

15 JUNE 1958

BRAZIL 2–0 **USSR**

VAVA 3, 77

I T IS WISE TO BEWARE of latter-day embellishments. But a glance at the newspapers published on 16 June 1958 leaves no room for doubt: the journalists and 51,000 spectators present at the Ullevi Stadium in Gothenburg on the previous day believed they had witnessed "superhuman" football, "the most brilliant firework display in the history of the game". The Soviet selector Gavriil Kachalin, definitely not a soul of wit, expressed it in this way: "Garrincha is an extra-terrestrial."

What had happened? After a solid victory over Austria (3–0) and a tense draw with England (0–0), coach Vicente Feola had brought two new players into his team: Manoel Francisco dos Santos, nicknamed Garrincha, and Édson Arantes do Nascimento, known as Pelé. To date, it was Brazil's defence that had been impressive; now, with the devastating attacking formation of Didi-Garrincha-Vavá-Pelé-Zagallo, they were set to play the USSR off the park. In the first minute, Garrincha dribbled round Boris Kuznetsov and struck Lev Yashin's left-hand post. In the second, Pelé shot and found the other upright. In the third minute, Didi, surrounded by Soviet players, stopped dead, arms swinging, before making a quick run and laying on a through-ball to Vavá, who opened the scoring. Ball control, good positioning, technical skill… the Brazilians had it all. The Soviet captain, Igor Netto, detailed to mark Didi but suffering from injury, was distressing to watch. The play of the Olympic champions was reduced to long clearances, into touch if necessary. Garrincha, a "devil with crooked legs", was highly elusive. At one point, full-back Nílton Santos was heard to shout, "Garrincha, stop inventing new dribbles!" as no further goals were forthcoming. Pelé missed several opportunities, before his masterpiece in the 77th minute: a series of one-twos, in the air and on the ground, between him and Vavá leading up to the second goal, scored by Vavá.

So why were Garrincha and Pelé not included in the team for the first two matches? Brazil's captain Hideraldo Bellini was evasive: "Some questions are better not asked." In Pelé's case, there were two reasons: firstly, the teenager, a surprise inclusion in the Brazilian squad, was recovering from a knee injury; secondly, the psychologist who had accompanied the team to Sweden regarded Pelé as childish and lacking in fighting spirit. He advised Feola not to play him against the virile "comrades" from the USSR. Feola, as Pelé himself tells the story, replied: "You may be right, doctor, but you know nothing about football. If Pelé's knee is alright, he will play!"

Garrincha, aged 24, already had something of a reputation in Brazil, and various stories were doing the rounds: he was the son of country people and hardly knew how to read and write; he was incapable of understanding a tactical plan; and his only interest was in girls… He was, in fact, paying for some disciplinary issues. Djalma Santos, on the bench against the USSR, spilled the beans some years later: "Before the World Cup, we played against Fiorentina, in Italy. Garrincha received the ball, dribbled round one full-back, the sweeper, the goalkeeper, then stopped dead on the goal-line. A defender moved towards him and only then did Garrincha back-heel the ball into the net. The coach was not amused. He took this to mean that Garrincha was not mature enough to play in a World Cup." But after Joel was injured playing against England, Feola gave the winger from Botafogo a second chance…

The Brazil-USSR game was not the first match in which Pelé and Garrincha had played together; they had both been selected for a friendly against Bulgaria on 18 May (3–1). But it was the start of an amazing partnership: they played together in 40 internationals for Brazil, recording 36 victories, 4 draws and no defeats.

▲ Just Fontaine scores the first of his two goals during the quarter-final against Northern Ireland.

▲ The Brazilians congratulate Pelé on his first World Cup goal.

Fontaine puts paid to Northern Ireland

19 JUNE 1958

FRANCE ▮▮ 4–0 ┿ **NORTHERN IRELAND**

WISNIESKI 44, FONTAINE 55, 63, PIANTONI 68

"WE SHALL WIN by one goal or suffer a disaster," announced Danny Blanchflower, the Northern Ireland captain. He knew his team were exhausted at the end of the group stage. They had beaten Czechoslovakia (1–0), been dictated to by the Argentinians (1–3), and "won" a heroic draw against West Germany (2–2). Their great strengths were their fighting spirit and an inspired goalkeeper, Harry Gregg, a hero of Munich. On 6 February 1958, when the plane carrying the Manchester United back from Belgrade made a stop in Munich and crashed at the end of the runway, claiming 23 lives, he had climbed back into the burning fuselage to rescue a Yugoslav mother and her daughter, as well as his teammates Bobby Charlton and Dennis Viollet.

In Sweden, Gregg was injured in the game against the Germans and was forced to give up his place to Norman Uprichard for the playoff against Czechoslovakia. But the whole Northern Ireland team were suffering: just two days after their final group game in Malmö, it had taken them 120 hard-fought minutes to overcome Josef Masopust and his team, thanks to Peter McParland's fourth and fifth goals of the tournament, with night falling in an unlit stadium. Now they had to play the French on 19 June in Norrköping, 400 km farther north, their third game in five days.

The French, meanwhile, had arrived by a very different route: a flamboyant victory over Paraguay (7–3) after being behind until the 52nd minute; an honourable defeat to the Yugoslavs (2–3); and a predictable success against the Scots (2–1). The French style of play was elegant and free-flowing. They boasted one of the best attacks in the tournament, having scored 11 goals, six from the boot of Just Fontaine. The understanding between the striker from Reims and Raymond Kopa, who played for the great Real Madrid team, was something to behold. According to Fontaine: "It is so easy to play with Raymond. You just launch yourself into free space, and you can be sure of receiving the ball."

But, at the Idrottsparken, the Northern Irish put up a stiff resistance. Gregg returned to the team, hobbling but in magnificent form, but left-half Bertie Peacock was out injured. The French opened the scoring at the end of the first half, when their young right-winger Maryan Wisnieski shot from a tight angle, rather than cross the ball.

After half-time, the French moved the ball about to exhaust their opponents. Inevitably, Fontaine scored the second goal, heading in a cross from Armand Penverne in the 55th minute, then, eight minutes later, the third, with his left foot, after Kopa had laid on a delicate pass for his room-mate. Roger Piantoni completed the scoring with a solo effort from the right wing (4–0). France were in the semi-finals of the World Cup for the first time. "I played my best-ever match in Sweden," concluded Kopa. "During the first three games, I fought, worked hard, sorted things out, organized. On this occasion, I was able to follow my own inspiration."

Harry Gregg, who again made many great saves, was elected best World Cup goalkeeper, despite the presence in Sweden of the Soviet Lev Yashin and the Brazilian Gylmar.

4

In the entire history of the World Cup, France have only twice won matches with a goal difference of four or more, both in 1958 (7–3 against Paraguay and 4–0 against Northern Ireland), and on both occasions at the Idrottsparken in Norrköping.

Pelé's first goal

19 JUNE 1958

BRAZIL ◉ 1–0 🏴󠁧󠁢󠁷󠁬󠁳󠁿 **WALES**

PELÉ 66

IN MEETING the Brazilians in Gothenburg, the Welsh, like the Northern Irish, were playing their third match in five days. They were weakened, their main striker John Charles having been injured in the playoff against Hungary (2–1). But they fiercely resisted a Brazilian team who by this point were favourites to win the tournament. After 65 minutes, the score was still 0–0.

Changing this situation was the work of one man, or rather one teenager: Pelé, officially inside-left, but, in fact, second centre-forward to José Altafini, right- or left-winger as the fancy took him, and sweeper as soon as Brazil lost the ball. Having featured in the match against the USSR (2–0), he was already the youngest player to take part in the World Cup. In the 66th minute, Didi headed the ball to him at chest height in the Welsh penalty area. Pelé had his back to the goal. He controlled the ball with his body, flicking it past his left shoulder before it touched the ground, bamboozled a Welsh defender and beat Jack Kelsey with a well-placed right-foot shot. After a merry dance, he dived into the goal to recover the ball and was then buried alive by his team-mates!

In his joy, Pelé did not realize that, at the age of 17 years and 239 days, he had become the youngest player to score a World Cup goal, a record that still stands today. Wales's only venture into the knockout stages of the World Cup had come to an end.

Yashin overcome by Hamrin

19 JUNE 1958

SWEDEN 2-0 **USSR**

HAMRIN 49, SIMONSSON 88

T WAS A WEEK that must have been indelibly printed on Boris Kuznetzov's memory. Four days after the closest of close-up views of the budding genius of Garrincha in the USSR's match against Brazil (2–0), the Soviet left-back found himself up against Kurt Hamrin in the quarter-final of the World Cup at Solna. Now it was the turn of the Swedish right-winger to put on one of the finest performances of his career.

Kurt Hamrin, like centre-half Bengt "Julle" Gustavsson (Atalanta) and left-winger Lennart "Nacka" Skoglund (Inter Milan), was part of the Swedish diaspora in Italy. For their home World Cup, the Scandinavian association, abandoning several decades of resolute amateurism, had decided to include "mercenaries" who had left to seek fame and fortune abroad in their squad, and Hamrin, who had transferred to Padova after just one season with Juventus, was the Swedish player showing the sharpest form. Against Hungary in the group stage, he scored both the goals in a 2–1 win. Rested against Wales, his sharpness was clearly on display from the start of the quarter-final against the USSR, goading a Soviet defence that had been involved in a playoff against England just two days earlier. Only four minutes had been played when his first shot was stopped by Lev Yashin; others were to follow in a constant stream.

Anything but the popular image of a Swede, Hamrin was short in stature (1.68m), dark, animated and as modest as his team-mate Skoglund, on the left wing, was flamboyant and self-confident. Hamrin's right leg was slightly shorter than his left, the result of a car accident several years before. He wore an orthopaedic insole to compensate. At half-time, despite the Swedish domi-

nance, the score was still 0–0. As in the USSR's earlier matches, Lev Yashin was their outstanding player. In their first group game against England (2–2), he had been concussed after a collision with inside-forward Bobby Robson, who had made a lunge for the ball. Against Austria (2–0), the Moscow Dynamo keeper made one of the great saves of the tournament, stopping a shot from Walter Horak from close range. In the playoff against England, his desperate dive to gather the ball at the feet of Derek Kevan was decisive. Yashin was another player who did not fit the national stereotype. A man of exceptional vigour, reflexes and authority, he also showed a humorous side in the game against Austria, standing and gesturing, like a policeman, as the ball passed wide of his goal-post.

But with Hamrin in such devilish form, there was little he could do. At the beginning of the second half, a pass from Hamrin to Skoglund was blocked by Konstantin Krizhevsky. The ball bounced back to Hamrin and he headed it past Yashin (1–0). Shortly afterwards, he was denied a second goal when the referee whistled following a foul by Kuznetsov, even though he was able to play on. Then, in the 70th minute, Kuznetsov collared the Swedish will-o'-the-wisp again, just as he was about to score. The Soviets' man-handling of the Swedish star was all in vain, however: in the 88th minute, Hamrin, out on the left wing, dribbled round Krizhevsky, made his way along the goal-line and passed back to Agne Simonsson, in space in front of Yashin, who rifled the ball home to make it 2–0. Just as had been the case in 1938 and 1950, Sweden were in the last four of the World Cup.

▲▲ Caricature of Kurt Hamrin, published during the World Cup.

▲ Lev Yashin is beaten by Kurt Hamrin's header in the quarter-final between the Soviet Union and Sweden.

▲ Helmut Rahn and Fritz Walter after West Germany's quarter-final victory over Yugoslavia.

A repeat of 1954

Behind 1–0 to Argentina, 2–0 to Czechoslovakia and 2–1 to Northern Ireland, the defending champions West Germany had certainly not covered themselves with glory in the group stage, but neither had they lost a game, recording one victory and two draws (3–1, 2–2 and 2–2). Helmut Rahn, still as good a dribbler and striker as he had been in 1954, had scored four of the seven West German goals. Yugoslavia owed their place in the

quarter-finals to a famous victory over France (3–2, thanks to an 88th-minute goal from Veselinović), and draws with Scotland (1–1) and Paraguay (3–3).

In a repeat of the 1954 tournament (a game which West Germany had won 2–0), the quarter-final between West Germany and Yugoslavia quickly turned in Germany's favour as a result of a Yugoslav error. Four years earlier, in Geneva, Ivan Horvat had scored an own goal. In this case, the guilty party was Srboljub

Krivokuća, a last-minute replacement for long-standing regular goalkeeper Vladimir Beara (who was suffering from a cartilage injury). In the 12th minute, Krivokuća let an admittedly fierce shot from a tight angle creep in under his body (1–0). It was, nevertheless, a magnificent sequence of play, the goalscorer having first slipped the attentions of his marker on the left wing, before slaloming between two defenders and evading a sliding tackle. His name? Helmut Rahn, of course!

Pele's tracksuit top

The tracksuit top worn by Pelé during his first appearance at the World Cup finals.

▲ **FIFA World Football Museum collection.**

French chivalry

▲ Raymond Kopa gets the better of goalkeeper Gilmar in the France-Brazil semi-final.

24 JUNE 1958

BRAZIL 5–2 **FRANCE**

VAVÁ 2	FONTAINE 9
DIDI 39	PIANTONI 83
PELÉ 52, 64, 75	

Pelé, an amazing hat-trick

At the age of 17 (and now 244 days), Pelé made history again in the game against France, becoming the youngest player to score a hat-trick in the World Cup finals.
Two of his goals were testimony to his sense of positioning and coolness under pressure. In the first instance, he seized on a ball dropped in front of him by goalkeeper Claude Abbes, scoring with his left foot (3–1). In the second, he took advantage of a misunderstanding in the penalty area between Jean Vincent and Armand Penverne, dashing in to beat the French goalkeeper to make it 4–1. And what about the third goal? Pelé ran onto a ball just outside the penalty area, taking it acrobatically on his thigh before volleying it into the net with his right foot (5–1). "This Pelé of mine is proving to be ever more extraordinary," enthused Brazilian manager Vicente Feola. His French counterpart regarded him as a prodigy: "This lad controls the ball, swerves, dribbles and dummies in the most amazing way. If he is tackled hard, he rises above it, regains his balance in the air, falls on his feet and recovers the ball. In all my career, few players have impressed me as much as this Pelé." Since this match in 1958, no Brazilian has scored a hat-trick at the World Cup finals.

N JUST THE SECOND MINUTE of the match, a poor pass by Robert Jonquet to right-back André Lerond was intercepted by Garrincha. Jonquet tackled him, but the ball fell to Didi, who immediately laid on a through-ball to Vavá. The Brazilian forward, rested in the quarter-final against Wales, controlled the ball with his chest and scored with a right-footed shot (1–0).

The name of the striker and the timing of the goal at the Råsunda Stadium in Solna were reminiscent of the start of Brazil's group game against the USSR, and the one-sided match that followed (2–0). The final scoreline between Brazil and France (5–2 after the final goal in the 83rd minute) suggests a walk in the park for the Brazilians, but this is wrong on two counts: France proved to be a real handful for Bellini and his men, and the Brazilians benefited from a stroke of French ill-fortune.

Gylmar had managed to keep a clean sheet for 368 minutes, until Just Fontaine became the first player to score against him in this World Cup. And what a goal it was. In the ninth minute, Fontaine passed to Raymond Kopa, who dummied a defender and returned the ball to his eager partner. The top scorer in the competition rounded Gylmar and equalized with his left foot (1–1). It was Fontaine's ninth goal in five matches. During the period that followed, the match hung in the balance: Mário Zagallo stuck the bar with a long shot, while Kopa awed the crowd with his ball-carrying skills and clinical passes (he won the Ballon d'Or at the end of the season). Garrincha was denied a goal because Zagallo was offside. Then, in the 35th minute, disaster struck: there was a collision in midfield between Jonquet and Vavá, who made a lunging tackle. The French centre-half immediately clutched his leg and then held his head in his hands. His team-mates Raymond Kaelbel and Armand Penverne

helped him off the field. Jonquet, the French captain, must have remembered the 1954 World Cup match, lost to Yugoslavia in the group phase (0–1), when he had suffered a broken nose. Pale-faced, he returned to the field, but was unable to run, and spent the rest of the game limping up and down the right wing. Later, once in hospital, he was diagnosed with a double fracture of the fibula. Without Jonquet, the French could not hold out for long, and, in the 39th minute, Didi soon sent a searing shot into the top corner of the net (2–1). In the second half, 11 against ten, Garrincha, Vavá, Didi, Pelé and Zagallo were able to dance a menacing ballet, with new choreography for each attack. They were more efficient than they had been at any other time in the tournament and Pelé scored the final Brazilian goal, before Roger Piantoni got one back with a solo effort, after dribbling past three players *à la brésilienne* in the 83rd minute (5–2). This was the lively French left-winger's only effective moment of the game, although he had a good excuse: since the quarter-final against Northern Ireland (4–0), he had been playing with a rumbling appendix, which made any contact with his abdomen painful. In fact, Piantoni returned home for an operation after the match and took no part in the third-place playoff.

This enthralling but cruel game evoked sincere admiration between the two teams. "Victory has gone to the most formidable team in the competition", judged Armand Penverne. "You have to be honest and recognise the superiority of the Brazilians," concluded Raymond Kopa. On the other side, Vavá praised the qualities of left-half Jean-Jacques Marcel, who took Jonquet's place in central defence. But it was Didi who had the final word: "The French are a chivalrous team. We don't often come across players who are so gracious in defeat."

◀◀ Lennart Skoglund gets the better of Germany's Georg Stollenwerk.

◀ Gunnar Gren battling Horst Eckel in front of Lennart Skoglund.

Sweden rule on home turf

24 JUNE 1958

SWEDEN 🇸🇪 3–1 🇩🇪 **WEST GERMANY**

SKOGLUND 32, GREN 81, HAMRIN 88   SCHÄFER 24

BEFORE THE MATCH, George Raynor, brandishing a file stuffed full of notes, joked: "I know all there is to know about Germany: how they train, what their tactics are, and even the shoe size of each player. In fact, I know so much about them, I really don't see much point in playing the match." As well as studying his opponents in such detail, the English coach of the Sweden team had put together a competitive squad, despite having to draw on a mix of local players, old hands (Gunnar Gren, Nils Liedholm) and stars playing for Italian championship sides.

Raynor knew that West Germany were a physical side with an intractable defence led by the ruthless Hebert Erhardt (they had been penalized 22 times in the quarter-final against Yugoslavia), and were dangerous both on and off the ball. At the Ullevi Stadium in Gothenburg, however, Sweden took the game by the scruff of the neck: five corners to none in the first 15 minutes. Then, in the 24th minute and against the run of play, Germany opened the scoring with a fine shot from their captain Hans Schäfer (0–1).

But the Swedes had resources which the Germans lacked. In the 32nd minute, Nacka Skoglund received a pass from Liedholm. German defender Georg Stollenwerk was slow to intervene and the Swede fired off a left-footed shot which beat Fritz Herkenrath (1–1). In the second half, the pace slackened as the number of fouls increased. Kurt Hamrin weaving his way between defenders, collided with Erich Juskowiak. The German full-back responded to the Swedish winger's provocation with a kick. Hamrin, who has been playing in Italy for the last two seasons, rolled on the ground in pain. The Hungarian referee, István Zsolt, sent Juskowiak off... and Hamrin was immediately on his feet again, running and jumping around freely. With ten men against 11, West Germany could not resist for long, especially since Fritz Walter had picked up an injury, and it was Gunnar Gren, with a searing shot from 25 metres, who eventually put the host team ahead in the 81st minute (2–1). Then, in the 88th minute, Hamrin, again the man of the match, strolled down the right wing, dribbled into the penalty area and scored the goal that made sure of Sweden's place in the final (3–1). Valiant as ever but ageing, West Germany had surrendered their world title.

Born on the same day

Sweden and West Germany both picked a 37-year-old for their line-up in the semi-final. The amazing thing is that the two men were born on the same day, 31 October 1920, one in Gothenburg, the other in Kaiserslautern. Both were footballing giants, but on 24 June 1958 their fortunes turned out to be very different. On the German side, while Fritz Walter had maintained all his old skills, his legs were no longer so dependable. The leader of the 1954 World Cup champions had passed on the captain's armband to Hans Schäfer. Manager Sepp Herberger had nevertheless entrusted him with a key role in the team: sharing a room with *enfant terrible* Helmut Rahn, whose fondness for beer was well known... Against Sweden, Walter played his finest game of the tournament, but he injured both knee and ankle in the second half. When Juskowiak was sent off, Walter was left feeling impotent. This was his 61st cap and his 11th appearance in the World Cup finals, and the Kaiserslautern playmaker rightly reckoned it would be his last. In fact, he did not play in the match to decide third place.

On the Swedish side, despite his advancing years, Gunnar Gren was playing in his first World Cup. His glory days were even further behind him: he had scored two goals against Yugoslavia in the London Olympic Final in 1948 (won by Sweden, 3–1). Why did he not play in the 1950 World Cup in Brazil? Because, having left to play in Italy, he was no longer eligible for selection. And, in 1954, Sweden had not qualified. After seven seasons in *Serie A* (Milan, Fiorentina, Genoa), Gren had returned home in 1956, as player-manager for Örgryte, in the Swedish second division, a club in Gothenburg, where this semi-final was played. Gren was denied the captaincy: the Swedish team was led by Nils Liedholm, another Italian "exile" and his former partner at Milan. But Gren was his country's hero: his well-judged shot into the top corner of the German goal in the 81st minute gave Sweden a decisive advantage (2–1). And he still had another match to play: a World Cup final, on home turf, against Brazil.

▲ Brazil's Garrincha, neck and neck with Swedish defender Sven Axbom.

▲ Vavá, Didi and Pelé with the Jules Rimet trophy.

Brazil the kings of football at last

29 JUNE 1958

BRAZIL 5–2 **SWEDEN**

VAVÁ 9, 32, PELÉ 55, 90, ZAGALLO 68   LIEDHOLM 4, SIMONSSON 80

EIGHT YEARS after the disaster at the Maracanã (1–2 against Uruguay), would Brazil fail once again in the attempt to win their first World Cup title? At the start of the match, there were plenty of negative signs. By drawing lots, the Swedes had won the right to wear their own colours, yellow jerseys and blue shorts, while the Brazilians exchanged their yellow jerseys for an all-blue strip. The heavy, greasy surface of the Råsunda Stadium in Stockholm also favoured the European style of play. Finally, in the first few minutes the Brazilians seemed strangely intimidated, not so much by the presence of King Gustav VI as by the surprisingly aggressive approach of the Swedish team. George Raynor, the Scandinavians' English coach, was counting on an quick goal to: "Plunge the Brazilians into panic for the whole of the match." According to plan, a pass from Agne Simonsson in the fourth minute found Nils Liedholm, the veteran Swedish captain, who dribbled his way round Orlando, then Bellini, and put the ball past Gylmar (1–0). Brazil found themselves a goal down for the first time in the tournament.

But unlike in 1950, when Juan Schiaffino equalized for Uruguay (1–1), shock and discouragement were not written all over the faces of the Brazilian team. Didi plucked the ball out of the net and walked back to the centre spot. Although Bellini, at centre-back, was the captain, Didi, Brazil's play-maker, called the team together. According to Djalma Santos: "He told us we were good enough to win the match, and his words had a settling effect on the team."

Indeed, the Brazilians immediately upped their game, and Garrincha set about tormenting his latest victim, Sven Axbom. In the ninth minute, the "Bent-Legged Angel" (Garrincha had one leg shorter than the other) broke through on the right and centred to Vavá, who slotted the ball home (1–1). If any of the 49,737 spectators missed this piece of action, they were to see a repeat in the 32nd minute. Again on the right, Garrincha broke through, centred and found Vavá in the goalmouth (1–2). The only difference was that, this time, he swept the ball home with his left foot…

As in the semi-final against France, the second half was more of a demonstration than a battle. But what about Kurt Hamrin and Nacka Skoglund? The two Swedish wingers were effectively neutralized by the Brazilians' 4-2-4 formation, especially since Vicente Feola had replaced De Sordi in defence with the tough Djalma Santos, making a perfectly timed debut in the tournament. Strangely, there was no man-marking of Didi. Raynor countered him using his two inside-forwards, between whom the wizard tacked happily back and forth.

And what about Pelé? The youngest player ever to feature in a World Cup final (a record which still stands) left an indelible mark on the game. In the first half, he struck the Swedish goalpost with a lobbed shot from 20 metres. In the second, he chested a pass from Nílton Santos to elude Sigge Parling in the penalty area, lobbed the ball over Julle Gustavsson and volleyed the ball into the net with his right foot before it could hit the ground, giving Svensson no chance at all (1–3). How could such a prodigious miracle be performed in less than two seconds? "The rainbow kick was something the Europeans were not familiar with," Pelé explained later. "They generally committed themselves to the tackle, because everyone shot at the first touch. I therefore juggled the ball to send it over the head of the defender. Then, without waiting for it to land, I shot and scored. It will always be one of the best goals of my career."

This was followed by a shot from Garrincha, which Svensson diverted against the crossbar, then Mário Zagallo added a fourth goal for Brazil in the 68th minute, having run in from the left wing to win a loose ball (1–4). Simonsson reduced the deficit in the 80th minute following some fine work by Liedholm (2–4), but it was Pelé who ended the scoring, rising between two Swedish defenders to meet a long centre from Zagallo and place a lobbed header beyond the reach of Svensson in the final minute if the match (2–5).

Brazil were at last the kings of football, and the world's most popular sport had just discovered its absolute monarch: he was just 17 years old and bore the name of Édson Arantes do Nascimento, better known as Pelé.

▲ Bengt Gustavsson and Pelé battle it out for the ball.

Just Fontaine's Jersey

The jersey worn by Just Fontaine, record-holder for the most goals scored in a single finals phase.

▲ FIFA World Football Museum collection.

PLAY-OFF FOR THIRD PLACE

▲ Just Fontaine held aloft by his team-mates after scoring four times against West Germany.

Fontaine, the all-time record-holder

28 JUNE 1958

FRANCE 6-3 **WEST GERMANY**

FONTAINE 16, 36, 78, 89, KOPA 27 (PEN), DOUIS 50   CIESCLARCZYK 18, RAHN 52, SCHÄFER 84

The legend created on 28 June 1958 at the Ullevi Stadium in Gothenburg could have had another hero. Helmut Rahn, for example. The double goalscorer in the 1954 final scored his tenth World Cup goal (four in 1954, six in 1958). After the "Miracle of Berne", the down-to-earth footballer from Essen became a national idol, but lost his way. Rahn put on weight, was disqualified for drunk driving, and got into a fracas with the police. The Rot-Weiss Essen fans began calling him "Prosit Helmut" because of his tendency to ship a lot of beer. But Sepp Herberger, the West German manager, continued to believe in him. In preparation for the 1958 World Cup, he ordered him to lose 8kg, and convinced him that he was still capable of being *"der Boss"*. And Rahn went on to play a heroic role in the tournament. His goal in the third-place playoff match against France certainly bore his unmistakable trademark: a tricky dribble down the right wing and a scorching shot from a tight angle. But this only brought Germany back to 4–2. The fact was, another striker had been in the ascendant for the previous three weeks: Just Fontaine.

It has been claimed that Fontaine, who was born in Morocco, then a French colony, on 18 August 1933, was not an automatic choice for the team (he had been selected for the national team only five times before this World Cup). It is true that Thadée Cisowski (nine goals in ten matches up to that point) had broken his leg, but an injury to René Bliard (no goals in seven matches) had nothing to do with the selection. The French selectors had assured Fontaine, before the tournament that he would be included in the squad, even though he would wear number 17. The Stade de Reims striker had just enjoyed a remarkable season, scoring 34 goals in only 26 league matches. Having undergone an operation on his right knee in December 1957, he did not play again until February 1958. The inside-right later stated that this period of recuperation had been the "fuel" that enabled him to put on such an explosive display in Sweden.

In France's opening game against Paraguay (7–3), he scored three goals and laid on two others. Concentrating their attentions on Raymond Kopa, the Paraguayans left too much space for Fontaine. The other teams they played did not make the same mistake… but to no avail. "Justo" scored a pair against Yugoslavia (2–3), another goal against Scotland (2–1), then two against Northern Ireland (4–0) and one against Brazil (2–5). What were his strengths? Speed, strength and efficiency. Fontaine's understanding with Kopa was miraculous, even though the two men were not acquainted before the World Cup. Albert Batteux, the French coach, had had the bright idea of getting them to share a room. It was not all roses: "Between the two of us, it was love at first sight, but only in a footballing sense," said Fontaine. "Raymond, who was playing for Real Madrid, lived by Spanish time and went to bed two hours after me. And as I was not an easy person to get on with…"

Playing against West Germany, Just Fontaine scored four goals. The first was from a cross from Kopa during a counter-attack, easily converted with a right-foot shot (1–0). The second: a shot from André Lerond was pushed away by German goalkeeper Heinz Kwiatkowski; Fontaine recovered the ball, turned and put it in the net (3–1). The third was all his own work: Fontaine gathered the ball 50 metres from goal, accelerated, beat Rahn, ran on, accelerated again and scored (5–2). Then the fourth: Fontaine received a long pass from Maryan Wisnieski on the halfway line. The German defence thought he was offside. Fontaine charged towards Kwiatkowski and beat him again (6–3). At the final whistle, the French striker was carried in triumph by his team-mates. And why did Fontaine not take the French penalty in the 27th minute, converted by Kopa ? "Raymond had been appointed to take it", explained Fontaine in 2014. "At 1–1, it was normal that he should take it. It would never have occurred to me to ask him to leave it to me." Just Fontaine's record of 13 goals in the tournament is likely to remain forever out of reach.

1962

Two years before hosting the 1962 World Cup, Chile suffered the most powerful earthquake ever measured. Four of the eight venues were destroyed – but with passionate support behind them, Chile's team finished third. The inspirational Garrincha led Brazil to victories over England and Chile, then in the Final they beat Czechoslovakia 3–1 to become the second country to retain the trophy.

The World Cup, pride of the Chilean people

◄ Garrincha, one of Brazil's key players, poses with the Jules Rimet trophy.

▼ Two years on, Chile was still recovering from the terrible earthquake that took place on 22 May 1960.

"IT IS PRECISELY because we have nothing that we will move heaven and Earth." With these words, in 1956, Carlos Dittborn, the Chilean president of CONMEBOL (the South American football confederation), persuaded FIFA to entrust Chile with the organization of the 1962 World Cup. Their main rivals, Argentina, deployed exactly the opposite argument: "We could stage the World Cup tomorrow. We already have all it takes."

But Chile was a poor country. To cap it all, on 21 and 22 May 1960, the country was struck by the most powerful earthquake of the 20th century: 9.5 on the Richter scale. The ground shook for ten minutes 600 kilometres south of Santiago and a tidal wave completed the work of destruction. The earthquake claimed three thousand victims; almost two million Chileans were left without a roof over their heads. But Chile was not to be deterred: it was decided that four venues, rather than the original eight, would be used to host the competition; roads and bridges were reconstructed. The World Cup became a focus of national pride... But foreign observers were struck by the poverty of a country which, though politically stable, was economically underdeveloped. There were, for example, a mere 120,000 motor cars for a population of 7.5 million. Carlos Dittborn did not live to see the success of "his" World Cup: he died of a heart attack a month before the start of the competition, at the age of 38. The stadium at Arica was immediately renamed the Estadio Carlos Dittborn.

CHILE 1962

WORLD CHAMPIONSHIP
JULES RIMET CUP 1962 IN CHILE

Regulations

No more play-offs

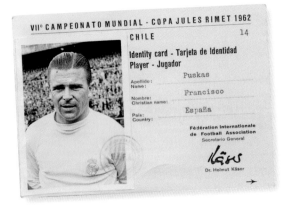

Identity card of "Spanish" player "Francisco" Puskás for the 1962 World Cup.

▲ **FIFA World Football Museum Collection.**

T HE FORMAT of the tournament was the same as in 1958, except that there were no playoffs between teams on equal points at the end of the group stage. The old arrangement had unfairly penalized those condemned to play extra matches. Instead, goal average was used to decide which teams should progress to the quarter-finals. This system was used again in 1966 and 1970, after which goal difference replaced goal average.

But the World Cup was bedevilled by another problem: the unfair recruitment of foreign players. The Argentinian Alfredo Di Stéfano, the Uruguayan José Santamaría and the Hungarian Ferenc Puskás, all three playing for Real Madrid, featured in the Spanish squad, while the Argentinians Humberto Maschio (Atalanta) and Omar Sivori (Juventus), plus the Brazilians José Altafini (AC Milan) and Angelo Sormani (Mantova) were included in the Italian squad. FIFA reacted even before the competition began: to prevent opportunist changes of citizenship, they decided that from the start of the 1962–63 season international players would not be permitted to compete for a country other than their country of birth or origin.

Story of the qualifiers

South America well served

▼ Stanley Rous, Carlos Dittborn and Ernst Thommem at the draw for the 1962 World Cup.

T WO OF THE SEMI-FINALISTS from the previous World Cup failed to qualify: Sweden and France. The Swedes, runners-up in 1958, had been defeated by Switzerland in a playoff in West Berlin (2–1) and the French had lost in Milan to unfancied Bulgaria (1–0), who therefore became the latest country from the Eastern bloc to make their debut in the tournament. The other debutants were Colombia, who only had to beat Peru. With three countries qualifying (Argentina, Uruguay and Colombia), plus Brazil (the title holders) and Chile (the hosts), South America was well served by the qualification system.

Group stage

GROUP 1	
URU 2–1 COL	
URS 2–0 YUG	
YUG 3–1 URU	
URS 4–4 COL	
URS 2–1 URU	
YUG 5–0 COL	

	W	D	L	+	–	PTS
URS	2	1	0	8	5	5
YUG	2	0	1	8	3	4
URU	1	0	2	4	6	2
COL	0	1	2	5	11	1

GROUP 2	
CHI 3–1 SUI	
FRG 0–0 ITA	
CHI 2–0 ITA	
FRG 2–1 SUI	
FRG 2–0 CHI	
ITA 3–0 SUI	

	W	D	L	+	–	PTS
FRG	2	1	0	4	1	5
CHI	2	0	1	5	3	4
ITA	1	1	1	3	2	3
SUI	0	0	3	2	8	0

GROUP 3	
BRA 2–0 MEX	
TCH 1–0 ESP	
BRA 0–0 TCH	
ESP 1–0 MEX	
BRA 2–1 ESP	
MEX 3–1 TCH	

	W	D	L	+	–	PTS
BRA	2	1	0	4	1	5
TCH	1	1	1	2	3	3
MEX	1	0	2	3	4	2
ESP	1	0	2	2	3	2

GROUP 4	
ARG 1–0 BUL	
HUN 2–1 ENG	
ENG 3–1 ARG	
HUN 6–1 BUL	
HUN 0–0 ARG	
ENG 0–0 BUL	

	W	D	L	+	–	PTS
HUN	2	1	0	8	2	5
ENG	1	1	1	4	3	3
ARG	1	1	1	2	3	3
BUL	0	1	2	1	7	1

Knockout stages

QUARTER-FINAL	QUARTER-FINAL	QUARTER-FINAL	QUARTER-FINAL
BRA 3–1 ENG	CHI 2–1 URS	TCH 1–0 HUN	YUG 1–0 FRG

SEMI-FINAL	SEMI-FINAL
BRA 4–2 CHI	TCH 3–1 YUG

PLAY-OFF FOR THIRD PLACE

CHI 1–0 YUG

FINAL

BRA 3–1 TCH

ARG BRA BUL CHI
COL ENG ESP FRG
HUN ITA MEX SUI
TCH URS URU YUG

16 TEAMS

32
MATCHES PLAYED

6
CARDS

893 172
SPECTATORS

×4

**ALBERT, IVANOV, GARRINCHA,
SÁNCHEZ, JERKOVIĆ, VAVÁ**
LEADING GOALSCORERS

BRAZIL
WINNERS

OFFICIAL LOGO

2.8
AVERAGE GOALS
PER MATCH

CRACK
OFFICIAL MATCH BALL

Host towns, cities and stadiums

Four stadiums, one per group

ARICA

**ESTADIO CARLOS
DITTBORN** (25,000)

ESTADIO SAUSALITO
(32,000)

VIÑA DEL MAR — SANTIAGO DE CHILE

RANCAGUA

ESTADIO NACIONAL
(75,000)

**ESTADIO BRADEN
COOPER CO.** (25,000)

The original plan had been for eight cities to host matches at the 1962 World Cup but, following the earthquake of 1950, four venues were dropped. Talca, Concepción, Talcahuano and Valdivia had been left badly damaged and were discarded in favour of hosting each of the tournament's four groups in one location only – Santiago, Viña del Mar, Rancagua and Arica. The three venues outside the capital Santiago varied dramatically – the seaside town of Viña del Mar with its casinos, the mines of Rancagua and the frontier city and port of Arica in the arid north of the Atacama desert, recognised as the driest inhabited place on Earth. The modest capacities of the three stadiums outside Santiago proved sufficient as an average of just 10,427 spectators turned up to matches outside the capital. The Estadio Nacional, on the other hand, was full for most of the games played there, even when the hosts were not involved.

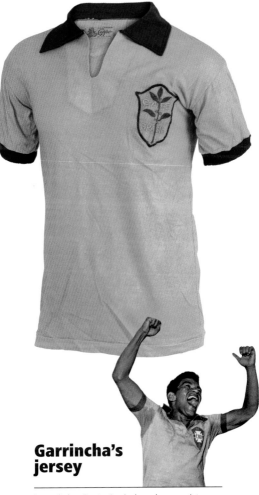

Garrincha's jersey

Jersey belonging to Garrincha, who won sixty caps for Brazil. He wore this jersey in a warm-up match played in Chile before the tournament started.

▲ **FIFA World Football Museum Collection.**

◀ Soviet Eduard Dubinski is carried off the pitch following an aggressive tackle by Yugoslavia's Muhamed Mujić.

▶ After playing the first two games for Brazil, an injury meant Pelé had to watch the rest of the tournament from the sidelines.

Horrific injury at Arica

31 MAY 1962

USSR 🇷🇺 2–0 🇾🇺 **YUGOSLAVIA**

IVANOV 51, PONEDELNIK 83

FEATURING the finalists of the 1960 European Championship (won 2–1 by the USSR), the opening confrontation between the Soviets and Yugoslavs at Arica, in the north of Chile, was a real needle match. The Yugoslavs Josip Skoblar and Dragoslav Šekularac mounted some slick attacks, but they were foiled by Lev Yashin, impeccable in the Soviet goal. The tension rose. Fouls were committed, becoming systematic, especially when the USSR opened the scoring in the 51st minute thanks to a goal by Valentin Ivanov (1–0). Believing a free-kick had been wrongly awarded, the Yugoslav Dražan Jerković took hold of the West German referee, Albert Dusch, and shook him violently. Then horror struck: Yugoslav winger Muhamed Mujić felled Soviet right-back Eduard Dubinsky with a crunching tackle. His team-mates gathered round, visibly shocked: he had sustained an open fracture of the tibia. Dubinsky was carried off the field and sent straight to hospital.

After the match, horrified by what he had done, Mujić could neither eat nor sleep. It was announced that the Yugoslav Federation had taken the initiative of suspending him for a year, but manager Ljubomir Lovrić denied it. In any case, Mujić would never play for Yugoslavia again. As for Dubinsky, although the surgeons at first thought his playing days were over, he was eventually able to make a comeback, after a long convalescence. However, he died in 1969 of a malignant tumour at the age of just 34, a rare complication resulting from the injury he had suffered in Chile.

The number of goals scored by 20-year-old Hungarian Flórián Albert in his country's victory over Bulgaria (6–1), on 3 June at Rancagua. This was the only hat-trick scored in a World Cup in which no single player scored more than four goals in total.

Pelé: a masterpiece of a goal, then out of action

In Brazil's opening game against Mexico (2–0), Pelé resumed his World Cup role where he had left off in 1958: producing a decisive cross that enabled Mário Zagallo to open the scoring with a header in the 56th minute (1–0); and then, in the 73rd minute, scoring a goal that bore his special trademark – the young prodigy gathered the ball 40 metres out, set off, dribbled round four opponents, entered the penalty area, shot between two Mexican defenders and beat the experienced Antonio Carbajal.

Against Czechoslovakia in a poorly attended Viña del Mar stadium (14,000 spectators), Santos and Brazil's star player fired off a left-foot shot in the 25th minute. The ball crashed against Viliam Schrojf's goal post. But Pelé, left holding his thigh, made a face and limped towards the touchline: the 21-year-old had pulled a muscle in his groin. He played out the remainder of the game on the wing in a match that offered few scoring opportunities. When the ball came Pelé's way, Jan Lála and Ján Popluhár refrained from tackling him so as not to aggravate his injury – an attitude that touched Pelé deeply.

In the third group match against Spain, Brazilian coach Aymoré Moreira replaced him with another youngster, Amarildo, also aged 21. The move paid off: the Botafogo striker turned the score round in the last quarter of the match, after the Spaniards had led since the 35th minute thanks to a goal from Adelardo. Amarildo first volleyed home a cross from Zagallo in the 72nd minute (1–1), then scored with his head following some fine work by Garrincha in the 86th minute (2–1). The Spanish team of Ferenc Puskás and Alfredo Di Stéfano (who was apparently injured and did not play at all in Chile) were eliminated. Brazil, meanwhile, were preparing to write another chapter in their World Cup history. But without Pelé.

The "Battle of Santiago"

2 JUNE 1962

CHILE 2–0 **ITALY**

RAMIREZ 73, TORO 87

IT WAS AN ARTICLE in a Florence daily newspaper that lit the blue touchpaper. Published in the days prior to the competition, it described the poverty of certain districts of Santiago, deplored the general level of illiteracy and cast doubt on the morality of Chilean women. The whole country was up in arms and determined to take revenge on the Italian squad. The 11 Chilean players lined up on the pitch with the whole country behind them.

Barely five minutes had elapsed when, in a seething national stadium (the Estadio Nacional in Santiago), with 66,000 spectators booing the Italians whenever they got the ball, the Italian right-back Mario David was fouled by Eladio Rojas and delivered a kick in return. Players congregated, punches were thrown. Three minutes later, Giorgio Ferrini and the Chilean Leonel Sánchez, who had scored two goals in the opening match against Switzerland (3–1), exchanged kicks. In the scrum that followed, the Italian striker attacked Honorino Landa. The English referee, Ken Aston, gave Ferrini his marching orders, but the Italian refused to leave the pitch. The game was stopped for eight minutes and the Chilean police had to intervene to remove the Torino midfielder.

But order was not restored. On the contrary, the Argentinian-Italian Humberto Maschio, who had just had his nose broken by an anonymous fist, struck Jorge Toro but received no more than a reprimand. The referee seemed overwhelmed by the fury that swirled around him.

And the worst was yet to come. Towards the end of the first half, Leonel Sánchez, having dribbled round David, held the ball tight clenched between his feet. David kicked out at both ball and player. Sánchez reacted by turning and giving David a punch in the face, in full sight of the linesman, before collapsing and clutching his leg. Again the referee did nothing, failing to send Sánchez off. David subsequently took his own revenge by driving his boot into the neck of the player who had punched him. Aston sent David back to the dressing-room: the Italians were down to nine men.

The referee blew for half-time after yet another incident: the Chilean Jorge Toro rugby-tackled Italy's captain, Bruno Mora, then fought with him on the ground until Aston separated the pair. The first half had lasted 57 minutes.

And what of the football? Strangely, the Italians had selected a second-string team, making seven changes after their match against West Germany (0–0) and leaving out their goalkeeper and captain Lorenzo Buffon, as well as Omar Sivori and Cesare Maldini. In the second half, even with nine men, they often looked more likely to score, but, despite the talents of Maschio and the Brazilian world champion José Altafini, who was playing his final game for Italy, they ended up conceding two late goals, scored by Jaime Ramírez and Jorge Toro.

"It is a sad thing to have travelled 16,000 km to see something like that," said the head of the Italian delegation. The players complained that the Chileans spat in their faces from the start of the game, and in the days that followed stones were thrown into their training camp, besieged by 500 "supporters".

As for Ken Aston, he came up with the system of red and yellow cards which was introduced at the 1970 World Cup in Mexico.

The softest corner ever

3 JUNE 1962

USSR 4–4 **COLOMBIA**

IVANOV 8, 11, CHISLENKO 10, PONEDELNIK 56   ACEROS 21, COLL 68, RADA 72, KLINGER 76

IN 1954, another game had ended with the very unusual scoreline of 4–4: a match between England and Belgium involving a goal-chase and extra-time. But the encounter between the USSR and Colombia at Arica defied all known logic. After 13 minutes, the Soviets, the clear favourites, were leading 3–0. After 57 minutes, the score had progressed to 4–1.

Gavril Kachalin's men then lost concentration and, in the 68th minute, let in an absurd goal direct from a corner taken by Marcos Coll (4–2). Hardly a fierce shot into the top corner of the net; rather a weak cross that bounced gently towards Lev Yashin's goal… Defender Givi Chokheli left it for Yashin, but the ball went straight in. The Colombians immediately sprang to life, winning every tackle and started to fire in accurate shots. It was Marino Klinger who finally equalized in the 76th minutr, drawing Yashin out of his goal (4–4). A catastrophic match for the Dynamo Moscow goalkeeper? Not entirely: for without an extraordinary save on his part in the final minutes, the Colombians might have won 5–4.

23

The number worn by Uruguayan striker Guillermo Escalada… despite the 22-player limit on World Cup squads. The Uruguayans, being superstitious, had all refused to wear the number 13… Even so, luck was not on their side: although they beat Colombia (2–1), they were then defeated by Yugoslavia (3–1), then the USSR (2–1). Escalada did not play in any of the three matches.

Schrojf unbeatable

10 JUNE 1962

CZECHOSLOVAKIA 1–0 **HUNGARY**

SCHERER 13

EW PEOPLE had been extolling the merits of Viliam Schrojf a fortnight earlier. But after four matches in Chile, the Slovan Bratislava goalkeeper had established himself as the world number one in that position. He was the player on whom Czechoslovakia had relied to get through the group stage (only three goals conceded, all against Mexico). And it was thanks to him that they beat Hungary at Rancagua.

After their inside-right, Adolf Scherer, had scored in a counter-attack in the 14th minute (1–0), the Czechs drew down an (iron) curtain to shut out the Hungarians, who responded by throwing eight men forward in attack. In the first World Cup quarter-final between two Eastern bloc teams, Schrojf manoeuvred his defensive forces like pieces in a game of chess, his great passion. In the middle of the pitch, Andrej Kvašňák and Josef Masopust cut off all routes forward. Immediately in front of Schrojf, the towering Svatopluk Pluskal and Ján Popluhár dealt with high balls. At full-back, the ultra-tough Jan Lála and highly experienced Ladislav Novák (who, at the age of 30, was in his third World Cup as captain) threw themselves at any Hungarian attacker who dared to break through. On his goal-line and, when necessary, charging out into his penalty area, Schrojf was the last line of defence, denying Flórián Albert and Lajos Tichy with some brilliant saves. He preferred to risk catching the ball, rather than punching it clear, which surprised many commentators. But Schrojf, aged 30, was quite sure of himself: although he had not actually played in 1954 and 1958, this was the third World Cup for which he had been selected.

At the end of the match, it was probably true that the better team had lost, but Czechoslovakia were through to the semi-finals… having scored only three goals in four games.

▲ Viliam Schrojf, the Czechslovak keeper, was man of the match in the quarter-final against Hungary.

Sepp Herberger bows out

Cover of German magazine *Kicker*, May 1962.

▲ **FIFA World Football Museum Collection.**

10 JUNE 1962

YUGOSLAVIA 1–0 **WEST GERMANY**

RADAKOVIC 85

HIS WAS the third meeting between West Germany and Yugoslavia in consecutive World Cup quarter-finals. In 1954 (2–0), and again in 1958 (1–0), the West Germans, managed by the long-serving Sepp Herberger, had won by narrow margins. In Santiago, the tables were turned. The crowd at the Estadio Nacional were somewhat disappointed, as they had anticipated a Chilean victory over Germany at the group stage (rather than a 0–2 defeat) and a quarter-final featuring their national team in Santiago. In the event, they were to witness one of the finest displays in the competition between two European teams with opposing styles of play: long and physical, in the case of West Germany; quick, inventive passing and skilful dribbling, in the case of Yugoslavia. The result was an intense, close but fairly fought match. The winners finally emerged in the 86th minute, when a cross from Yugoslav captain Milan Galić found Petar Radaković, his head swathed in bandages since he had sustained a cut over the eyebrow in a clash with Uwe Seeler. Radaković duly volleyed the ball into the net.

In the dressing-room afterwards, Sepp Herberger was in a state of depression for nearly two hours. At half-time, some of his players had dared to complain that the West German approach was too defensive. This he could not accept. Born in 1897, a PE teacher who had been called up for the national team three times as a player, Sepp Herberger had taken charge of the German team in 1936, after their defeat in the quarter-finals of the Berlin Olympic Games. He had led them at the 1938 World Cup, at a time when the German squad – as a result of the Anschluss – included many Austrian players. He had spent the war trying to prevent his players from being called up for military service. Not for ideological reasons, but to be able to build the best possible team when peace was restored… The Miracle of Berne in 1954 was his crowning achievement. So what was the Herberger method? Selecting versatile players whom he could re-position to counter different opponents, subjecting them to intense physical and tactical training, while showing total confidence in them over the long term. His watchwords? Determination, punctuality, and discipline. His great strength? Enormous charisma. In 1954 and 1958, his men had hung on his every word. But on 10 June 1962, only one of his world champion players was on the pitch in Santiago: the durable Hans Schäfer.

Up to this point, Herr Herberger had been enjoying the Chilean World Cup. The *West Germans* were staying at the Santiago military training school, in a disciplined, formal environment that suited them down to the ground. In the group stage, he had taken revenge on Switzerland (2–1) and his old rival Karl Rappan, who in 1938 had eliminated the German team 4–2, a defeat he had never come to terms with. The defeat by Yugoslavia affected him just as deeply. The next day, 11 June, Herberger presented himself to the press in a simple tracksuit. The atmosphere was calm and dignified, as the journalists awaited the comments of this sage of the footballing world. He criticized the failings of one of his players, Horst Szymaniak, which was not at all like him. "Our preparations for the 1966 World Cup begin right here and now," he concluded. Herberger finally resigned in 1964 after 28 years in the job.

▼ Garrincha shoots straight past English defender Ray Wilson.

▲ A surprise intruder on the pitch! Garrincha later adopted the dog.

Garrincha and a dog steal the show

10 JUNE 1962

BRAZIL 3–1 ENGLAND

GARRINCHA 31, 59, VAVÁ 53   HITCHENS 38

THE QUESTION that faced England in the very British sea-fog that smothered the Estadio Sausalito in Viña del Mar before the kick-off, was whether they could perform the same feat as in 1958, when they were the only team to hold Brazil in check (0–0)? Pelé was absent, nursing an injury, and after just 20 minutes his replacement, Amarildo, was hampered in his movements by a pulled muscle. But danger, when you are playing Brazil, can come from any quarter. The amazing Garrincha, famous for his dribbling skills, opened the scoring with a header from a corner taken by Mário Zagallo in the 31st minute. The English, however, responded seven minutes later: a free-kick by captain Johnny Haynes was headed against the bar by Jimmy Greaves, and Gerry Hitchens was there in front of goal to put the ball in the net (1–1).

But the fact that the English held out until half-time was because their long-standing manager, Walter Winterbottom (in charge for a fourth World Cup), required all his players to come back and defend, time and time again. Exhaustion ensued. After the break,

the Brazilians upped the tempo and, attacking in waves, eventually wore down their opponents. In the 53rd minute, a sharp free-kick by Garrincha was poorly dealt with by Ron Springett, and Vavá took advantage (2–1). Five minutes later, Garrincha sent a magnificent shot into the top corner of the net from a distance of 25 metres (3–1).

However, the *Brazil* right-winger was not in total control. At a certain point, a stray dog gate-crashed the match, forcing the referee to stop play. The animal avoided an Springett's attempt to gather him, then wove his way around Garrincha, much to the amusement of the crowd. Eventually Jimmy Greaves had a bright idea. "I got down on all fours, because I love dogs", the Tottenham striker recalled, "and he came to me straight away… I picked up the dog and stroked him. But at that moment, he forgot himself and messed all over my jersey. We didn't have a change of strip in those days… So I had to play on just as I was. It didn't smell too good, I can tell you." As for Garrincha, after the match he asked if he could adopt the dog, and later took it back with him to Brazil.

The "black spider" discomfited

10 JUNE 1962

CHILE 2–1 USSR

SANCHEZ 11, ROJAS 29   CHISLENKO 26

FROM ALL OVER the north of Chile, for hundreds of miles, buses and lorries brought thousands of spectators to the desert town of Arica, on the frontier with Peru. The local shop and hotels were literally besieged. The dressing-rooms of the Carlos Dittborn Stadium, packed to the rafters with 20,000 spectators, were guarded by police. All because Chile, regarded as outsiders, were playing the strong USSR team of Igor Netto, Valentin Ivanov (who had already scored four goals in the tournament), and Lev Yashin.

In the 11th minute, Armando Tobar was awarded a free-kick, to the right of the Soviet penalty area. Leonel Sánchez prepared to take it, his teammates jockeying for position in the area. But the Chilean left-wing decided to go straight for goal, firing in an incredibly powerful shot. The "Black Spider", Lev Yashin, who was expecting a cross, was poorly positioned on his line and reacted too late (1–0). Sánchez had gone it alone, but that was just what coach Fernando Riera wanted from him. For a long time, Sánchez had been in contention for the left-wing role with his best friend, Bernardo Bello. Their rivalry had inhibited him, prevented him from asserting himself. Riera, trusting in Sánchez and his powerful shot, had therefore decided not to select Bello for the Chilean World Cup squad. And Sánchez played with a new-found freedom. The switch was cruel, but effective.

After Chislenko had equalized for the Soviet Union in the 26th minute (1–1), it was the turn of Chilean inside-left Eladio Rojas to try his luck from distance. In the 29th minute, he delivered a sharp, accurate right-footed shot, at mid-height, just inside the left-hand post. Yashin dived, arm outstretched, but in vain (2–1). Chile had caused one of the great upsets of the tournament.

▲ Chile's Leonel Sánchez shoots, watched by Brazil's Djalma Santos.

▲ Amarildo watches as the ball hits the top corner of the net for the third Brazilian goal.

"It's a great thing that we have come so far. Let's keep our feet on the ground."

Fernando Riera, Chile's manager, after his team's semi-final defeat.

Garrincha allowed to play in the Final

Why did Garrincha's sending-off in the game against Chile not result in his exclusion from the Final? Because, in 1962, this was not an automatic sanction, but subject to the decision of a FIFA committee. In Garrincha's case, in spite of the player's comic denials ("I raised my leg to sell Rojas a dummy and, unintentionally, my knee connected with his stomach"), the committee members took three factors into account: 1. Garrincha had never previously been sent off; 2. He was reacting to provocation, unlike the Chilean Landa, who was excluded from the third-place playoff; and 3. The Brazilian prime minister, Tancredo Neves, sent a telegram begging the FIFA committee to allow Garrincha to play against Czechoslovakia.

Blood red and pure gold

13 JUNE 1962

BRAZIL 🔵 4-2 🔴 **CHILE**

GARRINCHA 9, 32, VAVÁ 47, 78   TORO 42, L SANCHEZ 61 (PEN)

AFTER TWO HOURS of traffic jams and jostling, the spectators who made it to the immense Estadio Nacional in Santiago felt as if they were entering a bullfighting arena. The jerseys of the Chilean team were blood red, those of the Brazilians golden yellow. Both had come for an event far more important than a World Cup semi-final. Before they left home, the Brazilian president, João Goulart, had addressed the players with these words: "If you win the World Cup, for four years our people will not complain of hardship. Your victory will make up for our lack of rice and beans." The Chileans, for their part, were playing to restore the dignity they saw as compromised by the devastating earthquake of 1960. After their victory over the USSR, a bitter slogan had appeared on walls throughout Arica : *"Subdessarrollados: 2, Europa: 1."* (*"Underdeveloped world: 2, Europe: 1"*).

Brazil were fielding the same side as against England. Pelé, still injured, remained on the bench, while Nílton Santos (aged 37), Djalma Santos (33) and Didi (33) were playing their fifth match in a fortnight. And then, of course, there was Garrincha. What could the Chileans do to counter so unpredictable a player? Nothing, as the inventive winger was to prove after only nine minutes of play: receiving the ball on the edge of the Chilean penalty area, he unleashed a left-footed shot which flew into the top corner of Misael Escuti's net (1–0). For the thankless task of left-back, marking Garrincha, the Chilean manager Fernando Riera had no option but to select the young Manuel Rodríguez as a replacement for the injured captain Sergio Navarro. In the 14th minute, Garrincha bamboozled him with his celebrated manoeuvre of feinting to go to the left and dribbling past on the right. Rodríguez, left standing by the Brazilian like so many other defenders before him, brought him down with his shoulder. Was it in the penalty area? The Peru-

vian referee, Arturo Yamasaki, whistled for an indirect free-kick, a decision which gave rise to lasting controversy. Especially since Chile came very close to equalizing with a shot from Eladio Rojas that struck Gylmar's goal post. Then Vavá was denied a goal on the counter for a dubious offside. But, in the 32nd minute, Garrincha eventually found a way to open up a two-goal lead, scoring with a header at the near post from a Mário Zagallo corner (0–2).

The Chileans, urged on by a crowd of 76,594 who would not accept defeat, refused to roll over, getting a goal back in the 42nd minute with an extraordinary swerving free-kick by their captain Jorge Toro (1–2). With Toro, Honorino Landa and Leonel Sánchez in their line-up, Chile were not deficient in attack; it was their defence that let them down, such as when they allowed an unmarked Vavá to score with a header from a corner by Garrincha two minutes into the second half (1–3). Any other team would have given up at this point, but Chile refused to lie down and, in the 61st minute, were awarded a penalty following a handball by Zózimo. Leonel Sánchez converted (3–2) and the Estadio Nacional went into meltdown. On two occasions, Armando Tobar nearly beat Gylmar. But the Brazilians soon opened up the gap once again. Twice already, they had scored from high balls; why not do it again? Zagallo crossed from the left and Vavá headed in to make it 2-4 in the 78th minute.

In the anger and disappointment that ensued, the Chilean Landa was sent off for unsportsmanlike behaviour, as was Garrincha, who was struck by a stone thrown from the stands on his way to the dressing-room. When the referee blew the final whistle, seven million Chileans grieved. "It's a great thing that we have come so far. Let's keep our feet on the ground." Fernando Riera, the Chilean manager, after the host country's defeat.

▲ Czechoslovakia's Jan Lála tries to save Dražan Jerković's equalizer for Yugoslavia.

Chile 1962 medal

This commemorative medal lists the four World Cup host cities.

◀ **FIFA World Football Museum collection.**

Defence in control

13 JUNE 1962

CZECHOSLOVAKIA ▶ 3–1 **YUGOSLAVIA**

KADRABA 48, SCHERER 80, 84 (PEN)   JERKOVIĆ 69

TOGETHER WITH BRAZIL, Yugoslavia played the most imaginative attacking football in the world. The dribbling of Dragoslav Šekularac, the swerving and goals of Milan Galić, and the shooting of Josip Skoblar and Dražan Jerković were a delight to watch. But the Yugoslav attack often lacked a cutting edge, and their defence suffered from worrying omissions. In the semi-final at Viña del Mar, the youngest team in the competition were to express all their strengths and all their weaknesses, faced with a Czech side faithful to their principles, in other words concerned purely with defence.

Although several of their players were out injured (defender Vasilije Šijaković was brought in to play on the right wing), the Yugoslavs dominated a rather sterile first half. Even when on target, Galić and Šekularac were foiled by Viliam Schrojf, who was as efficient as ever in the Czech goal. And it was, in fact, the Czechs who opened the scoring soon after the break: culpable slowness on the part of the Yugoslav left-half Vladimir Popović allowed Tomáš Pospíchal to centre for Josef Kadraba, who beat Milutin Šoškić at the second attempt. Czechoslovakia were leading 1–0, even though they were playing with only one real striker, Adolf Scherer; their other centre-forward, Andrej Kvašňák, spent most of his time playing in midfield.

A goal down, the Yugoslavs piled on the pressure: Jerković first headed the ball onto the crossbar, then scored in the 69th minute with another header, after a superb deep pass from Petar Radaković, which Schrojf charged out to field but, for once, failed to gather (1–1). There were 21 minutes left for the Yugoslavs to secure victory. They kept pressing, but Jerković then Skoblar were again denied by Schrojf. The Czechs eventually took the lead following a counter-attack in the 80th minute: Scherer cut through a passive and poorly positioned Yugoslav defence to calmly beat Šoškić (2–1). Four minutes later, Vlatko Marković concluded the string of Yugoslav defensive gaffes by absurdly handling the ball in the penalty area, well away from goal and barely under pressure from Kvašňák. Scherer converted the penalty (3–1). When the final whistle blew, the Czechs headed for the dressing-room, shouting words they could hardly believe themselves: "We're in the final; we're in the final!"

PLAY-OFF FOR THIRD PLACE

A medal in the dying seconds

16 JUNE 1962

CHILE 1–0 **YUGOSLAVIA**

ROJAS 90

Is it true that a match for third place is not really important? The day before the game, the Chilean coach Fernando Riera and his team received an unexpected visit at the secluded house of Las Condes, in the suburbs of Santiago, where they had been staying for the last month. According to legend, the man who pushed his way in, without warning and without escort, was none other than the president of Chile, Jorge Alessandri. "We can be proud of you," he said to the team members. "You have done for our nation something that has not been done before. And I hope you will win the third place you have merited, you and your coach."

More easily said than done… because Chile would be appearing at the Estadio Nacional in Santiago much weakened after a month of competition. Sent off in the game against Brazil, Honorino Landa had not been treated with the same clemency as Garrincha; defender Sergio Navarro and midfielder Alberto Fouilloux, first choices at the start of the tournament, were still unfit. Meanwhile, right-wing Jaime Ramírez had learned of the death of his father just two days before the game, but insisted that he should play all the same. In fact, the Chileans had lost nothing of their motivation, unlike the Yugoslavs, who were still digesting their semi-final defeat at the hands of Czechoslovakia. As Milan Galić and Dražan Jerković failed to rediscover their effectiveness in front of goal, the Chileans were able to hold firm throughout the game, despite picking up some fresh injuries. Their captain Jorge Toro twisted his knee in the first half, restricting his movements; centre-forward Carlos Campos began limping soon after the break; and, finally, full-back Manuel Rodríguez hurt his leg as a result of a foul he himself committed on Dragoslav Šekularac. But the Chileans, for all their fatigue, had the drive and willpower that gave them a decisive edge. Having stopped the game ten minutes earlier for a (probable) dive by left-half Eladio Rojas, the referee decreed one minute of extra-time. Restored to life, Rojas gathered the ball in midfield, charged forward one last time and aimed a shot at Milutin Šoškić's goal. The centre-back Vlatko Marković got something on it and the deflection caught his goalkeeper off-balance (1–0). Chile, before an ecstatic semi-crowd, had won their place on the podium of world football.

▲ Amarildo, who replaced Pelé, scored the first Brazil goal in the Final.

▲ Garrincha tries to make a break between Ján Popluhár and Josef Masopust.

Without Pelé but not without class

17 JUNE 1962

BRAZIL ⬤ 3–1 ▬ **CZECHOSLOVAKIA**

AMARILDO 17, ZITO 69, VAVÁ 78   MASOPUST 15

3

Having got two goals against Sweden in 1958, Vavá was the first player to score in two World Cup Finals. His total of three goals in finals would later be equalled by Englishman Geoff Hurst (a hat-trick in 1966), Pelé (two goals in 1958, one in 1970), and Frenchman Zinedine Zidane (two goals in 1998, one in 2006), but has never been beaten.

THE FINAL ARRIVED and still no one knew whether Pelé, injured in the group match against Czechoslovakia, would be in the Brazilian line-up. With the agreement of manager Aymoré Moreira, the world's star player decided to undergo a final test in training. "I felt well enough and my leg was barely hurting," he later explained. "But, when taking a corner, I felt a sharp pain in my adductor muscles. I don't think I have ever been in such agony… That's when I knew I would not be able to play in the Final."

The day before the match, he spent some time with his replacement, Amarildo. They were both 21 years old, but the young Botafogo striker did not have the same self-confidence or the same aura, though he had got Brazil out of a hole when they were playing Spain in the group stage. Pelé knew that Amarildo was sometimes undisciplined, a defect that had resulted in his being sacked by Flamengo a few years earlier. Hence his heartfelt appeal: "God has given you my place. Make sure you are worthy of it."

Amarildo was one of the heroes of the Final. But not the only one – because the discreet Czechoslovakian manager Rudolf Vytlačil surprised Brazil and the Santiago crowd by choosing a team that was prepared to play the game, pass the ball around and even go on the attack. After 15 minutes, their right-wing Tomáš Pospíchal received the ball in midfield and slid an intelligent pass through to half-back Josef Masopust, who, anticipating the move, pounced on the ball and beat Gylmar (0–1). As had been the case in the 1958 Final, Brazil were a goal down; as in Sweden, they were also quick to reply. Just two minutes later, Djalma Santos, on the left-wing, found Amarildo from a throw-in. Amarildo worked his way round Svatopluk Pluskal and, instead of crossing the ball, shot into the yawning gap that Viliam Schrojf had left between himself and his near post (1-1).

The best goalkeeper in the tournament had a poor match, and Brazil's best player, Garrincha, restricted in his movements by the combined efforts of Masopust and left-back Ladislav Novák, lacked the cutting edge he had shown in the quarter- and semi-finals. This fine match, probably the most technical in the competition, was nothing like the commentators had anticipated. And the move that gave Brazil the advantage came from an unexpected source. As Zito later recounted: "In a counter-attack, the ball came to Mauro and I shouted: 'Pass it to me, pass it to me.' He passed me the ball, I sent it to Mário Zagallo, who had advanced on the left, and ran upfield. Zagallo carried the ball forward and I told him to give it to Amarildo, who was unmarked on the left. Zagallo passed to him and I continued towards goal. Amarildo beat an opponent and launched a wonderful cross. I hardly needed to jump to head the ball into the back of the net." This was Zito's first goal for Brazil for five years (2–1).

There were 20 minutes still to play and it seemed as though nothing was going to stop the Brazilians from winning their second world title. Even the sun played a part. In the 78th minute, Djalma Santos launched a long looping cross, not particularly dangerous, towards Schrojf. The ball came down exactly in the line of the sun. Blinded, Schrojf dropped the ball, leaving Vavá the easy task of poking it into the net to hand Brazil an unassailable two-goal lead (3-1).

After the victory over Spain in the group stage, Pelé had gone to congratulate Amarildo under the shower, posing for the photographers with his replacement naked as the day he was born. This time, Amarildo himself ran towards Pelé, who embraced him on the touchline. Both were world champions. Like their 20 team-mates. Like millions of Brazilians. It was becoming a habit.

▲ Brazil, world champions in 1962. Back row, left to right: Djalma Santos, Zito, Gilmar, Zozimo, Nílton Santos and Mauro Ramos. Front row, left to right: Garrincha, Didi, Vavá, Amarildo and Mário Zagallo.

▲ Didi and Pelé celebrate their second World Cup victory in a row.

◄ Training or no training, Nílton Santos takes time out to relax.

An average age of 30

Replaced by Aymoré Moreira, Vicente Feola was no longer manager of the Brazilian team; he had left to train Boca Juniors in Argentina before being afflicted by health problems. But the composition of the team, from one tournament to the next, was characterized by amazing stability: eight of the 11 players in the 1962 Final (Gylmar, Djalma Santos, Nílton Santos, Zito, Garrincha, Didi, Vavá and Mário Zagallo) had played in the Final in 1958, and 14 of the players in the 22-man squad had made the journey to Sweden. In Chile, Moreira used only 12 members of the squad: the 11 finalists, plus Pelé. The average age of 30 was the highest for any World Cup-winning team. Three of the 11 ended their international careers on this note of triumph: Nílton Santos (aged 37), Zózimo (29) and Didi (33).

Masopust in line for the Ballon d'Or

When the Czechoslovakian team booked in at their hotel in Chile in May 1962, Josef Masopust was unpleasantly surprised to find his name wrongly spelt in the register. "Joseph Masapost", as he was recorded, was hardly known outside Czechoslovakia, though he had played for his country since 1954. A defensive half-back for Dukla Prague, playing for a club and a national team that rarely attracted much attention, he had not had much opportunity to make a reputation for himself abroad. But his excellent performances in Chile, particularly in the Final, revealed him as one of the finest players of his era. He scored a goal, held Garrincha in check and showed such calmness, ability to read the game and skill with both feet that his opponents were astounded. From the side-lines, Pelé, who had already encountered Masopust in a friendly with Santos in 1959, was all agog: "Masopust is one of the greatest players I have come across," he exclaimed. "But I can't believe he was born in Europe. To dribble like that, you have to have been born in Brazil!" Josef Masopust was awarded the Ballon d'Or for 1962, as European Footballer of the Year.

1966

Celebrated as the motherland of football, England staged and won the World Cup in a tournament noted for shocks and controversial incidents. North Korea knocked out two-time world champions Italy and then led Portugal 3–0 in the quarter-finals before losing 5–3. In the Final at Wembley, England beat West Germany 4–2 in a match remembered for a Geoff Hurst hat-trick and a hotly disputed goal.

Football comes home

◀ Captain Bobby Moore kisses the World Cup as team-mates Jack Charlton and Geoff Hurst look on.

▼ My generation: English bands like The Who helped change youth culture around the world.

WITH THE TOURNAMENT landing in England, football was returning home. The time had passed when teams from Great Britain ignored the World Cup. Since 1950, the British nations had joined the great world festival, without ever shining in it. In four events, from 1950 to 1962, none of them got beyond the quarter-finals. World football was no longer within the empire of the nation that gave it life, just as the United Kingdom no longer had its immense Empire. The name of the famous Wembley Stadium, which was to host the World Cup Final, resonated like an echo from the past: the Empire Stadium. However, England was on the move. Mary Quant had popularized the miniskirt, taking her inspiration from the name of a car which was all the rage, the Mini. The Beatles and other English pop groups were making the youth of the world shriek. Even English football was being revamped. Since 1963, the team had a manager granted full powers, Alf Ramsey. The same year, to celebrate its centenary, the Football Association welcomed a team from the "Rest of the World" for a match televized across the globe. Also in 1963, an English club, Tottenham, won a European trophy (the Cup Winners' Cup) for the first time. From now on, English football was international. And Alf Ramsey made a prediction when taking up his job: England will win its World Cup.

ENGLAND 1966

WORLD CHAMPIONSHIP
JULES RIMET CUP 1966 IN ENGLAND

Story of the qualifiers

Africa withdraws

INDEPENDENCE for numerous African countries, starting at the end of the 1950s, should have opened the door to the World Cup for them. For the 1962 competition, five countries (Ethiopia, Ghana, Morocco, Nigeria and Tunisia) had taken part, although none of them would qualify for the finals tournament. For the 1966 tournament, 15 nations were involved. But FIFA only gave a minor role to Africa, Asia and Oceania (one team each). As a protest, all the African associations withdrew and left the way open for North Korea and Australia, who confronted each other in two encounters on neutral territory, in Phnom Penh. The North Koreans won twice (6–1 and 3–1) and became the first Asian team to qualify for the finals tournament since their neighbours, South Korea, in 1954.

As for the Europeans, would the curse hang over the teams beaten by Brazil in the finals of the World Cup? Sweden, beaten in the 1958 Final, had not qualified for the following World Cup, in 1962. They still didn't appear in 1966, after their elimination by West Germany in the qualifying rounds. The same applied to Czechoslovakia, the losing finalists in 1962. Beaten by Portugal in the qualifying stage, they were deprived of a place in the finals for the first time since 1950. For Portugal, on the other hand, it was a first appearance in the tournament.

▶ Agenda for the meeting of FIFA's Emergency Committee. On the list was the theft of the Jules Rimet Cup the previous month.

Regulations

Geographical "hats"

THE DRAW for the four groups in the first round of the World Cup was largely based on geographical criteria, blended with essentially hierarchical considerations. After lengthy discussions, FIFA created four hats:

1. The four South American countries (Argentina, Brazil, Chile, Uruguay).
2. The four Latin-European countries (Spain, France, Italy, Portugal).
3. The four large European countries (West Germany, England, Hungary, USSR).
4. The four "smaller" countries (Bulgaria, North Korea, Mexico, Switzerland). England and Brazil were automatically put in Groups I and III, and would play their first-round matches in the same stadium, Wembley and Goodison Park (Everton) respectively. This distribution of the four hats gave rise to a balanced draw in the four groups.

(Agenda document shown:)

Fédération Internationale de Football Association

A G E N D A

of Meeting No. 9 of the EMERGENCY COMMITTEE to be held at the Hotel Quirinale in Rome on 24th April, 1966, commencing at 10 a.m.

I. ROLL CALL
II. CHAIRMAN'S REMARKS
III. MINUTES
To approve the Minutes of the January, February and March meetings, circulated in April.

INDEX OF ITEMS
Since the January meetings the following matters requiring attention have arisen:
IV. WORLD CUP
  1. Trophy
     To hear that the Jules Rimet Cup was stolen on Sunday 20th March and recovered on 27th March.
     To confirm that a replica in base metal be made to avoid future mishaps.
  2. Television
     2.1 To hear a progress report concerning TV contracts signed since the last meeting (Argentine, Brazil, Peru) and those still under negotiation (U.S.A., Canada, Sudan, Lebanon, etc.)
     2.2 To confirm that for smaller countries the rate card as established on 16th August, 1965 may be subject to alteration, based on suggestions to be submitted by the BBC/ITV Consortium.
     2.3 To confirm that for small countries the exclusive rights fee should be fixed at 10 times the rate for one match.
     2.4 Closed circuit TV: to discuss this problem.
  3. Radio
     To hear a progress report and to decide any outstanding problems.
  4. Colours of Teams
     To confirm the action taken concerning the colours of teams in the 1/8th finals (matches nos. 1 to 24) (List will be provided at the meeting)
  5. Travel Expenses
     To confirm the action taken concerning the air fares and ports of embarcation and disembarcation.

Group stage

GROUP 1	GROUP 2	GROUP 3	GROUP 4
ENG 0–0 URU	FRG 5–0 SUI	BRA 2–0 BUL	URS 3–0 PRK
FRA 1–1 MEX	ARG 2–1 ESP	POR 3–1 HUN	ITA 2–0 CHI
URU 2–1 FRA	ESP 2–1 SUI	HUN 3–1 BRA	CHI 1–1 PRK
ENG 2–0 MEX	ARG 0–0 FRG	POR 3–0 BUL	URS 1–0 ITA
MEX 0–0 URU	ARG 2–0 SUI	POR 3–1 BRA	PRK 1–0 ITA
ENG 2–0 FRA	FRG 2–1 ESP	HUN 3–1 BUL	URS 2–1 CHI

	W	D	L	+	−	PTS		W	D	L	+	−	PTS		W	D	L	+	−	PTS		W	D	L	+	−	PTS
ENG	2	1	0	4	0	5	FRG	2	1	0	7	1	5	POR	3	0	0	9	2	6	URS	3	0	0	6	1	6
URU	1	2	0	2	1	4	ARG	2	1	0	4	1	5	HUN	2	0	1	7	5	4	PRK	1	1	1	2	4	3
MEX	0	2	1	1	3	2	ESP	1	0	2	4	5	2	BRA	1	0	2	4	6	2	ITA	1	0	2	2	2	2
FRA	0	1	2	2	5	1	SUI	0	0	3	1	9	0	BUL	0	0	3	1	8	0	CHI	0	1	2	2	5	1

Knockout stage

QUARTER-FINAL	QUARTER-FINAL	QUARTER-FINAL	QUARTER-FINAL
ENG 1–0 ARG	POR 5–3 PRK	FRG 4–0 URU	URS 2–1 HUN

SEMI-FINAL	SEMI-FINAL
ENG 2–1 POR	FRG 2–1 URS

PLAY-OFF FOR THIRD PLACE

POR 2–1 URS

FINAL

ENG 4–2 FRG
A.E.T.

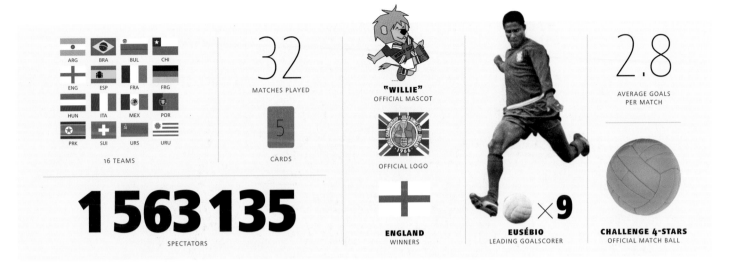

ARG BRA BUL CHI
ENG ESP FRA FRG
HUN ITA MEX POR
PRK SUI URS URU

16 TEAMS

32
MATCHES PLAYED

5
CARDS

1 563 135
SPECTATORS

"WILLIE"
OFFICIAL MASCOT

OFFICIAL LOGO

ENGLAND
WINNERS

EUSÉBIO ×9
LEADING GOALSCORER

2.8
AVERAGE GOALS
PER MATCH

CHALLENGE 4-STARS
OFFICIAL MATCH BALL

Host cities and stadiums

Northern lights

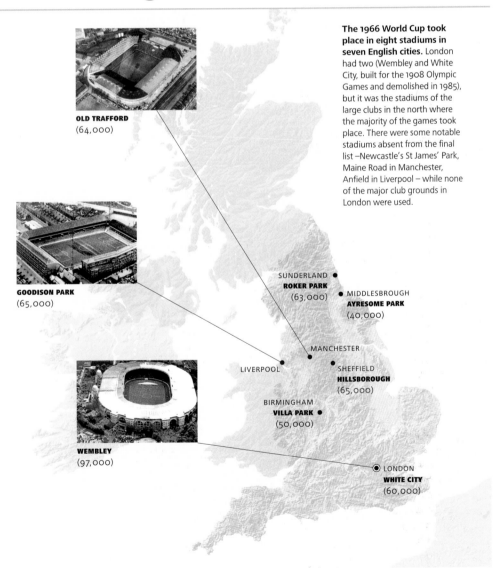

OLD TRAFFORD
(64,000)

GOODISON PARK
(65,000)

WEMBLEY
(97,000)

SUNDERLAND
ROKER PARK
(63,000)

MIDDLESBROUGH
AYRESOME PARK
(40,000)

MANCHESTER

LIVERPOOL

SHEFFIELD
HILLSBOROUGH
(65,000)

BIRMINGHAM
VILLA PARK
(50,000)

LONDON
WHITE CITY
(60,000)

The 1966 World Cup took place in eight stadiums in seven English cities. London had two (Wembley and White City, built for the 1908 Olympic Games and demolished in 1985), but it was the stadiums of the large clubs in the north where the majority of the games took place. There were some notable stadiums absent from the final list –Newcastle's St James' Park, Maine Road in Manchester, Anfield in Liverpool – while none of the major club grounds in London were used.

World Cup Willie, the first mascot

The 1966 tournament saw the World Cup's first mascot. It had been designed by the British illustrator Reg Hoye and was a lion wearing a football shirt in the colours of the Union Jack, the United Kingdom's national flag. Its distant descendant was Goaliath, another lion with a white shirt, the mascot for Euro 1996 which was also staged in England.

▲ **FIFA World Football Museum collection.**

▲ Hungary's Kálmán Mészöly leaves the pitch after Hungary's 3–1 win over Brazil.

▲ Jairzinho, Brazil's new shining star, breaks through the Hungarian defence.

Hungary-Brazil, a marvellous match!

15 JULY 1966

HUNGARY 3–1 BRAZIL

BENE 2, FARKAS 64, MESZOLY 73 (PEN)   TOSTAO 14

98 270

This was the official number of spectators watching the England-France match in the first round, at Wembley. It was the largest crowd at the 1966 World Cup, larger than the 96,924 spectators who saw the England-West Germany Final.

0–0 in the opening match

The 1966 World Cup inaugurated the tradition of the ceremonial aspect of opening matches. After Queen Elizabeth II declared the tournament open, England and Uruguay met in a disappointing and defensive match. No one knew at the time that the score, 0–0, was going to become a tradition of sorts for opening matches. This was to be the result of the opening matches in 1970 (Mexico-USSR), 1974 (Brazil-Yugoslavia) and 1978 (West Germany-Poland).

WHEN THE HUNGARIANS and Brazilians came to Goodison Park, spectators with long memories recalled that their last clash in the World Cup, in 1954, gave rise to the Battle of Berne. They also noted that that was Brazil's last defeat in the World Cup (2–4). In that game, Hungary played without Ferenc Puskás. This time, Brazil had to do without Pelé, handled roughly by the Bulgarians during their first match. From the 2nd minute, Ferenc Bene, a winger with Újpest, put the encounter on a pinnacle from which it would never descend. Following a series of dazzling dribbles, he opened the scoring. Close on the heels of the goal, both Gyula Rákosi and János Farkas came close for Hungary, but these were just cleared by the 1958 and 1962 world champions Djalma Santos and Gylmar. In the 14th minute, Brazil levelled the score. Following a free-kick by Lima that was poorly cleared by the Hungarian defence, Tostão, Pelé's 19-year-old replacement, put the ball into the back of the net. The match increased in intensity. Alcindo missed a massive chance for the Brazilians, but the Hungarians dominated. In the 21st minute, Flórián Albert and Bene performed a breathtaking headed one-two during a sequence of seven passes without the ball touching the ground. But Gylmar intervened to save the situation twice from Farkas.

Hungary then displayed their clear domination of a Brazilian team that had lost its magic of yesteryear. In the 64th minute, following a cross by Bene, Farkas scored with a perfect volley from near the penalty spot. Then, in the 74th minute, following a foul on Bene, Hungary increased their lead with a penalty converted by Kálmán Mészöly, who ended the encounter with his injured arm in a sling. In the 78th minute, Rákosi had a goal disallowed for a questionable offside. From then on, the Brazilian double world champions looked shaky on their throne, and those who felt nostalgic for the 1950s thought that they had rediscovered the magnificent Hungary of former times.

◄ North Korean players defend their goal in the group match at Ayresome Park against Italy.

▲ The North Koreans celebrate after beating Italy in one of the greatest World Cup upsets.

The sensation of Middlesbrough

19 JULY 1966

NORTH KOREA 1-0 **ITALY**

PAK DOO IK 42

ON THE MORNING of the last matches in the first round, everything seemed more or less settled in Group 4. The USSR were top with four points, and Italy had beaten Chile but lost to the Soviets (1–0). North Korea had probably surpassed their own expectations by drawing against Chile (1-1). They now had to meet Italy, for whom a draw would be enough to qualify. No one saw the unknowns from Asia threatening the stars of Italian football. And, in fact, even with the support of the Middlesbrough crowd, the Koreans had to put up with Italian attacks during all of the opening period of the match. Marino Perani, a winger with Bologna, had already created two excellent chances, from which the young keeper Lee Chang Myung (19 years old) made fine saves. But in the 33rd minute the Italian captain Giacomo Bulgarelli was injured in a clash with Pak Doo Ik. He had to leave the field on a stretcher and his absence

disrupted the attacking game of the Italians, all the more so since the two stars from the two Milan clubs, Sandro Mazzola and Gianni Rivera, were not at their best. From then on the Koreans started to believe they had a chance to win the game. They continued to defend with discipline, while their counter-attacks showed their newfound confidence. In one of them, just before half-time (41st minute), Pak Doo Ik received a pass from Im Seung Hwi and deceived Enrico Albertosi with a cross-shot. Almost 50 minutes remained for the Italians, but they did not score the goal that would save them. Rivera, Perani and Fogli all had great opportunities to equalize, but could not beat Lee Chang Myung. Towards the end, Kim Bong Hwan missed a great chance to double North Korea's lead, but the unfancied Asians held on. Italy left the World Cup by the back door. Pak Doo Ik, Lee Chang Myung and their teammates had just stepped through the front door into history.

At the 1962 World Cup the Mexican goalkeeper Antonio Carbajal had become the first player to take part in four World Cups. He had started in 1950, against Brazil. He then played in the World Cup competitions of 1954 in Switzerland and 1958 in Sweden. In 1966 he beat his own record when he played in Mexico's third match, against Uruguay. In total, he played in 11 World Cup matches. Along with the Mexican, Germany's Lothar Matthäus is the only other player to have participated in five finals.

Pelé: "I will not go to Mexico"

For Pelé, his third World Cup was a great disappointment. Badly fouled in the first match, Brazil-Bulgaria (2–0), he could not play in the following match (Hungary-Brazil, 3–1). He returned against Portugal (a 3–1 defeat), during which he was man-handled by the Portuguese players in a match that saw the Brazilians eliminated from the competition. At the end of the game, he told the *Sunday Telegraph*: "I will not go to Mexico in 1970." So the reign of Pelé was thought to be over…

▲ Bobby Charlton, in action during the England-Argentina quarter-final, was one of the stars of the tournament.

Latin America claims a conspiracy

Both banks of the River Plate commented furiously on the incidents that took place during the two quarter-finals between the Europeans (England and West Germany) and South Americans (Argentina and Uruguay). There were claims of conspiracy. The sendings-off of the Argentinian Rattín and the Uruguayans Troche and Silva seemed scandalous. The appointment of the two referees "proved" that there was collusion to eliminate the last representatives from the Americas: a German, Rudolf Kreitlein, was in charge of the England-Argentina match, and an Englishman, Jim Finney, severely sanctioned the Uruguayans. In Buenos Aires, the British embassy had to receive military protection. And before matches in the Argentinian capital played on the Sunday following the confrontation, teams playing at home were asked to come onto the ground with a national flag, in honour of the "moral victory" won by Argentina at Wembley.

The "animals" of Wembley

23 JULY 1966

ENGLAND ✚ 1–0 🇦🇷 ARGENTINA

HURST 78

THERE WAS overwhelming heat that afternoon, 23 July, at Wembley. And in the rows of seats at the venerable stadium, the atmosphere would also reach boiling point. The English fans became increasingly incensed with the spectacle of an Argentinian team that used every possible means to constrict their beloved team. The South Americans used obvious technical tactics, such as keeping the ball and breaking up the rhythm of play, but they also resorted to less laudable tricks, which upset not only the most phlegmatic of Englishmen but also a diminutive tailor from Stuttgart, which is what the match referee Rudolf Kreitlein was when he wasn't officiating football matches. He cautioned two Argentinian players in the first 35 minutes – yellow and red cards did not yet exist; they would be introduced after the tournament. The Argentinians did not stop complaining about the roughness of the

English team in the tackle and thought that every decision the referee made was going against them. On the 30-minute mark, the huge Argentinian captain, the sublime technician Antonio Rattín, pulled the referee by the arm… and Kreitlein sent him off. The whole Argentinian team descended on the referee, pleading the case for their captain. The English, hands on hips, waited for calm to return… It took six minutes before play could eventually restart, and four minutes more before Rattín finally reached the tunnel, in the face of the shouts of the outraged public. The match restarted, although it was poisoned by the incident. England narrowly won, thanks to a goal from Geoff Hurst in the 78th minute. At the press conference, the English manager described the Argentinians as "animals". In Buenos Aires, thousands of people hailed their team's triumphant success on their return from England.

Kreitlein's whistle

The whistle used by Rudolf Kreitlein in the quarter-final between England and Argentina.

▲ **FIFA World Football Museum Collection.**

▶ German referee Rudolf Kreitlein sent off Argentina's captain Antonio Rattín. The Argentinian initially refused to go.

▲ The police are obliged to intervene to force Héctor Silva to leave the pitch.

West Germany, by elimination'

23 JULY 1966

WEST GERMANY 4–0 **URUGUAY**

HALLER 11, 83, BECKENBAUER 70, SEELER 75

THE SCORELINE, 4–0, might suggest that the German victory over Uruguay was easy. But the margin of four goals is deceptive. First, West Germany needed a good dose of luck in the opening minutes. Uruguay started the encounter with a remarkable burst of energy and a short passing game in the Sky Blue tradition. In the fourth minute, a fierce long-distance shot from Cortés hit the post. In the seventh minute, the elegant Pedro Rocha headed the ball from a corner. Karl-Heinz Schnellinger on the goal-line handled the ball which was destined for the top corner of the net. The Uruguayans claimed a penalty. Tempers were already rising.

West Germany opened the scoring in the 11th minute during a period of Uruguayan domination. Sigi Held took a speculative shot from long range, but Helmut Haller, in deflecting it, caught Ladislao Mazurkiewicz on the wrong foot. This piece of luck did not reassure the Germans, but they had one

quality that the Uruguayans did not. They kept calm. In the 50th minute there was an altercation between the Uruguayan captain Horacio Troche and Lothar Emmerich. The Uruguayan kneed the German striker, which would have gone almost unnoticed without the intervention of the Egyptian linesman Ali Kandil. When told about it, the English referee Jim Finney sent off the defender. Five minutes later, Silva badly fouled Haller, who rolled on the ground. Silva, warned at the start of the match, was also sent off.

With 11 men against nine, the Germans finally relaxed. In the 70th minute, Franz Beckenbauer scored a second goal following a straightforward attacking move. Two more goals followed, scored by Uwe Seeler and Haller. West Germany had benefitted from the Uruguayans' inability to control their nerves. With more composure, the Uruguayans would have been better placed to exploit their technical superiority.

Beckenbauer, the revelation

▲ Franz Beckenbauer, 21, takes part in his first World Cup.

When the 1966 World Cup started, Franz Beckenbauer was barely known on the international scene. But in Germany he had become an undisputed team member ever since his debut in the team at the age of 20 against Sweden (2–1) in September 1965. The Germans viewed him as the finest talent from the country since Fritz Walter. But his club, Bayern Munich, only reached the Bundesliga in 1965 and did not have the reputation of Munich 1860. So the young midfield player revealed himself to the world in the very first match of these finals, against Switzerland (5–0), during which he scored two goals. A huge career was underway. An observer of the World Cup, Just Fontaine immediately placed him in his World Cup XI, and said: "Beckenbauer is exceptional, a player such as him is rarely seen." In his position, Fontaine considered him the successor of the great József Bozsik, who had been a key member of the marvellous Hungarian side of the 1950s.

▲ Goodison Park's score-board shows a dramatic score. In the 25th minute, the North Koreans had established a 3–0 lead over Portugal.

► Eusébio caricatured as a panther in a brochure for the 1966 World Cup.

◄ Eusébio retrieves the ball after scoring his fourth goal.

Eusébio saves Portugal's blushes

23 JULY 1966

PORTUGAL 5–3 **NORTH KOREA**

EUSÉBIO 27, 43 (PEN), 56, 59 (PEN)	PAK SEUNG ZIN 1
JOSÉ AUGUSTO 80	LI DONG WOON 22
	YANG SEUNG KOOK 25

A S THE FOUR quarter-finals took place on the same day at the same time, Saturday 23 July, television viewers could only watch one encounter live. Few of them saw what on paper seemed to be most uneven match, between Portugal and North Korea. But the commentators of the other encounters kept viewers informed of the amazing events that were unfolding in Liverpool. They announced that the Koreans opened the scoring in the 1st minute through Pak Seung Zin; that they added a second goal in the 22nd minute through Li Dong Woon; and then a third, two minutes later, through Yang Seung Kook. Was it conceivable that after depriving the Italians of their place in the quarter-finals, the Cup's unknowns were going to reach the semi-finals at the expense of Portugal? The tension among the Portuguese was extreme. They played unnaturally, wasting lofted passes towards the tall José Torres. But Portugal had Eusébio and North Korea lacked experience. A team used to international tussles would know how to protect so great an advantage. At this point the Koreans continued to play without closing down the game… and this would be their undoing. But the Portuguese owed a huge debt of thanks to Eusébio. The magnificent Benfica striker made the most of the opposing defence's generosity. From the 27th to the 59th minute, he scored four goals, two of them from the penalty-spot. In the 80th minute, José Augusto headed a fifth goal. But the first 25 minutes will remain forever in World Cup folklore.

▲ A supporter from the Soviet Union outside Roker Park in Sunderland.

▲ Players in action as Hungary's Flórián Albert looks on.

The East European "final"

23 JULY 1966

USSR 🇷🇺 2-1 🇭🇺 **HUNGARY**

CHISLENKO 5, PORKUYAN 46   BENE 57

THE HUNGARY-USSR match was a sort of East European final, played in Sunderland. The Soviets had devised a plan to thwart Flórián Albert, the Hungarian team's playmaker, with Valery Voronin assigned to mark him. The tactic was the right one. Albert was very much less in evidence in this match than he had been against Brazil. The Soviet Union dominated the beginning of the encounter and opened the scoring in the fifth minute through Igor Chislenko, following an error by the Hungarian goalkeeper, József Gelei. Just before half-time, Eduard Malofeyev saw his header hit the crossbar. It was Valery Porkujan who scored the second goal in the 47th minute, from a free-kick taken by Khusainov. The wake-up call for the Hungarian team sounded too late. In the 58th minute Albert finally succeeded in getting away from Voronin. After an exchange of passes with Kálmán Mészöly, the ball reached Ferenc Bene who scored with a cross-shot. Mészöly left the defensive line more and more often to make the extra man. He even had a chance to level the score, in the 83rd minute, from a free-kick taken by Ferenc Sipos. But, once again, Lev Yashin kept it out.

Yashin, at last

At 36 years old, Lev Yashin was taking part in his third World Cup.
Up to now, he had not enjoyed great success in the world's greatest football competition. A quarter-finalist in 1958, when the USSR first took part, and again in 1962, he seemed in decline during the Chilean World Cup. On the other hand, he had a long list of international achievements in the other competitions: an Olympic title in 1956, a European title in 1960 and a European final in 1964. Considered one of the best goalkeepers in football history, he remains the only player in that position to have won the Ballon d'Or (in 1963) and played for two World XIs. In England, handicapped by a recurrent knee injury, he played just one match out of three in the first round. He played an important role against Italy, and a crucial one in the victory over Hungary which hoisted the USSR into the semi-finals. The Soviet team thus secured its best performance in history, and Yashin was voted the best goalkeeper at the tournament.

▲ 1966 was Lev Yashin's most successful World Cup finals. The Soviet Union got as far as the semi-finals for the first – and only – time.

▲ West Germany's Franz Beckenbauer takes on the USSR's Albert Shesternev.

◥ Helmut Haller et Wolfgand Overath celebrate the first goal for West Germany.

West Germany win the battle

25 JULY 1966

WEST GERMANY ▬ 2-1 ▬ **USSR**

HALLER 43, BECKENBAUER 67   PORKUYAN 88

Goodison Park, graveyard for idols

The Everton stadium was the stage for the two best matches in the World Cup, Hungary-Brazil (3–1) in the first round, and Portugal-North Korea (5–3) in the quarter-finals. It was also the graveyard for two idols of world football. It was at Goodison Park that Pelé was the victim of a number of assaults during the two matches he took part in, against Bulgaria and Portugal. He lost his "crown" there. It is there, too, that Lev Yashin was unable to prevent the USSR's elimination in the semi-final. But it was also there that new idols were born. Just before the semi-final between West Germany and the Soviet Union, the North Korean players, the revelations of the competition who were present at the match, received a massive ovation when they came into the stadium. A French journalist was able to write at the time: "Having arrived incognito in England, there they were, almost as famous in Liverpool as the Beatles!"

THE LIVERPOOL PUBLIC were still spellbound by the fine quarter-final played at Goodison Park between Portugal and North Korea. Two days later, an entirely different spectacle was inflicted on them in the semi-finals. The similarities were too great and the ambitions too identical between the teams from West Germany and the USSR to produce anything other than a fierce encounter. The German team of Helmut Schön were a mixture of defensive rigour and attacking appeal, the balance between the two being most often held by Franz Beckenbauer, depending on the instructions that he had been given. His Soviet opponents had as great a desire to defend, and did not lack attacking qualities, under the direction of midfield players Voronin and Sabo, who knew perfectly how to exploit the talent of winger Chislenko and strikers Malofeyev and Porkujan. But it was a fear of their opponents and a desire to impose themselves by force which motivated the two protagonists. This was evident from the outset in an insipid, highly physical clash that the Italian referee, Concetto Lo Bello, although experienced, had difficulty in controlling. Every bit of technical artistry was drowned in a deluge of crunching tackles: Beckenbauer, Seeler and Emmerich were fouled, but Sabo most of all. Injured in the

14th minute, he was no longer any use. In the furious battle West Germany dominated, under the leadership of their captain Uwe Seeler. But Beckenbauer was too often confined to defence for his team to really move forward and when they did manage to do so, the great Lev Yashin intervened with brio.

The match changed dramatically before half-time. In the 43rd minute, Helmut Haller handed the West Germans the lead. In the following minute, Chislenko, annoyed by the knock he had just received, fouled Sigi Held, right next to the referee, who sent him off. Given the injury to Sabo, the USSR had to play the whole of the second half with nine men against 11. They tried their luck several times, but their numerical inferiority was too great to threaten a German defence that was as uncompromising as their own. The departure of Chislenko allowed Beckenbauer to take more attacking initiatives and the partnership that he formed in midfield with Wolfgang Overath was clearly dominant. In the 67th minute, the maestro from Munich gave the Germans a decisive advantage with a fierce shot that deceived Yashin. Towards the end, Soviet efforts were rewarded with a goal from Porkujan, but it was too late. There were only two minutes left to play.

▲ The England team before their semi-final against Portugal.

Stiles as Eusébio's watchdog

On the day before the England-Portugal semi-final, as the English press was designating Eusébio as the prime threat to his team, manager Alf Ramsey was reassuring: "Calm down, Eusébio will not score four goals as he did against Korea." He recalled that when Manchester United beat Benfica 5–1 in the European Cup, on 9 March the same year, it was Nobby Stiles who marked the Portuguese star. He was to have the same mission at Wembley. Although he was not short of technical qualities, the small midfield player from Manchester United had a reputation as a hard player, not just because, in removing his dentures to play, he had a vampire's smile on the pitch! In the first round, he had savagely tackled the Frenchman Jacky Simon. Was Eusébio going to receive the same treatment? In fact, Stiles played the perfect game against the Benfica star, having the intelligence never to jump in, as he tried to stop the Portuguese's dribbling. Luckily for Eusébio's ankles and also luckily for the collective English defence.

Charlton shines as England reach Final

26 JULY 1966		
ENGLAND ✚ 2–1 ▮ PORTUGAL		
CHARLTON 30, 80	EUSEBIO 82 (PEN)	

THE ENGLAND-PORTUGAL semi-final was one of football's great games. In their fifth match of the competition at Wembley, Alf Ramsey's team produced their best performance of the tournament. Their opponents were no doubt largely responsible for this. Portugal's gameplan was clearly to attack. Their defensive system, zonal and with no cover, was badly suited to stifle England's lively attack. England had employed an innovative 4-4-2 formation, that contained no traditional wingers, but in which their centre-forward duo (Liverpool's Roger Hunt and West Ham's Geoff Hurst) thrived, particularly when playing against a defence that lacked a sweeper. However, it was Bobby Charlton, Manchester United's playmaker, free to play instinctively, who held the key to this encounter. In the 30th minute, he opened the scoring after latching on to a ball which the Belenenses goalkeeper, José Pereira, had spilled. He then scored the winning goal ten minutes from time, picking up a pass from Hurst and slamming the ball home with his right foot to seal England's victory.

Even though they lost, Portugal did honour to their burgeoning reputation. Having appeared awed at the start of the match, Otto Glória's team was practically on equal terms with their hosts. At the end of the first half, Torres, Augusto and Eusébio were threatening. After half-time the Portuguese frankly dominated, with Mário Coluna to the fore, but their endeavours always came up against an impeccable Gordon Banks.

Bobby Charlton's second goal did not put a brake on Portuguese efforts. The brother of the English goalscorer, Jack "the Giraffe", even rekindled their vigour. In the 82nd minute, from a Simões cross, Torres sent a header over Banks. Jack Charlton, on his line, pushed the ball away with his hand and Eusébio converted the resulting penalty. In the closing minutes, Simões and Coluna both came close to equalizing, but Banks's athleticism proved decisive.

PLAY-OFF FOR THIRD PLACE

▲ Mario Coluna and Lev Yashin before the start of the third-place play-off.

Eusébio and Coluna, the African presence in England

28 JULY 1966		
PORTUGAL ▮ 2–1 ▬ USSR		
EUSEBIO 12 (PEN), JOSE TORRES 89	MALOFEYEV 43	

Despite the absence of teams from the African continent, it was indirectly represented in the World Cup. The Benfica striker Eusébio scored nine goals, approaching the unassailable record of 13 goals set by Just Fontaine in 1958. After scoring once against Bulgaria and twice against Brazil in the group stage, he scored four against North Korea in the quarter-finals, a penalty against England in the semi-final, and rounding it off with another penalty against the legendary Soviet goalkeeper Lev Yashin in the match for third place (2–1). Eusébio was born in Lourenço Marques, the capital of Mozambique, at that time a Portuguese African colony. He took his first steps as a footballer in a local club, and was spotted there by talent scouts from Benfica, who brought him to Lisbon aged 18 years old. The captain of Portugal, Mário Coluna, more than six years older than Eusébio, also hailed from Mozambique. This remarkable midfield player was nicknamed the "Sacred Monster". After his playing career was over (he finished at Lyon at the start of the 1970s), he returned to Mozambique, where he went on to become a coach and President of the football federation.

▲ Bobby Moore with the Jules Rimet Cup after England's 4–2 victory over West Germany in the 1966 World Cup Final. Left to right: Jack Charlton, Nobby Stiles, Gordon Banks (behind), Alan Ball, Martin Peters, Roger Hunt (hidden), Geoff Hurst, Bobby Moore, Ray Wilson, George Cohen and Bobby Charlton.

Ramsey's vindication

Many people scoffed at Alf Ramsey when he stated, when he was installed as manager of the English team in 1963, that he was going to win the World Cup three years later at Wembley. So the victory in 1966 was a personal triumph for the man who faced fierce criticism from the moment he took up his post. It would also have done much to eliminate the nightmares he suffered when he had played for England. He was in the team that went through two of the most painful episodes in the history of the English team. A full-back with Tottenham, he played in the defeat by the United States in the 1950 World Cup, the first in which the English took part. Three years later, he was selected to play at Wembley for the 32nd and last time, in England's first defeat at home by a non-British team, Hungary (6–3), in what was dubbed the "match of the century".

4-4-2 breaks down rigid defence

30 JULY 1966

ENGLAND ✚ **4–2** A.E.T. 🏴 **WEST GERMANY**

HURST 18, 101, 120   HALLER 12
PETERS 78   WEBER 89

THE 1966 WORLD CUP and its final came at a pivotal period in the evolution of the game. England under Alf Ramsey had made a choice that appeared iconoclastic: the withdrawal of traditional wingers, transformed into additional midfield players. From this emerged a 4-4-2 formation which became common over the following decade. England used a mixed defence, within which certain players had the job of man-marking (Jack Charlton on the centre-forward, or Nobby Stiles, in the semi-final against Portugal), while others had an expanded role (the two full-backs, or Bobby Moore, moving forward into midfield). In attack, the disappearance of the wingers meant that the English played with two centre-forwards, Roger Hunt and Geoff Hurst, who often disrupted the opposing defensive systems. In the face of this much more supple system of playing, West Germany retained individual marking. They were uncompromising in defence, with a remarkable duo in the axis of play, Wolfgang Weber as the centre-half and Willi Schulz as the last line of defence. The only drawback with this system of integral marking was that it had the effect, in midfield, of constraining the dazzling Franz Beckenbauer, sometimes restricting him to an exaggerated defensive role against the opposing playmaker. In the Final he had to sacrifice himself again, facing Bobby Charlton. So much so that the best German player in the Final was arguably the tireless left-footed player from Cologne, Wolfgang Overath. But the numerical superiority of the English in the centre, their capacity for switching positions and de-zoning, contributed to destabilizing the rigid organization of the Germans. In the years that followed, they learned the lessons from that day, while remaining true to their defensive principles.

◄ Referee Gottfried Dienst consults with his linesman Tofik Bachramov before awarding England's third goal.

◄ A captain's duel: Bobby Moore and Uwe Seeler battle it out during the Final.

Dienst: "I was doubtful…"

"I was quite far from the goal, about 20 metres. It seemed to me that the ball crossed the line, but I wasn't sure. No doubt I would not have given the goal if I had not seen my linesman, the Russian [sic] Tofik Bakhramov, take a step towards the centre circle. So I consulted him and he confirmed it. He showed me with his two hands that the ball had rebounded onto the ground about 20 centimetres behind the goal-line. I could no longer hesitate."

The Swiss Gottfried Dienst, the referee for the Final.

The "true" score in the final

Hurst, for all time

DESPITE THE PASSAGE of more than 50 years, the debate over Geoff Hurst's second goal shows no sign of diminishing. The award of the goal, which gave England the lead in extra-time, caused consternation in West Germany, but there really shouldn't have been extra-time played in the first place! With just a minute of the match remaining, the Germans were given a very dubious free-kick when Jack Charlton was judged to have fouled Sigi Held. Wolfgang Weber scored from a free-kick that should not have been given. The true score of the final? 2–1!

On 30 July 1966, Geoff Hurst scored the most talked about goal in the history of the World Cup finals. Debate still rages as to whether his second goal, and England's third, actually crossed the line. But Hurst secured his place in history for another reason: he is the only player to score a hat-trick in a World Cup Final. Before the World Cup, Hurst was barely known outside the United Kingdom, in spite of the fact that he was part of the West Ham side that won the Cup-Winners' Cup in 1965. He had first appeared for the national team on 23 February 1966, in a friendly against… West Germany (1–0). Hurst was selected for the tournament as a back-up for Tottenham's Jimmy Greaves, who played in the three group matches. Hurst replaced the injured Greaves in the quarter-final against Argentina, scored the winner and kept his place.

► Geoff Hurst's "famous" Wembley goal. Did it cross the line? The debate still rages today.

1970

The heat and thin air made conditions difficult, but Mexico 1970 is regarded as one of the very best World Cups, garnished with epic matches. In the first finals broadcast in colour, all five past winners fielded strong teams – and Brazil, once again led by Pelé, beat Italy 4–1 in the Final. This was Brazil's third title, earning them the right to keep the Jules Rimet Cup forever.

A World Cup full of colour

◀ Pelé celebrates Brazil's third world title.

▼ At the final whistle, there were chaotic scenes as fans and journalists mobbed the Brazilian team.

MEXICO HAD BEEN the centre of the sporting world for two years. After the Olympic Games in 1968, the country hosted the football World Cup· It was the first time that the great world rendezvous was held somewhere other than in Europe or South America. And this time, it was the World Cup for the whole world: Africa had joined the Americas, Asia and Europe at the top table of world football. From now on, thanks to satellite communications, more people than ever could tune in to watch the tournament live, and in colour.

In discovering new countries, the World Cup was also going to discover new playing conditions. For the first time, the event was taking place at altitude. Four of the five sites were at heights of between 1,800 and 2,600 metres. In addition, the finals took place in scorching heat, with matches taking place in the daytime, with kick-offs at midday or at four in the afternoon. The European teams, in particular, dreaded the double effect of these playing conditions on their bodies. They had to prepare themselves in a specific way to resist the particular climatic conditions of the country. The experience of the 1968 Games had been useful for them. Scrutinized from now on by the whole world, football was entering the era of science, but this did not prevent it from becoming a legendary World Cup.

WORLD CHAMPIONSHIP
JULES RIMET CUP 1970 IN MEXICO

Story of the qualifiers

Honduras-El Salvador, "The Football War"

▼ As a result of the armed conflict between El Salvador and Honduras that had been going on since July, thousands of Salvadorans sought refuge at the Red Cross headquarters in San Miguel (Honduras).

THE CONFLICT between two neighbouring nations in Central America, Honduras and El Salvador, quickly became known as "The Football War". Hostilities had been brewing between the two countries for a number of years, and the tension had risen over several months. On 8 and 15 June 1969, the two countries clashed in the qualifying phase of the World Cup. The two meetings (1–0 to Honduras in Tegucigalpa, 3–0 to El Salvador in San Salvador) took place in a context of great violence. Because the two teams had each won at home, a playoff took place in Mexico, in an atmosphere of riots, fanned by the governments and the press of the two countries. El Salvador's victory (3–2) was contested by the Hondurans. In the hours following the match, incidents occurred on the frontier between the two countries, inflated by propaganda on both sides. The escalation ended in a war which lasted for four days,

from 14 to 18 July (hence the expression "The Hundred Hour War"), and caused 3,000 deaths. The two countries didn't sign a peace treaty until 1990.

On another note, while each of the five countries to have won the World Cup (Uruguay, Italy, West Germany, Brazil and England) had qualified for the tournament in Mexico, the 1970 World Cup was also notable for another fact: only nine teams from Europe qualified. It was the first time since 1950 that Europe had so few entrants in the finals tournament. What it lost in comparison to 1966 was given to the African continent, represented (by Morocco) for the first time since 1934 (Egypt). Eight of the participants from 1966 failed to qualify for the tournament: Argentina, Chile, North Korea, Spain, France, Hungary, Portugal and Switzerland. On the other hand, three countries qualified for the first time: Israel, Morocco and, of course, El Salvador.

Regulations

The appearance of cards

There were two major innovations introduced for the 1970 World Cup.
From now on, cautions and sendings-off were indicated by yellow and red cards. The decision to use them had been taken following the refereeing incidents during the previous World Cup, notably the heated dismissal of the Argentinian Rattín during the England-Argentina quarter-final. The first referee to wave a yellow card was the West German Kurt Tschenscher, who brought it out five times during the opening match between Mexico and the USSR (0–0), the Soviet midfielder Kakhi Asatiani having the dubious honour of the first player to be shown a card. On the other hand, no red card was brought out during the whole tournament. The other innovation was the authorization for two substitutions per team in a match. The first player substituted, during the Mexico-USSR match, was the Soviet Viktor Serebrianikov, replaced at half-time by Anatoly Puzach.

Group stage

GROUP 1

MEX	0–0	URS
BEL	3–0	SLV
URS	4–1	BEL
MEX	4–0	SLV
URS	2–0	SLV
MEX	1–0	BEL

	W	D	L	+	–	PTS
URS	2	1	0	6	1	5
MEX	2	1	0	5	0	5
BEL	1	0	2	4	5	2
SLV	0	0	3	0	9	0

GROUP 2

URU	2–0	ISR
ITA	1–0	SWE
URU	0–0	ITA
ISR	1–1	SWE
SWE	1–0	URU
ITA	0–0	ISR

	W	D	L	+	–	PTS
ITA	1	2	0	1	0	4
URU	1	1	1	2	1	3
SWE	1	1	1	2	2	3
ISR	0	2	1	1	3	2

GROUP 3

ENG	1–0	ROU
BRA	4–1	TCH
ROU	2–1	TCH
BRA	1–0	ENG
BRA	3–2	ROU
ENG	1–0	TCH

	W	D	L	+	–	PTS
BRA	3	0	0	8	3	6
ENG	2	0	1	2	1	4
ROU	1	0	2	4	5	2
TCH	0	0	3	2	7	0

GROUP 4

PER	3–2	BUL
FRG	2–1	MAR
PER	3–0	MAR
FRG	5–2	BUL
FRG	3–1	PER
MAR	1–1	BUL

	W	D	L	+	–	PTS
FRG	3	0	0	10	4	6
PER	2	0	1	7	5	4
BUL	0	1	2	5	9	1
MAR	0	1	2	2		1

Knockout stages

QUARTER-FINAL	QUARTER-FINAL	QUARTER-FINAL	QUARTER-FINAL
BRA 4–2 PER	URU 1–0 A.E.T. URS	ITA 4–1 MEX	FRG 3–2 A.E.T. ENG

SEMI-FINAL	SEMI-FINAL
BRA 3–1 URU	ITA 4–3 A.E.T. FRG

PLAY-OFF FOR THIRD PLACE
FRG 1–0 URU

FINAL
BRA 4–1 ITA

BEL	BRA	BUL	ENG
FRG	ISR	ITA	MAR
MEX	PER	ROU	SLV
SWE	TCH	URS	URU

16 TEAMS

32
MATCHES PLAYED

47 0

CARDS

"JUANITO"
OFFICIAL MASCOTT

MEXICO 70
OFFICAL LOGO

BRAZIL
WINNERS

GERD MÜLLER
LEADING GOALSCORER

× **10**

3
AVERAGE GOALS
PER MATCH

TELSTAR
OFFICIAL MATCH BALL

1 500 000
SPECTATORS

Presentation whistle

This whistle was presented to Austrian referee Ferdinand Marschall. He refereed the group game between Brazil and Romania in Guadalajara.

◀ **FIFA World Football Museum collection.**

Host cities and stadiums
Matches played at 2,651 metres

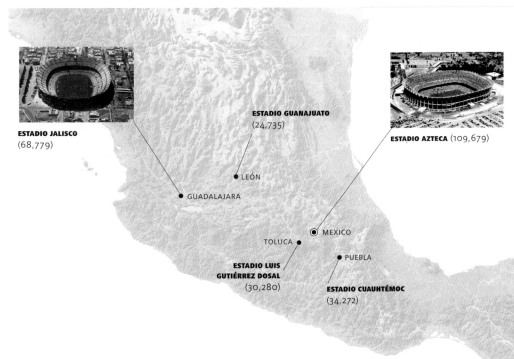

ESTADIO JALISCO
(68,779)

ESTADIO GUANAJUATO
(24,735)

ESTADIO AZTECA (109,679)

● LEÓN

● GUADALAJARA

◉ MEXICO

TOLUCA ●

**ESTADIO LUIS
GUTIÉRREZ DOSAL**
(30,280)

● PUEBLA

ESTADIO CUAUHTÉMOC
(34,272)

Mexico 1970 was a World Cup played at altitude and in intense heat. Of the five stadiums chosen, the Jalisco in Guadalajara was the lowest at 1680 meters, while the Estadio Luis Gutiérrez Dosal in Toluca was the highest at 2651 meters. Mexico City's Azteca, venue of the 1968 Olympic football Final stood at 2240 meters. The Azteca had the biggest crowds with 1,006,199 watching the ten games played there. The highest attendance was 108,192 for the group game between Mexico and Belgium, followed by 107,412 for the Final

7

Gerd Müller, the centre-forward from Bayern Munich and West Germany, played prodigiously in the first round. After scoring West Germany's winning goal against Morocco (2–1), he subsequently scored hat-tricks against Bulgaria (5–2) and Peru (3–1). With seven goals from his first three matches, he was one goal ahead of the France's Just Fontaine, who had scored six times during the first round in 1958.

◄ The streets of Mexico bedecked with World Cup decorations.

Mexican passion

TWO YEARS EARLIER, the Olympic Games had seen the world become accustomed to hearing the spectators chant "Me-hi-co, Me-hi-co!" During the 1970 World Cup, this chant echoed around the immense Azteca Stadium in which Mexico played their three group-stage matches, and in the streets of Mexico during the nights following their encounters. More than 100,000 spectators filled the Azteca Stadium for these matches: 107,160 for the opening match, Mexico-USSR (0–0), 103,058 for Mexico-El Salvador (4–0) and 108,192 for Mexico-Belgium (1–0). At the end of the group stage, the USSR and Mexico were level on points and goal difference. Lots had to be drawn to decide which of the two teams would play its quarter-final in Mexico City. The USSR won the draw, to the considerable dismay of the Mexicans, who would lose the fanatic support of the Azteca for their quarter-final clash against Italy and be exiled to Toluca and its smaller stadium (26,851).

Far from the marvels of Guadalajara and the frenzy of the Azteca Stadium, Group 2, whose matches took place at Puebla and Toluca, was dominated by ennui. Italy, who did not want to relive the misfortune of 1966, tightened their game. Uruguay closed theirs down, and both teams had that effect on their opponents, Israel and Sweden. Italy finished top of the group despite scoring only one goal (against Sweden). Uruguay also went through, after an insipid 0–0 draw with Italy and defeat by Sweden. Sweden were beaten by a single goal by Italy and Israel made an honourable start, but their draws against Italy (0–0) and Sweden (1–1) saw them fail to qualify.

▲ Duel between Morocco's Houmane Jarir and Germany's Hennes Löhr.

Jarir, a historic goalscorer

3 JUNE 1970

WEST GERMANY 🇩🇪	2–1	🇲🇦 MOROCCO
SEELER 56, MÜLLER 80		JARIR 21

IN THEIR FIRST appearance in the World Cup finals, Morocco made West Germany, one of the tournament favourites, tremble. In the 21st minute, Morocco took the lead, which they held for 35 minutes. A striker from Raja Casablanca, Houmane Jarir, scored the first African goal in the World Cup finals since Fawzy's goal for Egypt in 1934. The Germans took control of the match in the last half-hour (thanks to goals from Uwe Seeler and Gerd Müller), but the Moroccans went on to win their first point in the finals when they drew with Bulgaria (1–1).

▶ Peru's Teófilo Cubillas poses before training.

◀ Pelé and Bobby Moore exchange shirts at the end of the Brazil–England match.

A magnificent transfer of power

---

7 JUNE 1970

BRAZIL 🇧🇷 1–0 ➕ **ENGLAND**

JAIRZINHO 59

THE SCENE HAS been immortalized by a dozen photographers surrounding the two men, in the centre of the Jalisco ground, in Guadalajara. Stripped to the waist, smiling, as if happy to have taken part in so great an expenditure of energy and talent, the England captain Bobby Moore and the Brazilian King Pelé congratulate each other after exchanging shirts. The image illustrates the conclusion of a magnificent battle, fought in scorching heat and in an atmosphere totally favourable to Brazil, winners by a single goal… but what a goal. In the 59th minute, Tostão crossed the ball to Pelé, who controlled it with astounding calmness before delivering a pass of amazing simplicity to his right, where Jairzinho completed the sequence with a thunderbolt of a shot. The victory virtually assured Brazil's place in the quarter-finals. The defeat did not eliminate England, but the photographers who surrounded the two players as they congratulated each other had the feeling of being present at a transfer of power from the 1966 champions to the new 1970 favourites.

Peru spring a surprise

---

2 JUNE 1970

PERU 🇵🇪 3–2 🇧🇬 **BULGARIA**

GALLARDO 50, CHUMPITÁZ 55, CUBILLAS 73　　DERMENDJIEV 13, BONEV 49

THE PERUVIAN TEAM was the revelation of the opening round of the World Cup. Forty years after their only other participation in the finals, they were more or less unknown outside South America. In their qualifying group, they had eliminated Bolivia and, notably, Argentina, beating them in Lima (1–0, goal by Perico León) and drawing (2–2) in Buenos Aires. The best-known member of the Peruvian squad was its manager, the Brazilian double world champion Didi, who imposed a Brazilian style of play on the team. This style was revealed in Peru's first match, against Bulgaria: 2–0 down by the 49th minute, they rapidly levelled the score at 2–2, through Alberto Gallardo (in the 50th minute) and their captain Héctor Chumpitáz (in the 55th minute). In the 73rd minute, Teófilo Cubillas handed Peru the lead with a fine individual goal. Four days later, Cubillas scored twice and propelled Peru, winners over Morocco (3–0), into the quarter-finals.

"From the moment I headed it, I was sure it had gone in."

Pelé, Brazil striker

Save of the century

During the group game between Brazil and England in Guadalajara, Gordon Banks pulled off what was described as the save of the century. Pelé could not believe what he had seen. "From the moment I headed it, I was sure it had gone in. After I headed the ball, I had already began to jump to celebrate the goal … I looked back and I couldn't believe it hadn't gone in. I have scored more than a thousand goals in my life and the thing people always talk to me about is the one I didn't score."

▲ Franz Beckenbauer tackles Colin Bell in the quarter-final between West Germany and England.

▶ Gerd Müller scores the winner for West Germany in extra-time.

▼ The heroes of the day, Gerd Müller and Uwe Seeler, after their quarter-final victory over England.

West Germany gains its revenge

14 JUNE 1970

WEST GERMANY ▬ **3-2** ✚ **ENGLAND**
A.E.T.

BECKENBAUER 68, SEELER 82, MÜLLER 108   MULLERY 31, PETERS 49

4

The number of World Cups in which the German Uwe Seeler and the Brazilian Pelé scored. The two players took part in the World Cups of 1958, 1962, 1966 and 1970 and scored in each one. The only other player to have matched this feat is Miroslav Klose, who scored in 2002, 2006, 2010 and 2014. Pelé, the scorer of four goals in 1970, had a total of 12 goals in 14 matches in the World Cup and Seeler notched up nine goals in 21 matches (including three in 1970).

FOR FOUR YEARS German footballers had been dreaming of it. On 14 June 1970, in the stadium at Léon, they gained their revenge for the unhappy final in 1966. On 1 June 1968, for the first time in history, Germany had beaten England, 1–0 in a friendly (goal by Franz Beckenbauer). This time, it was for real. As in 1966, England were playing in red and Germany in white. At the start of the match, five players from each side remained from the Wembley final. A sixth, in the English team, had to withdraw. Gordon Banks, the heroic goalkeeper, had a stomach upset and was replaced by Chelsea's Peter Bonetti.

A terrific match took place, in terrible heat (the kick-off was at 12.00pm) and on a hard and patchy pitch. The defending champions did not want to give anything away, while the challengers were tense as a result of their desire to avenge the Wembley defeat. In this tough trial of strength England seemed to gain a decisive advantage. In the 31st minute Alan Mullery scored a first goal, latching on to a cross from Keith Newton. Then, in the 49th minute, following another attack by Newton down the right wing, Martin Peters scored a second goal. At 2–0, the English team seemed to be in a position to protect its advantage and conserve

their strength. Shortly afterwards, however, the German manager, Helmut Schön, chose to bring on Jürgen Grabowski in place of Stan Libuda. Franz Beckenbauer pulled one back for the Germans in the 68th minute when he beat Mullery with a cross-shot. This was the point at which England manager Alf Ramsey, made a critical change that would affect the outcome of the game. Sensing that his midfield players were tired, he took off 32-year-old Bobby Charlton. But the departure of their playmaker deprived the English team of their best strategist, at a time when the Germans were undoubtedly on top. West Germany started to bombard the English goal. In the 82nd minute, from a high cross by Karl-Heinz Schnellinger, Uwe Seeler got the better of Mullery in the air; with his back to goal, he lobbed Bonetti with an extraordinary header.

During extra-time the battle lost nothing of its intensity. Both teams had chances to score, but only West Germany succeeded. In the 108th minute, Grabowski broke through on the right and sent over a long cross which Hennes Löhr, beyond the far post, headed back into the centre. Gerd Müller was once again supreme in front of goal and his eighth goal of the tournament put an end to England's reign.

The first adidas ball

The World Cup used an adidas ball for the first time in 1970. The white ball with the 12 black pentagonal panels carried the name Telstar. This was because it recalled the shape of the telecommunications satellite which made the first transcontinental television transmissions possible.

▶ Uruguay's Victor Espárrago scores the only goal of their quarter-final against the USSR.

The affair of the Bogotá bracelet

A trivial event marked the England team's preparations. To acclimatize to the high altitude in Mexico, the world champions played two matches in Colombia and Ecuador before moving to Mexico. In Bogotá, the English captain, Bobby Moore, was accused by an employee of the hotel where the team was staying of having stolen a bracelet from a jewellery shop in the shopping arcade. Arrested on his return from Quito, Moore was detained for four days at the home of the president of the Colombian Football Federation, and the affair took on a diplomatic aspect. Moore was finally found innocent. He was then able to re-join the English squad at their base in Guadalajara.

Uruguayan pragmatism

14 JUNE 1970

URUGUAY 🇺🇾 **1-0** A.E.T. **USSR** 🇷🇺

ESPÁRRAGO 117

THE SOVIET UNION had shown the solidity of their football during the group stage when they stoically resisted Mexican fever (0–0), before dominating Belgium (4–1) and El Salvador (2–0). But no one was sure whether the team's uneconomical style of play had left its mark on the players' bodies, worn down by Mexico's challenging climactic conditions. The USSR's opponents in the quarter-finals, Uruguay, had scraped through Group 2. Deprived at the start of the first match by an injury to their star, the magnificent Pedro Rocha, Uruguay resorted to a negative game whose principal aim was to stifle the opposition. And the Soviet team would become their latest victims. They exhausted themselves in trying to overcome the resistance and the numerous fouls of the Uruguayans, whose behaviour was met by incessant whistling from the referee, broke up the rhythm of the match. That the game went into extra-time merely prolonged the Soviets' agony. In the 117th minute, after a free-kick and a long cross delivered by Luis Ubiña, the ball finally reached Luis Cubilla, who was hemmed in between two defenders on the goal-line. He somehow got the ball off them and managed to find a cross, which was headed into the back of the net by substitute Víctor Espárrago. The USSR protested, but the referee did not reverse his decision, and the linesman, on the opposite side, did not contradict him. After scoring just three goals in 390 minutes of play, Uruguay were in the semi-final. At least the winner had not been decided by the toss of a coin...

▲ Rivera in action during
Italy's 4–1 quarter-final
victory over hosts Mexico.

▲▲ Italians Gigi Riva and
Pierluigi Cera celebrate
their win.

▲ Italian coach Ferruccio Valcareggi, flanked by
his team's playmakers Sandro Mazzola and Gianni Rivera.

Italy dampen Mexican enthusiasm

14 JUNE 1970		
ITALY	4-1	**MEXICO**
GUZMAN 25 (O.G.)		GONZÁLEZ 13
RIVA 63, 76		
RIVERA 70		

THE NIGHTS following the matches involving Mexico during the group stage had been marked by scenes of unbounded enthusiasm, most notably in Mexico City. During the afternoon of 14 June, when the Mexico-Italy quarter-final was taking place, the country was strangely calm and quiet. At the same time, the Azteca Stadium was only half-full for the Uruguay-USSR encounter. The Mexican supporters stayed at home to follow their team's match on television. And unlike the preceding matches, the silence was to continue well after the final whistle. The heavy defeat by Italy (4–1) dampened the national passion for their team. There would not be any further sleepless nights in Mexican towns.

First Mazzola, then Rivera

FOR YEARS ITALIAN FOOTBALL had been wondering how to play Sandro Mazzola and Gianni Rivera together, to give impetus to the national team's attack. In 1966, their partnership had suffered defeat by North Korea during the World Cup held in England. In 1968, Italy won the European title with Mazzola but without Rivera, who was injured during the semi-final. For two years the manager, Ferruccio Valcareggi, had seldom put them together, the last time just before their departure for Mexico, and only for 45 minutes (Portugal-Italy, 2–2). During their preparations, Rivera complained of usually being left on the substitute's bench. In Mexico, Mazzola was first choice, with Rivera only used for the second half of the match against Israel. The choice was the same for the quarter-final: Mazzola started the match, with Rivera on the bench. Mexico opened the scoring, and Italy equalized. At half-time, Mazzola was replaced by Rivera. The Italian game lit up. The playmaker from AC Milan, whom the Mexicans did not mark closely, made the most of his freedom to show off his passing game. Gigi Riva, the Cagliari striker, was transformed by it. Having failed to score since the start of the competition, he became the marksman of the Italian team again. In a quarter of an hour he scored two goals and Rivera scored one. Italy had rediscovered the joys of attacking and Valcareggi had found his formula: using his two famous players, but not at the same time…

◀ Jairzinho tries to steal the ball from Peru's Nicolás Fuentes.

▲ Didi, world champion with Brazil in 1958 and 1962, and coach of Peru in 1970.

Didi beaten by his Brazil

14 JUNE 1970

BRAZIL 🇧🇷 4–2 🇵🇪 PERU

RIVELINO 11   GALLARDO 28, CUBILLAS 70
TOSTÃO 15, 52
JAIRZINHO 75

D IDI WAS THE GREAT PLAYMAKER of the Brazilian double world champions (1958 and 1962). In Mexico, in the quarter-final, Brazil met up with him again, but on the bench, and in the opposing camp, as the coach of Peru. At Guadalajara, Didi confronted Mário Zagallo, his former teammate in the Brazilian team, and he dreamt of a spectacular exploit. In the days preceding their reunion, he asserted that his team was the best and that the Brazilian defence resembled a "pack of cards". In reality, it was Peru who would show the greater defensive shortcomings. At the end of the first quarter of an hour, it was Rivelino, with a curling shot from the left, then Tostão, from a narrow angle, who handed Brazil a 2–0 advantage. Zagallo had asked his players not to draw on their reserves of energy. From then on, they controlled the game. But the Peruvians refused to surrender, and managed to respond. In the 28th minute, Alberto Gallardo, having got away on the left, reduced the margin. Perhaps Didi was right about the Brazilian defence. At the start of the second half, Tostão restored Brazil's two-goal advantage, but Teófilo Cubillas scored his fifth goal of the tournament, with a straightforward volley. That did not really worry Brazil, who scored a fourth goal following a solo run by Jairzinho (75th minute). Peru lost with honour and the Brazilians admitted they were doubly happy: firstly, for having beaten Didi; and secondly, for knowing that England had been eliminated at the hands of West Germany. Who could now prevent them from becoming world champions?

The first Panini stickers

The first World Cup trading card album was produced for the 1970 competition.

▲ FIFA World Football Museum collection.

> **"We were looking for a significant victory because we had just made fools of our opponents in the second half. We were eliminated by the sin of pride."**
>
> **West Germany captain Uwe Seeler.**

4

The number of previous winners of the World Cup present in the 1970 semi-finals: West Germany (1954), Brazil (1958 and 1962), Italy (1934 and 1938) and Uruguay (1930 and 1950). This domination by former champions had never happened before and has only happened once since, in 1990 (West Germany, Argentina, England and Italy).

The mythical photo

This is one of the legendary images in the history of the World Cup. Franz Beckenbauer played the half-hour of extra time against Italy with his arm in a sling. He had injured his shoulder at the end of full time, when Helmut Schön had already used his two permitted substitutes.

▲ Things get heated beween Wolfgang Overath and Angelo Domenghini after a foul on Sigfried Held.

A World Cup classic

17 JUNE 1970

ITALY ▮▮ **4–3** ▬▬ **WEST GERMANY**
A.E.T.

BONINSEGNA 8, BURGNICH 98, RIVA 104, RIVERA 111   SCHNELLINGER 90, MÜLLER 94, 110

THE SEMI-FINAL in Mexico City, between two representatives from Europe, was shaping up to be a tight match. West Germany and Italy were both believers in ruthless, man-to-man marking. They knew this method by heart, and each team's sweeper was used to the Italian style of play. Pierluigi Cera played for Cagliari, who had just won the national title. Karl-Heinz Schnellinger had just completed his seventh season in Italian football. At AC Milan, he formed the pair of central defenders with his adversary this day, Roberto Rosato.

The start of the match met pre-match expectations. The two teams watched each other carefully, without doing battle. Prudence was acceptable. But rapidly, Italy found themselves in a situation that suited them perfectly. In the eighth minute, Roberto Boninsegna penetrated the German defence and deceived Sepp Maier with a shot from the left. The Italian footballers knew all the tricks of the trade when it came to defending a small lead, even for 80 minutes.

However, the German pressure became more and more intense during the second half. Helmut Schön made resolutely attacking choices, bringing on Stan Libuda and Sigi Held. The Overath-Beckenbauer duo laid down the law in midfield, a part of the field in which, as in the preceding round, Gianni Rivera had replaced Sandro Mazzola for Italy. Overath hit the crossbar, Gerd Müller had three chances, and Enrico Albertosi saved a header from Seeler that seemed destined for the top corner. The Italians held on, sometimes it seemed as if by a miracle. There were a few seconds left to play. After a final throw-in, Jürgen Grabowski, from the left wing, sent over a lofted cross. Karl-Heinz Schnellinger suddenly appeared in front of goal, on his own, forgotten by the Italian defenders. The sweeper from Milan pushed the ball into the goal, with a lunge that looked like a tackle.

The period of extra-time will go down in the annals of World Cup history. The exchanges between the two teams were breathless, going against everything people knew about German and Italian football. Their defensive rigour, their realism, their well-known dependability were exploded. Five goals were scored in 17 minutes and each team led in turn before Italy eventually won 4–3. At the end of the match, the players were heaving with fatigue and emotion. "We were looking for a significant victory because we had just made fools of our opponents during the second half. We were knocked out by the sin of pride," said the German captain Uwe Seeler after his team's elimination.

▲ Uruguayan captain Luis Ubiña and his Brazilian counterpart Carlos Alberto shake hands before this all-South American semi-final.

A change of grounds

On the day following the quarter-finals, the committee organizing the tournament decided, left, after a proposal from the President of FIFA, Sir Stanley Rous, to reverse the stadiums planned for the semi-finals. In January, at the time of the draw, it was planned for the winner of the Mexico City quarter of the draw (Uruguay) to meet the winner from Guadalajara (Brazil), and the winner from Toluca (Italy) to meet the one from Léon (West Germany). The reason for this change was to limit the amount of movement for the four teams.

Brazil "champions of America"

17 JUNE 1970

BRAZIL 3–1 **URUGUAY**

CLODOALDO 44, JAIRZINHO 76, RIVELINO 89   CUBILLA 19

THE SEMI-FINAL in Guadalajara brought together the most admired team since the beginning of the World Cup, Brazil, and the hardest to like, Uruguay. In Brazilian memories there remained the nightmare of the 1950 World Cup, even though they had not lost against Uruguay for ten years. The start of the match confirmed the extreme difficulty of a team trying to impose itself on the Uruguayans, and it was Uruguay who imposed their rhythm on the game, striving to retain the ball thanks to their impeccable technique and, as a result, even posing the greater threat. In the 19th minute, following a poor start to an attack by Brito, Julio César Morales, on the left, hit a long centre, which Luis Cubilla did not entirely control. But the Brazilian goalkeeper Félix, who was badly placed by the near post, was deceived by the Uruguayan's flick and, against all the odds, Uruguay had taken the lead.

Uruguay's defence became more and more impenetrable and more and more corrosive. Fouls on the Brazilian strikers proliferated, it rained yellow cards, and goalkeeper Ladislao Mazurkiewicz held steady behind the blue wall. Just before half-time, however, Brazil developed an attack on the left. Clodoaldo linked up with Tostão, who launched him into the heart of the defence. The young midfielder from Santos equalized with a cross-shot.

Even though Cubilla created a huge chance for himself and saw his point-blank header saved by Félix, the second half was all about Brazil. Having hoped for a penalty for a foul by Atilio Ancheta on Pelé, it was in the last quarter of an hour that Brazil finally took the lead. In the 76th minute, a magnificent three-man move involving Pelé and Tostão allowed Jairzinho to escape on the right wing. He resisted Ancheta and scored in the corner. From then on, Uruguayan resistance lost its determination and Brazil's attacking moves became more agile. Some of them entered the annals, like the Pelé's famous dummy on Mazurkiewicz. In the 89th minute Rivelino, calmly fed by a regal Pelé, scored with a cross-shot that Mazurkiewicz could only get his fingers to. So the finalists from South America were Brazil.

PLAY-OFF FOR THIRD PLACE

▲ Wolfang Overath secures third place for West Germany at the 1970 World Cup.

West Germany's collection of podium finishes

20 JUNE 1970

WEST GERMANY 1–0 **URUGUAY**

OVERATH 26

In beating Uruguay 1–0, thanks to a 26th-minute goal by Wolfgang Overath (from his left foot, naturally), the best player in the match, West Germany completed its collection of places on the world podium. World champions in 1954, they finished fourth in 1958, second in 1966, and now third in 1970.

▲ Pennants are exchanged by Giacinto Facchetti and Carlos Alberto before the Final.

◥ Carlos Alberto celebrates scoring Brazil's fourth goal of the Final, a goal remembered as one of the greatest in World Cup history.

Three-star success for Brazil

21 JUNE 1970

BRAZIL 🔵 4–1 🟦 **ITALY**

PELÉ 18, GÉRSON 66   BONINSEGNA 37
JAIRZINHO 71
CARLOS ALBERTO 86

Jairzinho, the new Garrincha

Since 1958, the Brazilian team had often played with a true winger (on the right) and a ghost winger (on the left). The ghosts were Mario Zagallo in 1958 and 1962 and Rivelino in 1970. The true winger was Garrincha from 1958 to 1966. Jairzinho succeeded him. Jairzinho watched Garrincha during his first years at Botafogo. He took his place on the wing when the latter left for Corinthians in 1966. They played together in the 1966 World Cup (Jairzinho was then 21 years old, Garrincha 11 years older), then Jairzinho became first choice in 1968. The two players were very dissimilar in their physique and their style. More powerful than his predecessor, Jairzinho's game was more varied than Garrincha's, for whom just a dribble was sufficient to deceive his opponent. In Mexico, Jairzinho brought a formidable sense of where the goal was; he scored in each match – two goals against Czechoslovakia, and one each against England, Romania, Peru, Uruguay and Italy.

I N REACHING their final rendezvous, Brazil and Italy had taken very different routes. Brazil had beaten England only 1–0 during the group stage – but in the knockout phase theyvhad clearly dominated their two South American opponents, Peru (4–2) and Uruguay (3–1). In contrast, Italy had only just got through the first round, and had been obliged to bring their Mexican hosts to their senses (4–1), before undergoing the exhausting clash in the semi-final against West Germany. This made Brazil inevitable favourites for the Final – and the match played out according to the forecasts. Deprived of the spice of suspense, which was extinguished far too early, it was not a great event, being far from the spellbinding semi-final that had taken place in the same Azteca Stadium four days before. Standing by his previous choices, the Italian manager Ferruccio Valcareggi again preferred Sandro Mazzola to Gianni Rivera, who only came on in the last few minutes, when the result of the match had long since been decided.

The main attraction of the match was the performance of Pelé, whose slightest movement was scrutinized by the entire world in this Final which everybody – apart from Italians, of course – hoped would be his. He was going to enclose the match within two sumptuous brackets. In the 18th minute, leaping to meet a centre from Rivelino, Pelé rose extraordinarily high to get the better of Tarcisio Burgnich and head his 12th goal in the World Cup finals. Sixty-nine minutes later, when he received a pass from Jairzinho, he released Carlos Alberto down the right for Brazil's fourth and final goal, with a pass of extraordinary simplicity.

Between these two moves by Pelé, which ultimately define the story of the game, Italy's principal virtue was to bring a touch of the unexpected in equalizing, through Boninsegna, thanks to a gross error by Clodoaldo in defence. But, even though there were 80 minutes still to play, the result seemed inevitable. It therefore came as no surprise when first Gérson, with a left-foot shot in the 66th minute, and then Jairzinho in the 71st minute, who had been played in by Pelé, opened the way for Brazil's third world title.

▲ Pelé apologizes to goal-keeper Enrico Albertosi after fouling the Italian goalkeeper.

▲ Pelé is carried triumphantly after the match. *O Rei.*

▶ Brazil captain Carlos Alberto lifts the Jules Rimet Cup.

Which was better – Brazil 1958 or 1970?

The Brazil team of 1970 is regarded by many as the best in the history of football. But in Brazil itself, it has a rival – the 1958 World Cup winning team. Mario Zagallo featured in both, in 1958 as a player and in 1970 as the coach, and he rates them as good as each other for different reasons. In 1958, Brazil were tactically innovative and changed the way the game was played. "When Brazil had the ball I would leave my role as the third midfielder to play on the left wing in a 4-2-4 formation," Zagallo remembers. "When we lost the ball, I would drop back into a defensive role." Shades of the Total Football to come in the 1970s. And 1958 was the World Cup that first introduced Pelé to the world. "Despite being just 17 years old, you could see by what he did, he was a level higher than everyone else. He had the 'tranquility' of a veteran."

Pelé was also the star of the 1970 team. He had played in 1958 only from the third match, and was injured in the second match of 1962. In 1966 he was on the end of some rough tackles as Brazil exited at the group stage. But in 1970 he played every game. "The cup that gave him the international prestige for everything that he did was 1970. Pelé played from the beginning to the end of this tournament," says Zagallo. "When Brazil became world champions for the third time in 1970, he came up to me and hugged me. He said 'Zagallo, we needed to be together to become champions for a third time.' That was something that has always stuck with me."

Pelé's view? "Because of the 1958 World Cup, Brazil became known around the world as it had not been known before. That victory was important for the social and economical life of Brazil. Regarding 1970… Brazil had the best team of all time. No doubt about it."

100

Brazil's 100th goal in the World Cup finals was scored by Pelé in the 18th minute of the Final against Italy. It was Brazil's 38th match in the finals. They failed to score in only two of them (0–0 against England in 1958 and Czechoslovakia in 1962).

Zagallo, from the wing to the bench

Mário Zagallo, coach of the 1970 world champions, had twice won the World Cup as a player, in 1958 and 1962, playing on the left wing. He was the first man to win the world title as both player and manager. Franz Beckenbauer was the second: as a player in 1974 and as manager in 1990.

The Winged Victory Trophy flies off to Brazil

What was certain before the final of the ninth World Cup, was that the winner would keep the Jules Rimet Cup forever. From the start, the rules had stipulated that the first nation to win it three times would become the permanent owner of the trophy designed by the French sculptor Abel Lafleur. Italy (in 1934 and 1938) and Brazil (1958 and 1962) had been world champions twice. When he raised the trophy aloft after the Final, Carlos Alberto took the gold statuette to Brazil for good. Stolen in 1983, it was never found. The Brazilian Federation had a replica made. As for the new trophy, introduced in 1974, it remains the property of FIFA.

1974

In Munich's iconic Olympiastadion, West Germany beat the Netherlands 2–1 to become the first team to win the new FIFA World Cup Trophy. The West Germans lost a match – against neighbours East Germany – but in the Final overcame the "Total Football" of Johan Cruijff's Dutch team, despite conceding a first-minute penalty. Their winner was Gerd Müller's 14th finals goal, a new World Cup record.

The shadow of terrorism

A COUNTRY AT PEACE and growing strongly. In 1966, when the 1974 World Cup was awarded to West Germany, it did not seem as though FIFA were taking any risks. But on 5 September 1972, Palestinian terrorists assassinated 11 Israeli athletes at the Munich Olympic Games. The World Cup would, therefore, be marked by security, all the more so since the West Germany of the 1970s was also grappling with extreme left-wing terrorism. Squads moved under police escort, certain training camps were protected by barbed-wire fencing, personnel were systematically searched and at every location journalists were obliged to show an identity card with a colour photo... During matches presumed to be at risk, marksmen were posted on the roofs of the stadiums. For the Final, two thousand men and seven helicopters were dispatched to Munich. As for the spectators, the cost of their ticket included disability and life insurance. Just one incident would catch out the perfect German organization: just before the Final, the referee realized that the corner flags had disappeared during the opening ceremony! By the time they were found, kick-off had been delayed by a few minutes.

WEST GERMANY 74

1974 FIFA WORLD CUP
FEDERAL REPUBLIC OF GERMANY

Regulations

New cup and new format

BRAZIL'S THIRD WORLD TRIUMPH in 1970 entitled them to keep the Jules Rimet Cup. Fifty-three proposals for the new trophy were submitted to FIFA, who chose the design by the Italian artist Silvio Gazzaniga, who worked for the Milan firm Bartoni. Called "The FIFA World Cup Trophy", it is 36.8 cm high but weighs 6,142 grams, including 5,092 grams of pure 18-carat gold. A new regulation decreed that the World Cup would always remain the property of FIFA, with the winning team retaining a gold-plated replica.

From a sporting point of view, the major innovation was the return to first and second round groups, as in 1950. But there were two groups in the second round, with the winners confronting each other for the title. The advantage in terms of receipts was certain: 38 matches, compared to 32 in 1970. But with only the Final resulting in direct elimination, the huge thrill of "sudden death" in 90 or 120 minutes was the major casualty of the new format.

▲ Silvio Gazzaniga with the new FIFA World Cup trophy.

Story of the qualifiers

East Germany's only final phase

FOR THE FIRST TIME, a country from Oceania qualified for the World Cup finals, after Australia disposed of South Korea in a playoff in Hong Kong (1–0). The 1974 finals also saw the first participation of a Sub-Saharan country in the tournament, after Zaire, playing in its first qualifying campaign, won the slot for Africa ahead of Morocco and Zambia. Another new arrival: Haiti, hosts of the final round of the CONCACAF tournament and the beneficiaries of Mexico's disastrous 4–0 defeat by Trinidad and Tobago). The European zone marked the return of two nations absent from the world tournament since 1938: the Netherlands, winners on goal difference ahead of Belgium, and Poland, who put out England. Chile benefitted from the withdrawal of the Soviet Union, who had refused to play in Santiago's Estadio Nacional two months after the coup d'état against Salvador Allende, claiming political prisoners had been tortured there. East Germany were drawn in a winnable group (Romania, Finland, Albania), and qualified for the first and only time. The presence of East Germany in West Germany, with a match scheduled for West Berlin, marked a spectacular diplomatic victory for football.

First group stage

GROUP 1

FRG	1–0	CHI
GDR	2–0	AUS
CHI	1–1	GDR
AUS	0–3	FRG
AUS	0–0	CHI
GDR	1–0	FRG

	W	D	L	+	–	PTS
GDR	2	1	0	4	1	5
FRG	2	0	1	4	1	4
CHI	0	2	1	1	2	2
AUS	0	1	2	0	5	1

GROUP 2

BRA	0–0	YUG
ZAI	0–2	SCO
YUG	9–0	ZAI
SCO	0–0	BRA
SCO	1–1	YUG
ZAI	0–3	BRA

	W	D	L	+	–	PTS
YUG	1	2	0	10	1	4
BRA	1	2	0	3	0	4
SCO	1	2	0	3	1	4
ZAI	0	0	3	0	14	0

GROUP 3

URU	0–2	NED
SWE	0–0	BUL
NED	0–0	SWE
BUL	1–1	URU
BUL	1–4	NED
SWE	3–0	URU

	W	D	L	+	–	PTS
NED	2	1	0	6	1	5
SWE	1	2	0	3	0	4
BUL	0	2	1	2	5	2
URU	0	1	2	1	6	1

GROUP 4

ITA	3–1	HAI
POL	3–2	ARG
HAI	0–7	POL
ARG	1–1	ITA
ARG	4–1	HAI
POL	2–1	ITA

	W	D	L	+	–	PTS
POL	3	0	0	12	3	6
ARG	1	1	1	7	5	3
ITA	1	1	1	5	4	3
HAI	0	0	3	2	14	0

Second group stage

GROUP A

BRA	1–0	GDR
NED	4–0	ARG
GDR	0–2	NED
ARG	1–2	BRA
ARG	1–1	GDR
NED	2–0	BRA

	W	D	L	+	–	PTS
NED	3	0	0	8	0	6
BRA	2	0	1	3	3	4
GDR	0	1	2	1	4	1
ARG	0	1	2	2	7	1

GROUP B

YUG	0–2	FRG
SWE	0–1	POL
FRG	4–2	SWE
POL	2–1	YUG
POL	0–1	FRG
SWE	2–1	YUG

	W	D	L	+	–	PTS
FRG	3	0	0	7	2	6
POL	2	0	1	3	2	4
SWE	1	0	2	4	6	2
YUG	0	0	3	2	6	0

Knockout stages

PLAY-OFF FOR THIRD PLACE

BRA	0–1	POL

FINAL

NED	1–2	FRG

ARG	AUS	BRA	BUL
CHI	FRG	GDR	HAI
ITA	NED	POL	SCO
SWE	URU	YUG	ZAI

16 TEAMS

38
MATCHES PLAYED

23　4
CARDS

1 865 753
SPECTATORS

TIP AND TAP
OFFICIAL MASCOT

WM 74
OFFICIAL LOGO

WEST GERMANY
WINNERS

GRZEGORZ LATO ×7
LEADING GOALSCORER

2.6
AVERAGE GOALS
PER MATCH

TELSTAR DURLAST
OFFICIAL BALL

Host cities and stadiums

A wet summer in West Germany

▼ The 1974 World Cup was notable for heavy rain and waterlogged pitches.

HAMBURG
● **VOLKSPARKSTADION**
(60,200)

HANOVER
● **NIEDERSACHSENSTADION**
(59,900)

BERLIN
◉ **OLYMPIASTADION**
(84,100)

GELSENKIRCHEN
PARKSTADION ●
(69,600)

DORTMUND
● **WESTFALENSTADION**
(53,700)

DÜSSELDORF
RHEINSTADION
(67,800)

FRANKFURT
● **WALDSTADION**
(62,000)

STUTTGART
● **NECKARSTADION**
(70,100)

MUNICH
OLYMPIASTADION
(79,000)

No stadium was built or enlarged for the 1974 World Cup. Instead, the organizing committee endeavoured to reduce their capacity, in order to improve comfort and security. The nine cites used were well-equipped: all the fenced-in areas, including the Olympic Stadium at Munich where the Final would be played, and its venerable counterpart in Berlin, could comfortably hold more than 50,000 spectators. This meant that the attendance record would be broken: 1,820 million spectators, at an average of nearly 48,000 per match. The fans deserve great credit, considering the torrential rain storms that struck Germany in the summer of 1974. The conditions for the players were also challenging at times. The matches between the Netherlands and Argentina in the first round, the Netherlands and East Germany, West Germany and Sweden and West Germany and Poland in the second were played on turf that was first waterlogged and then muddy. And, throughout the competition, all the pitches were heavy and greasy.

▲ Grzegorz Lato in action for Poland against Argentina.

◥ A young Mario Kempes takes on defenders Jerzy Gorgoń and Antoni Szymanowski in Argentina's 3–2 defeat at the hands of Poland in Stuttgart.

From the outset, a pinnacle of the game

15 JUNE 1974

POLAND ▬ 3–2 ▀ **ARGENTINA**

LATO 7, 62, SZARMACH 8   HEREDIA 60, BABINGTON 66

I N A GRIM OPENING MATCH, the Brazilian holders, unrecognizable from 1970, removed themselves from the list of favourites by conceding a sad draw to Yugoslavia (0–0) in the rain at Frankfurt. Two days later, the match at the Neckarstadion in Stuttgart between Poland and Argentina reassured those concerned for the 1974 World Cup. In South America as in Europe, there were still players who knew how to play football…

All eyes were turned in particular to Poland, both in expectation, because they were the Olympic champions and had overcome England in the qualifying rounds (2–0 at home before an heroic 1–1 draw at Wembley), and curiosity, because they had not played in the finals since 1938. These eyes showed an even keener interest after eight minutes, because Poland were already leading 2–0. From a sixth-minute corner, the Argentinian goal-keeper Daniel Carnevali, impeded by one of his defenders, released the ball right in front of Grzegorz Lato (1–0). Then, two minutes later, a failed Argentinian pass offered Andrzej Szarmach a counter-attack from a pass by Lato (2–0). For an hour, manager Kazimierz Gorski's men played more varied, lively and inspired football than the physical and team

football often associated with countries from Eastern Europe. Argentina, as slow as in the past, were not far from foundering, with Polish shots hitting the post in the 22nd and 46th minutes and a save by Enrique Wolff on the line in the 37th minute.

If Argentina did not go under, it was because their cohesion, a big talking point for commentators before the start of the tournament, did not fail. The last half-hour was transformed into a catch-up: Ramón Heredia reduced the deficit in the 60th minute with a fine curling strike after a move involving 19-year-old Mario Kempes (2–1) before Poland restored their two-goal lead through the formidable Lato in the 62nd minute (3–1). An opportunist goal by Carlos Babington after a mix-up in the Polish penalty area made it 3–2 in the 66th minute.

"In order to remain a bit longer in Germany, we now have no other choice than to beat Italy in the next match," the Argentinian manager Vladislao Cap lamented… but he was wrong. As for the Poles, their only reward was to be denied television in their base camp in Württemberg, so they could concentrate on the rest of the tournament.

1142

In minutes, this is the playing time (more than 12 matches) during which the Italian goalkeeper Dino Zoff had not let in a goal at international level before conceding in the 46th minute of the Italy-Haiti match, on 15 June in Munich. On a lightning counter-attack, the Haitian striker Emmanuel Sanon beat Italian defender Luciano Spinosi for speed, dribbled past Zoff to his left and then shot into the empty goal. Italy won the match 3–1, thus avoiding another trauma as suffered eight years earlier against the North Koreans, but the goal did cost them dearly: after a draw with Argentina (1–1) and a defeat by Poland (1–2), Italy were eliminated on goal difference by Argentina (+ 1 against + 2 for the Argentinians).

After playing against Italy, Ernst Jean-Joseph became the first player to test positive for drugs during a World Cup. The Haitian sweeper, who had taken a psychomotor stimulant, was banned from the competition.

▶ The Dutch team before the match against Uruguay. Back row: Jan Jongbloed, Wim Rijsbergen, Arie Haan, Johan Neeskens, Ruud Krol, Wim Suurbier; front row: Johnny Rep, Johan Cruijff, Rob Rensenbrink, Wim Jansen and Wim Van Hanegem.

Press passes

Media passes for journalists.

▲ FIFA World Football Museum collection.

The first red card

The introduction of red and yellow cards in the World Cup went back to 1970, but no one was sent off in Mexico. So the first red card ever shown at the World Cup finals dates to 14 June 1974. It was brandished in West Berlin by Turkish referee Dogan Babaçan in the face of Carlos Caszely during Chile's defeat by West Germany (1–0). The error by the Chilean had nothing to do with a serious foul: already warned in the first half, he received a second yellow card for refusing to move away from the ball at a free-kick.

The Netherlands did not go on strike

15 JUNE 1974

URUGUAY 0–2 NETHERLANDS

REP 7, 86

WERE THEY GOING to withdraw? A few days before the Netherlands entered the tournament, this unbelievable question was asked for real. The Dutch players were threatening not to go to Germany, in protest against the non-payment of bonuses for qualification promised by their federation and its sponsors. In reply, Rinus Michels, the manager of Barcelona and the Dutch national team, responded that he would return to Catalonia by the first plane. The affair of the bonuses would be sorted out on 11 June … with their first match to be played four days later against Uruguay (semi-finalists in 1970) in Hanover.

This carry-on was not the only one to undermine the team. Feyenoord then Ajax had carried off all the European Cups from 1970 to 1973, but the players from the two clubs did not get along well together. In addition, the idol Johan Cruijff, transferred from Ajax to Barça a year earlier, did not get on with his former teammate Piet Keizer, who had to play beside him in attack. Michels acceded to his request in putting Rob Rensenbrink and Johnny Rep on either side of him, in an untried starting line-up. The Netherlands demolished a Uruguay side that, without its fantastic goalkeeper Ladislao Mazurkiewicz, dressed all in black like his hero Lev Yashin, might have conceded five or six goals. Between the two goals by Rep, the 22-year-old winger from Ajax, who opened the scoring with a seventh-minute header and closed it in the 69th minute, the Dutch rang rings round a Uruguayan side who seemed to be playing the game at walking pace. The Dutch pressed every opposition player in possession, their strikers defended, the two wing-backs Suurbier and Ruud Krol attacked and Cruijff went wherever he wanted to…

▲▲ Detlev Lange, aged 11, performs the draw for the 1974 FIFA World Cup.

▲ Jürgen Sparwasser leads out the East Germany team for the match against West Germany in Hamburg.

◥ Franz Beckenbauer and Bernd Bransch shake hands before the West Germany against East Germany match.

The match of the two Germanys

22 JUNE 1974

EAST GERMANY ▬ 1–0 ▬ **WEST GERMANY**

SPARWASSER 77

"If one day 'Hamburg '74' is written on my grave, everyone will know who is underneath."

Jürgen Sparwasser, East Germany's goalscorer in their match against West Germany.

THE PERSON responsible was called Detlef Lange, he was 11 years old and an altar boy in Frankfurt. At the draw for the 1974 World Cup, he put the German Democratic Republic in Group 1, the same group as the German Federal Republic, the host nation. Since the division of the country, the East and West German football teams had never met each other. And, up to reunification, they would never come up against each other again.

Throughout the first round, the East Germans had intrigued. They had set up at Quickborn, a small town to the north of Hamburg, in a hotel in which they demanded sole occupancy. Pressed with questions about the host country, their manager Georg Buschner hadn't really given anything away: "West Germany has some great qualities." Just 18,000 curious people had watched the East Germany-Australia match in Hamburg (2–0). The following day, the East German players had visited the city and gone to the cinema. The following match, against Chile (1–1), despite being played in West Berlin, had again attracted a disappointing total of 28,000 spectators.

There remained the fraternal encounter against the West Germany of Franz Beckenbauer. "In what way is it different?" Buschner was asked. "It's not a match like any other because it is decisive for our qualification for the second round," he replied, in impeccable waffle. In fact, just before the kick-off, the draw between Australia and Chile (0–0) ensured the presence of both teams in the next round. They were only playing for first place.

The Volksparkstadion in Hamburg was, this time, absolutely full (60,200 spectators). Marksmen were stationed on the roof of the stadium. They put down their arms and stood to attention for the national anthems, which were completely respected by the public. West Germany dominated, but without scoring, Gerd Müller hitting a post in the 38th minute. East Germany resisted. West Germany, undermined by internal dissentions, disappointed. East Germany, about whom little was known, were surprising. One player, in particular, impressed with his speed: Jürgen Sparwasser. On a counter-attack, in the 77th minute, the striker from 1. FC Magdeburg burst through between Berti Vogts and Horst-Dieter Höttges, intelligently headed the ball sideways and deceived Sepp Maier. East Germany were leading … and their defence was going to hold firm until the final whistle.

The Hamburg public applauded the winners. With the players too, the East Germans had won the respect of the 1972 European Champions. But there was no question of publicly exchanging shirts. Paul Breitner would wait until he got to the dressing-room before he swapped his for Sparwasser's, from then on the eternal hero of East German football: "If one day 'Hamburg '74' is written on my grave, everyone will know who is underneath," he said after the match. From the West German perspective, the defeat would force manager Helmut Schön to readjust his team. "Sparwasser's goal woke us up," Franz Beckenbauer himself would say. "Without it, we would never have become world champions."

▲ Cruijff on the way to scoring the fourth Dutch goal against Argentina.

◥ Johnny Rep relaxes with his wife in the German sunshine.

Cruijff at the pinnacle of his genius

26 JUNE 1974

NETHERLANDS 4–0 ARGENTINA

CRUIJFF 10, 90, KROL 25 , REP 73

THE NETHERLANDS could do anything, risk anything and try anything. After their dazzling victory against Bulgaria (4–1) in their final group match, the team had hardly trained. The Dutch team had been visited by their wives, with whom they had been able to share some down time… It must be said that their manager, Rinus Michels, had left West Germany for two days. Still in his job at Barcelona, he had gone to Madrid to take charge of Barça, who were facing Atlético Madrid in the semi-finals of the Spanish Cup. Although deprived of Johan Cruijff, the Catalans qualified (they would lose the final on 29 June against Real Madrid). In Germany, the players, very laid-back, had given often funny and provocative interviews, like the rock stars that they almost were. Cruijff had justified the low intensity of the training by emphasizing the amount of work the squad had done before the tournament, but had laughed as he explained that the replacements, for their part, would have to throw themselves into it "otherwise they were going to get fat". In contrast, however, Rob Rensenbrink hadn't minced his words: "Everything has not been rosy for me since my arrival. The players from Ajax are a group of mates who are difficult to mix with. And I have also had to change my game. At Anderlecht, like Cruijff here, I can do what I like. But in the national team, my position and style are imposed on me."

One would think that any team approaching a major match in the World Cup in that frame of mind would fall apart. But the Dutch reinvented the norms of football. Away from and especially on the pitch. At Gelsenkirchen, it was a rather lucky Argentina who were offered up to them as their next victims. They had come out of the first round with just one victory (4–1 against Haiti), and they were not going to resist for long against a team that contained a Johan Cruijff who still hadn't scored in the World Cup, but who was about to make up for it rapidly. Having presented the first chance of the match to Rensenbrink, following a feint with his eyes that had sent the Argentinian defence the wrong way, Cruijff received a superb lob from Wim van Hanegem in the tenth minute. He acrobatically controlled the ball, deceived the Argentinian goalkeeper Daniel Carnevali and scored with his left foot (1–0). Cruijff directed the incessant Dutch attacks like a conductor, changing the position of his team members and even telling the goalkeeper, Jan Jongbloed, where to stand. A second goal followed in the 25th minute, from a strike by Ruud Krol (2–0). Johan Neeskens's game tailed off, perhaps following a clash? Cruijff had put him at centre forward, so as to position himself in midfield. A terrible storm broke in the second half, making the pitch slippery. The Dutch adapted immediately, and started to play a longer game. In the 73rd minute, a centre from the left by Cruijff gave the impression that the Dutch genius had anticipated everything: how the Argentinian defenders were going to move, how Johnny Rep was going to rise at the far post. The ball landed right on the Ajax winger's head as he came hurtling in (3–0). But the Cruijff legend demanded one last spectacular feat, and he was going to deliver it. Carnevali blocked a shot from Van Hanegem. The Dutch number 14 instantly volleyed the ball with his right foot from the left-hand edge of the penalty area (4–0).

The rout of Zaire by Yugoslavia, on 18 June at Gelsenkirchen, equalled the biggest defeat in the history of the World Cup, the 9–0 beating taken by South Korea against Hungary in 1954. After a more than honourable 2–0 defeat by Scotland, the Zaire team capitulated against the Yugoslavs. In protest against the fourth Yugoslav goal, Mwepu Ilunga even kicked the Colombian referee on the backside. Omar Delgado not having been able to see who had attacked him, sent off… Ndaye Mulamba. During Zaire's third defeat, by Brazil (3–0), Ilunga produced a moment that entered World Cup folklore: he charged out of the wall at a free-kick and cleared the ball before any Brazilian had touched it.

Unlucky Scotland

▲ A devastated Billy Bremner leaves the pitch after Scotland are knocked out on goal difference.

With one win (2–0 against Zaire) and two draws (0–0 against Brazil, 1–1 against Yugoslavia), Scotland became the first unbeaten team to be eliminated from a World Cup, after scoring fewer goals against Zaire than Brazil or Yugoslavia.

▶ ▼ Both Jairzinho (right) and Rivellino (below right) were playing in their third World Cup. Both scored against Argentina, but neither could inspire Brazil to the heights of 1970.

▼ ▼ Mário Zagallo, two-time world champion and Brazil's coach in 1974. Victory over the Dutch would have taken Brazil to the Final, and for coach Mário Zagallo the chance of a fourth world title.

Brazil win the "Copa América"

30 JUNE 1974

ARGENTINA 🇦🇷 1–2 🇧🇷 BRAZIL

BRINDISI 35   RIVELINO 32, JAIRZINHO 49

W HEN BRAZIL and Argentina met in this second round group game, it was, remarkably, the first time that they had played each other in the World Cup. The world champions had only made it through a dull first group stage on goal difference, characterized by 0–0 draws with Yugoslavia and Scotland, before recording a narrow win over East Germany (1–0) in the first match of the second group stage. In attack not much had happened, and the stars Rivelino and Jairzinho had disappointed. Argentina had been even more painful to watch, and their heavy defeat against the Netherlands had virtually wiped out their chances of reaching the Final. Worse, as defender Ángel Bargas recognized, the Argentinian team felt their football lagged "a generation behind".

However, in a far from full Hanover Niedersachsenstadion (just 39,400 spectators turned up to watch the match, the lowest crowd of any of the six encounters in Pool A), Brazil and Argentina played a splendid match of high quality, a festival of impossible ball control, unexpected dribbles and powerful long-range strikes. A subtle series of passes put Rivelino in position for the first goal in the 32nd minute, a shot skimming the surface from outside the penalty area (1–0). Argentina replied from a direct free-kick three minutes later through their captain Miguel Ángel Brindisi (1–1). But Jairzinho headed home the winner in the 49th minute (2–1), after Zé Maria had won back the ball and outflanked the defence. The Brazil of manager Mário Zagallo, double world champions, in 1958 and 1962, had become Brazil again… and just at the right moment.

The triumph of "Total Football"

3 JULY 1974

NETHERLANDS 2–0 **BRAZIL**

NEESKENS 50, CRUIJFF 65

THE WINS by the Netherlands and Brazil in their first two matches in the second group stage offered both teams a semi-final in all but name: the winner of the encounter in Dortmund would play in the Final, the loser in the match for third place. And if it was a draw? It would be the Dutch who would have the honour of heading for the Olympiastadion in Munich, thanks to their goal average. So, for the Brazilians, no calculations were necessary. Relying on their rock-solid defence (only a single goal conceded), Brazil would have to impose their technique, their fluidity and their imaginative game on a different school of thought: the Dutch "Total Football", developed by Rinus Michels and Johan Cruijff from the time of their first successes at Ajax, before the coach (in 1971) then the player (in 1973) left for Barcelona.

What were its principles? "During a match, a player is only in possession of the ball for three or four minutes," explained Rinus Michels. "Total football is explaining to him what to do and how to move during the other 86 or 87." The Dutch players were constantly on the move, changing places all the time, improvising according to the situation of the game and not to predetermined placings. The strikers put pressure on the opposition defender in possession, the midfielders pushed forward and the wing-backs overlapped. In defence, Michels played a sweeper who was a converted midfielder, Arie Haan, whose job it was to push the defensive line forward so as to win back the ball as far as possible from the goal area, or else to play offside. The tactic pre-supposes a goalkeeper who is a first-class distributor and who excels with his feet. Michels gave the job to a returnee, Jan Jongbloed, 33 years old, who had the triple peculiarity of playing without gloves, wearing number 8 and having been capped on only one other occasion, as a late substitute in 1962, before Michels called him up in May 1974 for a friendly in preparation for the World Cup. Between the triple world champions, in blue, and the Dutch, in white, there was, therefore, the prospect of a duel between different philosophies, for the probable handing over of power. It would indeed be that…But also a very physical match too. Brazil had chosen to respond to the verbal provocations of Michels ("Since the Brazilians do not like playing on Sundays, they are going to arrange to qualify for the losers' final, played on Saturday") and to the assaults of Johan Neeskens and his consorts with a very tough game. Elbows, two-footed tackles, dives in the penalty area (Valdomiro) and even a tackle by Zé Maria on Cruijff more suited to rugby. In goal, Leão pulled off some staggering saves, from point-blank volleys by Cruijff and then Wim Suurbier, so the score remained 0–0 at half-time. Just before the break, Jairzinho, the best Brazilian player on the pitch, had his team's best chance, with a shot blocked in extremis by Wim Rijsbergen. But during all the action, Johan Neeskens had remained stretched out near the Brazilian goal area, the victim of a blow in the face from Marinho Peres…

The second half would sometimes veer towards a fist fight, all the more so because the Dutch were not novices in that type of game either. But it was also going to see the better of the two teams take off. First of all Johan Neeskens, the young and shy protégé of Cruijff (he had just signed for Barça to rejoin him) who had been one of the most dazzling players in the tournament, latched on to a centre from his mentor in the 50th minute and, with a spectacular aerial thrust, lobbed the ball over Leão (1–0). Then, 15 minutes later, Cruijff himself, after a rapid counter-attack led by Rob Rensenbrink, volleyed at top speed a perfect centre from wing-back Ruud Krol (2–0). The world champions were on the ropes. A free-kick from Valdomiro skimmed past the post in the 83rd minute, but the last notable event was unfortunately down to Luis Pereira, already warned in the first half, who made a late and knee-high tackle on Neeskens in the 84th minute. The red card for the foul was fully justified. In Dortmund, Brazil lost more than just a match: the gaze of admiration of football fans from all over the world had shifted from them to the men in orange.

▼ Johan Cruijff confirms that it is indeed Luis Pereira who should receive a second yellow card and be sent off.

◀ Johan Neeskens shoots as Paulo César Carpegiani looks on.

1

Thanks to their victory against Brazil, the Netherlands reached their first World Cup Final. In their last appearance in the finals, in 1938, they had been beaten in the first round 3–0 by Czechoslovakia…

▲ Sweden's Kent Karlsson marks Gerd Müller.

◥ Rainer Bonhof scores Germany's second goal despite the efforts of the Swedish defence.

The Ghost of Malente is laid to rest

30 JUNE 1974

WEST GERMANY 🇩🇪 4–2 🇸🇪 **SWEDEN**

OVERATH 51, BONHOF 52, GRABOWSKI 76, HOENESS 89 (PEN)   EDSTROM 24, SANDBERG 53

Overath, the other giant

Five West German players in 1974 were appearing in their third World Cup following on from 1966 and 1970. Neither Sepp Maier nor Jürgen Grabowski had actually played in 1966, and in 1974 Hans-Dieter Höttges appeared only once, in the defeat by East Germany. The other two were Franz Beckenbauer and Wolfgang Overath. Overath played for 1. FC Köln, the only club in his long professional career (536 matches from 1962 to 1977). He was the only German used by Helmut Schön in all the 19 matches played by West Germany in those three World Cups. The Kaiser would only play in 18 (five goals), missing the third-place playoff against Uruguay in 1970 (1–0, goal… by Overath).

However, in 1974, there was competition for Wolfgang Overath's place. He did not play for Bayern Munich, and had not taken part in the European Nations Cup, won by West Germany in 1972. Certain people preferred Günter Netzer to him. Since Overath was 30 years old, he was criticized for his lack of speed and some missed passes, even sometimes by teammates in training… Overath was not part of the clan of Beckenbauer, who reigned over the team. But he remained indispensable to West Germany for his vision of the game, the flawlessness of his left foot and his endurance. Schön knew it, and Beckenbauer knew it. During two of the three World Cups Beckenbauer played alongside him, the famous sweeper shared a room with Overath. "We have slept together more often than with our wives," quipped Beckenbauer one day, "but nothing ever happened."

I N THE FIRST ROUND WEST GERMANY had only beaten Chile by one goal (1–0), saved energy against Australia (3–0) and lost to East Germany (1–0). The "Ghost of Malente" was said to be haunting West Germany's national team. Because, at their training camp situated in this small town in the far north of the country, the players had confronted their training personnel before the start of the tournament on the matter of bonuses, following the example of the Dutch. They had been ready to quit – Paul Breitner had even packed his suitcase – before a compromise was found. Franz Beckenbauer dented his relative popularity as a result of the affair (Gerd Müller was the idol of the German crowds). During his third World Cup, Beckenbauer was even whistled by his own crowd at the Volksparkstadion in Hamburg, and said unfortunate things about the Australians, for which he later had to apologize. Because it was him, captain of West Germany, the European champions, captain of Bayern Munich, also European champions, who pulled the team's strings. The defeat by East Germany had allegedly given him full powers, to the detriment of Helmut Schön. When the manager missed a press conference, German journalists joked: "Beckenbauer hasn't given him the team line-up yet…"

Against Yugoslavia, at the start of the second round, Bernd Cullmann, Jürgen Grabowski, Uli Hoeness and Heinz Flohe had not been selected; Schön (and The Kaiser, his captain) preferred Herbert Wimmer, Rainer Bonhof, Bernd Hölzenbein and Dieter Herzog. West Germany prevailed, with brio (2–0). In the following match, at the Rheinstadion in Düsseldorf, they played

Sweden, who had just lost to Poland (1–0) conceding their first goal in the tournament in the process. It poured with rain, the pitch was heavy, and the Swedish central defence, made up of Björn Nordqvist and Kent Karlsson, kept a close watch. At half-time, in spite of ten German chances saved by Ronnie Hellström, it was Sweden who were leading, after a poor headed clearance by Georg Schwarzenbeck was immaculately volleyed home by Ralf Edström in the 24th minute (0–1).

The second half was one of the finest in the whole competition. Beckenbauer's Green Shirts attacked constantly, following the example of their leader. They equalized six minutes after the break thanks to a goal which Wolfgang Overath scored with his right foot (1–1), a rarity for the West German veteran. Then it was down to Rainer Bonhof to raise the roof of the stadium, with a goal straight out of table football: his 52nd-minute, right-foot strike from 16 metres, was deflected by Hellström, and ricocheted off both posts before going in (2–1). But Sweden replied immediately through Roland Sandberg, after a defensive error by Berti Vogts (2–2). Were West Germany going to lose their composure? On the contrary: they reacted as a team, firm, determined and irresistible. Beckenbauer hurled himself to the ground to tackle Inge Ejderstedt. Then, in the 76th minute, Grabowski, left on the bench since the start of the second group stage, but who had just replaced Herzog, scored with a fierce shot after a fine advance by Hölzenbein (3–2). Uli Hoeness made the result safe from the penalty spot in the 89th minute (4–2). If West Germany could beat Poland in their final group match, they would secure a place in the Final.

▲ Poland's Grzegorz Lato (left) finished the tournament as top scorer; Franz Beckenbauer (right) finished as the winning captain.

◥ Poland's Robert Gadocha shoots past Beckenbauer and Berti Vogts but fails to beat keeper Sepp Maier.

Thank you, Maier... and the rain

▲ Heavy rain before and during the crucial West Germany-Poland match meant the pitch in Frankfurt was almost unplayable.

3 JULY 1974

POLAND 0–1 **WEST GERMANY**

MÜLLER 76

Tomaszewski, the goalkeeper who saved two penalties

A famous World Cup exploit: Jan Tomaszewski saved two penalties in a row. The Polish goalkeeper, considered *"the man who eliminated England"* in a masterly performance during a qualifying match at Wembley (1–1), first of all saved a penalty from the Swede Staffan Tapper during the first encounter in the second round. The shot from Tapper, to the right of Tomaszewski, at mid-height and near the post, was perfect. But just before the strike Tomaszewski had made a feint to the left which may perhaps have encouraged Tapper to shoot in the other direction. It was the direction chosen by the goalkeeper with long hair kept in place by a lace in the form of a headband to throw his 1.93 m frame… and push the ball away. Facing West Germany and Uli Hoeness, Tomaszewski repeated his feint to the left. Like Tapper, the powerful West German midfielder, perhaps disconcerted, shot to the right of the Polish keeper, not strongly enough and a bit too much to the centre. Tomaszewski again threw himself to the correct side. He remains to this day, with 63 appearances, the most capped goalkeeper in history of Polish football.

SOMETIMES, the ball stuck in a pool of water, or just refused to bounce, or else it skidded on a patch of slippery grass. It was unthinkable to guide it with your foot, because each soaked square centimetre of the Waldstadion in Frankfurt was liable to bring down the most skilful of ball players. The passes slowed down, then accelerated again … Shortly before the scheduled kick-off, a cloudburst hit Frankfurt, in a Wagnerian deluge streaked with flashes of lightning and claps of thunder. Play was impossible. But it had to go on. Because it was the World Cup.

Floodlights were switched on, even though it was only 5.00 pm, in high summer. Absorbent rollers were applied to a pitch which had become a marsh, but they hardly dried it. Fire engines tried to pump out the thousands of litres of water that had accumulated. After half-an-hour of effort and as long a delay, the whistle for the kick-off of the West Germany-Poland match was blown, but assumptions about the match had changed. In some quarters, Poland were considered the favourites to win. Since the start of the tournament, like Brazil in 1970, they had accumulated five victories from their first five matches. They had scored 15 goals in the tournament to date, an average of three per match. Their solid game, with wingers (Grzegorz Lato and Robert Gadocha) playing like wingers, had allowed them to defeat more famous teams, like Italy in the first group stage (2–1) and Yugoslavia in the second (2–1). But in that rain, and without their centre-forward Andrzej Szarmach, Poland no longer presented the same attacking potential. In the mud, West Germany surpassed themselves, even if the two teams had to use unbelievable energy to overcome the skidding caused by changes of body position, in order to extract themselves from the mud sticking to studs, forgetting the water seeping into boots and the streams of water that must have made their shirts freezing cold.

It was Sepp Maier, in the first half, who produced the most impressive save, flying across the mire to deflect a thunderous free-kick by Gadocha, which was hurtling towards the top corner of the net. After the break, the Germans seemed to gain the advantage, since it was their turn to attack on the driest part of the pitch. With tiredness creeping in, chances became more clear-cut. In the 53rd minute, Bernd Hölzenbein broke into the penalty area, only to be brought down by Władysław Żmuda for a clear penalty. However, Polish goalkeeper Jan Tomaszewski pushed away Uli Hoeness's kick. At the other end of the pitch, Maier, impassable, held on to a thunderbolt of a shot from the Polish captain Kazimierz Deyna. With a quarter of an hour to go, the score was still 0–0. West Germany's hopes of making it to the Final hung in the balance. But, in the 76th minute, Franz Beckenbauer advanced into midfield, and an exchange of passes took place between Hölzenbein and Rainer Bonhof, who fed Gerd Müller in the penalty area. The leading goalscorer at the 1970 World Cup had only scored two goals in the 1974 tournament. Now he added a third.

Poland still had a chance to force a draw, but Maier got an impossible hand to a final shot from Kazimierz Kmiecik. "It all depends on my level of concentration," the whimsical German goalkeeper would say. The next day, when the West German team arrived at Munich airport, where the Final was to be played, Sepp Maier kissed the tarmac, in front of his astonished team members. "I had promised to do it if we got into the Final."

▲ Franz Beckenbauer battles for the ball with Johan
Cruijff during the 1974 Final.

▲ Beckenbauer sends a free-kick over the Dutch wall.

Beckenbauer beats Cruijff

7 JULY 1974

NETHERLANDS 1–2 **WEST GERMANY**

NEESKENS 2 (PEN)   BREITNER 25 (PEN) , MÜLLER 43

PELÉ NEVER played against Puskás in the World Cup, and Platini and Maradona avoided each other in 1982 and 1986, as did Messi and Cristiano Ronaldo in 2006, 2010 and 2014. But Franz Beckenbauer and Johan Cruijff, the two greatest footballers of their time, confronted each other in the supreme competition. It was 7 July 1974, in Munich, and it was the World Cup Final. Throughout the previous week, tension had mounted between the two camps. The West German tabloid press had tried to unearth shocking revelations about the Dutch; Cruijff had complained in return about the meagre quota of seats allotted to Dutch fans… When the final started, only 7,000 supporters of the team in orange took their places in an Olympic Stadium filled with 78,000 spectators who started whistling Cruijff and his team from the kick-off. For one minute Rinus Michels's players passed the ball to each other in front of a static, stunned West Germany. Fifteen Dutch passes without opposition. Cruijff, from the centre circle, accelerated. He shook off Berti Vogts, accelerated again and moved into the West German penalty area, where Uli Hoeness brought him down with a tackle from the side. The English referee, Jack Taylor, blew for a penalty, the first ever awarded in a World Cup Final. Johan Neeskens stepped forward to face Sepp Maier and deceived him with a powerful shot, straight down the middle. The Dutch were now leading 1–0 with only two minutes on the clock, and the Germans had not even touched the ball…

One minute later Berti Vogts, marking Cruijff very tightly, was warned by the referee. The Final seemed almost over. Except that the Dutch, suddenly, no longer attacked. They redoubled their passing, and seemed to taunt their opponents. "We gave the Germans the runaround," Johnny Rep would say later. "It wasn't a conscious tactic, but we started knocking the ball around, and we forgot to score a second goal." West Germany had neither possession nor chances, but stayed in touch with the Dutch. "Going a goal down so early did us good," Beckenbauer later admitted. "The Dutch released the pressure and we got back into the match."

As against Poland in the last encounter of the second round, Bernd Hölzenbein plunged into the Dutch defence. As against Poland, he was brought down, a controversial foul by Wim Jansen. Penalty. Against Jan Tomaszewski, Uli Hoeness had failed to score. Authoritatively, coldly, Paul Breitner took the ball. Jan Jongbloed, in the Dutch goal, tried a feint. With an air of indifference, the German right-back side-footed the ball into the corner of the net. It was 1–1 after 25 minutes.

The Dutch machine seized up. First Vogts went past Cruijff to spread terror in a counter-attack and, fed by Jürgen Grabowski, shot at Jongbloed, who managed to pull off an astonishing save. Then it was Beckenbauer, with a finely taken free-kick, who forced the Dutch goalkeeper to make an athletic save under the crossbar. Two minutes before the interval, Rainer Bonhof charged down the right wing and centred for Gerd Müller. "The Bomber" stopped the ball with an exaggerated action that looked like a miskick, then hooked it from behind him and low across Jongbloed to put West Germany 2–1 up.

Even though there was an entire half of the match left to play, it seemed as though the Dutch were starting to get on each other's nerves. At half-time Cruijff was cautioned by Mr Taylor for complaining too strongly about the treatment being inflicted on him by Vogts. Rob Rensenbrink, carrying a thigh injury from the match against Brazil, but played by Rinus Michels with presumptuous optimism, had to leave the field. René van de Kerkhof took his place. Then the exhausted Wim Rijsbergen was replaced by Theo de Jong. And Cruijff? To escape Vogts, he pulled back, moved around behind his own midfielders and went missing in attack. "It was the first time we were playing against a team which had perfected a very rigorous system and which knew how to apply it to the letter," he would reckon. "For our part, we hadn't got a player like Gerd Müller." But the Dutch did create a few chances. Breitner cleared the ball off the line following a Dutch corner; a tremendous volley from Neeskens was kept out by Maier; Rep missed when he was put clean through by Cruijff… And then nerves took over and the game broke up: 41 free-kicks were given, 27 of them in favour of West Germany. The Germans had the final flourish. A goal was disallowed for offside against Gerd Müller, who wasn't. A penalty was not given for another foul by Jansen on Hölzenbein. But what did it matter? The final whistle sounded. Cruijff shook his head, hands on hips, head down. The best attacking player in the world would never be a world champion. The Germans hugged each other. Franz Beckenbauer, of all people, ran towards the fans. He had just delivered West Germany, at home, its second World Cup.

Captain's armband worn by Franz Beckenbauer during the 1975-76 season.

▲ **FIFA World Football Museum collection.**

Minus a stripe

All the players in the World Cup were equipped by Adidas. But there was no question of Johan Cruijff (No. 14), under contract with his own equipment supplier, of wearing the brand with three stripes. He would, therefore, play the whole competition, including the Final, with a shirt and shorts made specially for him, and having… only two stripes.

Gerd Müller moved ahead of Just Fontaine

"I am not in the least afraid for my record. The time has passed for goals galore," Just Fontaine had declared midway through the competition. The highest goalscorer of all time in a World Cup (13 goals for France in 1958) would certainly not be dispossessed of his auspicious record, since the goal by Grzegorz Lato in the match for third place crowned the Pole as the best goalscorer in the 1974 finals with "only" seven goals. But Gerd Müller, thanks to his winning goal in the Final, passed Fontaine in another list: the total number of goals scored in World Cup tournaments. The German striker finished with 14: ten in 1970 and four in 1974, whereas Fontaine played in just one tournament. Only the Brazilian Ronaldo (15 goals) and then the German Miroslav Klose (16) would subsequently exceed Gerd Müller's total.

3

Second in 1966, third in 1970 and first in 1974, West Germany appeared on the podium for the third time in a row. Five German players concurrently held gold, silver and bronze medals: Franz Beckenbauer, Wolfgang Overath, Jürgen Grabowski, Horst-Dieter Höttges and Sepp Maier.

PLAY-OFF FOR THIRD PLACE

Lato, one more for the road

▲ Grzegorz Lato scores the only goal of the game, his seventh of the finals.

6 JULY 1974

BRAZIL 0–1 POLAND

LATO 76

With their last group matches respectively lost against the Netherlands (0–2) and West Germany (0–1), the Brazilians and Poles were wiped out, both physically and mentally. With a day's recovery less than the two finalists, it was clear, on the turf of the Olympic Stadium in Munich, that the players were exhausted. Brazil only distinguished themselves with a few fancy touches from Rivelino (who hit the post in the second half), spurts by Zé Maria and feeble shots by an attacking Valdomiro-Jairzinho-Dirceu trio of chronic ineffectiveness (it was Rivelino who finished as the top Brazilian goalscorer in the tournament with three goals in seven matches). The Polish side attacked as always via the wings, but without much success.

Only two moments marked out the encounter. The first came from Henryk Kasperczak. In the 73rd minute, during a Brazilian counter-attack led by Mirandinha, the Polish midfielder, running alongside him, held him back by the arm for 30 metres. "Footballers using their arms like that, what a scandal!" people immediately sounded off indignantly… in those innocent and blessed times. The second moment was a masterpiece by Grzegorz Lato. In the 76th minute, the young (24 years old) but balding Polish right-winger received the ball 60 metres from the Brazilian goal. He took off, beat Alfredo, entered the penalty area and scored with a cross-shot (1–0). It was his seventh goal in the competition and the finest. He was its sole creator, but always attributed his success to the Polish squad. "We had an exceptional team, on the pitch and off it," he would say in 2001. "The atmosphere in it contributed a lot to our success. Add to it the genius of Kazimierz Deyna, for me one of the best footballers in history, the great game of Andrzej Szarmach, my all-time mate, the raids on the left-wing by Robert Gadocha, the saves by Jan Tomaszewski, without forgetting the knowledge of Kazimierz Gorski, our manager, plus my seven goals, and you have the ingredients of our success." Since 1974, only the Brazilian Ronaldo, in 2002, has scored more goals in a World Cup tournament (eight to Lato's seven). The Pole would score two more in 1978 and once in 1982.

1978

In a winter World Cup, Argentina were greeted by a snowstorm of tickertape at the start of their matches, one of the enduring football images. And the euphoric mood of the nation carried the team to the Final. The Netherlands joined them there, once again as outsiders facing the home country. In stoppage time, Rob Rensenbrink hit a post for the Dutch. And Argentina won the trophy with two goals in extra-time.

A competition to serve the regime?

ARGENTINA WAS CHOSEN to host the 1978 World Cup in 1966. But ten years later, on 24 March 1976, Isabel Perón's government was overthrown in a military coup d'état. The chief of the armed forces, General Jorge Rafael Videla, then ruled with an iron fist. Opponents were tortured and many simply disappeared. At the start of 1978, Amnesty International reported some 10,000 murders, 15,000 disappearances, and 8,000 prisoners.

Throughout Europe, the question of boycotting the event was raised. The Swedish parliament asked its football association to state its position. The Swedish Football Association put the question to its players, and the players chose to go to Argentina. Germans Sepp Maier and Paul Breitner took a public stand against Videla's dictatorship, while three-time Golden Ball winner Johan Cruijff announced that he would be pulling out of the World Cup in solidarity with the

regime's victims (although later on, in late 1977, the Dutchman admitted that his decision was the result of an attempted kidnapping at home in Barcelona). In France, a protest movement was starting to gather momentum, supported by notable left-wing figures such as Jean-Paul Sartre, Louis Aragon and Yves Montand.

A notable feature of the finals were the daily marches by the Mothers of the Plaza de Mayo, protesting about the disappearance of their sons. They were glad of the publicity. Manager César Luis Menotti, who made no bones about his ideological opposition to the dictatorship, stood his ground during his pre-Final interview. "We are the people, we come from the victimized classes and we represent the only thing that is legitimate in this country – football. We are not playing for the expensive seats full of military officers. We represent freedom, not the dictatorship." In 2010, Videla was convicted for crimes against humanity and died in prison three years later.

◄ An ecstatic Daniel Passarella, the Argentine captain, after his team's win over the Netherlands in the Final.

▲ General Jorge Videla, senior commander of the Argentine Army, during the 1978 World Cup's opening ceremony.

Argentina '78

Story of the qualifiers

Tunisia makes its debut

SEVERAL NEW African and Asian countries were formed in the 1970s following decolonization. As a result, 95 national teams appeared in the qualifying rounds of the 1978 World Cup, with 107 having entered. Nine European countries made it through to the finals (Netherlands, France, Poland, Sweden, Scotland, Italy, Spain and defending champions Germany, along with Hungary, who won the Europe versus South America intercontinental play-off against Bolivia (6–0 in the home leg, 3–2 away). However, England – who had suffered only one defeat in six matches and came second in Group 2 behind Italy on goal difference – Portugal, Czechoslovakia and the USSR all missed out on a spot. The place reserved for Africa went to Tunisia for the first time, ahead of Egypt and Nigeria. South America had three representatives – Brazil, Peru, and Argentina as the host country – with Uruguay failing to qualify. Having remained undefeated throughout the qualifiers, Iran (Asia and Oceania zone) earned a place in the World Cup for the first time. At home, Mexico breezed through the qualifiers for the North, Central American and Caribbean zone (with five wins out of five) ahead of Haiti and El Salvador.

Letter from the Tunisian Football Association to FIFA, announcing the squad list for a qualifying match against Egypt in December 1977.

▶ **FIFA World Football Museum collection.**

First group stage

GROUP 1		
ITA	2–1	FRA
ARG	2–1	HUN
ITA	3–1	HUN
ARG	2–1	FRA
FRA	3–1	HUN
ARG	0–1	ITA

	W	D	L	+	–	PTS
ITA	3	0	0	6	2	6
ARG	2	0	1	4	3	4
FRA	1	0	2	5	5	2
HUN	0	0	3	3	8	0

GROUP 2		
POL	0–0	FRG
TUN	3–1	MEX
POL	1–0	TUN
FRG	6–0	MEX
TUN	0–0	FRG
POL	3–1	MEX

	W	D	L	+	–	PTS
POL	2	1	0	4	1	5
FRG	1	2	0	6	0	4
TUN	1	1	1	3	2	3
MEX	0	0	3	2	12	0

GROUP 3		
BRA	1–1	SWE
AUT	2–1	ESP
AUT	1–0	SWE
BRA	0–0	ESP
BRA	1–0	AUT
ESP	1–0	SWE

	W	D	L	+	–	PTS
AUT	2	0	1	3	2	4
BRA	1	2	0	2	1	4
ESP	1	1	1	2	2	3
SWE	0	1	2	1	3	1

GROUP 4		
NED	3–0	IRN
PER	3–1	SCO
NED	0–0	PER
SCO	1–1	IRN
SCO	3–2	NED
PER	4–1	IRN

	W	D	L	+	–	PTS
PER	2	1	0	7	2	5
NED	1	1	1	5	3	3
SCO	1	1	1	5	6	3
IRN	0	1	2	2	8	1

Second group stage

GROUP A		
ITA	0–0	FRG
NED	5–1	AUT
FRG	2–2	NED
ITA	1–0	AUT
NED	2–1	ITA
AUT	3–2	FRG

	W	D	L	+	–	PTS
NED	2	1	0	9	4	5
ITA	1	1	1	2	2	3
FRG	0	2	1	4	5	2
AUT	1	0	2	4	8	2

GROUP B		
BRA	3–0	PER
ARG	2–0	POL
POL	1–0	PER
ARG	0–0	BRA
BRA	3–1	POL
ARG	6–0	PER

	W	D	L	+	–	PTS
ARG	2	1	0	8	0	5
BRA	2	1	0	6	1	5
POL	1	0	2	2	5	2
PER	0	0	3	0	10	0

Final and play-off for third place

THIRD-PLACE PLAYOFF

BRA	2–1	ITA

FINAL

ARG	3–1 A.E.T.	NED

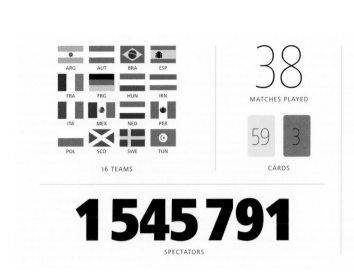

ARG AUT BRA ESP
FRA FRG HUN IRN
ITA MEX NED PER
POL SCO SWE TUN

16 TEAMS

38
MATCHES PLAYED

59 3
CARDS

1 545 791
SPECTATORS

GAUCHITO
OFFICIAL MASCOT

Argentina '78
OFFICIAL LOGO

ARGENTINA
WINNERS

MARIO KEMPES ×6
LEADING GOALSCORER

2.7
AVERAGE GOALS
PER MATCH

TANGO DURLAST
OFFICIAL BALL

Host cities and stadiums

A Monumental renovation

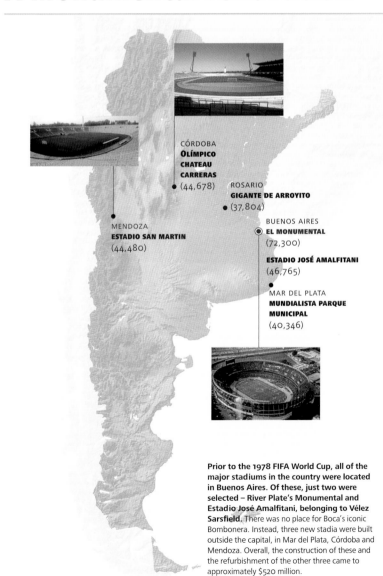

CÓRDOBA
OLÍMPICO CHATEAU CARRERAS
(44,678)

ROSARIO
GIGANTE DE ARROYITO
(37,804)

MENDOZA
ESTADIO SAN MARTIN
(44,480)

BUENOS AIRES
EL MONUMENTAL
(72,300)

ESTADIO JOSÉ AMALFITANI
(46,765)

MAR DEL PLATA
MUNDIALISTA PARQUE MUNICIPAL
(40,346)

Prior to the 1978 FIFA World Cup, all of the major stadiums in the country were located in Buenos Aires. Of these, just two were selected – River Plate's Monumental and Estadio José Amalfitani, belonging to Vélez Sarsfield. There was no place for Boca's iconic Bombonera. Instead, three new stadia were built outside the capital, in Mar del Plata, Córdoba and Mendoza. Overall, the construction of these and the refurbishment of the other three came to approximately $520 million.

Papelitos

A TRADITION IN ARGENTINA and South America, these little scraps of paper, cut up by supporters and thrown from the stands, highlighted the party atmosphere among Argentinian spectators, but littered the pitch, particularly during the Final.

Argentine 20 peso pieces in copper, nickel and aluminium, specially minted in 1977 for the World Cup.

▲ **FIFA World Football Museum collection.**

▲▲ Nejib Ghommidh in an aerial battle with Mexico's Antonio de la Torre.

▲ Players and coaching staff congratulate one another after the match.

◥ Ali Kaabi and Tarak Dhiab celebrate the first African victory at a World Cup.

Tarak makes his name

In the match against Mexico, Tunisian number 10 Tarak Dhiab dazzled with his technical finesse. The African Footballer of the Year for 1977, nicknamed the "Emperor of Football," charmed the crowds with the quality of his passes and the precision of his left foot. Despite not scoring himself, he provided the assist for Ghommidh to score Tunisia's second goal. At 23, Tarak was both an altruist and a strong player in his own right, making him one of the breakthrough stars of the tournament.

A first World Cup win for Africa

2 JUNE 1978

TUNISIA 3–1 **MEXICO**

KAABI 55, GHOMMIDH 79, DOUIEB 87   VÁZQUEZ AYALA 45 (PEN)

TUNISIA'S WORLD CUP victory on 2 June marked a historic moment for African football. The best result by an African team up to that point had been in 1970, when Morocco clinched a draw with Bulgaria. It looked to be going badly in Rosario for Tunisia when they conceded a penalty that was put away by Mexico's captain Arturo Vázquez Ayala, at the end of the first half (0–1). But the second half saw the North Africans on the offensive. The goals followed from Ali Kaabi, Nejib Ghommidh, and Mokhtar Dhouib (3–1). Abdelmajid Chetali's men achieved a monumental feat, and the consistency, creativity and discipline they had displayed during the qualifying rounds was on display.

Tunisia had already knocked out Morocco, Algeria and Guinea before winning a round robin against Egypt and Nigeria to secure their place in Argentina. "Ten matches to qualify. Two years of training and all sorts of sacrifices. For us it's a success. And as our coach keeps telling us, we've already won because we're here," said Ali Kaabi before the match. Tunisia were beaten by Poland during their second game (0–1) but did well to hold defending champions West Germany to a 0–0 draw in their third match. Third in Group 2, they were eliminated, but they left the tournament with their heads held high. "The world tended to make fun of African football. I think that's over now," said manager Chetali.

Lacombe scores after just 31 seconds

2 JUNE 1978

ITALY ▌ 2–1 ▌ **FRANCE**

ROSSI 29, ZACCARELLI 54   LACOMBE 1

THE FIRST GOAL of the tournament was scored during the match at Mar del Plata on 2 June by Frenchman Bernard Lacombe after a mere 31 seconds of play. The Italians took the kick-off, with Didier Six soon outflanking them on the left and delivering a perfect curling cross for Lacombe to head the ball wide of Dino Zoff. It still wasn't the fastest goal in World Cup history – that accolade was held by Czechoslovakia's Václav Mašek, who opened the scoring on 7 June 1962 against Mexico, at Viña del Mar in Chile, after just 15 seconds of play.

▲ Bernard Lacombe, scoring after just 31 seconds, celebrates with team-mates Henri Michel and Christian Dalger.

Gauchito superstar

Keyrings depicting the mascot Gauchito, named after the famous Gauchos – cowboys from the Argentine Pampas.

▲ **FIFA World Football Museum collection.**

Spain weathers the storm

7 JUNE 1978

BRAZIL 0–0 **SPAIN**

Having been beaten by Austria in their opening match (1–2) Spain's campaign was left hanging in the balance, especially as they faced Brazil in the second round of games in group 3. The Brazilians had drawn their opening match (1–1 with Sweden), and they were under early pressure from a determined Spanish team. The poor state of the pitch in Mar del Plata contributed to a scrappy first half, though it was not to blame when Brazil almost took the lead after 28 minutes. Edinho's deep cross from the left was met by Spanish defender Antonio Olmo, whose looping header hit his own crossbar before falling into the grateful arms of goalkeeper Miguel Ángel. Not long after, Nelihno's free kick from 20 metres out looked to be on target before curling away wide of the post.

After half-time Zico found the perfect gap to Reinaldo, who was blocked by Miguel Ángel. Another spectacular long-range free-kick from Nelinho saw the Spanish keeper pull off a spectacular save as Brazil dominated the half. But there were no goals and it was the Spanish who almost stole it near the end. Santillana headed down a long Francisco Uria cross into the path of an unmarked Julio Cardeñosa. Brazilian keeper Leão was out of position and Cardeñosa had just Amaral on the line to beat but shot straight at the defender. Leal followed up but by then the Leão was back to save. In their third match, Brazil beat the already qualified Austria (1–0), their victory seeing them through to the next stage. Despite winning 1–0 against Sweden, Spain finished in third place and were out.

▲ Scottish Manager Ally MacLeod, after his side's loss to Peru.

▶ Peru's Teófilo Cubillas scores from a free-kick with the outside of his foot. The Scottish wall formed by Kenneth Burns, Stuart Kennedy, Archie Gemmill, Kenny Dalglish and Lou Macari is beaten.

▼ The Peruvian players celebrate.

MacLeod's hopes dashed

3 JUNE 1978

PERU 🇵🇪 3–1 🏴󠁧󠁢󠁳󠁣󠁴󠁿 **SCOTLAND**

CUETO 43, CUBILLAS 70, 76   JORDAN 19

6711

The record for the number of press passes handed out to newspaper, radio and television journalists and photographers was beaten in Argentina, with 6,711 passes. In 1974 in Germany, 4,616 had been granted.

FOLLOWING THEIR impressive performances during qualification, in particular knocking out European champions Czechoslovakia, Scotland went into the tournament with high hopes. The team featured stars such as Graeme Souness and Kenny Dalglish, who had just brought home the 1978 European Cup for Liverpool (1–0 in the final against Bruges). Manager Ally MacLeod confidently announced his intention to return from Argentina, "with at least a medal", and when asked what he planned to do after the World Cup he replied simply, "retain it!" But things did not go as planned. Scotland crumbled during their opening match against Peru, losing 3–1, despite having taken the lead through a 19th-minute goal from Joe Jordan. "Our main fault was not having marked Cubillas well," remarked MacLeod. Cubillas had scored twice. After a mediocre 1–1 draw against Iran, Scotland succeeded in beating the Netherlands 3–2 thanks to a memorable goal from Archie Gemmill, who beat three men before lifting the ball over the goalkeeper. Yet it was not quite enough to see the Scots through to the second group stage: they were eliminated on goal difference, with the Netherlands, a team they had beaten, going through at their expense. It was a heartbreaking finish. "I've still got a lot to learn," said MacLeod at the end of the tournament.

Kubala's triple citizenship

1

Sweden came bottom of the overall table with only one goal, and were knocked out in the first round. Spain, Mexico and Iran scored only twice each.

▶ The Swedish captain, Björn Nordqvist, during his side's group match against Spain.

L ÁSZLÓ KUBALA, Spain's manager for the 1978 tournament, was also the only footballer to play for three different countries: Czechoslovakia (1946–47), his native Hungary (1948), and Spain (1953–61), for whom he won 19 caps and scored 11 goals. However, the former Barcelona forward never played in the World Cup finals.

▼ Goalkeeper Ronnie Hellström collects the ball while Spain's Santillana looks on.

Nordqvist makes it 111

11 JUNE 1978

SPAIN 🇪🇸 1–0 🇸🇪 **SWEDEN**

ASENSI 75

B JÖRN NORDQVIST was hoping to leave on a high after his third World Cup with Sweden, having already played in 1970 and 1974. The 1–1 draw with Brazil in Mar del Plata on 3 June saw the Swedish captain's win his 109th cap, a new European record. His 110th was against Austria (0–1) and his 111th against Spain (0–1). Sadly it was not enough to get past the first round. By the end of the year the 35-year-old centre-back had racked up a total of 115 caps, having started his international career in 1963.

▲ Iraj Danayfar dribbles past Archie Gemmill before scoring Iran's first-ever goal in the World Cup.

▲ Mohammad Sadeqi congratulates Iraj Danayfar on his goal.

Iran's premiere

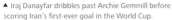

7 JUNE 1978

SCOTLAND ✕ 1–1 ▭ **IRAN**

ESKANDARIAN 43 (O.G.)   DANAYFAR 60

SINCE THE 1960S, Iran had dominated Asian football, having taken home the AFC Asian Cup three times (1968, 1972 and 1976), and qualified for their first FIFA World Cup by topping a group consisting of South Korea, Kuwait, Australia and Hong Kong (recording six wins and two draws in the eight matches they played). In their first match at the 1978 World Cup they suffered a predictable 3–0 defeat against the Netherlands, the 1974 runners-up. Iran's second match took place on 7 June in Córdoba. Spurred on by their keeper Nasser Hejazi and captain Ali Parvin, they drew 1–1 with Scotland despite falling behind in the 43rd minute following defender Andranik Eskandarian's own goal. But Iran fought back, and equalized in the 60th minute with a shot from a tight angle by Iraj Danayfar. They hung on for a draw and secured their first-ever point at a World Cup finals tournament. And although they went on to lose again to Peru (1–4), the Iranian team had displayed real

progress. "We have learned a lot in Argentina, not all of it pleasant," said manager Heshmat Mohajerani. "Our players are amateurs and have never experienced anything like this before. They rubbed shoulders with the best teams in the world, sampling the atmosphere of the big time for the first time. Now we must use the experience we have gained as we begin the four-year cycle all over again. We cannot afford to rest on our laurels. We must keep playing top teams if we want to carry on improving." Although Iran seemed to be capable of holding their own on the international scene, the Iranian Revolution began five months later. The National Championships stopped and football, which was considered to be a Western sport by the new authorities, was barely tolerated. Despite qualifying for the 1980 Olympics, the national team was not allowed to participate. It was a blow for Iranian football, and the national team did not appear at a World Cup finals again until 1998.

Rensenbrink is one in a thousand

His goal against Scotland on 11 June in Mendoza earned Dutchman Rob Rensenbrink a place in World Cup history. Following a tackle on Johnny Rep, Austrian referee Erich Linemayr awarded a penalty. The Dutchman scored with a low shot to the left, allowing his team to open the scoring with the 1,000th goal in the World Cup finals. Yet Anderlecht's winger barely even batted an eyelid at his historic feat.

11 JUNE 1978

SCOTLAND ✕ 3–2 ▭ **NETHERLANDS**

DALGLISH 44   RENSENBRINK 34 (PEN)
GEMMILL 46 (PEN), 68   REP 71

▶ Holland's Rob Rensenbrink scores the 1000th goal in the history of the World Cup finals – a penalty against Scotland.

Les Bleus in green and white

10 JUNE 1978

FRANCE ▮▮ 3–1 ▬HUNGARY

LOPEZ 22, BERDOLL 37,   ZOMBORI 41
ROCHETEAU 42

N THE WARM-UP for their third match, the French – who had already been eliminated from the tournament – found themselves wearing white shirts. The reason? Their normal shirts had been left in their previous hotel 400 kilometres away. But Hungary were also playing in white, as FIFA had planned for France to be in blue. French official Henri Patrelle was duly dispatched in a police car to search the city of Mar del Plata for a set of football shirts. He finally found some at local club CA Kimberley. The match started 45 minutes late, with France wearing the green-and-white strip of the club from the suburbs of Mar del Plata. The numbers on the shirts didn't match the numbers on the players' shorts, but France still went on to win the game 3–1.

▲ Hungary's András Törőcsik manages to shake off France's Christian Lopez.

Cubillas racks up the records

11 JUNE 1978

PERU ▮•▮ 4–1 ▬IRAN

VELÁSQUEZ 2   ROWSHAN 41
CUBILLAS 36 (PEN), 39 (PEN), 79

RGENTINA 1978 was the second World Cup for Teófilo Cubillas, who had turned heads in 1970 by scoring five goals. In his first match on 3 June in Cordoba, the Peruvian number 10 performed an astonishing move, taking a free-kick with the outside of his right foot, floating it over the Scottish wall and landing it in the top corner of Alan Rough's goal (3–1 in the 77th minute). "Seeing the positioning of the wall and the keeper, I was convinced that I could get the ball in from this unexpected angle," explained Cubillas, who had scored another superb goal six minutes earlier (2–1). "What is more, I managed not to give it too much power." On 11 June, a hat-trick against Iran (4–1) made him the first footballer to score five goals in two separate World Cups. However, his second-round matches were less successful. "It was a surprise to lose our last three matches and I know that there has been a lot of talk about that," said the so-called "Peruvian Pelé". "But we lost to Brazil and to Argentina, the home side who went on to win the competition."

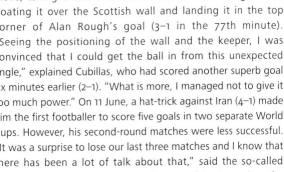

◀ Peruvian forward Teófilo Cubillas scored a hat-trick against Iran.

3

Over the course of the tournament, only three players received red cards. They were Hungarians András Törőcsik and Tibor Nyilasi, and Dutchman Dick Nanninga.

145

▲ Brazilian coach
Cláudio Coutinho.

▲ Brazil's Gil battles it out
with Argentina's Américo
Gallego.

"My team is the moral victor of this tournament."

Claudio Coutinho,
Brazilian coach.

Should first-round results count in the second round?

"A national coach said that in order to encourage the teams to win all of their first-round matches, these results should be taken into account during the second round," said FIFA's technical report. "This could be reasonable if the groups in the first round were balanced and all of the teams had a good change of qualifying. But if, as was the case in West Germany in 1974, certain groups contained weaker teams, the teams that qualified from these groups would have an unfair advantage during the second round of the competition." The idea, therefore, did not take off.

Brazil's elimination leaves a sour taste

18 JUNE 1978

ARGENTINA 0–0 🇧🇷 BRAZIL

AFTER AN AVERAGE first round (two draws followed by a 1–0 victory against Austria), Brazil found themselves in Group B. They kicked off the second round with a solid win against Peru (3–0) before facing Argentina on 18 June in Rosario. It was a match that was as violent as it was defensive, featuring no fewer than 59 free-kicks. Following the success of the class of 1970, manager Cláudio Coutinho had had trouble finding the right formula. A timid Brazil played uncharacteristically poorly, while the team's stars, Dirceu and Zico, were simply not on their best form. An injured, ageing, 32-year-old Rivelino spent most of his time on the bench. To reach the Final, Brazil had to finish first out of the four Group B teams. During their third match against Poland, they won 3–1 (thanks to a double from Roberto Dinamite), but had to wait for Argentina's game against Peru to learn their fate. "The Argentines will know the results of our match," argued Coutinho. "And they will therefore know exactly what they need to do and how many goals they need to score to reach the final." The Brazilian manager was right. Later on that night, Argentina knew that they had to beat Peru by four goals, won 6–0, and qualified thanks to their superior goal difference (+8 versus +5). Brazil were knocked out of the tournament without having lost a match. They went on to take third place by beating Italy 2–1 on 24 June in Buenos Aires, but a frustrated Coutinho considered his team to be the "moral victors" of the tournament.

Osvaldo Ardiles, a man who preferred to keep out of the spotlight was one of the stars of the Argentina team.

Ardiles: the invisible star

TOGETHER WITH Ubaldo Fillol, Daniel Passarella and Mario Kempes, his friend since the age of 11 and his room-mate during the 1978 World Cup, Osvaldo "Ossie" Ardiles was a stalwart of the Argentinian team. "My position is difficult to describe: half playmaker, half defender. Not a wide player as they have nowadays, but a true midfielder that you rarely see in the penalty area. My job was to relieve the number 10 [of his defensive duties] to help him create pressure," said Ardiles, nicknamed the "Python" because of his serpentine movements that deprived his "prey" of the ball.

As one of Menotti's key players, Ardiles played every match in the tournament except his team's 6–0 victory over Peru in the final round of matches in the second group stage. A comparative featherweight in football teams,

standing at a mere 1.69 m, the Huracán midfielder had been called up to the national team as a 23-year-old in 1975 and had gone on to become a lynchpin of the Argentina side. He symbolized intelligent play, accurate passing and anticipation. "The loss to Italy [1–0 during the first group stage] forced us to play the second round in Rosario, in a stadium that suited us better than the one in Buenos Aires," claimed Ardiles. "Gradually, we began to believe we could do it. We were depending more on the team than on the individuals. But there really was a lot of pressure and expectation on the team."

Ardiles signed for English club Tottenham Hotspur shortly after the tournament (along with compatriot Ricki Villa) and went on to become a cult figure during a ten-year stint at the North London club.

A controversial victory

21 JUNE 1978		
ARGENTINA	6–0	PERU

KEMPES 21, 49
TARANTINI 43, LUQUE 50, 72
HOUSEMAN 67

Rarely has there been so much conjecture about a single match. When Argentina began their third and final Group B match against Peru, they knew that they needed to win by four goals to reach the Final. On 21 June in Rosario, César Luis Menotti's men faced a strangely absent opponent, with Mario Kempes and Leopoldo Luque scoring twice each. Suspicion fell on the shoulders of Ramón Quiroga, the Peruvian keeper, who had held Argentinian citizenship until a few months before the start of the tournament. Other rumours had it that money had changed hands between the two countries, that the match was thrown to partially write off Peruvian debt, that Peru had been gifted thousands of tonnes of grain, and even that the Argentinian dictatorship had sent political opponents to Peru so that the military junta could "disappear" them. César Luis Menotti's team denied that any such bribery took place. "We simply played our best match of the tournament," said Leopoldo Luque.

▲ Hans Krankl scores
despite the best efforts
of Sepp Maier.

▲▲ Tackle by Germany's
Bernd Hölzenbein on
Austrian Willy Kreuz.

▲ The last international
match for German captain
Berti Vogts.

Germany under no more illusions

21 JUNE 1978

AUSTRIA 3–2 **WEST GERMANY**

VOGTS 59 (O.G.), KRANKL 66, 87   RUMMENIGGE 19, HÖLZENBEIN 72

DESPITE BEING the defending champions, West Germany never really got into the swing of things during this tournament, with two 0–0 draws in the first round against Poland and Tunisia. It was hardly a surprise given that the big names (Wolfgang Overath, Uli Hoeness, Gerd Müller, Günter Netzer and the iconic "Kaiser" Franz Beckenbauer) had left the *national team*, while Paul Breitner decided to take a break. In this transitional period, the pressure rested on the shoulders of striker Karl-Heinz Rummenigge. During the second group stage, after two more draws against Italy (0–0) and the Netherlands (2–2), the West Germans were still in with a chance of qualifying for what would have been their fifth Final. But they needed to beat Austria on 21 June in Cordoba and hope the other result went their way. Instead, two goals from Krankl and an own goal from captain Berti Vogts led to a 3–2 defeat. It marked the last international match for both Vogts and manager Helmut Schoen. With two draws and one loss, West Germany finished bottom of Group A. For Austria however, it was their first win over the Germans since 1931.

Happel versus Senekowitsch

14 JUNE 1978

AUSTRIA 1–5 **NETHERLANDS**

OBERMAYER 80   BRANDTS 6, RENSENBRINK 35 (PEN)
                REP 36, 53,
                W. VAN DE KERKHOF 82

THE NETHERLANDS' second-round victory over Austria on 14 June in Córdoba led to a surprising head to head: Austrian Ernst Happel, who was now managing the Netherlands, found himself facing his fellow countryman Helmut Senekowitsch, who had been Austria manager since 1976. Twenty years earlier, as players, the two men had represented Austria in the 1958 World Cup in Sweden (although they were knocked out in the first round), with Senekowitsch up front and Happel in defence.

▲ Italian Roberto Bettega and Dutchman Ernie Brandts scramble to catch the ball.

"I didn't live up to the public's expectations."

Dino Zoff,
Italy goalkeeper

Even the best goalkeeper in the world can make mistakes. This was certainly the case for Italian keeper Dino Zoff against the Netherlands. "We had a great World Cup, even though, on a personal level, I didn't live up to the public's expectations. They still hold that long shot from Arie Haan against me. I admit that we could have done better: reaching the Final, for example, even if winning it would have been a challenge. Argentina were always very strong and they were playing at home." Zoff, who only let in six goals in seven matches during the 1978 FIFA World Cup, also had his highlights in Argentina. "I remember that spectacular dive against Germany [to stop a volley]. People had always thought I wasn't very unrestrained or spontaneous. That was my response."

Double Dutch

21 JUNE 1978

ITALY 1-2 **NETHERLANDS**

BRANDTS 19 (o.g.)   BRANDTS 49, HAAN 76

HAVING BEATEN AUSTRIA 5–1, before being kept in check by West Germany (2–2), the Dutch needed to win to be certain of reaching their second consecutive Final when they faced Italy in Buenos Aires on 21 June. Things got off to a bad start for them as Ernie Brandts, while attempting to stop Roberto Bettega from challenging goalkeeper Piet Schrijvers, sent the ball into his own net from outside the penalty box to hand the Italians the lead (0–1). However, four minutes after the start of the second half, Brandts made up for his error by finding the top corner of Dino Zoff's goal with a bullet off his right foot. Another long-distance shot – from more than 35 metres – by Arie Haan put the Netherlands in the lead (2–1). The Anderlecht midfielder caught

Juventus keeper Zoff off guard with a fierce shot that bounced off the post before landing in the back of the net. "It was a really beautiful goal, particularly as I'd already scored a long-distance goal three days earlier against Germany. I received a pass, ran about five metres with the ball and, seeing that no-one was tackling me, thought I could score a goal. It worked," recalled Haan. "Scoring against such a skilled keeper from a great footballing nation who had trained so many talented goalies was a really special moment." Thanks to this goal, the Dutch finished top of Group A with 5 points, ahead of Italy, to qualify for the Final against Argentina, which was due to take place in Buenos Aires four days later.

PLAY-OFF FOR THIRD PLACE

▲ Brazilian forwards struggle with the Italian defence.

24 JUNE 1978

BRAZIL 2–1 **ITALY**

NELINHO 64, DIRCEU 72   CAUSIO 38

Brazil were disappointed not to reach the Final. Along with their suspicions over Argentina's 6–0 win over Peru, had Zico's "winner" against Sweden been allowed to stand, instead of being disallowed by Clive Thomas who blew for time as the ball was on its way in, Brazil would have found themselves in a different group to Argentina. Nevertheless, manager Claudio Coutinho's men took the play-off for third place seriously. After Italy's Franco Causio scored in the first half, Nelinho equalized with a shot from the outside of his right foot. The ball floated into the side of the net behind Dino Zoff (1–1, 64th minute). A few minutes after missing a volley from the right, Dirceu took aim at Zoff from the left with a masterful half-volley from outside the penalty area (2–1, 72nd minute). Leão's unbeaten team (four victories, three draws), took third place.

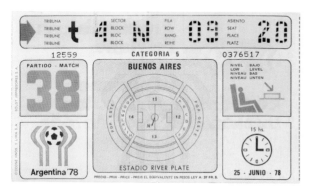

Tickets for the 1978
FIFA World Cup Final.

▲ FIFA World Football
Museum collection.

▲▲ Argentina's goal-
keeper Fillol holds on
to cross to bring an
end to a Dutch attack.

▲ Mario Kempes, centre,
scores the second
Argentina goal of the final.

"Why don't you get rid of the moustache?"

Luis Cesar Menotti to Mario Kempes

**"I couldn't be bothered with the whole
shaving-every-couple-of-days routine,'
Kempes recalled.** "After nearly three weeks I had
a pretty decent beard and moustache going. "I
played like that in our first two games, but shaved
the beard off before our third." Yet he had not
scored a single goal. "We were heading back to
our camp after that match, thinking ahead to our
next assignment in Rosario, when the coach said
to me, 'Mario, why don't you get rid of the
moustache and see if your luck changes?' The
coach had been over to see me before the World
Cup to see how I was getting on in Valencia. So he
said to me, 'You didn't have a beard or moustache
when you were playing for Valencia, so why don't
you shave when we get to Rosario and you might
start scoring again?' I don't know if it was luck or
coincidence, but it marked the start of a new
chapter for me. I started scoring goals during the
first match of the second round against Poland in
Rosario, then against Peru and the Netherlands."

Kempes on Argentinian team spirit

25 JUNE 1978

NETHERLANDS ⬜ 1–3 A.E.T. ⬛ ARGENTINA

NANNINGA 82   KEMPES 37°, 104, BERTONI 115

ALTHOUGH HE SCORED SIX GOALS,
making him the tournament's leaing
goalscorer, Mario Kempes almost
didn't make the cut. The military junta
wanted César Luis Menotti to select only
players from Argentinian teams, but the
manager stood his ground. The former Rosario Central forward had been in Spain playing for Valencia for two seasons and had
ended each of those seasons as the top
scorer in the championship. When he arrived
in Argentina, Kempes, 23, encountered a
tightly-knit group. "I joined up not long
before the World Cup: I landed in Argentina
on 8 May and we had our first game on 2
June," recalled Kempes, who had played in
the 1974 finals. "My team-mates, in contrast,
had been training together since February.
But the best thing was that as soon as I
arrived, they treated me as if I'd been there
for the previous three months. There was
no selfishness, no adverse reaction and none
of those sneaks who run blabbing to the
coach to tell him what everybody has been
saying. Everybody was free to talk to the
coach or just get on with their lives." Bolstered
by this team spirit, the player known as "El
Matador" scored twice in three out of Argentina's last four matches – including the
winning goal in the Final. It earned him the
Adidas Golden Shoe, matching the achievement of his compatriot Guillermo Stábile who
scored eight goals during the first World Cup
in 1930.

The iconic photo

One of the most famous photos in Argentinian sporting history, left, was taken just after their victory in the Final. Defender Alberto Tarantini, who was pictured embracing Ubaldo Fillol, explained, "There was a kid who came over to hug me after the match. He came onto the pitch and, when he got close to me, I realized he had no arms. It alone encapsulates the bond between us and the supporters." The "kid" was Víctor dell'Aquila, who had lost his arms at the age of 12.

Bitter *Oranjes*

SOMETIMES IT TAKES a stroke of luck to bring home the cup. But this is exactly what the Netherlands were missing in the 89th minute, when Rob Rensenbrink hit the post of Ubaldo Fillol's goal. The score stood at 1–1, thanks to Dutch substitute Dick Nanninga who headed an equalizer after Mario Kempes had opened the scoring for Argentina. Kempes, who had already scored five goals during the tournament, and Daniel Bertoni went on to score from two successful crosses in the 105th and 115th minutes to give Argentina their first world title. Buenos Aires's Estadio Monumental, with its turf covered in *papelitos*, erupted. The Argentinians joined Uruguay and Brazil as South American world champions. Excluding Kempes's goals, Argentina owed their success to their pluck, the saves made by keeper Fillol, and the aggressive defence of Daniel Passarella and Alberto Tarantini (only four goals conceded in seven matches). The Argentinian manager did not even need to call up a promising 17-year-old by the name of Diego Maradona.

For the Netherlands, who had also lost to West Germany in the 1974 Final, this defeat was hard to swallow. The *Dutch* were probably the best team of the 1970s, but without Johan Cruijff, who had ended his international career, the spark had gone out of their attack. Despite this, their team play was a delight to watch, thanks to the likes of Rob Rensenbrink, Johnny Rep, Ruud Krol and twins René and Willy van de Kerkhof. The Netherlands left with a bitter taste in their mouths – not only from their loss, but also from the particularly hostile atmosphere and questionable refereeing decisions. "Security was non-existent. The Argentinian supporters were insane. What would have happened if we had won? How would we have got back to the hotel?" complained Rensenbrink. The frustrated Dutch team refused to attend the closing ceremony.

▲ The Dutch players distraught after their defeat in extra-time.

1982

With 24 teams, the 1982 World Cup in Spain was the largest gathering of football nations so far. It featured entertaining teams from Brazil and France, but both were knocked out in epic matches by more organized sides: Brazil by Italy, and France by West Germany in the first World Cup penalty shoot-out. In the Final, the Italians beat the Germans 3–1 to win the title for a record equalling third time.

Spanish hopes dashed

◀ Paolo Rossi kisses the FIFA World Cup trophy on the plane back to Italy.

▼ Madrid residents reading the newspapers after the death of General Franco in November 1975.

WHEN GENERAL FRANCISCO FRANCO died in 1975, having been in power since 1939, Spain was restored to a democracy. Hosting the World Cup was a symbolic celebration of this change. Unfortunately, the national team failed to live up to expectations, winning just one match out of five and becoming the first host country since Chile in 1962 to lose two.

The shift from 16 to 24 teams gave Africa and Asia two places each. South America was given three qualifying places and the North, Central American and Caribbean zone two. Europe, meanwhile, had four additional qualifiers, bringing their total to 14. Five countries – Algeria, Cameroon, Honduras, Kuwait and rugby-mad New Zealand – made their first appearance at the World Cup finals.

Españə 82

Story of the qualifiers

Two of the newcomers: Kuwait and New Zealand

A S WELL AS HOSTS SPAIN, 13 European countries earned their ticket to the finals by either finishing in the top two of their group of five teams (West Germany, with eight wins, Austria, Belgium, France, USSR, Czechoslovakia, Hungary, England, Yugoslavia, Italy, Scotland, and Northern Ireland) or first in a group of three (Poland). The great footballing nations of the Netherlands and Portugal did not qualify. As for South America, three teams got through (Brazil, Chile and Peru) together with Argentina who qualified automatically as defending champions. Africa now had two qualifiers: Cameroon, victors against Morocco, and Algeria who had beaten Nigeria. Kuwait and New Zealand, who had played China, represented the Asia-Oceania zone for the first time. North America, Central America and the Caribbean sent Honduras and El Salvador, but in a surprise upset Mexico finished third in the qualifiers and were knocked out. In total, 103 countries took part in the qualifying rounds (out of 109 who entered), playing 306 matches and scoring 797 goals.

▲ Steve Sumner defends for World Cup debutants New Zealand during their group match against Brazil. The All-Whites lost 4–0.

It was the first time that all six Confederations had been represented at the finals.

First group stage

GROUP 1		
ITA	0–0	POL
PER	0–0	CMR
ITA	1–1	PER
POL	0–0	CMR
POL	5–1	PER
ITA	1–1	CMR

	W	D	L	+	–	PTS
POL	1	2	0	5	1	4
ITA	0	3	0	2	2	3
CMR	0	3	0	1	1	3
PER	0	2	1	2	6	2

GROUP 2		
FRG	1–2	ALG
CHI	0–1	AUT
FRG	4–1	CHI
ALG	0–2	AUT
ALG	3–2	CHI
FRG	1–0	AUT

	W	D	L	+	–	PTS
FRG	2	0	1	6	3	4
AUT	2	0	1	3	1	4
ALG	2	0	1	5	5	4
CHI	0	0	3	3	8	0

GROUP 3		
ARG	0–1	BEL
HUN	10–1	SLV
ARG	4–1	HUN
BEL	1–0	SLV
BEL	1–1	HUN
ARG	2–0	SLV

	W	D	L	+	–	PTS
BEL	2	1	0	3	1	5
ARG	2	0	1	6	2	4
HUN	1	1	1	12	6	3
SLV	0	0	3	1	13	0

GROUP 4		
ENG	3–1	FRA
TCH	1–1	KUW
ENG	2–0	TCH
FRA	4–1	KUW
FRA	1–1	TCH
ENG	1–0	KUW

	W	D	L	+	–	PTS
ENG	3	0	0	6	1	6
FRA	1	1	1	6	5	3
TCH	0	2	1	2	4	2
KUW	0	1	2	2	6	1

GROUP 5		
ESP	1–1	HON
YUG	0–0	NIR
ESP	2–1	YUG
HON	1–1	NIR
HON	0–1	YUG
ESP	0–1	NIR

	W	D	L	+	–	PTS
NIR	1	2	0	2	1	4
ESP	1	1	1	3	3	3
YUG	1	1	1	2	2	3
HON	0	2	1	2	3	2

GROUP 6		
BRA	2–1	URS
SCO	5–2	NZL
BRA	4–1	SCO
URS	3–0	NZL
URS	2–2	SCO
BRA	4–0	NZL

	W	D	L	+	–	PTS
BRA	3	0	0	10	2	6
URS	1	1	1	6	4	3
SCO	1	1	1	8	8	3
NZL	0	0	3	2	12	0

Second group stage

GROUP A		
POL	3–0	BEL
BEL	0–1	URS
POL	0–0	URS

	W	D	L	+	–	PTS
POL	1	1	0	3	0	3
URS	1	1	0	1	0	3
BEL	0	0	2	0	4	0

GROUP B		
FRG	0–0	ENG
FRG	2–1	ESP
ESP	0–0	ENG

	W	D	L	+	–	PTS
FRG	1	1	0	2	1	3
ENG	0	2	0	0	0	2
ESP	0	1	1	1	2	1

GROUP C		
ITA	2–1	ARG
ARG	1–3	BRA
ITA	3–2	BRA

	W	D	L	+	–	PTS
ITA	2	0	0	5	3	4
BRA	1	0	1	5	4	2
ARG	0	0	2	2	5	0

GROUP D		
AUT	0–1	FRA
AUT	2–2	NIR
NIR	1–4	FRA

	W	D	L	+	–	PTS
FRA	2	0	0	5	1	4
AUT	0	1	1	2	3	1
NIR	0	1	1	3	6	1

Knockout stages

SEMI-FINAL

POL	0–2	ITA

SEMI-FINAL

FRG	3–3 / 5–4	FRA

PLAY-OFF FOR THIRD PLACE

POL	3–2	FRA

FINAL

ITA	3–1	FRG

ALG	ARG	AUT	BEL	BRA	CHI
CMR	ENG	ESP	FRA	FRG	HON
HUN	ITA	KUW	NIR	NZL	PER
POL	SCO	SLV	TCH	URS	YUG

24 TEAMS

52
MATCHES PLAYED

99 **5**
CARDS

NARANJITO
OFFICIAL MASCOT

ESPAÑA 82
OFFICIAL LOGO

ITALY
WINNERS

×**6**

PAOLO ROSSI
LEADING GOALSCORER

2.8
AVERAGE GOALS
PER MATCH

TANGO
OFFICIAL BALL

2 109 723
SPECTATORS

▲ German goalkeeper Toni Schumacher is beaten by Michel Platini during the penalty shoot out after the semi-final between West Germany and France.

Innovation: The penalty shoot-out

THE TAKING OF penalties to decide matches had been introduced for the 1974 finals in West Germany. However, the first time that they were needed was after the 1982 semi-final between France and West Germany. The Germans were the first to win by this method, winning further shoot-outs in 1986, 1990 and 2006.

Host cities and stadiums

120,000 seats at Camp Nou

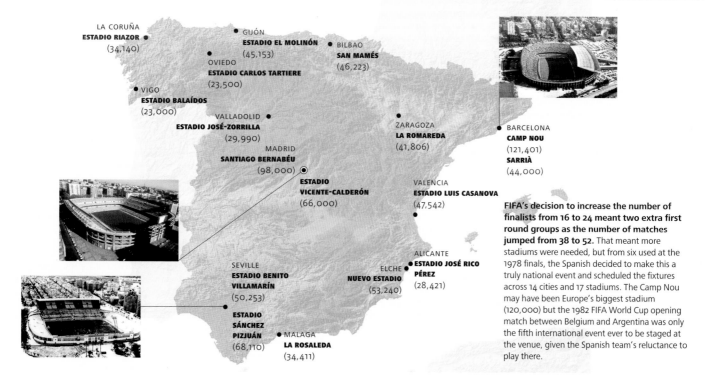

LA CORUÑA
ESTADIO RIAZOR
(34,140)

GIJÓN
ESTADIO EL MOLINÓN
(45,153)

BILBAO
SAN MAMÉS
(46,223)

OVIEDO
ESTADIO CARLOS TARTIERE
(23,500)

VIGO
ESTADIO BALAÍDOS
(23,000)

VALLADOLID
ESTADIO JOSÉ-ZORRILLA
(29,990)

ZARAGOZA
LA ROMAREDA
(41,806)

BARCELONA
CAMP NOU
(121,401)
SARRIÀ
(44,000)

MADRID
SANTIAGO BERNABÉU
(98,000)

ESTADIO VICENTE-CALDERÓN
(66,000)

VALENCIA
ESTADIO LUIS CASANOVA
(47,542)

ALICANTE
ESTADIO JOSÉ RICO PÉREZ
(28,421)

SEVILLE
ESTADIO BENITO VILLAMARÍN
(50,253)

ELCHE
NUEVO ESTADIO
(53,240)

ESTADIO SÁNCHEZ PIZJUÁN
(68,110)

MALAGA
LA ROSALEDA
(34,411)

FIFA's decision to increase the number of finalists from 16 to 24 meant two extra first round groups as the number of matches jumped from 38 to 52. That meant more stadiums were needed, but from six used at the 1978 finals, the Spanish decided to make this a truly national event and scheduled the fixtures across 14 cities and 17 stadiums. The Camp Nou may have been Europe's biggest stadium (120,000) but the 1982 FIFA World Cup opening match between Belgium and Argentina was only the fifth international event ever to be staged at the venue, given the Spanish team's reluctance to play there.

▲ Lakhdar Belloumi finds a way past Harald Schumacher and Karlheinz Förster to score Algeria's second goal of the match against West Germany.

▲ Rabah Madjer, the first Algerian to score a World Cup goal, seeks a way around Hans-Peter Briegel.

Italy draw through

In 1980, the Italian leagues had been affected by the *Totonero* match-fixing scandal, which led to AC Milan and Lazio being relegated to Serie B. The scandal seemed to affect the Italian team, which got off to a slow start with three draws (0–0 versus Poland, during which Dino Zoff celebrated his 100th cap, then 1–1 against Peru and Cameroon). Paolo Rossi failed to score, but Italy still made it to the second group stage by finishing runners-up in Group 1, beating Cameroon only on goal difference.

"If we lose this match, I'm catching the first plane home."

German manager Jupp Derwall before playing Algeria.

Algerian magic

16 JUNE 1982

WEST GERMANY 🇩🇪 1–2 🇩🇿 **ALGERIA**

RUMMENIGGE 67   MADJER 54, BELLOUMI 68

ON PAPER, Algeria's World Cup debut in Group 2 was a tricky one, as the rookies faced European champions West Germany. The German team boasted such players as Karl-Heinz Rummenigge, two-time European Footballer of the Year (1980 and 1981), yet, on 16 June in Gijón, in front of a 25,000-strong crowd, the debutants caused a sensation. In the 54th minute, after a goalless first half, Algeria made their move. Djamel Zidane shrewdly took up the attack, with Lakhdar Belloumi losing a one-on-one against Harald Schumacher only for Rabah Madjer to follow through with a chip straight into the German net (1–0). Rummenigge equalized from Magath's low cross in the 67th minute, but, one minute later, *Algeria took the lead again*. Salah Assad sent a straight cross to Belloumi who hammered it past Schumacher. It was an enormous upset and the first-ever win by an African side over a European line-up in the World Cup. "We were a solid group that had been together since 1979. We played with no inferiority complex and won that match with our own brand of football. In my opinion, Germany had the best team in that tournament, which made the victory a very special one," Madjer said.

Robson in the fast lane

▲ England's Bryan Robson jumps to score his second goal in the 3–1 victory over France.

16 JUNE 1982

ENGLAND ✚ 3–1 ▮▮ **FRANCE**

ROBSON 1, 67   SOLER 23
MARINER 83

T TOOK ENGLAND just 27 seconds to score against France on 16 June in Bilbao. An English throw-in from the right found its way to Terry Butcher. Butcher headed the ball to Bryan Robson who volleyed it past French keeper Jean-Luc Ettori. It was the fastest goal in the finals since 1962.

Honduras's first steps

16 JUNE 1982

SPAIN 🇪🇸 1–1 ▬▬ **HONDURAS**

LÓPEZ UFARTE 65 (PEN)   ZELAYA 8

HONDURAS KICKED OFF their first World Cup finals on 16 June in Valencia – against the hosts. With the Central American team in fine form, Héctor Zelaya opened the scoring in the eighth minute of the game, but Spain equalized after half time through a Roberto López Ufarte penalty. Five days later in Zaragoza, Honduras surprised people once again with a 1–1 draw against Northern Ireland, their goal scored by substitute Tony Laing. But José de la Paz's men just missed out on qualifying, losing 1–0 to Yugoslavia in their final group match following an 88th-minute penalty. Their lack of experience no doubt played a part, with only Gilberto Yearwood (Elche and Real Valladolid) having played abroad out of the 22-strong Honduran squad.

"The papers were saying that we were going to lose 7–0 or 8–0."

Jean-Marie Pfaff, Belgium goalkeeper

On 13 June in Barcelona, Belgium caused a stir by beating Argentina 1–0, a team including Diego Maradona who was making his first finals appearance. Erwin Vandenbergh scored the only goal of the match in the 62nd minute. "This first test against Maradona's Argentina, just after he had signed for Barcelona, was particularly special. What's more, it was the defending champions' opening match. The papers were saying that we were going to lose 7–0 or 8–0, but I knew that they'd only score a goal over my dead body," recalled Belgian keeper Jean-Marie Pfaff, who made several crucial saves. "No one, not even the great Diego, managed to do it. My ten years' experience at Beveren helped me in this match. Then there was the opening ceremony – which was really well organized – and above all the chance to play in front of millions of TV viewers. In that situation, you either crumble or you raise your game, and that's what happened with Belgium on that day."

▲ Belgian keeper Jean-Marie Pfaff and striker Marc Baecke, wearing an Argentina shirt, celebrate after Belgium's 1–0 victory in the opening match of España 82.

El Salvador concede ten

15 JUNE 1982

HUNGARY 🇭🇺 10–1 ▬▬ **EL SALVADOR**

NYILASI 4, 83, PÖLÖSKEI 11,   RAMÍREZ 64
FAZEKAS 23, 54, TÓTH 50,
KISS 69, 72, 76, SZENTES 72

EL SALVADOR made their World Cup debut in 1970 without scoring a single goal. On 15 June in Elche, in their first FIFA World Cup 1982 match against Hungary, history looked set to repeat itself, until Baltazar Ramírez Zapata brought the score to 1–5 in the 64th minute. Manager Mauricio Rodríguez and his men celebrated passionately, but their celebrations were short-lived as they continued to be totally outclassed.

For Hungary, the scoreboard broke numerous records. They became the first and only team to hit double figures in a World Cup finals match; their seven goals during the second half also entered the record books; and László Kiss became the first substitute to score a hat-trick, a feat he achieved in just seven minutes and 4 seconds (in the 69th, 72nd and 76th minutes) – the fastest hat-trick in any World Cup finals.

▲ French coach Michel Hidalgo during the confusion over Giresse's disallowed goal.

▲ Sheikh Ahmed Al-Fahad Al-Jaber Al-Sabah, brother of the Emir of Kuwait, smiles after having France's fourth goal, scored by Alain Giresse, overturned.

44

There were 41 referees and three stand-ins at the ready at the 1982 World Cup finals.
Between them, the referees, 25 of whom were Europeans, represented the six continental confederations. Twenty-nine of them had already officiated in one or more FIFA tournaments (World Cup, Olympic Football tournament, Junior World Championships). The average age of the men in black was 39.

A Sheikh on the pitch

21 JUNE 1982

FRANCE ▮▮ 4–1 ▮▮ **KUWAIT**

GENGHINI 31, PLATINI 43, SIX 48, BOSSIS 89   AL-BULOUSHI 75

WHEN ALAIN GIRESSE scored the fourth French goal against Kuwait (4–1) in the 78th minute on 21 June in Valladolid, no one could have imagined the incredible scenes that were about to play out. The Kuwaiti players surrounded the referee, explaining that they had stopped playing because they had heard a whistle blown from the direction of the stands. Sheikh Fahad Al-Sabah, president of the Kuwaiti Football Association and brother of the Emir, then descended from the stands and ordered his players to leave the pitch. It worked, as Soviet referee Myroslav Stupar agreed to his demands and restarted play with a dropped ball. A dumbfounded French team protested, with manager Michel Hidalgo also trying to step onto the pitch to find out what was going on before being pushed back by security. The 3–1 score stood. Nevertheless, the French went on to take the victory 4–1 thanks to a final solo effort by Maxime Bossis. In the end, Kuwait were landed with a €10,000 fine and Stupar never refereed a World Cup match again. As for Sheikh Fahad Ahmad Al-Jaber Al-Sabah, he was killed while trying to protect the Royal Palace during the Iraqi invasion of 1990.

Scotland scuppered

22 JUNE 1982

USSR 2–2 SCOTLAND

CHIVADZE 59, SHENGELIA 84   JORDAN 15, SOUNESS 86

WITH HIS GOAL against the USSR (1–0) on 22 June in Malaga, Scotsman Joe Jordan became the first British footballer to score in three different World Cup tournaments. The score stood at 1–1 when, in the 84th minute, disaster struck for Scotland. Alan Hansen and Willie Miller collided while chasing down a stray ball, leaving Ramaz Shengelia free to dribble his way past goalkeeper Allan Rough and hand the Soviets a 2–1 lead. Two minutes later, captain Graeme Souness provided the Scots with a glimmer of hope by squeezing the ball between Rinat Dasayev and the post. Despite a thrilling four minutes Scotland were knocked out. They had beaten New Zealand 5–2 and lost 4–1 to Brazil to finish third in Group 6, beaten by the Russians only on goal difference.

"We pressed the self-destruct button."

Scottish captain Graeme Souness, referring to the defensive error that cost the team the chance to qualify.

World Cup pennant

Pennant depicting "Naranjito", the official mascot of the World Cup 1982.

◄ FIFA World Football Museum collection.

Maradona returns to form

18 JUNE 1982

ARGENTINA 4–1 HUNGARY

BERTONI 26, MARADONA 28, 57, ARDILES 60   PÖLÖSKEI 76

FRUSTRATED BY his team's initial 1–0 defeat by Belgium, during which he was fouled multiple times, Diego Maradona set his sights on Argentina's second match, against Hungary, as the chance to show off his talents to the world. On 18 June in Alicante, "El Pibe de Oro" wowed the crowds with an acrobatic volley, a lobbed header saved by keeper Ferenc Mészáros, and a delicately curled free-kick. It was Argentina's Daniel Bertoni who opened the scoring, with Maradona doubling their lead after another shot from Bertoni was only half saved by the Hungarian keeper. Maradona's low shot from the left, after a one-two with Mario Kempes, brought the score to 3–0 on the way to a 4–1 win. Five days later, in Alicante, César Luis Menotti's men took their place in the second round with a comfortable 2–0 win over El Salvador.

▼ Diego Maradona scored twice in the Argentina-Hungary match.

Brothers in arms

The Belgian squad included a pair of brothers, Luc and Marc Millecamps. Luc, a defender, was a regular on the pitch while Marc, a midfielder, only made one appearancs during the tournament. West Germany had also enlisted a pair of siblings: Bernd and Karlheinz Förster, both defenders. Karlheinz played in every match of the competition, while Bernd was not called up until the second group stage, but then kept his place in the side until the end of the tournament. The Försters, therefore, became the last brothers to play in a World Cup Final.

▲ Brothers Karlheinz and Bernd Förster keep a close eye on Paolo Rossi during the West Germany-Italy World Cup Final.

▲ Algerian supporters wave banknotes during the West Germany-Austria match.

The match of shame

25 JUNE 1982

WEST GERMANY ▬ 1–0 ▬ **AUSTRIA**

HRUBESCH 10

AS THEY KICKED OFF for their third and final group match in Gijón on 25 June, West Germany and Austria knew exactly what score they needed to qualify for the second round, following Algeria's 3–2 victory over Chile a day earlier. The Germans had to win, while Austria could make do with a draw or a loss by no more than three goals. Whether tacitly or on purpose, the two teams came to an arrangement that would scupper Algeria. After Horst Hrubesch's rapid goal, the match descended into a farce. Neither team attacked, several players were walking, and the spectators in the stands were far from happy. Over the course of the next 80 minutes there were virtually no attempts to score, barely any tackles were made, and there seemed to be absolutely no desire to move things along. The 41,000 spectators shouted, "Out!" and "Algeria! Algeria!" or teased the players by yelling, "Let them kiss!" Algerian supporters waved banknotes in the stands to imply that the match had

been fixed. On German channel ARD, commentator Eberhard Stanjek remained silent for several minutes in protest, while Austria reporter Robert Seeger from ORF encouraged viewers to turn off their televisions. In spite of the absurd situation, West Germany and Austria finished first and second in Group 2 and both qualified for the second group stage. Algeria were knocked out on goal difference, even though they had won two out of three matches. The media referred to it as the "Disgrace of Gijón". But far from keeping a low profile, the Germans seemed completely at ease. "The reaction is stupid. We didn't come here to put on a show, but to win the tournament," said Paul Breitner. According to manager Jupp Derwall: "We just wanted to qualify, not play football." Neither team was sanctioned, but to avoid such arrangements being repeated in future, FIFA ruled that the final two matches in a group of four teams would now always be played simultaneously.

 XII *Copa Mundial* **FIFA** ESPAÑA 82

▲ The protest letter from the Algerian officials written just after the "Disgrace of Gijón".

Cautious Cameroon

23 JUNE 1982

ITALY ▮▮ 1–1 🔳 **CAMEROON**

GRAZIANI 60   M'BIDA 61

C AMEROON had qualified for the World Cup finals for the very first time, and goalkeeper Thomas N'Kono and his team put on a solid performance in the opening two games with draws against Peru (0–0) and Poland (0–0). To reach the second group stage, they needed to beat Italy in their third match on 23 June in Vigo. Francesco Graziani was the first to score with a looping header. Grégoire M'Bida replied a minute later, but that's how it finished. Despite having the same number of points and goal difference as the Italians, Cameroon were knocked out, having scored one goal less than their opponents.

▲ Cameroon goalkeeper Thomas N'kono catches the ball under pressure from Italy's Francesco Graziani.

A Group of Death for the brave Kiwis

They may have been the kings of rugby, but New Zealand weren't so successful with a round ball. Defeat followed defeat for manager John Adshead and his team at their first-ever World Cup: 5–2 v Scotland, 3–0 v USSR and 4–0 v Brazil. Just two goals scored versus 12 conceded – even though they had their moments in a very difficult group.

Heroic Northern Ireland

25 JUNE 1982

SPAIN ▧ 0–1 ✛ **NORTHERN IRELAND**

ARMSTRONG 47

O N 25 JUNE IN VALENCIA, Northern Ireland played their third match, against Spain, knowing that they had to win to reach the second group stage. Spurred on by their fans, the Spanish dominated, but found themselves up against a vigilant Pat Jennings. Gerry Armstrong scored from a mistake by goalkeeper Luis Arconada and converted one of the Irishmen's first opportunities. And neither Mal Donaghy's sending off in the 62nd minute nor the repeated Spanish attacks made a mark, with the Irish coming out on top. They finished first in their group with four points. The defeated hosts, who came second in their group thanks to having scored one goal more than Yugoslavia, also qualified.

17

Born on 7 May 1965, Norman Whiteside became the youngest player to take part in a World Cup finals phase, breaking the record set by Pelé in 1958 (17 years 235 days). On the day of his first appearance, against Yugoslavia on 17 June in Zaragoza, the Manchester United midfielder was 17 years and 41 days old.

▶ Gerry Armstrong celebrates Northern Ireland's win over Spain with coach Billy Bingham.

▲ Zbigniew Boniek is tackled by Belgium's Luc Millecamps. Boniek scored a hat-trick in the match in Barcelona.

Boniek shines

28 JUNE 1982

POLAND 3-0 **BELGIUM**

BONIEK 4, 26, 53

WITH A BULLET of a shot that grazed the underside of the bar (1–0), a smooth looping header (2–0) and a sneaky sidestep past the keeper to drive the ball into an open goal (3–0), Zbigniew Boniek almost single-handedly overwhelmed Belgium on 28 June at the Camp Nou during Poland's first match of the second group stage. The Widzew Łódź striker wowed the crowds with his bursts of speed and fancy footwork. But during their next encounter, on 4 July against the Soviet Union (0–0), Boniek was booked in the 88th minute: his second caution of the tournament after having already received one in Poland's first-round match against Italy. "That yellow card should never have happened. In my opinion, the referee wanted to give it to me. But I don't want to create controversy after the fact." Poland qualified for the semi-finals, but a suspended "Zibi" missed the match against Italy, who won 2–0. Back on the pitch to face France in the third-place playoff (3–2), the Pole, who scored four goals in the tournament and showed undeniable leadership, ended on a high as one of the stars of the show. "That third place is an excellent memory. I was really on very good form," said Boniek. At the end of the tournament, the 26-year-old striker quit his club for Juventus, where he and Michel Platini forged a formidable partnership.

▲ Zbigniew Boniek had a great tournament at the 1982 World Cup, scoring four goals as Poland finished third.

▲ Pierre Littbarski scores the first West German goal past Spanish keeper Luis Arconada. He set up Fischer for the second.

Littbarski knocks out the hosts

2 JULY 1982

WEST GERMANY 2–1 **SPAIN**

LITTBARSKI 50, FISHER 75   ZAMORA 82

GERMAN FORWARD PIERRE LITTBARSKI was easy to spot on the pitch. His bow legs gave him a limp that made him look as if he was constantly about to fall over. But this pint-sized winger (1.68 m) also stood out for his remarkable dribbling skills and constant movement. On 2 July at the Santiago Bernabéu Stadium in Madrid, the 1. FC Köln player scored the first goal of the game against Spain from a shot parried by Luis Arconada (1–0). For Germany's second goal, "Litti" pulled out all the stops. Picking up a pass from Paul Breitner, he deceived his marker by changing direction at lightning speed before outpacing Arconada and passing to Klaus Fischer who only had to finish the job. Spain were on the back foot, but pulled a goal back in the 82nd minute thanks to a Jesús Zamora header into the top corner. But it was not enough to save the hosts, who were knocked out before they had even played their second match against England (0–0). It was a bitter disappointment.

Ricardo Gallego's shattered dreams

Hosting a tournament can either make or break a team. Spain in 1982 broke. After years of living under Franco's rule, the country experienced a resurgence. There was a huge weight of expectation on the shoulders of the national team. José Santamaría's men – who had spent two months at a training camp in the Pyrenees – were cheered wherever they went. But an unexceptional campaign got off to a shaky start in the first group stage (1–1 against Honduras, 2–1 versus Yugoslavia then a 1–0 loss to Northern Ireland) before being eliminated in the second (losing 2–1 to West Germany and drawing 0–0 against England). "The fans and the journalists were harassing us. They were phoning up constantly, sometimes in the middle of the night. It was both hard and incredibly flattering, as if we'd been given a task that was beyond our abilities," recalls Ricardo Gallego, the Real Madrid midfielder. "I just think that we didn't have the team we needed. The squad was far too inexperienced since only three players – Juanito, Miguel and Arconada – had played in the Argentina World Cup four years earlier. And you forget we were facing teams composed of exceptional players."

▲ Santiago Urquiaga Pérez in action with Pierre Littbarski. Spain lost 2–1 to West Germany and were knocked out.

The invincible Shilton

During this World Cup, English goalkeeper Peter Shilton equalled a record by not conceding a single goal in four finals matches in a row. After letting in a Gérard Soler goal in the 24th minute of their first-round match against France (which England won 3–1), the Nottingham Forest keeper was unbeatable. Unfortunately, despite his four consecutive clean sheets, the English attack was failing to keep up, scoring three goals in their first group-stage match, two in the second, and only one in the third. Their two 0–0 draws against West Germany and Spain in the second group stage were not enough to see England through to the semis. Ron Greenwood's team left the competition without losing a single match and having conceded only one goal in five games.

▲ Claudio Gentile marked Diego Maradona closely during Italy and Argentina's second group-stage match.

"Mark Maradona? No problem!"

Claudio Gentile, Italian defender.

◄ Alberto Tarantini consoles Diego Maradona after the Argentina number 10 was sent off against Brazil.

Reigning champions on their way out

Beaten first by Italy (2–1) and then by Brazil (3–1) in the second group stage, Argentina finished with no points, in third and last place in Group 3. It was a disappointing end for the defending champions. After the tournament, 13 players including Mario Kempes and Osvaldo Ardiles bade farewell to the national team. The closing minutes of their last match against Brazil on 2 July in Barcelona were marred by a red card for Maradona. Frustrated by his performance and feeling cheated out of a penalty, "Dieguito" took matters into his own hands and kicked Batista, who had only just come onto the pitch, in the stomach. He was sent off in the 85th minute.

// I WAS WATCHING TELEVISION in my room when the manager, Enzo Bearzot, came to see me and asked, 'What do you think about marking Maradona?' I jokingly responded, 'No problem.' But the coach didn't realize I was joking. So for two days I watched videos to study his style and potential. I realized it was impossible to stop him. You just had to control him and stop him changing direction. The match went really well since we beat the titleholders [2–1]." Italian number six Claudio Gentile did not shy away from fouling Maradona, to the point that he was booked in the very first minute for dangerous play. Romanian referee Nicolae Rainea then seemed to go easier on him and even handed out a yellow card to Maradona in the 35th minute, who was rather flustered by the treatment inflicted on him by his marker. "Before we faced Brazil, this time Bearzot hadn't warned me that I was going to be dealing with Zico," said Gentile. "But thankfully things swung in our favour [a 3–2 victory thanks to a hat-trick from Paolo Rossi]. I think it was a turning point in this World Cup because we wanted to show that we were not just a defensive team." Once again, Gentile kept up the fouls. He was booked for tackling Zico from behind in the 13th minute, but the referee couldn't send him off when he ripped the Brazilian number 10's shirt shortly before half time, because a linesman had flagged for offside.

▲▲ Italy's Paolo Rossi scored a hat-trick against Brazil in the second round group match.

▲ Italians Francesco Graziani, Claudio Gentile and Antonio Cabrini defend against Brazil's Zico and Serginho.

▲ Midfielders Bruno Conti and Socrates clash.

Brazil enchant but fail to go through

5 JULY 1982

ITALY ▮ 3–2 🇧🇷 **BRAZIL**

ROSSI 5, 25, 74   SÓCRATES 12, FALCÃO 68

An eternal five seconds

Italy were leading 3–2, but in the last minute Brazil were awarded a free-kick. Oscar met it with a thumping header but it was not enough to beat Dino Zoff, who caught it on the line.

"Even though the ball was still trapped underneath me, the Brazilian players were celebrating the goal. I was sure it hadn't gone in, but I was terrified of the idea that the referee could wrongly think the ball had gone over the line. That's why I stayed on the ground, clutching the ball as if my life depended on it – so that the referee would see exactly where it was," explained the Italian keeper. "The same thing had happened to me nine years earlier in Romania. That day, the referee was wrong: he'd awarded the goal. Those four or five seconds against Brazil seemed like an eternity, and because I couldn't locate the referee, I prayed that he'd seen that the ball hadn't gone in."

FOR MANY PEOPLE, Brazil's class of '82 was one of the best in history. Telê Santana's team boasted an incredible, hard-working yet creative midfield (Zico, Sócrates, Falcão, Cerezo) who embraced the Total Football approach. In Portuguese, this all-round style of play is known as *Futebol do Arte* (artistic football) or *jogo bonito* (beautiful game). By the time their final second group-stage match came around, against Italy on 5 July in Barcelona, Brazil had proven themselves to be formidable opponents (2–1 versus USSR, 4–1 against Scotland, 4–0 against New Zealand and 3–1 versus defending champions Argentina). Had they become complacent? Was there too much focus on attacking? The Brazilians spent the game chasing a score, with an in-form Paolo Rossi exploiting a poor Cerezo pass across the Brazilian goal (1–2). Although they scored two exquisite goals, Brazil lost the game 3–2 and were unexpectedly knocked out of the competition.

"This World Cup should have been the pinnacle of three years of hard work. When you've worked hard you're naturally confident. It's like at school: if you've worked hard in class you're not worried in the exam," explained captain Sócrates. "We changed nothing about our style against Italy and we got ready like we had for the other matches. We played our football like we did in the previous matches, and the only thing that was different was that Italy somehow scored more goals than us."

Rossi's hat-trick

Paolo Rossi had failed to score in any of the previous four matches, but now was his moment to shine. In Italy's decisive match against Brazil, the Juventus centre-forward scored a memorable hat-trick (5', 25' and 74') to send the *Azzurri* into the semis. It was a first-rate return for Rossi who had finished a two-year suspension in April 1982 for his involvement in the *Totonero* scandal.

▲ ▲ Jean-Luc Ettori in the French goal fails to prevent Karl-Heinz Rummenigge scoring the second West German goal as Christian Lopez looks on.

▲ Germany's third goal, in extra-time, scored by Klaus Fischer.

▲ Michel Platini scored France's equalizing goal in the 26th minute.

▼ The official referee's report for the Germany-France semi-final.

Crème de la crème

8 JULY 1982

WEST GERMANY 🇩🇪 3–3 A.E.T. 🇫🇷 **FRANCE**

LITTBARSKI 17, RUMMENIGGE 102, FISCHER 108   PLATINI 26 (PEN), TRÉSOR 92, GIRESSE 98

⚽⚽✗⚽⚽⚽ 5–4 ⚽⚽⚽✗⚽✗

THE QUALITY, individual technical skills on show, the suspense and the unforeseen twists and turns made the France-West Germany semi-final one of the most memorable encounters of the tournament. On 8 July in Seville, the clash between French creativity and German discipline lived up to expectations. West Germany had the upper hand to begin with thanks to Pierre Littbarski, who scored from a rebound that bounced off Jean-Luc Ettori (1–0). France responded with a penalty taken by Michel Platini, which was given for a foul on Dominique Rocheteau. Following the second-half incident involving Patrick Battiston, tensions were running high. Then, during

extra-time, France saw a chance to take a decisive lead. Marius Trésor hit the back of the net with a beautiful volley followed swiftly by Alain Giresse, whose shot bounced off the post and into the German goal. But the Germans refused to give in. Their comeback was led by Karl-Heinz Rummenigge, who had only been on the pitch for five minutes, and Klaus Fischer who performed a magnificent bicycle kick. The finalists would be the winners of the first penalty shoot-out in World Cup history. At four-all (Didier Six and Uli Stielike missed), each team had one more shot. Maxime Bossis failed to score, while Horst Hrubesch succeeded (5–4). West Germany were in the Final.

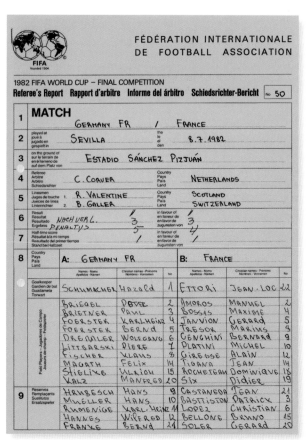

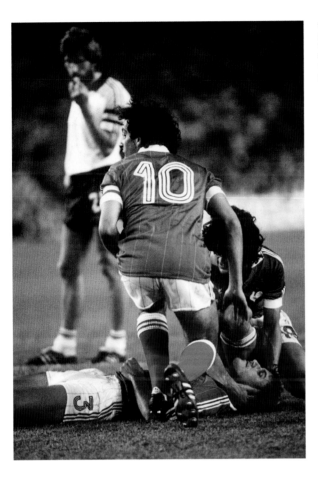

◀ Patrick Battiston lies prostrate on the ground following a reckless challenge by German keeper Harald Schumacher.

Italy cruise through

8 JULY 1982

ITALY ▌ 2–0 ▬ POLAND

ROSSI 22, 73

WITH A WIN against Brazil under their belts, Italy made short work of Poland, whose star player Zbigniew Boniek had been suspended for the match. Paolo Rossi scored twice in their 8 June match in Barcelona, bringing his total number of goals in the tournament to five. Italy found themselves in the Final for the first time since 1970. In the interests of fairness, both semi-finals were played on the same day.

▶ Italy's Francesco Graziani and Marco Tardelli congratulate Paolo Rossi after he scores in the semi-final against Poland.

Battiston and Schumacher collide

In the 57th minute and with the score at 1–1, Patrick Battiston, who had come on seven minutes earlier, found himself face to face with West Germany's goalkeeper, Harald Schumacher, who piled into him at full speed without touching the ball. The French defender lay immobile on the turf. "We quickly realized that Patrick was in serious trouble. He was unconscious, his teeth had been knocked out and the referee didn't call the foul or a penalty," explained Michel Platini. "Schumacher had been beaten. He couldn't get to the ball. So he tried to wipe Battiston out. The players, the public, everyone saw the foul. The only one who didn't see it was the ref. For me, it was completely unfair," added Alain Giresse. An unconscious Battiston was stretchered off the pitch with a cracked vertebra in his neck and broken teeth, Platini holding his hand. He was replaced by Christian Lopez. Schumacher, meanwhile, enraged the French supporters by pretending to kick the ball to them.

PLAY-OFF FOR THIRD PLACE

▲ Gérard Janvion tries to intercept a shot from Zbigniew Boniek in the third-place playoff.

"A lot of tears in the dressing room."

Michel Hidalgo, French team manager

10

"Naturally, we have bad memories of that game. We were happy with our campaign and the quality of the match, which was enjoyable to watch and fiercely contested. Battiston leaving the pitch, his arms trembling, affected the team," recalled Michel Hidalgo, the French manager. "Schumacher didn't even ask how he was. We couldn't understand how the referee didn't punish it. Losing on penalties, after having led 3–1 in extra-time, was very hard to accept. In the dressing room my team were like a youth team. There were a lot of tears, but also a feeling of indignation because of what had happened, particularly from Michel Platini. He was right."

▲ Michel Platini returns to the locker room in tears after missing out on the World Cup Final.

The tournament's top goalscorers, France, with 16 goals to Brazil's 15, had a record-breaking ten different scorers (Gérard Soler, Bernard Genghini, Michel Platini, Didier Six, Maxime Bossis, Alain Giresse, Dominique Rocheteau, Marius Trésor, René Girard, and Alain Couriol).

10 JULY 1982

POLAND ▬ 3–2 ▌ FRANCE

SZARMACH 40   GIRARD 13
MAJEWSKI 44   COURIOL 72
KUPCEWICZ 46

AFTER 1974, Poland once again found themselves third in the World Cup having beaten France on 10 July in Alicante. The Poles won 3–2 after scoring three times in six minutes. Their first goal was the work of Andrzej Szarmach, who had also played in 1974 and 1978. It was to be Szarmach and his teammate Grzegorz Lato's last international match. France's line-up on the other hand consisted mainly of replacements.

Italy on top of the world

11 JULY 1982

ITALY ▌ 3–1 ▬ **WEST GERMANY**

ROSSI 57, TARDELLI 69, ALTOBELLI 80   BREITNER 83

TALY HAD BEEN ON A ROLL since the start of the second group stage and ended their World Cup campaign on a high on 11 July in Madrid. After an average first half that saw the Italians miss a penalty, the *Azzurri* began to pull away, thanks to Paolo Rossi, who scored from a quick free-kick, Marco Tardelli (2–0), and then Alessandro Altobelli, after a storming counter-attack (3–0). Paul Breitner converted a volley from the right to allow the Germans, who had long since given up hope, to save face. Italy took home their third world title and their first since 1938. Paolo Rossi's six goals crowned him the tournament's top scorer, ahead of Karl-Heinz Rummenigge (five).

▲ Italy, world champions for a record-equalling third time. Manager Enzo Bearzot is carried on his players' shoulders.

▲ Marco Tardelli's scores for Italy in the 1982 World Cup Final against West Germany.

▲ West Germany's keeper Harald Schumacher is helpless as Tardelli scores Italy's second goal in the Final.

Bearzot defends his image

Although he is sometimes considered to be a coach more concerned with defence than attack, the pipe-smoking Italian manager Enzo Bearzot believed that this view of him was inaccurate: "For me, football should be played with two wingers, a centre-forward and a playmaker. That's the way I see the game. I select my players and then I let them play the game, without trying to impose tactical plans on them. You can't tell Maradona, 'Play the way I tell you.' You have to leave him free to express himself. The rest will take care of itself."

The pipe belonging to Italian manager Enzo Bearzot.

▲ **FIFA World Football Museum collection.**

Tardelli's roar

In the 69th minute, Marco Tardelli turned to his left. Although he was off-balance, his shot found its way into Harald Schumacher's goal (2–0). Italy had scored a decisive goal and what followed was to become the most famous celebration in World Cup history. His *urlo* (shout or roar) became legendary. "I was born with the roar, it didn't just emerge at that moment. You live your life and have some good experiences and some bad ones. Then it all comes out at that moment," explained Tardelli. "Scoring in the Final was a dream come true. I never saw my job as work, but as a game. I never experienced any mental pain from my job. Physical pain, yes, but it was always fun to get up in the morning and go training. I also felt released from a certain section of the press that had always lambasted us. It was like we were at war with them. But we won in the end. It was only once the referee had blown the final whistle that I realized what had happened. We were absolutely exhausted after pushing ourselves to the asolute limit. You go into a kind of mental limbo. I don't quite remember what I did, but I remember that we hugged each other passionately. It was a victory for the team, but it was also my victory. A victory over my life."

▲ Paolo Rossi, the leading goalscorer at the 1982 World Cup with six goals, lifts the FIFA World Cup Trophy.

▶ President of the Italian Republic, Sandro Pertini, with Dino Zoff, Franco Causio and Enzo Bearzot on their flight back to Rome with the trophy.

Cabrini's missed penalty

Antonio Cabrini has the unfortunate distinction of being the first player to miss a penalty during a World Cup Final. The score was 0–0 in the 24th minute.
"Antognoni wasn't playing because of his injury against Poland and I was the second player on the list of penalty takers," recalled the Italian left-back. "I changed my mind at the last minute, which was a mistake. I was looking one way, but the keeper faked a dive that way. I adjusted the angle of the shot, but the ball went past the goal. Still, I had the chance to be part of a world championship-winning team. Everyone makes mistakes from time to time. It didn't stop me becoming a world champion. But I haven't forgotten it. It's impossible."

The legendary photo: a card game on the president's plane

// That World Cup had a resounding impact throughout Italy. We flew back to Rome on President Sandro Pertini's plane," recalls Italy captain Dino Zoff. "The president hadn't been able to hold back his emotions in the stadium. I ended up playing cards with the president, Bearzot and Causio during the one-and-a-half-hour flight! Pertini had the gift of making you feel at ease. We felt like he was just one of us. When we reached Rome and went to the Quirinal Palace, there was an indescribable hullabaloo. Pertini insisted we stay for dinner. I still remember exactly what he said. 'I'm sitting here with Bearzot on one side and Zoff and his team on the other. If there's any space left for the ministers and members of parliament, even better. If not, they'll just have to go to the restaurant.' He knew how to talk, Pertini did."

1986

Following the withdrawal of Colombia, Mexico became the first country to host the World Cup twice. It was a tournament dominated by Argentina's Diego Maradona. In the quarter-final against England, he scored with his infamous "Hand of God", but followed that with a brilliant solo goal. In the Final against West Germany, his first-time pass put Jorge Burruchaga through to win the match 3–2.

The show must go on

◀ Diego Maradona holds the FIFA World Cup Trophy aloft after Argentina's victory over West Germany.

▼ The ruins of the Hotel Regis after the deadly earthquake of 19 September 1985 in Mexico.

N 1986 THE FIFA WORLD CUP returned to Mexico, just 16 years after Pelé and his team-mates had dazzled the world there. This time, a new star shone just as brightly, with Diego Maradona sealing his reputation as one of the all-time greats. But this was a World Cup played against the background of tragedy. Having beaten off the challenge of the USA, Brazil and Canada to replace Colombia as hosts, Mexico suffered one of the most powerful earthquakes in history. In September 1985, less than a year before the tournament was due to kick-off, Mexico City was rocked by shocks measuring 8.0, made worse by the city's location on an ancient lake bed. There were more than 10,000 casualties, but it was decided that the show should go on as none of the stadiums had been affected. The Azteca was unscathed and it went down in history as the first stadium to host two World Cup Finals, joined in 2014 by the Maracanã. Once again the heat and the altitude played a significant part in the tournament and, as in 1970, the were midday kick-offs to pander to the television audiences in Europe. But there were also some entertaining matches, none more so than the Final itself. Argentina's 3–2 victory was the only time after 1970 when more than four goals were scored. The next two Finals produced just one.

Story of the qualifiers

Belgium ousts the Netherlands

▲ Belgium celebrate their victory in a qualifying play-off against their Dutch neighbours.

N O FEWER THAN 100 TEAMS fought it out for the 22 qualifying spots in 308 matches. Mexico, as hosts, and Italy as defending champions were guaranteed a place. Algeria and Morocco were the African representatives, while Iraq, making their debut, and South Korea, returning after a 32-year absence, represented Asia. Europe sent Belgium, Bulgaria, England, France, Hungary, Italy, Northern Ireland, Poland, Portugal, Scotland, the Soviet Union, Spain and newcomers Denmark. But Yugoslavia, Austria and the Netherlands, who were knocked out in a playoff against Belgium, were left at home. The Dutch, who had been finalists in 1974 and 1978, had thought they had the match in the bag until Belgian Georges Grün scored the deciding away goal five minutes before the final whistle (0–1 away, 2–1 at home). For the first time, Canada (North, Central America and Caribbean zone) qualified for the finals. For South America, regulars Brazil and Argentina qualified, while Uruguay and Paraguay made their comebacks. In total, ten of the 24 teams were different from those who had appeared in 1982 – a turnover rate of 41.6 per cent.

Regulations

No more second round Groups

As in Spain in 1982, this was a 24-team competition. This time, however, the second round groups were cut. After a group stage (six groups of four), 16 teams would go into a knockout format. To qualify, teams needed to finish in the top two of their group or be one of the four best third-place teams. Another change, to avoid teams striking deals with one another as had allegedly happened between West Germany and Austria four years earlier, was that the final matches of each group would be played simultaneously.

▼ Mexico City's Azteca becomes the first stadium to host two World Cup Finals.

Group stage

GROUP A
ITA	1–1	BUL
ARG	3–1	KOR
ITA	1–1	ARG
BUL	1–1	KOR
ITA	3–2	KOR
ARG	2–0	BUL

	W	D	L	+	–	PTS
ARG	2	1	0	6	2	5
ITA	1	2	0	5	4	4
BUL	0	2	1	2	4	2
KOR	0	1	2	4	7	1

GROUP B
MEX	2–1	BEL
PAR	1–0	IRQ
MEX	1–1	PAR
BEL	2–1	IRQ
BEL	2–2	PAR
MEX	1–0	IRQ

	W	D	L	+	–	PTS
MEX	2	1	0	4	2	5
PAR	1	2	0	4	3	4
BEL	1	1	1	5	5	3
IRQ	0	0	3	1	4	0

GROUP C
FRA	1–0	CAN
URS	6–0	HUN
FRA	1–1	URS
CAN	0–2	HUN
FRA	3–0	HUN
CAN	0–2	URS

	W	D	L	+	–	PTS
URS	2	1	0	9	1	5
FRA	2	1	0	5	1	5
HUN	1	0	2	2	9	2
CAN	0	0	3	0	5	0

GROUP D
BRA	1–0	ESP
ALG	1–1	NIR
BRA	1–0	ALG
ESP	2–1	NIR
BRA	3–0	NIR
ESP	3–0	ALG

	W	D	L	+	–	PTS
BRA	3	0	0	5	0	6
ESP	2	0	1	5	2	4
NIR	0	1	2	2	6	1
ALG	0	1	2	1	5	1

GROUP E
FRG	1–1	URU
SCO	0–1	DEN
FRG	2–1	SCO
URU	1–6	DEN
FRG	0–2	DEN
URU	0–0	SCO

	W	D	L	+	–	PTS
DEN	3	0	0	9	1	6
FRG	1	1	1	3	4	3
URU	0	2	1	2	7	2
SCO	0	1	2	1	3	1

GROUP F
POL	0–0	MAR
POR	1–0	ENG
MAR	0–0	ENG
POL	1–0	POR
POL	0–3	ENG
MAR	3–1	POR

	W	D	L	+	–	PTS
MAR	1	2	0	3	1	4
ENG	1	1	1	3	1	3
POL	1	1	1	1	3	3
POR	1	0	2	2	4	2

Knockout stages

ROUND OF 16
ARG	1–0	URU
ENG	3–0	PAR

ROUND OF 16
DEN	1–5	ESP
URS	3–4 A.E.T.	BEL

ROUND OF 16
BRA	4–0	POL
ITA	0–2	FRA

ROUND OF 16
MAR	0–1	FRG
MEX	2–0	BUL

QUARTER-FINAL
ARG	2–1	ENG

QUARTER-FINAL
ESP	1–1 4–5	BEL

QUARTER-FINAL
BRA	1–1 3–4	FRA

QUARTER-FINAL
FRG	0–0 4–1	MEX

SEMI-FINAL
ARG	2–0	BEL

SEMI-FINAL
FRA	0–2	FRG

PLAY-OFF FOR THIRD PLACE
FRA	4–2 A.E.T.	BEL

FINAL
ARG	3–2	FRG

ALG ARG BEL BRA BUL CAN
DEN ENG ESP FRA FRG HUN
IRQ ITA KOR MAR MEX NIR
PAR POL POR SCO URS URU

24 TEAMS

52
MATCHES PLAYED

138 7
CARDS

2 394 031
SPECTATORS

PIQUÉ
OFFICIAL MASCOT

MEXICO86
OFFICIAL LOGO

ARGENTINA
WINNERS

×6

GARY LINEKER
LEADING GOALSCORER

2.5
AVERAGE GOALS
PER MATCH

AZTECA
OFFICIAL MATCH BALL

The Mexican wave

It was the tournament that introduced the world to the Mexican wave. This phenomenon, in which spectators stand up one after another to create the illusion of a rippling wave, was already extremely popular in Mexico and South America and has since spread to stadiums around the world.

Host cities and stadiums

Replacement hosts

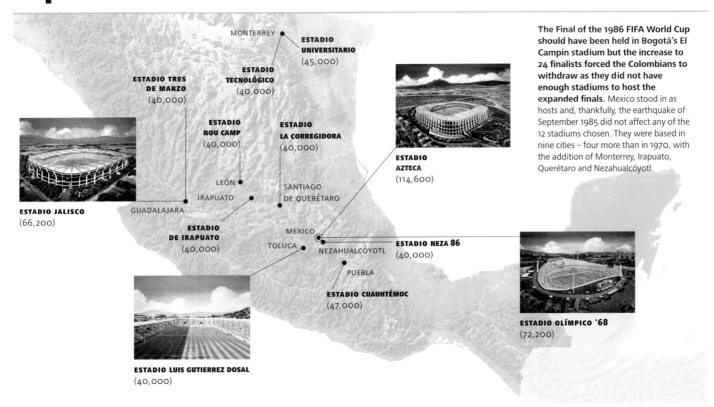

MONTERREY
ESTADIO UNIVERSITARIO
(45,000)

ESTADIO TECNOLÓGICO
(40,000)

ESTADIO TRES DE MARZO
(40,000)

ESTADIO NOU CAMP
(40,000)

ESTADIO LA CORREGIDORA
(40,000)

ESTADIO AZTECA
(114,600)

LEÓN

SANTIAGO DE QUERÉTARO

ESTADIO JALISCO
(66,200)

GUADALAJARA
IRAPUATO

ESTADIO DE IRAPUATO
(40,000)

MEXICO

TOLUCA

NEZAHUALCÓYOTL

ESTADIO NEZA 86
(40,000)

PUEBLA

ESTADIO CUAUHTÉMOC
(47,000)

ESTADIO OLÍMPICO '68
(72,200)

ESTADIO LUIS GUTIERREZ DOSAL
(40,000)

The Final of the 1986 FIFA World Cup should have been held in Bogotá's El Campín stadium but the increase to 24 finalists forced the Colombians to withdraw as they did not have enough stadiums to host the expanded finals. Mexico stood in as hosts and, thankfully, the earthquake of September 1985 did not affect any of the 12 stadiums chosen. They were based in nine cities – four more than in 1970, with the addition of Monterrey, Irapuato, Querétaro and Nezahualcóyotl.

Morocco on top

11 JUNE 1986

MOROCCO ▪ 3–1 ▪ **PORTUGAL**

KHAIRI 19, 26   DIAMANTINO 80
MERRY KRIMAU 62

WITH FOUR POINTS, the Moroccan team coached by Brazilian José Faria became the first African nation to finish top of their group in the finals phase. Thanks to stars such as goalkeeper and captain Ezzaki "Zaki" Badou, Aziz Bouderbala and striker Abdelkrim "Krimau" Merry, they went through to the last 16.

▲ Morocco surprised Portugal in Group F, winning 3–1 in Guadalajara.

Tigana's moment

French midfielder Jean Tigana scored his only goal for France during their third match at the finals in Mexico against Hungary, on **9 June** in **León**. It was his 43rd cap. The Bordeaux player scored with his left foot after a one-two with Dominique Rocheteau. He finished his career with 52 caps.

▲ Four years after thrashing El Salvador 10–1, Hungary are themselves on the wrong end of a big score.

▶ Igor Belanov beats Hungary's goalkeeper Péter Disztl from the penalty spot.

▲ Pavel Yakovenko brushes off a tackle by Hungary's Imre Garaba.

Six goals, six scorers

2 JUNE 1986

USSR ▪ 6–0 ▪ **HUNGARY**

YAKOVENKO 2, ALEINIKOV 4
BELANOV 24 (PEN), YAREMCHUK 66
DAJKA 73 (O.G.), RODIONOV 80

AS ONE OF THE "DARK HORSES", the USSR did not disappoint in their opening match against Hungary on 2 June in Irapuato (6–0). Built on the backbone of Dynamo Kyiv, who had recently won the Cup-Winners' Cup, the team coached by Valeriy Lobanovskyi had five different scorers (plus an own goal) in their opening match. Pavlo Yakovenko scored inside the box from the left following a corner; Sergei Aleinikov hit the back of the net with a spectacular goal from 20 metres; Igor Belanov converted a penalty; Ivan Yaremchuk scored after a strong run by Yakovenko; and Sergey Rodionov scored from a loose ball.

Hugo Sánchez
Mexican idol

RECENTLY CROWNED the top goal-scorer in the Spanish championship with Real Madrid, whom he had joined a year earlier after four seasons at Atlético Madrid, Hugo Sánchez was Mexico's not-so-secret weapon. At 1.78m, the left-footed striker was lethal in the opposition's box. His acrobatic goals (he had done gymnastics with his sisters for many years) and his somersault celebrations were iconic. During the group stages his fox-in-the-box style of play led to the team's second goal against Belgium. In their next game, against Paraguay, he was awarded a penalty in the closing minutes, but the goalkeeper pushed his effort onto a post. "I don't like missing penalties – I hate it – but as we finished top of our group it didn't get to me. And it also showed everyone I was human," he recalled. Sánchez was suspended for Mexico's third match against Iraq after picking up a yellow card in each of his side's opening two games: for sending the ball into the crowd after the first Mexican goal against Belgium and then, in the 75th minute of the Para-

guay match, for challenging the opposing goalkeeper.

The finals took place just eight months after the devastating loss of life in the 1985 earthquake. "The earthquake hadn't affected us directly, but our job involved bringing a bit of joy to people who had suffered a lot," he explained. "I also think that playing at home is an advantage because we ended up top seeds, which meant we advanced in the competition. Our fans' support also helped." On his performance during the group stage, Sánchez said: "Since I was the star of the team and Pichichi [the top scorer in the Spanish championships] for the last two seasons, perhaps people thought I was going to be scoring in every match and be the tournament's leading goalscorer, but playing with Mexico is very different to playing for Real." He was also suffering the after-effects of an ankle injury he had picked up during the UEFA Cup Final, which Real won against West German side Cologne (5–1 at home and 0–2 away).

▲ Hugo Sánchez, one of the all-time greats of Mexican football.

Mexico on a roll

3 JUNE 1986

MEXICO 2-1 **BELGIUM**

QUIRARTE 23   VANDENBERGH 45
SÁNCHEZ 39

Mexico found themselves in arguably one of the easiest groups of the tournament and capitalized on their good fortune with a successful group stage. Under their Yugoslavian manager Bora Milutinović, they beat Belgium, drew against Paraguay (1–1, with a goal from Luis Flores and a last-minute missed penalty from Sánchez), then beat Iraq (1–0, thanks to a goal from Quirarte). Their results secured them first place in Group B, one point ahead of Paraguay. The Mexicans benefited enormously from the 100,000-plus enthusiastic fans who turned out to support them at the Estadio Azteca. With 4-4-2 their formation of choice, they relied heavily on their three star attackers – Hugo Sánchez (Real Madrid), Luis Flores (Sporting de Gijón) and Manuel Negrete. With a blend of South American passion and European tactical discipline, Milutinović gave his team a sense of identity, which served them well at these finals.

◄ Mexico got their campaign off to a great start with a 2–1 victory over Belgium. Forward Luis Flores is watched by Belgium's Enzo Scifo

114 600

For the Mexico versus Paraguay game on 7 June, 114,600 people packed into the Estadio Azteca. It was the highest attendance for a World Cup finals match, with the exception of games not played at Rio's Maracanã Stadium.

▲ Jean-Pierre Papin had already missed five clear-cut chances before he finally broke through Canada's solid defence and scored past keeper Paul Dolan.

A heroic first for Canada

1 JUNE 1986

FRANCE ▌▌ 1–0 🍁 **CANADA**

PAPIN 79

WITH 15 MINUTES of their first World Cup finals match remaining, on 1 June in León, Canada saw a glimmer of hope, as France, one of the tournament favourites, had not yet scored. But Canadian keeper Paul Dolan failed to hold them off to the end. Jean-Pierre Papin, who had already had five clear shots, finally converted a pass from Yannick Stopyra. Despite their defeat, the Canadians, coached by Englishman Tony Waiters, impressed with their defensive skill. In their subsequent matches, they also defended well but lost 2–0 to both Hungary and the USSR.

"... The Mexicans were holding up their fingers to suggest we were going to lose 10–0."

**Bob Lenarduzzi,
Canada defender.**

"I remember the run-up to the tournament being tricky because half of the players no longer had a team after the North American Soccer League (NASL) closed down in March 1985. To keep in shape, some of them took part in the American Indoor Championships. But these difficulties only brought us closer together. I also remember the coach journey, being escorted by the Mexican police before the match against France. When we reached the stadium, the Mexicans were holding up their fingers to suggest we were going to lose 10–0. We thought, 'It's going to be a tough one!' I think that for the French goal, the altitude

slightly changed the trajectory of Manuel Amoros's pass and confused our keeper. But we were so happy to be at the World Cup and to have held our own against one of the favourites. We missed so many chances against Hungary that we deserved to get into the *Guinness Book of Records*. Me first: I went up for a corner, but the ball went straight over me. I had no one within a six-metre circle to bother me. I don't know why, but I panicked and kicked too quickly and not hard enough. I was devastated. You realize you could have scored the first Canadian goal in the World Cup!"

Against Italy on 10 June in Puebla, Korean Cha Bum-Kun played his 119th and final international game, a world record at the time

119

Two points are enough for Bulgaria and Uruguay

Alongside the top two teams from each group, the four best third-place teams also qualified for the tournament's knockout stages. In this virtual table, Belgium finished first with three points (one win, one draw, one defeat and a goal difference of 0), ahead of Poland (three points, -2), Bulgaria (two points, two draws, one defeat, -2) and Uruguay (two points, two draws, one defeat, -5). These four teams progressed to the round of 16, whereas Hungary (two points, two draws, one defeat, -7) and Northern Ireland (one point, one draw, two defeats, -4) did not.

Official mascot

Pennant with a picture of "Pique", the official mascot of the World Cup 1986.

▲ FIFA World Football Museum collection.

Iraq hold their heads high

8 JUNE 1986		
BELGIUM	2–1	IRAQ
SCIFO 16, CLAESEN 19 (PEN)		RADHI 59

RAQ WAS AT WAR with Iran at the time and the team played all of their home qualifying matches on neutral territory. Keen to impress at their first World Cup, the Iraqis embarked on a lengthy training regime which included 15 friendlies. But Evaristo de Macedo, the Brazilian manager, was only brought on board in May 1986 (he was their third manager in eight months). Thanks to their determination and technique, the Iraqis only lost by one goal in each match (1–0 to Paraguay, 2–1 to Belgium and then 1–0 to Mexico). In the Belgium game, Ahmed Radhi managed to score in the 59th minute to score Iraq's first-ever World Cup finals goal. Overall however, the Iraqi defenders were too hot-headed and lacked experienced, fouling multiple times. The team finished bottom of Group B, but they had nothing to be ashamed of.

▲ Ahmed Radhi was one of the stars for Iraq in this World Cup.

▶ Keeper Pat Jennings during his 119th and final match for Northern Ireland.

Pat Jennings bows out

12 JUNE 1986		
BRAZIL	3–0	NORTHERN IRELAND
CARECA 15, 87, JOSIMAR 42		

PAT JENNINGS, a Northern Ireland footballing legend, played his 119th and final international match against Brazil on 12 June in Guadalajara. In spite of some superb saves and his sure grasp of the ball he was unable to stop Brazil from finding a way through (3–0), in particular a bullet of a shot that full-back Josimar fired at him from 25 metres away in the 42nd minute. Jennings, who celebrated his 41st birthday that day, had made his senior international debut aged 18 on 15 April 1964. He also played the in the 1982 World Cup and participated in a record six qualifying phases, and was the oldest player to have appeared in the finals until overtaken by Roger Milla in 1990. He is still third on the list.

55

Just 55 seconds was all it took for Uruguay's José Batista to be sent off against Scotland in the game at the Estadio Nezahualcóyotl on 13 June. The French referee, Joël Quiniou, pulled out the fastest red card in World Cup finals history for the Uruguay number six's violent foul on Gordon Strachan. Despite being down to ten men for virtually the whole match, Uruguay managed to hold their opponents to a 0–0 draw and qualified for the round of 16 matches.

Negrete's masterpiece

15 JUNE 1986

MEXICO 2–0 **BULGARIA**

NEGRETE 34, SERVÍN 61

ON 15 JUNE, with Mexico and Bulgaria level pegging, it took an exceptional goal to break the stalemate. After a one-two in the air with Javier Aguirre, midfielder Manuel Negrete performed an acrobatic scissor kick that landed right in the back of Bulgarian keeper Borislav Mihaylov's net. This perfect volley in the 34th minute brought the Estadio Azteca to its feet (1–0). "I remember it exactly. We were a bit nervous at the hotel because it was our first knockout match, but also very excited by the occasion, by the atmosphere in the tunnel that led onto the pitch. I received a ball from Rafael Amador which landed on my right-hand side," explained Manuel Negrete, the Mexican number 22. "I controlled the ball, gave it to Aguirre who caught it almost on the penalty box line, and he sent it back to me a little bit high. I didn't think. I just kicked it quite hard to fool Mihaylov. It was the perfect shot. I'd put everything into it, supported by our 111,000 fans. It was a really great moment, really special, and symbolized our journey through this home World Cup. It's one of the greatest goals ever scored in the World Cup."

▲ Against Buglaria, Mexico's Manuel Negrete scores one of the goals of the tournament with a spectacular scissor-kick.

26

The number of goals scored in the eight round of 16 matches – an average of 3.25 goals per game.

▼ Michel Platini scores the first goal as France knock out defending champions Italy.

Platini ousts the titleholders

17 JUNE 1986

ITALY 0–2 **FRANCE**

PLATINI 15, STOPYRA 57

HAVING BEEN CRITICIZED for his failure to score during the group stages, and hampered by a groin strain, Michel Platini was determined to set things straight in France's match against Italy on 17 June. The round-of-16 clash meant a lot to the Frenchman, who had Italian ancestry and had been playing for Juventus since 1982. The French number 10 found himself on the turf of Mexico's Olympic stadium opposite two of his club-mates, Antonio Cabrini and Gaetano Scirea. In the 15th minute, Luis Fernández sent the ball forward and found Dominique Rocheteau, who swung it round to Platini. The French captain beat Giovanni Galli with a shot from the right (1–0). One of his free-kicks forced Galli to punch the ball clear, while in the second half Platini narrowly missed scoring again after slalom-ing his way through the Italian defence. It did not matter: Italy conceded a second goal in the 57th minute following a Jean Tigana-Dominique Rocheteau-Yannick Stopyra move that Stopyra fired low past Galli. "I really wanted to beat Italy, more than any other team. In part it was because of my origins and in part because I was playing for Juve, but above all it was because if France had lost, my Italian teammates would have never let me forget about it. But to be honest, we were actually better than them," said Platini. The 1984 European champions ended up beating the 1982 World Cup champions, who lost their title. A sluggish Itay team had performed poorly in the group stages (1–1 draws with Bulgaria and Argentina, then a 3–2 victory over South Korea).

The Red Devils cause an upset

USSR ▮ 3–4 ▮▮ BELGIUM
A.E.T.

BELANOV 27, 70, 111 (PEN)   SCIFO 56, CEULEMANS 77, DEMOL 102, CLAESEN 110

◀ Spain's Emilio Butragueño scored four goals against Denmark.

I N THE RUN-UP to the Belgium v USSR round of 16 match, the two teams' form had been worlds apart. After some impressive performances during the group stage (two wins, one draw, nine goals scored, and only one conceded), the Soviets appeared confident in their team's strength, counting on stars such as Igor Belanov and Oleksandr Zavarov. The Belgians, on the other hand, seemed indecisive, finishing third in Group B thanks to their 2–1 victory over Iraq. And it was the USSR who twice held the lead on 15 June in León, before Belgium bounced back, twice capitalizing on errors by the Soviet defence. A cool Enzo Scifo found his way through Rinat Dasayev first (1–1), followed by their captain Jan Ceulemans from a long ball (2–2). The Belgians finally took the lead in extra-time following an incredible header from Stéphane Demol (3–2). Nico Claesen widened the gap with a volley from a Leo Clijsters header (4–2), before the Russians pulled one back through a Belanov penalty (4–3). But Belgium hung on to cause a genuine upset.

Butragueño times four

DENMARK ▮▮ 1–5 ▮ SPAIN

J.OLSEN 33 (PEN)   BUTRAGUEÑO 43, 56, 80, 88 (PEN) GOIKOETXEA 68 (PEN)

▶ Enzo Scifo was on the scoresheet in Belgium's thrilling 4–3 victory over the Soviet Union.

T HE 18 JUNE match in Querétaro saw Spain comfortably progress to the quarter-finals. Jesper Olsen handed Denmark the lead thanks to a 33rd-minute penalty (0–1), but soon afterwards Emilio Butragueño's team found their rhythm. The Real Madrid striker equalized two minutes before half time (1–1), and scored again in the 56th minute after Michel diverted a corner straight to him (2–1). *El Buitre* (The Vulture) then won a penalty that Goikoetxea put away with his left foot (3–1). Butragueño then received a textbook cross in the box to make it 4–1, before getting his fourth goal with another penalty in the 89th minute (5–1). The Spaniard became the sixth player to score four goals in a finals phase match. The Danes had many admirers with their performances in the group stages, but were knocked out of the competition.

Mexico 86 match ticket

Ticket for the round of 16 match between England and Paraguay.

▲ **FIFA World Football Museum collection.**

Belanov's hat-trick in vain

The Belgium-USSR match was the third World Cup game in history in which a player who scored at least three goals ended up on the losing team. After Pole Ernest Wilimowski in 1938 (four goals in a 6–5 loss during the first round against Brazil) and Swiss Seppe Hügi in 1954 (three goals in a 7–5 defeat to Austria in the quarter-finals), Igor Belanov joined the unhappy pair following the Soviet Union's defeat by Belgium.

▲ Diego Maradona's infamous "Hand of God" in the quarter-final between England and Argentina.

▲ Three minutes after the "Hand of God" Maradona scored what some describe as the goal of the century.

The Hand of God

22 JUNE 1986

ARGENTINA 2–1 ENGLAND

MARADONA 51, 54   LINEKER 81

ON 22 JUNE IN MEXICO CITY, an unusual action led to the birth of a legend. With the ball airborne, Diego Maradona clashed with England keeper Peter Shilton. Both players went up for it but the Argentinian number 10's left hand got there first, leading to a goal. To everyone's surprise, Tunisian referee Ali Bin Nasser let the goal stand because he had not seen Maradona's foul. In the press conference, *El Pibe de Oro* half admitted what had happened. "I scored it a little with the head of Maradona and a little with the hand of God," he said, before adding, "It was a final for us. It wasn't a question of winning a match; it was about knocking out the English." And to drive it home: "I don't regret and I will never regret the goal I scored with my hand against the English. I could apologize to them a thousand times, but at the end of the day I'd happily do the same thing a thousand and one times."

6

Gary Lineker closed the gap against Argentina in the 81st minute with a downward header (1–2). It was his sixth goal, making him the top scorer in the tournament despite England being knocked out in the quarter-finals.

The Goal of the Century,

as seen by Valdano

Five minutes after his "Hand of God" goal, Maradona went on to score one of the greatest goals in history. Picking up the ball in his own half, he dribbled past five English players (Peter Beardsley, Peter Reid, Glenn Hoddle, Terry Butcher and Terry Fenwick) before outmanoeuvring Peter Shilton (2–0). It was absolutely sensational. "For me, that goal felt like it was being filmed by a moving camera. Like any self-respecting forward, I'd mirrored him up the pitch and was over by the far post to give him an option," recalled Argentine centre-forward Jorge Valdano. "However, there was still a surprise in store for me. Once we'd got back to the locker room, Diego told me he'd been trying to catch my eye to give me the ball in the best possible position. As if that goal hadn't been impressive enough, he'd also taken the time to look around him to see if he should pass the ball. Talk about insulting for the rest of us mere mortals! It proves that we were in the presence of a genius. Of course, if he'd have passed the ball to me, it would have been a very easy goal to score, but in that case it wouldn't have been the most beautiful goal in World Cup history."

"One of the best matches in the history of the World Cup."

Pelé

◀ A clash between Brazilian star Socrates and Frenchman Jean Tigana during the quarter-final in Guadalajara.

▲ Michel Platini scores the French equalizer in the first half.

A legendary match

21 JUNE 1986

BRAZIL 1–1 **FRANCE**
A.E.T.

CARECA 17   PLATINI 40

✗◉◉◉✗ 3–4 ◉◉◉✗◉

THIS HOTLY-ANTICIPATED quarter-final, between Brazil and France in Guadalajara on 21 June, lived up to expectations and was rated "one of the best matches in World Cup history," by none other than Pelé. France were on top form. They had won the European Championships two years earlier and boasted their "magic square" of Platini, Giresse, Tigana and Fernández, while Telê Santana's Brazil were a mixture of old (Sócrates, Júnior, Zico) and young talent. Both placed the emphasis on attack and, as a result, it was an open game, despite the sweltering 45°C heat. Brazil were first to score with a textbook play: Müller executed a double one-two with Júnior, who nudged the ball forward to Careca. The striker fired it past Joël Bats (1–0) to score his fifth goal of the tournament. Thirty-two minutes in, he missed the chance to score Brazil's second when his shot hit the post.

But as the minutes ticked by, France began to claw back possession. In the 41st minute, Manuel Amoros passed to Alain Giresse who found Dominique Rocheteau on the right. However, Yannick Stopyra missed his pass and clattered into Brazilian keeper Oscar. Hanging wide on the far side, Michel Platini pushed the ball into the empty goal amid protests from Brazil (1–1). So Platini celebrated his 31st birthday with a goal.

It was a nail-biting match and could have gone either way. Brazil were awarded a penalty in the 71st minute, but Bats saved Zico's kick. Deep into extra-time, Platini beautifully set up Bruno Bellone who was brought down by goalkeeper Carlos, but the referee didn't give a penalty. The outcome of the game now rested on the penalty shoot-out. Unlike the semi-final against West Germany in Seville four years earlier, France came out victorious, with Luis Fernández converting the last kick (4–3) after Brazil's Sócrates and Júlio César and France's Platini had all failed to find the back of the net.

"Two incredible teams"

Branco, Brazil left back.

"**It was indisputably one of the greatest moments of that World Cup: a superb encounter between two extremely technical sides**. France had brought out their big guns – Platini, Amoros, Tigana, Rocheteau and Giresse. Not to be outdone, Brazil had Careca, Júnior, Edinho, Zico, Sócrates and Alemão, who was soon to make his name in Naples alongside Maradona. From a technical point of view, it was a beautiful duel. The first half ended 1–1 with both teams having every chance in the second. They each showed off their talents and put on a magnificent show. Both teams were absolutely incredible."

▲ For the second World Cup running, West Germany end the hopes of Michel Platini's France in the semi-final. The predicted Platini-Maradona final was not to be.

German realism

25 JUNE 1986

FRANCE ▮▮ 0–2 ▆▆ **WEST GERMANY**

BREHME 9, VÖLLER 89

O N 25 JUNE in Guadalajara, four years after facing West Germany in Seville, reigning European champions France, who had knocked out both Italy and Brazil, found themselves favourites against the Germans. Following a mediocre group stage (a draw with Uruguay, victory over Scotland and then a loss to Denmark), Franz Beckenbauer's team struggled against Morocco in the round of 16 (1–0) and even more so in their quarter-final against Mexico (winning 4–1 in the penalty shoot-out after the match had ended in a 0–0 stalemate). In the ninth minute, France were caught unprepared by a left-foot shot from a free-kick by Andreas Brehme (0–1). It was a catastrophe for Henri Michel and his team, who were forced to chase the game. They did take control, but Michel Platini and then Maxime Bossis, unchallenged in front of Harald Schumacher's goal, both squandered good chances. After half time, Yannick Stopyra launched a solo challenge, but lost his battle with the German keeper. With stoppage time upon them, goalkeeper Schumacher threw the ball long to Klaus Allofs who passed to Rudi Völler. The Werder Bremen centre-forward lobbed it over the head of Joël Bats and rolled it into the deserted net (2–0). One goal at the start of the game, another right at the end, saw the Germans qualify for consecutive Finals and the world was denied the opportunity to see Platini and Maradona face off in the biggest game of them all.

58%

During the Mexico World Cup, forwards scored 58 per cent of the 132 goals compared with 33 per cent by midfielders and 8 per cent by defenders. It was more than in 1982, when forwards only scored 49 per cent of goals.

Bats's "Arconada moment"

Nine minutes into the semi-final between West Germany and France, Andreas Brehme scored a free-kick, his shot slipping under the body of the French keeper Joël Bats (above). It was an error that called to mind Luis Arconada's mistake two years earlier in the France-Spain Euro 84 Final. "I made a mistake with my hands on Brehme's free-kick. We had our chances, but we never managed to equalize. It was a really frustrating match," said Bats. "I remember the goal perfectly," said Brehme, the German wing-back. "The free-kick was on the far right of the penalty area. Felix Magath set me up by nudging me the ball, which I shot in low on the right of the goal. I think Bats could have done better. The French had an excellent team, particularly in midfield."

Maradona's two strokes of genius

25 JUNE 1986		
ARGENTINA 2–0 BELGIUM		
MARADONA 51, 63		

Against Belgium, a Jorge Burruchaga pass led to Maradona beating Jean-Marie Pfaff with a flick from the right (1–0). The Argentine number 10 then gave the crowds a miniature replay of his goal against England, beating three Belgian defenders and scoring with a shot from the left (2–0). Superior on every level, Argentina qualified easily for the final – their first since 1978. As for the Belgians, they achieved their best-ever result at the World Cup.

▲ Belgian captain Jan Ceulemans at Mexico 86.

◥ Diego Maradona scores the first of his two goals against Belgium.

Belgium's original Golden Generation

JAN CEULEMANS was Belgium's captain throughout their most successful decade, culminating in their semi-final appearance in Mexico. The Belgians had been finalists at Euro 1980, reached the second round of the FIFA World Cup 1982, and qualified for Euro '84. The class of '86 were hungry for success. "We played very badly against Mexico and Iraq in the group stage," recalled Ceulemans, the Club Brugge forward or attacking midfielder. "But in the round of 16 against Igor Belanov's Soviet Union, who were one of the fastest teams of the time, I managed to equalize to 2–2 with a volley after catching the ball on my chest. I actually thought I was offside when I did it. At that point, we regained our confidence and started to play brilliantly. It was one of our best performances against one of the favourites in the competition." The Belgians won the match 4–3 after extra-time and went on to beat Spain in the quarter-finals. Ceulemans, measuring 1.88 m, opened the scoring with a header (1–1, 5–4 in the

penalty shoot-out). "I remember receiving a cross from the right that was perfectly controlled by Frank Vercauteren. I knew exactly where he was going to put the ball because we had been playing together in the team for so long. My timing was just right." Once again, his physical power, endurance and leadership skills worked wonders. Depite Ceulemans's exploits, and those of the likes of Pfaff, Gerets, Grün and the talented Scifo, Belgium's memorable run came to a halt in the semi-final against Diego Maradona's Argentina. "We knew that we stood a chance against them if we could stop Maradona. It worked once, but he evaded us twice in the second half. It was enough," explained Ceulemans, nicknamed "Captain Courageous" or "*Sterke Jan*" ("Jan the Strong"). Ceulemans scored his third goal during the third-place match against France (2–4 after extra-time). "It was a wonderful adventure. I'm really proud of our team performance and the spirit we showed in Mexico."

PLAY-OFF FOR THIRD PLACE

▲ Jean-Pierre Papin receives his third-place medal from FIFA president João Havelange.

France on the podium

28 JUNE 1986	
FRANCE 4–2 BELGIUM A.E.T.	
FERRERI 27, PAPIN 43	CEULEMANS 11
GENGHINI 104	CLAESEN 73
AMOROS 111 (PEN)	

On 28 June in Puebla, France had to do without Platini, Giresse, Rocheteau, Stopyra and Fernández, but, thanks to their reserves (Le Roux, Ferreri, Vercruysse, Genghini and others), they took third place, as they had in 1958, by beating Belgium. Manuel Amoros converted a penalty – his only goal from 82 caps.

▲ Argentina's Jorge Burruchaga scores the winning goal of the 1986 World Cup Final, past Hans-Peter Briegel and goalkeeper Harald Schumacher.

▲▲ Diego Maradona escapes Lothar Matthäus and Ditmar Jakobs.

▲ *El Pibe* celebrates Argentina's flawless World Cup journey.

Success in two halves

29 JUNE 1986

ARGENTINA 3–2 **WEST GERMANY**

BROWN 23, VALDANO 56, BURRUCHAGA 84   RUMMENIGGE 74, VÖLLER 81

D URING THE FINAL on 29 June, the Argentinians delivered a footballing masterclass. Defender José Luis Brown opened the scoring in the 23rd minute with a header from a Jorge Burruchaga free-kick (1–0) after Harald Schumacher came out and missed the ball. It was Brown's only goal for the national team. Eleven minutes into the second half, Jorge Valdano made it 2–0. The move began with keeper Nery Pumpido throwing to Valdano. The Real Madrid centre-forward found Diego Maradona, who fed Héctor Enrique. Enrique passed upfield to Valdano, who finished the move that he had started. Carlos Bilardo's men had a total

stranglehold on the game. But to everyone's surprise, the Germans made a late second-half comeback. Andreas Brehme took a corner from the left in the 74th minute, which was deflected by Rudi Völler to Karl-Heinz Rummenigge, who threw himself forward to score from up close (1–2). There was a sense of déjà vu seven minutes later, when Völler headed the ball in from another corner (2–2). But, in the 84th minute, Maradona found an opening to Burruchaga, who made a break for the goal. The Nantes playmaker kept a cool head to score (3–2). Argentina secured their second World Cup title in front of a 114,580-strong crowd.

"It was Jesus coming to tell me we were world champions…"

Jorge Burruchaga, scorer of Argentina's winning goal

"After scoring I ran to the touchline and dropped to my knees. The first one to come and congratulate me was Sergio Batista. He was exhausted. He knelt down next to me. With his beard, it looked to me like Jesus had come to tell me we were world champions…"

Maradona's shirt

Argentina shirt worn by Diego Maradona during the finals in Mexico.

▶ **FIFA World Football Museum collection.**

Relatively quiet in the Final, in spite of his decisive pass for Argentina's third goal, Diego Maradona nonetheless illuminated the 1986 World Cup with his class. The Argentine captain scored five goals and made five assists. Only the Soviet Union's Igor Belanov (with four goals and six assists), Brazil's Careca and Spain's Emilio Butragueno (five goals and three assists each) came close to matching his feats.

▲ Harald Schumacher helps Diego Maradona back onto his feet.

▼ Argentina coach Carlos Bilardo watches his captain Diego Maradona give advice.

The untold story

During the competition, Argentina's technical staff tried to stop Diego Maradona from spending all of his time on the training pitch. "Like all of us, Maradona was getting really bored stuck in the hotel. The only way to pass the time was to play football. However, Carlos Bilardo didn't want us to expend all of our energy on the training pitch, particularly as our camp in Mexico was at altitude," explained Jorge Valdano. "We needed to save our strength. Sometimes you find yourself in this strange situation where the players want to play and train but the coach won't let them. It's the world turned upside down!"

▲ Argentina and West Germany line-up before the Final.

Maradona according to Bilardo

"The World Cup draw took place on 18 and 19 November 1985. For everyone at the time, the players, the journalists and the coaches, it was all about Platini. He'd just won the European Championships with France and he was on great form. After him, there was Rummenigge, Zico and Maradona. I think that's what pushed Diego to reach the Final and deliver such good performances. But it wasn't just that. He felt good on the pitch and perfectly understood his teammates. What Diego achieved in Mexico was glorious."

Matthäus analyses the Final

"Our coach, Franz Beckenbauer, had a lot of respect for Maradona and he knew that I had played well in a number of matches against him. He therefore modified our system of play. I played just in front of the defenders, in the middle of the pitch. Felix Magath played at number 10, me at number 8 and Hans-Peter Briegel or Andreas Brehme were in charge of winning the ball behind us. As a result, Maradona was not as effective against us as he had been in other matches, but our attacking game suffered as a result. We changed the system after going 2–0 down, and I played higher up the pitch, which allowed us to exert more pressure on Argentina. We equalized through two set-pieces, but in our joy we forgot to hold a high defensive line and were undone by a long pass… If the match had gone into extra-time, we would have won it."

86

The number of seconds Argentina's Marcelo Trobbiani spent on the pitch in the Final – his only appearance in the tournament. The number 21 replaced match winner Jorge Burruchaga in stoppage time.

1990

In a sensational opening, Cameroon beat defending champions Argentina – but this was the World Cup with the fewest number of goals per game and a plague of red cards. Both semi-finals were decided on penalties, with Italy and England losing out, and another penalty gave West Germany a 1–0 win over Argentina in the Final. Franz Beckenbauer was the first to win the World Cup as both captain and coach.

An all-star cast

◄ Four years after their World Cup Final defeat to Argentina, Lothar Matthäus and Rudi Völler are world champions.

▼ Giant mural in honour of Diego Maradona on the streets of Naples.

ITALY, THE COUNTRY WHERE FOOTBALL REIGNS SUPREME, hosted its second World Cup in 1990, 56 years on from the first. It was a time when Italian sides dominated European football. Silvio Berlusconi's AC Milan had just won the European Cup for the second year running (1989 and 1990); Genoa's Sampdoria took home the 1990 Cup-Winners' Cup; while Juventus won the UEFA Cup by beating another Italian club, Fiorentina (winning 3–1 in the first leg before drawing 0–0 in the second). This impressive trio of victories made Italy one of the favourites, with big names across the pitch (Zenga, Maldini, Baresi, Bergomi, Ancelotti, Donadoni, Baggio, Vialli, and Mancini). But plenty of big names from these Italian club sides would, of course, be playing for countries other Italy: Diego Maradona, who had ushered in Napoli's heyday, would appear for Argentina; AC Milan's Ruud Gullit, Marco van Basten and Frank Rijkaard for the Netherlands; and Inter Milan's Lothar Matthäus, Andreas Brehme and Jürgen Klinsmann for Germany. And with every major footballing nation except France lined up to take part, it promised to be a great tournament.

ITALIA'90

1990 FIFA WORLD CUP ITALY

Story of the qualifiers

Mexico and Chile left at home for cheating

ONE HUNDRED AND THREE countries played in the qualifiers. In Europe, 1982 and 1986 semi-finalists France were knocked out, finishing third in their group behind Yugoslavia and Scotland. Poland, Denmark, Portugal and Hungary also failed to book their place, while the Republic of Ireland qualified for the first time. In total, European teams made up 14 out of the 24 finalists. In the North, Central America and Caribbean zone, newcomers Costa Rica were ready to step onto the World Cup stage, while the USA returned after a 40-year absence. It was a similar story in Asia, with newcomers United Arab Emirates accompanying old-timers South Korea. In South America, Brazil, Uruguay and Colombia (following a playoff against Israel),

as well as reigning champions Argentina, qualified. But Mexico, who had entered over-age players into the qualifiers of the 1989 FIFA U-20 championship, were banned from taking part. Chile entered but on 3 September 1989, during an away game in Brazil, Chilean goalkeeper Roberto Rojas pretended to have been injured by a firework that had been thrown from the stands. His team-mates quit the pitch, but it later emerged that Rojas had hidden a scalpel in his glove and had inflicted the wounds himself in an attempt to win the match by default. Chile were consequently banned from the 1990 and 1994 tournaments. As for Africa, Cameroon were joined by Egypt, who hadn't qualified since 1934 – the last time the tournament had taken place in Italy.

▲ Costa Rica enjoy their first appearance at the World Cup finals.

The format was the same as for the 1986 tournament, with 24 countries split into six groups comprising four teams each. The top two teams from each group, plus the top four third-placed teams would qualify for the round of 16, at which point the tournament became a straight knockout competition.

Group stage

GROUP A

ITA	1–0	AUT
USA	1–5	TCH
ITA	1–0	USA
AUT	0–1	TCH
AUT	2–1	USA
ITA	2–0	TCH

	W	D	L	+	–	PTS
ITA	3	0	0	4	0	6
TCH	2	0	1	6	3	4
AUT	1	0	2	2	3	2
USA	0	0	3	2	8	0

GROUP B

ARG	0–1	CMR
URS	0–2	ROU
ARG	2–0	URS
CMR	2–1	ROU
ARG	1–1	ROU
CMR	0–4	URS

	W	D	L	+	–	PTS
CMR	2	0	1	3	5	4
ROU	1	1	1	4	3	3
ARG	1	1	1	3	2	3
URS	1	0	2	4	4	2

GROUP C

BRA	2–1	SWE
CRC	1–0	SCO
BRA	1–0	CRC
SCO	2–1	SWE
BRA	1–0	SCO
SWE	1–2	CRC

	W	D	L	+	–	PTS
BRA	3	0	0	4	1	6
CRC	2	0	1	3	2	4
SCO	1	0	2	2	3	2
SWE	0	0	3	3	6	0

GROUP D

UAE	0–2	COL
FRG	4–1	YUG
YUG	1–0	COL
FRG	5–1	UAE
FRG	1–1	COL
YUG	4–1	UAE

	W	D	L	+	–	PTS
FRG	2	1	0	10	3	5
YUG	2	0	1	6	5	4
COL	1	1	1	3	2	3
UAE	0	0	3	2	11	0

GROUP E

BEL	2–0	KOR
URU	0–0	ESP
BEL	3–1	URU
ESP	3–1	KOR
BEL	1–2	ESP
KOR	0–1	URU

	W	D	L	+	–	PTS
ESP	2	1	0	5	2	5
BEL	2	0	1	6	3	4
URU	1	1	1	2	3	3
KOR	0	0	3	1	6	0

GROUP F

ENG	1–1	IRL
NED	1–1	EGY
ENG	0–0	NED
IRL	0–0	EGY
ENG	1–0	EGY
NED	1–1	IRL

	W	D	L	+	–	PTS
ENG	1	2	0	2	1	4
IRL	0	3	0	2	2	3
NED	0	3	0	2	2	3
EGY	0	2	1	1	2	2

Knockout stages

ROUND OF 16

FRG	2–1	NED
TCH	4–1	CRC

ROUND OF 16

ENG	1–0 A.E.T.	BEL
CMR	2–1 A.E.T.	COL

ROUND OF 16

ITA	2–0	URU
IRL	0–0 5–4	ROU

ROUND OF 16

ESP	1–2 A.E.T.	YUG
BRA	0–1	ARG

QUARTER-FINAL

FRG	1–0	TCH

QUARTER-FINAL

ENG	3–2 A.E.T.	CMR

QUARTER-FINAL

ITA	1–0	IRL

QUARTER-FINAL

YUG	0–0 2–3	ARG

SEMI-FINAL

FRG	1–1 4–3	ENG

SEMI-FINAL

ITA	1–1 3–4	ARG

PLAY-OFF FOR THIRD PLACE

ITA	2–1	ENG

FINAL

FRG	1–0	ARG

ARG · AUT · BEL · BRA · CMR · COL
CRC · EGY · ENG · ESP · FRG · IRL
ITA · KOR · NED · ROU · SCO · SWE
TCH · UAE · URS · URU · USA · YUG

24 TEAMS

52
MATCHES PLAYED

168 | 16

CARDS

2 527 348
SPECTATORS

CIAO
OFFICIAL MASCOT

ITALIA '90
OFFICIAL LOGO

WEST GERMANY
WINNERS

×6

SALVATORE SCHILLACI
LEADING GOALSCORER

2.2
AVERAGE GOALS
PER MATCH

ETRUSCO UNICO
OFFICIAL MATCH BALL

Host cities and stadiums

All-seater stadiums

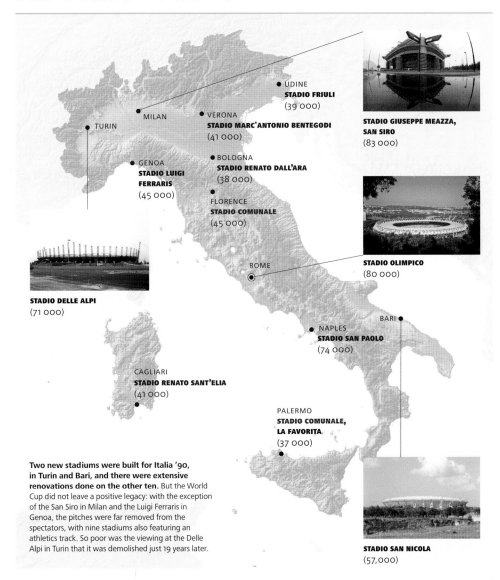

UDINE
STADIO FRIULI
(39 000)

MILAN

VERONA
STADIO MARC'ANTONIO BENTEGODI
(41 000)

TURIN

STADIO GIUSEPPE MEAZZA, SAN SIRO
(83 000)

GENOA
STADIO LUIGI FERRARIS
(45 000)

BOLOGNA
STADIO RENATO DALL'ARA
(38 000)

FLORENCE
STADIO COMUNALE
(45 000)

STADIO DELLE ALPI
(71 000)

ROME

STADIO OLIMPICO
(80 000)

BARI

NAPLES
STADIO SAN PAOLO
(74 000)

CAGLIARI
STADIO RENATO SANT'ELIA
(41 000)

PALERMO
STADIO COMUNALE, LA FAVORITA
(37 000)

STADIO SAN NICOLA
(57,000)

Two new stadiums were built for Italia '90, in Turin and Bari, and there were extensive renovations done on the other ten. But the World Cup did not leave a positive legacy: with the exception of the San Siro in Milan and the Luigi Ferraris in Genoa, the pitches were far removed from the spectators, with nine stadiums also featuring an athletics track. So poor was the viewing at the Delle Alpi in Turin that it was demolished just 19 years later.

A mixed bag

DESPITE THE INITIAL PROMISE, Italia '90 failed to live up to expectations. With some notable exceptions, the football was mediocre and predictable – the side that took the lead lost in just two of the 52 matches. And there were numerous fouls, lots of red cards (16 – twice as many as in 1986) and yellow cards (3.3 on average per match), professional fouls, dives, and lots of time-wasting. This became such an issue that the International Football Association Board responded by banning keepers from intercepting intentional back passes with their hands.

▼ The West Germany–Netherlands round of 16 saw many incidents.

◤ West Germany captain Lothar Matthäus celebrates his first goal against Yugoslavia as Jürgen Klinsmann looks on.

▲▲ Matthäus shoots and scores from the edge of the penalty area.

▲ Against Yugoslavia, Matthäus had the best game of his 150-cap international career, here recovering the ball from Safet Sušić.

Matthäus: German spirit

10 JUNE 1990

WEST GERMANY 4–1 **YUGOSLAVIA**

MATTHÄUS 28, 65, KLINSMANN 39, VÖLLER 71   JOZIĆ 55

AS A 21-YEAR-OLD ROOKIE IN 1982, Lothar Matthäus had only been brought on twice during the World Cup in Spain. By 1986, the German midfielder was a major influence as his team made it to the Final in Mexico. By 1990, Matthäus was captaining West Germany's national side. He set the tone in the team's first meeting against Yugoslavia (4–1). The Inter Milan player, wearing the number 10 shirt, was the first to put a score on the board after a quick change of direction. He then scored an absolute classic, storming up the pitch from inside his own half to net a low shot from the right that screamed past Tomislav Ivković (3–1). "I had a few good games, but the one that really stands out was our opener at the 1990 World Cup, when we laid the foundations for our winning campaign by beating Yugoslavia. We won 4–1 against a really strong Yugoslavia team who went on to the quarter-finals and only lost to Argentina on penalties. And I got two of the goals.

It was my 75th cap and I think it was the best of the 150 matches I played for Germany over the years."

The 29-year-old Matthäus, the life and soul of the team, was a skilled attacker and defender who never took his foot off the gas. He scored again against the United Arab Emirates and Czechoslovakia with a penalty in the quarter-finals (1–0). Standing at only 1.74 metres, this natural-born leader was fiercely competitive and was able to mobilize his troops. It paid off when he lifted the trophy on 8 July. "You never forget becoming a world champion. Everyone remembers it. You can take home all sorts of titles over the course of your career, but they've got nothing on it. All footballers dream of such a moment. And I was lucky enough to win a World Cup as captain," he said. After the competition, Matthäus was named Germany's Player of the Year, European Footballer of the Year, and *France Football's Ballon d'Or winner*. In 1991, he was named the first-ever FIFA World Player of the Year.

Coaches who played at the World Cup

German manager Franz Beckenbauer (below) played three World Cups himself (1966, 1970, and 1974), winning the third. The Republic of Ireland manager Jack Charlton, who coached his team to the quarter finals, won the 1966 Cup with England. As for Bobby Robson, he had played in 1958 and returned as manager in 1986 and 1990. Sweden's manager, Olle Nordin, played in the 1978 tournament, but he was unable to prevent his team losing three matches in 1990.

◀ Juan Cayasso celebrates Costa Rica's first-ever World Cup goal, against Scotland.

The Costa Rican tour de force

11 JUNE 1990

COSTA RICA 1–0 **SCOTLAND**

CAYASSO 49

PLAYING at their first World Cup finals, Costa Rica became the first Central American country to reach the second round. The team, coached by Bora Milutinović, beat Scotland in their first match and Sweden in their third (2–1, scored by Roger Flores and Hernán Medford), after losing narrowly to Brazil in their second game of the tournament (1–0). Their results placed them second in Group C behind Brazil. The Costa Rican team were incredibly disciplined and, while they had no stand-out players, goalkeeper Gabelo Conejo, a revelation in the group stages, proved invaluable. The modest keeper paid homage to Yugoslavian manager Bora Milutinović. "Bora had a long career behind him and he knew what he was getting into. There was no one like him for motivating you and he made us realize that the World Cup is something unique in your career. He never stopped believing in us. "

Bora Milutinović: miracle maker

Having coached Mexico to the quarter-finals four years earlier, Bora Milutinović was now on the Costa Rica payroll. Heading up this tiny country of three million people, which had no footballers playing abroad, the Yugoslavian sorcerer succeeded in winning two out of four matches. Thanks to his experience and the team's rigorous training, stars such as Ronald González, Juan Cayasso and Hernán Medford emerged. Milutinović had a method that seemed to work. "I always start by trying to understand the philosophy of the country, which is something that takes time. I have to understand how people think, learn to understand the decision-makers, and ensure that the training facilities are of good quality."

Cameroon's opening fanfare

8 JUNE 1990

ARGENTINA 0–1 **CAMEROON**

OMAM-BIYIK 67

TITLEHOLDERS ARGENTINA were in trouble right from their opening game against Cameroon on 8 June in Milan. Although the South Americans were dominant, Cameroon proved dangerous on the counter-attack. Down to 10 men after André Kana-Biyik was sent off in the 61st minute, then to nine after Benjamin Massing received his marching orders in the 88th, François Omam-Biyik still managed to score a header that was just too much for Nery Pumpido. It was an astonishing start to the World Cup. Bolstered by the win, Cameroon went on to beat Romania in their second match (2–1, both by Roger Milla) before losing 0–4 to the Soviet Union. But it didn't matter: Cameroon had got through the group stage for the first time.

▶ Cameroon's François Omam-Biyik scores the first goal of the 1990 World Cup, against defending champions Argentina.

> ## "If we're going to be knocked out like that, I hope our plane home crashes."

Carlos Bilardo, Argentina manager

"When we lost our opening match to Cameroon, we gathered in front of the blackboard at the hotel. Carlos Bilardo wasn't writing anything down. It seemed he was crying," recalled Argentina defender Oscar Ruggeri. "All of a sudden, he turned around and said to us, 'If we're going to be knocked out like that, I hope our plane home crashes.'"

▲ Argentine midfielder Pedro Troglio scores with a header – the first goal of the game against the USSR – after outjumping Andrei Zygmantovich and Igor Dobrovolski.

Maradona repeats the Hand of God

13 JUNE 1990

ARGENTINA 2–0 USSR

TROGLIO 27, BURRUCHAGA 79

FOUR YEARS after his famous "Hand of God" goal against England, Diego Maradona once more touched the ball with his hand, this time at his own end against Russia in their second match on 13 June. The score was 0–0. The referee did not award a penalty, even though the Napoli number 10, playing in front of a home crowd, appeared to deflect a Russian header that was flying towards the Argentinian net. With Sergio Goycochea standing in for keeper Nery Pumpido, who had broken his leg, the team pulled ahead thanks to a Pedro Troglio header from an Olarticoechea cross, and Jorge Burruchaga, who scored after Oleh Kuznetsov unintentionally sent the ball his way. They may have only drawn against Romania in an unconvincing third match (1–1), but Argentina still qualified by finishing third in Group B with three points.

A steep learning curve for the Emirates

The United Arab Emirates were the weakest team in the competition, conceding 11 goals in three matches against Colombia (0–2), West Germany (1–5) and Yugoslavia (1–4). The only consolation was that their two scorers, Khalid Ismaïl and Ali Thani Juma'a, received a Rolls Royce as a reward.

▲ Aerial duel between Costa Rica's Juan Cayasso and Sweden's Peter Larsson.

Another loss for Sweden

At Italia '90, Sweden became the first team to lose all three of their group-stage matches by the same score. The Swedes lost 2–1 to Brazil, Scotland and Costa Rica. It was their first appearance at the finals since 1978.

Draws that paid off

▲ Egypt's Hossam Hassan dribbles past the Netherlands' Graeme Rutjes.

Thanks to their three draws, against England, Egypt and the Netherlands (1–1), the Republic of Ireland finished second in Group F. It was a real coup for Jack Charlton's men. Ireland and the Netherlands found themselves level pegging with three draws and exactly the same scores. Lots were drawn and Ireland came out on top, with the Netherlands still qualifying as one of the best third-place teams.

Egypt's cracking campaign

12 JUNE 1990

NETHERLANDS 1–1 **EGYPT**

KIEFT 58   ABDELGHANI 83 (PEN)

HAVING PLAYED IN THE 1934 TOURNAMENT, Egypt had to wait 56 years to find themselves in the finals phase once more. It explains the sense of relief experienced by Hossam Hassan when he scored the only goal of their second-leg match against Algeria in the qualifiers (1-0) to earn his country their ticket to the finals. "That was the best moment of my career," said the Egyptian forward. "I remember that the whole country was behind us and supported us to achieve that dream."

Their opening match on 12 June in Palermo, against European champions the Netherlands, was a triumph for Egypt. After Egypt had spurned a number of chances, the Netherlands took the lead thanks to substitute Wim Kieft, but eight minutes before the final whistle Magdi Abdelghani converted a penalty. Egypt repeated the feat with a 0–0 draw against the Republic of Ireland in their second match, but lost their third to England (0–1). Manager Mahmoud El-Gohary's team nevertheless went out of the tournament with their heads high. "El-Gohary is like a father to me," said Hossam Hassan. "He's the greatest person I've ever met. We owe a great deal of the future success of Egyptian football to him."

◄ Uruguay's José Herrera controls the ball.

The Uruguayan miracle

21 JUNE 1990

SOUTH KOREA 0–1 **URUGUAY**

FONSECA 90

FACING elimination as the clock ticked past the 90th minute in their match against South Korea, Uruguay qualified in stoppage time thanks to a free-kick headed in by Daniel Fonseca. Uruguay had drawn 0–0 against Spain and lost 1–3 to Belgium, but the last-gasp victory left them third in Group E and they qualified for the knockout stages as one of the best third-placed teams. It was a close shave for Enzo Francescoli and co.

Both teams had already been eliminated when Austria played the United States (2–1) in Florence on 19 June. The match, refereed by Syrian Jamal Al Sharif, was notable for a then record number of yellow cards shown – nine in all. Five for Austria and four for the USA.

▶ Having dispossessed Colombian keeper René Higuita well outside the penalty area, Cameroon's Roger Milla ran on score the opening goal of the match in extra time.

▲ Roger Milla, the oldest goalscorer in the history of the World Cup, celebrates the first of his two goals against Colombia in his own inimitable style. The era of extravagant goal celebrations is launched!

The Old Lion roars again

23 JUNE 1990

CAMEROON 2–1 **COLOMBIA**
A.E.T.

MILLA 106, 109   REDÍN 115

Roger Milla's records

At 38 years and 20 days, Milla became the oldest scorer in a World Cup finals phase. The previous record was held by Sweden's Gunnar Gren, who scored in 1958 aged 37. Milla was also nearly twice as old as the youngest scorer in 1990, Costa Rica's 19-year-old Rónald González, who scored against Czechoslovakia.

ROGER MILLA should never have taken part in his second World Cup, after a first appearance in 1982. "I'd decided to end my international career, but the president ordered the sports minister to have me on the team," explained the forward, who played for JS Saint-Pierroise, a small team from La Réunion – hardly at the top of his sport. A predictably out-of-shape Milla was treated and used as a luxury substitute by Russian manager Valeri Nepomniashchi. "My only job was to come up with an action plan to ensure he'd be ready for the tournament. I also had to think about how best to use him. I told him he couldn't play the first half against such fit defenders. Roger would have been exhausted after 20 minutes. He said to me, 'OK coach. I'll do what you want.'"

When he scored against Romania in Cameroon's second group-stage match, 38-year-old Milla became the oldest goalscorer in World Cup history. Four minutes from time, he doubled the score by sending a bullet of a shot straight into the net. In the round of 16 match against Colombia (2–1, a.e.t.), the Old Lion gave fans two more memorable goals. "For the first goal I dribbled past three players before finding a way past René Higuita from the left. It was a classy goal," said Roger Milla. For the second, he plucked the ball from the Colombian goalkeeper's feet and sent it into the open goal.

Cameroon's trump card landed them in the quarter-finals for the first time ever. Milla did not score against England, but he did win a penalty and provided the assist for Eugène Ekéké's goal. Despite their defeat (2–3, a.e.t.), his four goals and idiosyncratic hip-wiggling celebrations made their mark on the tournament. "It's not magic; it's lots of work. I've always worked hard."

The European champions lose out

24 JUNE 1990

WEST GERMANY 2–1 **NETHERLANDS**

KLINSMANN 51, BREHME 82   R. KOEMAN 89 (PEN)

HAVING STOLEN THE SHOW AT EURO 1988, the Netherlands qualified for the round of 16 despite drawing all three Group matches. On 24 June in Milan they were knocked out after a tense match against West Germany. Frank Rijkaard and Rudi Völler were both sent off in the 22nd minute following an altercation.

◄ Red card for Germany's Rudi Völler and Dutchman Frank Rijkaard.

◄ Various official documents from the FIFA Archives refer to the consequences the fall of the Berlin Wall in 1989 had on world football. The 1990 World Cup was the last time the USSR and Yugoslavia would participate as unified countries.

Yugoslavia's last hurrah

The Yugoslavian team included a strong line-up of players with foreign clubs (Zlatko Vujović for PSG, Srečko Katanec for Sampdoria, and keeper Tomislav Ivković for Sporting CP). Two goals from Dragan Stojković, who scored the winning goal from a stunning free-kick, saw the team reach the quarter-finals for the first time since 1962. It was their last appearance as a team representing all of the Yugoslav states. Banned from the 1994 qualifiers, they returned in 1998 but in a much reduced form.

26 JUNE 1990

SPAIN 1–2 **YUGOSLAVIA**
A.E.T.

SALINAS 83   STOJKOVIĆ 78, 92

A tournament to forget for Brazil

24 JUNE 1990

BRAZIL 0–1 **ARGENTINA**

CANIGGIA 80

Italia '90 proved to be the biggest disappointment for Brazil since 1966. Brazil lost to Argentina on 24 June in Turin, in their only round of 16 defeat since the format was introduced in 1986. Maradona dribbled his way past three defenders and sent Claudio Caniggia the perfect assist, before being taken down by his Napoli team-mate Alemão. Caniggia shook off Brazilian keeper Cláudio Taffarel and made the most of the empty net. The Brazilians had been dominating the match, particularly during the first 20 minutes when Branco crossed to Dunga whose header hit the post.

◄ Claudio Caniggia dribbles his way past Brazil's keeper Taffarel to score the only goal of the match.

"The coach lost control of the situation"

Brazilian forward Bebeto, on his manager Sebastião Lazaroni

// AT THE TIME, the way things worked was that everyone would make suggestions on how to improve the team's game. Of course, everyone put their own interests first, which wasn't very productive. The coach lost control of the situation. Personally, I think it was up to him to make decisions and up to the players to accept them. In my case, I ended up top scorer in the Copa América and I was considered the best footballer in the South American qualifiers. But when the finals phase started, the coach decided to leave me out of the starting XI. He preferred to put his money on Müller and Careca, who were great players but who didn't understand each other like Romário and me. In my first match, against Costa Rica [Bebeto did not play the first match against Sweden], I only came on four minutes before the end. The team hadn't dazzled, including the two strikers. Then I injured myself ahead of the Scotland game, while Romário – who hadn't yet fully recovered from his pre-tournament operation – didn't play very well. Then, against Argentina, I didn't play and Romário wasn't even on the bench. We were eliminated."

▶ Cameroon celebrate their equalizer against England through an Emmanuel Kundé penalty.

▲ The Cameroon players make a lap of honour after their quarter-final defeat against England.

Twinkle-toed Cameroon

1 JULY 1990

ENGLAND ✚ 3–2 🔳 CAMEROON
A.E.T.

PLATT 25, LINEKER 83 (PEN), 105 (PEN)   KUNDÉ 61 (PEN), EKÉKÉ 65

N A WORLD CUP dominated by defences, this was a thrilling clash that could have gone either way. Deprived of André Kana-Biyik, Émile Mbouh, Victor N'Dip and Jules Onana, who were all suspended for this match in Naples, Cameroon went into their first-ever quarter-final with all guns blazing as François Omam-Biyik came up against an unbending Peter Shilton. It was, however, England who scored first, against the run of play, thanks to a cross from Stuart Pearce headed in by David Platt. After half time, substitute Roger Milla was brought down by Paul Gascoigne in the penalty box. A focused Emmanuel Kundé fired home the penalty past Shilton. Nicknamed the *Old Lion*, 38-year-old Milla was then involved in a world-class move. Turning around, he flew past the English rearguard and pushed the perfect pass to Eugène Ekéké, who chipped it into the goal (2–1). Cameroon seemed to have it

in the bag. Things were hotting up on both sides. Gary Lineker was brought down in the box and equalized with a beautiful penalty.

In extra-time, Lineker again made a break for the goal, but was tripped by goalkeeper Thomas N'Kono as he tried to snake past. The Tottenham striker was on fire, nailing his second penalty to hand England the lead (2–3). At no point in the match did Bobby Robson's squad break ranks. The English reached the semi-final four years after Diego Maradona's Argentina had snatched the opportunity away from them. "We were close to going out because of the quality of the Cameroonians, who attacked all the time, but our strength of character got us through," said Robson. "You have to give it to Cameroon and also Africa, showing their strength and quality," added Lineker. Cameroon's success meant that Africa would be represented by three teams at the finals from 1994 onwards.

"As if a dagger had been plunged into my heart."

Valeri Nepomniachi, Cameroon's Russian manager.

"**My regrets about that match will follow me my whole life**. It's as if a dagger had been plunged into my heart. I think I'm the one to blame. When we were leading 2–1, I didn't manage to convey to the players that they should take their time and stop attacking left, right and centre. The Cameroonians were very focused on offence. However, they didn't really like defending. Our central defenders weren't very fast and Lineker exploited this weakness twice. We should have shown more restraint and narrowed the gaps. But the tournament was still a wonderful experience. I was lucky enough to find myself in the right place at the right time. I was in charge of some very talented players. All I needed to do was let it show."

The official song becomes a golden disc

The official anthem "Un'estate italiana" by Edoardo Bennato and Gianna Nannini stayed at number one in Italy for 16 weeks.

◀ **FIFA World Football Museum collection.**

72%

Of the eighteen kicks taken during shoot-outs at Italia '90, 13 were successful (72 per cent), three were saved and two were missed.

◀ West Germany's Lothar Matthäus struggles to shake off Czechoslovakia's Ivo Knofliček.

▲ Diego Maradona congratulates his keeper, Sergio Goycochea, who had made two saves in the penalty shoot-out to see Argentina through to the semi-finals.

Goycochea: king of penalties

30 JUNE 1990

YUGOSLAVIA ▬ 0–0 ══ ARGENTINA
A.E.T.

xⓍⓍxx 2–3 ⓍⓍxxⓍ

ARGENTINA had to wait for the penalty shoot-out to qualify against Yugoslavia, who had been reduced to ten men after Refik Šabanadžović was sent off in the 31st minute, on 30 June in Florence (0–0, 3–2 on penalties). Goalkeeper Sergio Goycochea was called up to replace an injured Nery Pumpido and proved his worth by saving shots from Dragoljub Brnović and Faruk Hadžibegić, while Dragan Stojković hit the crossbar. But Argentina's last defence had a secret weapon. "We hadn't been able to go back to the locker room before the penalty shoot-out. Like a lot of the players, I'd drunk a lot of water during the 120 minutes, but hadn't got rid of it all because keepers run a lot less. Therefore, I really needed to go to the toilet. Since I wasn't allowed, I asked a teammate to stand next to me so I could urinate on the pitch. I did it again against Italy in the semi-final and it worked again…"

Czechoslovakia go down fighting

1 JULY 1990

WEST GERMANY ▬ 1–0 ▬ CZECHOSLOVAKIA

MATTHÄUS 25 (PEN)

THE FANTASTIC Czechoslovakian campaign, led by coach Jozef Venglöš, was brought to a halt on 1 July in Milan. After outclassing their opponents, with shots from captain Ivan Hašek and Michal Bílek saved on the line, Czechoslovakia only lost because of a penalty for Jürgen Klinsmann, taken by Lothar Matthäus in the 25th minute (1–0). Having been finalists in 1934 and 1962, this turned out to be Czechoslovakia's last World Cup, as the country was dissolved in 1993, although a combined team of Czechs and Slovaks participated unsuccessfully in the 1994 qualifiers.

3

Czech forward Tomáš Skuhravý scored a hat-trick in their 4–1 victory over Costa Rica. Only two hat-tricks were scored in Italy, the other one by the Spaniard Michel against South Korea in the group stage (3–1).

◄ Defender Giuseppe Bergomi stops Niall Quinn in the quarter-final between Italy and the Republic of Ireland in Rome.

Impenetrable Italian defence

30 JUNE 1990		
ITALY	1-0	REPUBLIC OF IRELAND
SCHILLACI 38		

TALY'S 1–0 QUARTER-FINAL WIN over the Republic of Ireland was their fifth consecutive match without conceding a goal. It was a record for the finals phase. Before this, six goalkeepers had kept four clean sheets in a row, starting with Gylmar of Brazil in 1958. Alongside Walter Zenga, Italy's defence consisted of Paolo Maldini on the left and Giuseppe Bergomi on the right, with Franco Baresi and Riccardo Ferri in the centre.

"Years later, people still talk about it"

David O'Leary, Republic of Ireland centre-back.

"Italy was an absolutely fantastic experience. I just think we got that little bit of luck. But the squad for Italia '90 was a strong one. If you go through the team, most of the players were playing for top clubs in what is now the Premier League. And there was a great atmosphere in the team, which was how we reached the quarters in our first World Cup campaign." The Arsenal centre-back proved a huge success on 25 June in Genoa, scoring the deciding goal in the round-of-16 penalty shoot-out against Romania (0–0, 5–4 on penalties). "I knew walking up to get the ball I was going to put it to the goalkeeper's left and that's what I made sure I did. There were about 20,000 brilliant Irish supporters behind the goal. They were so still and the eruption of green afterwards when the ball hit the net was absolutely amazing. It's a fantastic memory."

▲ Italian defender Paolo Maldini.

▲ Italian defender Giuseppe Bergomi.

3 The Italian team contained three veterans from their 1982 title-winning team in Spain – Franco Baresi, Giuseppe Bergomi and Pietro Vierchowod.

◄ Italy striker Salvatore "Totò" Schillaci celebrates scoring against Argentina in the semi-finals.

Totò's star turn for Italy

The Adidas Golden Ball for best player in the World Cup and the Golden Boot for top scorer went to Italy's Totò Schillaci.

◄ **FIFA World Football Museum collection.**

Totò Schillaci's Indian summer

20

In total, 20 of the 115 goals scored at this World Cup (17 per cent) were scored by substitutes.

THE MAN OF THE MOMENT at the 1990 World Cup was Salvatore "Totò" Schillaci. Going into the tournament, the Italian only had a single cap from a warm-up game against Switzerland. A year earlier, the striker had become the top scorer in Serie B, with Messina, before joining Juventus. "I was just delighted to be in the 22-man squad. And even if I hadn't played a single minute, I'd have been happy just to sit on the bench," he said. In their first match against Austria, the Italians were struggling. Seventy-five minutes in, coach Azeglio Vicini sent on Schillaci to replace Andrea Carnevale. Three minutes later, Totò had changed the host nation's fortunes with a powerful header (1–0). "I was a bit nervous. We were at the Stadio Olimpico [in Rome] in front of 73,000 *fans*. I just wanted to do my best. But it all happened very quickly when Gianluca Vialli passed to me and I scored. I didn't know where to run, so I ploughed into Stefano Tacconi, the substitute

goalkeeper, who was my team-mate at Juventus. I can't describe how it felt." The 25-year-old number 19 was on a roll, and the goals just kept coming. He was Italy's stand-out player against Czechoslovakia, their third match, when he headed in a volley from Giuseppe Giannini. Then, in Italy's round-of-16 encounter against Uruguay, his strike from the left in the 65th minute found the top of keeper Fernando Álvez's goal for Italy's first goal in a 2–0 win. In the quarter-finals, against the Republic of Ireland, it was Schillaci again who scored the winning goal in the 38th minute after a Roberto Donadoni strike bounced off the keeper's gloves. Poaching in the box, his right foot pushed the ball into the open Irish goal. It was his fourth goal of the tournament. He scored again in the semi-finals against Argentina, once more capitalizing on Sergio Goycochea's badly repelled save , but failed to prevent Italy from being knocked out, 4–3 on penalties after the match had ended 1–1

after extra-time. "It was as if a building had collapsed on me. I spent two hours in the dressing room crying. Our dream had slipped through our fingers."

Schillaci was not a fan of taking penalties, but agreed to do so in the third-place playoff match against England. "Roberto Baggio said to me, 'If you get it you'll be the top scorer.' I accepted his offer." With six goals under his belt, the Sicilian from Palermo took home the Adidas Golden Shoe (awarded to the tournament's leading goalscorer) and the Adidas Golden Ball (awarded to the tournament's best player). Over the course of the competition he had become the most effective centre-forward on the planet. What happened next, at club level, would be less extraordinary, but what did that matter? "Thanks to the World Cup, I became known. Playing for your country can change your life. It did for me. Although in some ways my career only lasted three weeks. But I wouldn't swap it for anything in the world."

▲ Claudio Caniggia scores Argentina's equalizer in the semi-final against Italy, despite best efforts made by Walter Zenga and defenders Pietro Vierchowod and Franco Baresi.

Italy miss their chance

3 JULY 1990

ITALY ❚ **1–1** 🇦🇷 **ARGENTINA**
A.E.T.

SCHILLACI 17   CANIGGIA 67

☺☺☺✕✕ 3–4 ☺☺☺☺

THERE WERE HIGH EXPECTATIONS in Naples on 3 July as the winners of the previous two tournaments fought for a place in the Final. It marked the first meeting between the host country and the defending champions since 1962. Emboldened by their five wins in a row, the Italians were the favourites against an inconsistent Argentina (only two wins in five games). Maradona, who had been playing for Napoli for the past two seasons, was as popular among the Neapolitans as their own national side. These split loyalties were summed up on the fans' banners, which read, "Diego in our hearts, Italy in our chants," and "Maradona: Naples loves you, but Italy is our homeland."

Salvatore Schillaci was the first to find his mark, scoring in the 17th minute from a ball parried by Sergio Goycochea after a Gianluca Vialli volley. Azeglio Vicini's men failed to build on their land, though. The fouls and tackles increased and the attitudes on the pitch were appalling. Yet the Argentinians refused to give up and levelled the score from one of the few opportunities to come their way. In the 67th minute, Maradona shifted play to Julio Olarticoechea, who crossed for Claudio Caniggia. Caniggia flicked the ball past Walter Zenga to equalize with a clever header. In extra-time, Roberto Baggio put Goycochea through his paces with a free-kick. But despite Ricardo Giusti being sent off, Argentina managed to hold out. For the first time in a World Cup, Italy were facing a penalty shoot-out. Roberto Donadoni and Aldo Serena both missed for the hosts, while the Argentinians scored all four of their spot-kicks to reach the Final.

517

After going five matches without conceding a single goal, Italy keeper Walter Zenga was finally beaten in the 67th minute of the semi-final against Argentina by a Claudio Caniggia header. Zenga had nevertheless just beaten a record for having gone 517 minutes without conceding in the finals phase. The previous record was 500 minutes, set by England's Peter Shilton in the 1982 and 1986 tournaments. In all, in spite of David Platt also finding a way through Zenga in the Italy-England third-place playoff match (2–1), the Inter Milan goalkeeper only let in two goals in seven matches.

◄ Paul Gascoigne in tears as England are knocked out in the semi-finals by West Germany.

The tears that started a revolution

The most famous tears in the history of the World Cup were shed by England's Paul Gascoigne during the semi-final in Turin against West Germany after he realised that he would miss the Final if England won the match. But those tears also sparked a revolution that would change English football for ever, the effects of which are still being felt the world over. During the 1980s England had fallen out of love with football. Constant stories of hooliganism at home and abroad, the Bradford fire, Heysel and Hillsborough all brought shame on the nation that had created the game. Football had become a dirty word: "A slum sport played in slum stadiums increasingly watched by slum people," had been the damning verdict of one newspaper. Yet here was England's star player showing that he cared. Football suddenly mattered. It became fashionable again. Stadiums were improved, attendances rose, and television money started to pour into a game that people wanted to be associated with. In 1992 the Premier League was formed and the rest, as they say, is history…

Three in a row for West Germany

4 JULY 1990

WEST GERMANY ▬ 1-1 ✚ ENGLAND
A.E.T.

BREHME 60   LINEKER 80

⊕⊕⊕⊕ 4–3 ⊕⊕⊕✗✗

THOMAS HÄSSLER launched a solo raid on the England defence, but was fouled by Stuart Pearce to give Andreas Brehme the free-kick. The German left-winger was lucky to hit the bullseye as his shot bounced off Paul Parker and looped over Peter Shilton. Brehme had also scored from a free-kick in the 1986 semi-final against France. With this second semi-final completely up for grabs, Gary Lineker capitalized as the ball bounced off the German defence, launching England's comeback with a beautiful touch and left-footed shot. In extra-time, both Chris Waddle and Guido Buchwald hit the post. England left-footers Pearce and Waddle each missed their penalty shots – the first found Bodo Illgner and the second flew over the crossbar – leaving West Germany to reach their third consecutive Final.

4

The number of matches that were settled on penalties: Argentina v Yugoslavia, Republic of Ireland v Romania and the two semi-finals.

PLAY-OFF FOR THIRD PLACE

▲ Roberto Baggio opens the scoring for Italy against England in the third-place play-off.

Italy finish third

7 JULY 1990

ITALY ▮▮ 2–1 ✚ ENGLAND

BAGGIO 70   PLATT 81
SCHILLACI 86 (PEN)

Italy took third place after beating England 2–1 on 7 July in Bari. Roberto Baggio and Salvatore Schillaci both scored, Schillaci from a penalty, with David Platt getting the English goal. Despite six victories in seven games, the Italians did not reap the rewards their performances deserved.

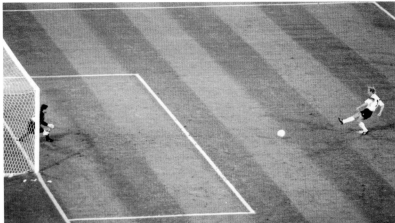

▲ Andreas Brehme's penalty beats Sergio Goycochea to give West Germany their winning 1–0 lead.

◄ Maradona's skill was not enough for Argentina to defend their title.

Germany take their revenge

8 JULY 1990

WEST GERMANY 1–0 **ARGENTINA**

BREHME 85 (PEN)

▲ Captains Lothar Matthäus and Diego Maradona lead West Germany and Argentina out before the 1990 FIFA World Cup Final.

0

This World Cup featured the least goals ever scored per match at 2.21, and it was the first since 1962 at which no own goals were scored.

WEST GERMANY were the first team to play three World Cup Finals in a row and this time, after their loss to the same opponents in Mexico, succeeded in lifting the trophy. It was their third title, having previously won in 1954 and 1974. The weakened Argentinians were missing four players, including Ricardo Giusti, who had been sent off against Italy, and Claudio Caniggia, their semi-final match-winner, who had picked up a second yellow card during the match. It was a desperately poor match – the first Final to feature less than three goals, the first in which one of the two teams failed to score and the first where there was no goal from open play. It was also the first in which a player was sent off. Not a great advert for the game. The defensive South Americans actually finished with nine men after Pedro Monzón (in the 64th minute) and Gustavo Dezotti (in the 87th minute) were both sent off. Defender Monzón, who was brought on at half time, only played 19 minutes of the Final.

Marked closely by Guido Buchwald, Diego Maradona kept out of the limelight. He was recovering from an injury to his left ankle and was not on top form. He was also whistled at every time he touched the ball, the Roman crowd seeing him as a double traitor: not only did he play for Napoli, but he had also been the main reason behind Italy's semi-final elimination. It made his tears at the end of the match all the more bitter. "It was the biggest disappointment of my career. I'd rather have lost 0–4 than have lost in that way," said Maradona.

Ultimately, Germany took the lead in the 85th minute when a penalty was awarded following a foul on Rudi Völler. Matthäus, who was an old hand at this, stood aside and let Andreas Brehme take centre stage. Just before he took his shot, Rudi Völler pulled him aside to say, "If you score it we'll be world champions." "Talk about pressure!" Brehme later commented when telling the tale. But the German defender, who was playing for Inter Milan at the time alongside Matthäus and Klinsmann, did not falter, calmly slotting the ball into the left-hand corner of the net. After losing out in two Finals, West Germany had finally come out on top. Brehme was elevated to the status of national hero. However, he refused to place too much importance on the penalty. "People talk about that penalty too much. At any rate, we deserved the victory because Argentina didn't show up to the Final. The rest is all hot air. "

▲ Four years on from the 1986 Final, it was the same teams but the opposite result. West Germany celebrate their third world title.

▶ There were tears from Gazza at the semi-final. Now, after the Final, it was Maradona's turn.

"As the minutes passed, I felt from his attitude that he was more and more resigned. Each time he looked at me, he seemed to be saying, 'Really? Is he still there?'"

Guido Buchwald, Maradona's marker in the 1990 Final.

Bilardo vs Beckenbauer: the rematch

Only two managers in World Cup history have faced each other in two Finals: Carlos Bilardo and Franz Beckenbauer. **In Mexico, the Argentinian got the upper hand when his side won 3–2, but four years later, in Italy, the West German took his revenge (1–0).** "At the end of the Final, I did the same as Beckenbauer had done four years earlier: I congratulated him," explained Bilardo. Both men also were in charge for 14 matches in the finals, winning eight. Beckenbauer, however, was the first person to win the World Cup as a captain and a coach – a feat matched by France's Didier Deschamps in 2018. Mário Zagallo was Brazil's winning coach in 1970, but he was not captain in either 1958 or 1962.

Peter Shilton's records

The third-place playoff was England keeper Peter Shilton's 125th and final international match. At the age of 40 (born 18 September 1949), the Derby County goalie was the oldest player in the tournament . The 0–0 draw against the Netherlands in the first round was his 120th international match. It enabled him to beat the European record set by Ireland's Pat Jennings in 1986. England's 1–0 win over Belgium in the round of 16 saw Shilton's goal remain untouched for the tenth time in the World Cup finals – another record, equalled only by Fabien Barthez of France in 2006.

1994

Although the USA hadn't fully embraced "soccer", the 1994 tournament was watched by more spectators than any other World Cup. Innovations included three points for a win and names on players' shirts, and there were great goals, especially Said Al Owairan's solo effort for Saudi Arabia against Belgium. But there were none in the Final for the first time, as Brazil won a record fourth title by beating Italy on penalties.

The United States embraces soccer

◄ Brazilian celebrations. A record fourth World Cup triumph for Brazil came 24 years after their third.

▼ Singer Diana Ross at the opening ceremony of the World Cup 1994.

USA '94 was yet another attempt to engage the American people with the world's game, following on from the American Soccer League of the 1920s and the NASL of the 1970s. It certainly represented a step in the right direction and led to the creation of Major League Soccer two years later. But although crowds were the biggest in the history of the World Cup, the tournament was strangely detached from a host nation gripped by the O.J. Simpson drama unfolding live on television at the same time.

Despite four time zones and 4000 kilometres between some venues, along with searing temperatures and humidity, the hosts put on a good show. Diana Ross missed a penalty in the opening ceremony and the tournament ended with another, Roberto Baggio's handing the title to Brazil.

Televised broadcasts on ABC and ESPN attracted 8.76 million American households, with a peak of 8.95 million for the round of 16 match between Brazil and the United States. For the Final, Univision, the Spanish-language channel, secured the best audience, with 1.62 million households.

*WorldCup*USA**94**

Story of the qualifiers

Zambia's tragedy

O N 27 APRIL 1993, Zambia travelled to Senegal to play a qualifying match. Their plane went down in the sea just after taking off from Libreville airport; everyone on board died. Captain Kalusha Bwalya, who had made his own arrangements to travel to the match, and Charly Musonda, who was injured at the time, were the lucky ones. A new team was quickly assembed, but they finished second behind Morocco in their final round group.

Having almost qualified with two games to spare, and needing only a draw against only Israel or Bulgaria, France went down twice at the Parc des Princes, after leading in both games. England, Uruguay, Czechoslovakia and Denmark, the defending European champions, were among other notable teams eliminated. For Africa, which was from now on allocated three places, the qualifiers were Cameroon, Morocco and Nigeria, the latter making their first finals appearance, alongside Saudi Arabia and Greece. Russia succeeded the USSR while a reunited Germany qualified automatically as the holders. In total, 130 countries took part. Among the smallest countries were the Faroe Islands and San Marino, while the Baltic countries (Estonia, Lithuania and Latvia), who had already taken part in 1934 and 1938, made their return. Chile, as a result of the Rojas affair (*see* 1990), remained suspended, while Yugoslavia were also suspended owing to the war affecting the country and to UN sanctions.

▲ With names now on shirts, fans were able to pay tribute to their favourite players.

Names on shirts

At USA '94, players had their names printed on the backs of their shirts for the first time at a World Cup. This was to make the game easier to follow. Long popular in American sports, names had first been used at Euro '92 in Sweden.

Group stage

GROUP A

USA	1–1	SUI
COL	1–3	ROU
ROU	1–4	SUI
USA	2–1	COL
SUI	0–2	COL
USA	0–1	ROU

	W	D	L	+	–	PTS
ROU	2	0	1	5	5	6
SUI	1	1	1	5	4	4
USA	1	1	1	3	3	4
COL	1	0	2	4	5	3

GROUP B

CMR	2–2	SWE
BRA	2–0	RUS
BRA	3–0	CMR
SWE	3–1	RUS
RUS	6–1	CMR
BRA	1–1	SWE

	W	D	L	+	–	PTS
BRA	2	1	0	6	1	7
SWE	1	2	0	6	4	5
RUS	1	0	2	7	6	3
CMR	0	1	2	3	11	1

GROUP C

GER	1–0	BOL
ESP	2–2	KOR
GER	1–1	ESP
KOR	0–0	BOL
BOL	1–3	ESP
GER	3–2	KOR

	W	D	L	+	–	PTS
GER	2	1	0	5	3	7
ESP	1	2	0	6	4	5
KOR	0	2	1	4	5	2
BOL	0	1	2	1	4	1

GROUP D

ARG	4–0	GRE
NGA	3–0	BUL
ARG	2–1	NGA
GRE	0–4	BUL
ARG	0–2	BUL
GRE	0–2	NGA

	W	D	L	+	–	PTS
NGA	2	0	1	6	2	6
BUL	2	0	1	6	3	6
ARG	2	0	1	6	3	6
GRE	0	0	3	0	10	0

GROUP E

ITA	0–1	IRL
NOR	1–0	MEX
ITA	1–0	NOR
MEX	2–1	IRL
ITA	1–1	MEX
IRL	0–0	NOR

	W	D	L	+	–	PTS
MEX	1	1	1	3	3	4
IRL	1	1	1	2	2	4
ITA	1	1	1	2	2	4
NOR	1	1	1	1	1	4

GROUP F

BEL	1–0	MAR
NED	2–1	KSA
KSA	2–1	MAR
BEL	1–0	NED
BEL	0–1	KSA
MAR	1–2	NED

	W	D	L	+	–	PTS
NED	2	0	1	4	3	6
KSA	2	0	1	4	3	6
BEL	2	0	1	2	1	6
MAR	0	0	3	2	5	0

Knockout stages

ROUND OF 16

ROU	3–2	ARG
KSA	1–3	SWE

ROUND OF 16

NED	2–0	IRL
BRA	1–0	USA

ROUND OF 16

MEX	1–1 / 1–3	BUL
GER	3–2	BEL

ROUND OF 16

NGA	1–2 A.E.T.	ITA
ESP	3–0	SUI

QUARTER-FINAL

ROU	2–2 / 4–5	SWE

QUARTER-FINAL

NED	2–3	BRA

QUARTER-FINAL

BUL	2–1	GER

QUARTER-FINAL

ITA	2–1	ESP

SEMI-FINAL

SWE	0–1	BRA

SEMI-FINAL

BUL	1–2	ITA

PLAY-OFF FOR THIRD PLACE

SWE	4–0	BUL

FINAL

BRA	0–0 / 3–2	ITA

ARG BEL BOL BRA BUL CMR
COL ESP GER GRE IRL ITA
KOR KSA MAR MEX NED NGA
NOR ROU RUS SUI SWE USA

24 TEAMS

52
MATCHES PLAYED

220 | 15
CARDS

3 587 538
SPECTATORS

STRIKER
OFFICIAL MASCOT

WorldCupUSA94
OFFICIAL LOGO

BRAZIL
WINNERS

×6

**HRISTO STOICHKOV
AND OLEG SALENKO**
LEADING GOALSCORERS

2.7
AVERAGE GOALS
PER MATCH

QUESTRA
OFFICIAL MATCH BALL

▲ USA players celebrate a goal scored in the group match against Colombia in Los Angeles.

Regulations

Three points for a win introduced

The tournament brought together 24 teams split into six groups of four. The top two from each group qualified for the round of 16, as did the four best third-placed sides. However, a win was now worth three points. Another innovation, to separate the teams, was that individual goal difference prevailed (except for the best third-placed teams where overall goal difference was used). Furthermore, no group could contain more than one team from the same geographic zone, with the exception of Europe. Lastly, with the deliberate backpass to the goalkeeper being prohibited, the role of the goalkeeper changed into that of a second sweeper.

Host cities and stadiums

Soccer's Stateside conversion

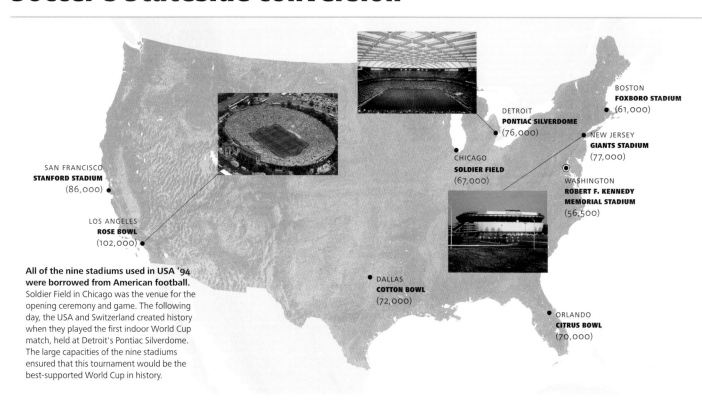

BOSTON
FOXBORO STADIUM
(61,000)

DETROIT
PONTIAC SILVERDOME
(76,000)

NEW JERSEY
GIANTS STADIUM
(77,000)

CHICAGO
SOLDIER FIELD
(67,000)

WASHINGTON
**ROBERT F. KENNEDY
MEMORIAL STADIUM**
(56,500)

SAN FRANCISCO
STANFORD STADIUM
(86,000)

LOS ANGELES
ROSE BOWL
(102,000)

DALLAS
COTTON BOWL
(72,000)

ORLANDO
CITRUS BOWL
(70,000)

All of the nine stadiums used in USA '94 were borrowed from American football. Soldier Field in Chicago was the venue for the opening ceremony and game. The following day, the USA and Switzerland created history when they played the first indoor World Cup match, held at Detroit's Pontiac Silverdome. The large capacities of the nine stadiums ensured that this tournament would be the best-supported World Cup in history.

The cover of American weekly *Newsweek* warmly welcomes soccer.

◄ **FIFA World Football Museum collection.**

▶ The American team line up before their game against Colombia.

"Magic"

**Alexi Lalas,
United States defender**

"That magical summer changed my life. We had been training for two years before the event, almost like a club. I remember our victory against Colombia, who were still one of the favourites for the tournament (2–1 in their second group-stage match). It was a magical moment in California in front of more than 100,000 people. Those flags, those screams and those cheers were things that I could never forget."

▶ American John Harkes chases Colombia's Carlos Valderrama.

Andrés Escobar

After scoring an own goal, from an interception at full stretch, during his side's 2–1 defeat to the United States, Colombian defender Andrés Escobar was assassinated on 2 July 1994 in the car park of a bar in Medellín. The assumption that the murder was a hit job by gamblers or even drug dealers, who would have lost money because of his unfortunate act against the USA, was neither ruled out nor proven. Escobar, aged 27 and capped 50 times, had also taken part in the 1990 World Cup. Around 80,000 people attended his funeral.

A welcome US surprise

22 JUNE 1994

UNITED STATES 🇺🇸 2–1 🇨🇴 **COLOMBIA**

ESCOBAR 34 (O.G.), STEWART 52   VALENCIA 89

THE US NATIONAL TEAM produced some encouraging performances in the group stages. They started off with a draw against Switzerland (1–1 with a goal by Eric Wynalda) and then beat a Colombia team containing the likes of Carlos Valderrama and Faustino Asprilla. The defeat against Romania in the third match (0–1) made no difference: the United States, third in Group A with four points, qualified for the round of 16. This was the first time that the Americans had progressed past the first round since 1930. "We raised awareness of football in the United States," Eric Wynalda was delighted to say. "It was a really special feeling." The USA also owed this qualification to their coach Bora Milutinović, who had been in the job since March 1991. The Serbian had a track record for getting the host nation through the group stages: he had done the same with Mexico in 1986. Playing a 4-4-2, the US team was highly disciplined team, very good on set-pieces and tremendously fit. Their only downside was a slight lack of attacking creativity. Personalities such as captain and goalkeeper Tony Meola, defensive linchpins Marcelo Balboa and Alexi Lalas, as well as attacking midfielders Tab Ramos and John Harkes, stood out.

Salenko's record

28 JUNE 1994

RUSSIA 6-1 CAMEROON

SALENKO 15, 41, 44(PEN), 72, 75   MILLA 46
RADCHENKO 81

DESPITE TWO OPENING DEFEATS (1–2 against Brazil and then 1–3 against Sweden), which left them no chance of finishing in the top three, Russia served up a treat for their final group match. Coach Pavel Sadyrin's men swept aside Cameroon 6–1, with five goals from Oleg Salenko. It was a record for the final stages of a World Cup for the Russian, who, despite Russia's group-stage elimination, ended up as the competition's joint top goalscorer with Bulgarian Hristo Stoichkov (six goals).

◀ Oleg Salenko scored a record five goals in a single World Cup match, against Cameroon.

Milla and the roaring 42s

Although Cameroon collapsed against Russia (1–6), Roger Milla pulled a goal back in the 46th minute (1–3), by wrong-footing Russian goalkeeper Cherchesov from close range. Having just come onto the pitch, the "Old Lion", 42 years old, thus broke his own record and became the tournament's oldest

scorer. Aged just 17, his teammate Rigobert Song became the youngest player ever to be sent off in a World Cup, against Brazil. For his part, American Fernando Clavijo, 37 years old, received a red card in the round of 16, again against Brazil, which made him the oldest player to be sent off in the final stages.

◀ Cameroon's Roger Milla and Russia's Oleg Salenko both set new records in the match between the two.

A debut to remember for Nigeria

21 JUNE 1994

NIGERIA 3-0 BULGARIA

YEKINI 21, AMOKACHI 43, AMUNIKE 55

ONLY TWO OF THE NIGERIAN TEAM played outside of Europe, which helped to offset their lack of World Cup experience. The technical quality of their players, particularly in attack, and their ability to move forward very quickly, thanks to master technicians such as Finidi George (Ajax), Emmanuel Amunike (Zamalek), Daniel Amokachi (Club Brugge) and Rashidi Yekini (Vitória Setúbal), were major assets. Their qualities enabled them to defeat Bulgaria (3–0) and Greece (2–0) and take second place in Group D, despite a defeat in their second match against Argentina (1–2).

▲ Nigeria's Rashidi Yekini celebrates his goal against Bulgaria.

"We were only thinking about having fun and the pleasure of playing."

Stephen Keshi, Nigerian defender.

"What was special about 1994 was that we had been playing together for six years. And although our team was made up of players who were already playing in top-level championships, on the pitch we were only thinking about having fun and the pleasure of playing. When Rashidi Yekini scored the first goal against Bulgaria (1–0), he clung onto the net as if he were on another planet. And, above all, we had beaten Bulgaria 3–0, who had an excellent player in Stoichkov. It remains a great moment for me."

▲ After three years out of the limelight, Diego Maradona made an extraordinary comeback, scoring against Greece.

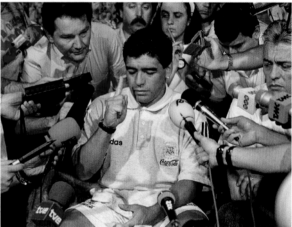

▲▲ Maradona celebrates scoring his goal against Greece.

▲ After Argentina's victory over Nigeria, Maradona failed a drugs test, testing positive for ephedrine. He was suspended and sent home

Commemorative coins

$1 and $5 coins issued in 1994 to celebrate the World Cup in America.

▲ **FIFA World Football Museum collection.**

Maradona's mad summer

21 JUNE 1994

ARGENTINA 4-0 **GREECE**

BATISTUTA 2, 45, 89 (PEN), MARADONA 60

ON SPARKLING FORM during Argentina's 4–0 victory over Greece, exploding a shot into the top corner of Antonis Minou's goal, Diego Maradona seemed to be back on top form for his last World Cup. However, when he celebrated his goal, screaming in front of a TV camera, Maradona seemed to have lost control of his emotions, driven as if in a frenzied trance. The Newell's Old Boys number 10 also played in Argentina's second match against Nigeria (a 2–1 win), during which he provided an assist for Claudio Caniggia, who scored both goals. However, at the end of this match, he tested positive for ephedrine as well as for four other banned substances. He was

immediately sent home from the World Cup.

Diego Maradona, 33 years of age, pleaded his good faith by asserting that, suffering from a cold, he had taken medicine containing the banned substance, not on the advice of Argentina's team doctor but of his dietician. The best player of the 1986 competition, he ended his fourth World Cup on a bad note. Without him, Argentina lost their third match against Bulgaria (2–0) but still qualified for the round of 16.

Maradona nevertheless managed to beat one record. He became the player to have played the most number of matches as captain (16) in the final stages, breaking Dino Zoff's record of 14 matches.

Italy get off to a quiet start

18 JUNE 1994

ITALY ▮▮ 0–1 ▮▮ **REPUBLIC OF IRELAND**

HOUGHTON 11

A S USUAL, Italy entered the competition quietly: Franco Baresi and his team-mates started with a surprise defeat against the Republic of Ireland (1–0), then recorded a narrow victory against Norway (1–0) before drawing their final group-stage match against Mexico (1–1). It was just enough to see them through to the round of 16 as one of the best third-placed teams.

▲ Italian goalkeeper Gianluca Pagliuca encourages his substitute Luca Marchegiani, after having been sent off.

Sad first for Pagliuca

Against Norway, Italy goalkeeper Gianluca Pagliuca became the first goalkeeper to be sent off in the World Cup finals. He received a red card for stopping a Norwegian shot outside his area in the 21st minute. Down to ten men, Italy nevertheless prevailed on 23 June in New York, thanks to a storming 69th-minute header from Dino Baggio.

Al-Owairan's magical slalom

29 JUNE 1994

BELGIUM ▮▮ 0–1 ▐ **SAUDI ARABIA**

AL-OWAIRAN 5

A GAINST BELGIUM in Washington on 29 June, Saudi Arabian striker Said Al-Owairan received the ball 40 yards from his own goal. He accelerated, crossed the halfway line and went past three Belgian players before nutmegging a fourth and then lining himself up to beat Michel Preud'homme from close range. This legendary goal enabled Saudi Arabia to become the first Asian team to win two matches in the final stages. Second in the group behind the Netherlands, the team coached by Argentinian Jorge Solari qualified for the round of 16 in its first tournament appearance.

◀ Saeed Al-Owairan swerves past Belgium's Rudi Smidts and scores the goal of the tournament.

Hagi's unexpected lob

18 JUNE 1994

COLOMBIA ▭ 1-3 ▮▮ **ROMANIA**

VALENCIA 43   RĂDUCIOIU 16, 89, HAGI 34

W ITH ROMANIA LEADING 1–0 AGAINST COLOMBIA, thanks to a powerful strike by Florin Răducioiu, Gheorghe Hagi produced a moment of pure class: instead of crossing, his left-footed lob from around 40 yards gave Colombian goalkeeper Oscar Cordoba no chance (2–0). "I scored quite a few goals, but that one was particularly important because I had made my mark in the World Cup," said the Romanian number 10 who was playing for Brescia at the time. "The slightly floating trajectory of the ball was quite special, but I had noted that Cordoba often left his goal-line. This was why, before this goal, I had tried a couple of similar strikes from the right-hand side. However, this time I succeeded." Thanks to this win, as well as a second victory in the third match against the United States (1–0, with a goal from Dan Petrescu), Romania secured their passage to the round of 16.

◀ Gheorghe Hagi scores Romania's second goal against Colombia with a lob from 40 metres.

1

In the 67th minute of their third match, in Chicago on 27 June, after a defeat to Germany (0–1) and a draw against South Korea (0–0), Bolivia finally managed to score their first World Cup goal after 517 unproductive minutes in the final stages. Erwin Sánchez reduced the deficit against Spain (1–3). The Bolivians had already taken part in 1930, without scoring in two losses (0–4) against Yugoslavia and Brazil, and in 1950, where they lost to Uruguay (0–8).

▲ Argentina's Diego Simeone in action against Romania.

▲ Gheorghe Hagi in action during Romania's match against Argentina.

Romania's huge achievement

3 JULY 1994

ROMANIA ▮▮ 3–2 ▭ **ARGENTINA**

DUMITRESCU 11, 18, HAGI 58   BATISTUTA 16 (PEN), BALBO 75

EVEN WITHOUT DIEGO MARADONA, suspended after testing positive for banned substances, Argentina lost little of their creativity, and this was reflected in the first minutes of the match, with a slaloming run by Diego Simeone, which Abel Balbo was unable to finish. However, it was Romania, without their striker, Florin Răducioiu, suspended after two yellow cards, who opened the scoring on 3 July in Pasadena: a superb right-footed free-kick taken by Ilie Dumitrescu floated over Luis Islas and ended up in the opponents' net. Barely five minutes later, Gabriel Batistuta won a penalty that he converted himself (1–1). Although Argentina controlled the game, Romania proved dangerous on the counter-attack: Gheorghe Hagi found Dumitrescu, whose brilliant side-footed deflection doubled their score (2–1). After the break, Dumitrescu fed Hagi, who finished with his right foot, another textbook counter-attack (3–1). Despite Balbo

reducing the deficit in the 75th minute, after a strike by Fernando Cáceres was pushed away by Romania's goalkeeper Prunea, Romania qualified for the quarter-finals for the first time in their history. It was a huge achievement.

"To be honest, we weren't expecting to go as far; it was amazing, even though we'd been playing together for a long time," explained Romanian sweeper Gheorghe Popescu, who was playing for PSV Eindhoven at the time. "We had matured as a team. After a group stage in which we suffered a heavy defeat against Switzerland by trying to attack too much and so leaving too much space at the back, we put it right. Against Argentina, we played the perfect game and created a lot of goalscoring opportunities. We were lucky that Maradona was suspended, but to come out on top against Argentina was still quite a performance. With Diego on the field, the result could have been different, but we seized our opportunity."

Andersson on cloud nine

3 JULY 1994

SAUDI ARABIA ▬ 1–3 ▮▮ **SWEDEN**

AL-GHESHEYAN 85   DAHLIN 6
                   K. ANDERSSON 51, 88

PROVIDER of the pass for Martin Dahlin's first goal, the giant Kennet Andersson pulled out all the stops on 3 July in Dallas. There was no holding the 1.93m centre forward, who demonstrated his technique and his burst of speed. In the 51st minute he flicked the ball over the head of his marker, dribbled past Ahmed Madani and then hit an unstoppable left-footed shot (2–0). After Fahad Al Ghesheyan reduced the deficit, Andersson scored his second following a clever pass from Dahlin (3–1). For the first time since 1958, Sweden were in the quarter-finals. Like Andersson, who was playing for Lille, the experience of senior Swedish players such as Tomas Brolin (Parma), Jonas Thern (Napoli) and Patrik Andersson (Borussia Mönchengladbach) made the difference.

▼ Swede Kennet Andersson celebrates scoring against Saudi Arabia.

Nigeria just two minutes away

5 JULY 1994

NIGERIA 🟩 1–2 🟦 **ITALY**
A.E.T.

AMUNIKE 25   R. BAGGIO 88, 100 (PEN)

TWO MINUTES from the end of the match, Nigeria were still leading (1–0) against Italy, thanks to a 25th-minute strike from Emmanuel Amunike. However, Roberto Mussi ran forward and then crossed the ball back for Roberto Baggio, who took the match into extra-time. In extra-time, the Italian number 10 converted a penalty (2–1). The Africans' first World Cup adventure was over.

◄ Duel between Italy's Paolo Maldini and Nigeria's Rashidi Yekini.

◄ Brazil striker Bebeto shoots past defender Alexi Lalas and keeper Tony Meola to knock out the hosts USA.

Bebeto unlocked it for Brazil

4 JULY 1994

BRAZIL 🔵 1–0 🇺🇸 **UNITED STATES**

BEBETO 72

AGAINST the fired-up Americans on 4 July, the country's national holiday, Brazil controlled the game, but goalkeeper Tony Meola pulled off a string of saves from the Romário-Bebeto strike pairing. Tempers flared as the minutes went by: in a tussle with Tab Ramos, Leonardo struck him violently with his elbow. Sent off by French referee Joël Quiniou in the 43rd minute, Brazil were down to ten men. Brazil pressed on in the second half and ended up finding the opening when Bebeto, well fed by Romário, put the ball in Meola's net from an angled shot.

"At half-time, when we got back into the dressing room, I found Leonardo – with whom I had started out at Flamengo – sobbing all alone," related Bebeto. "I told him not to worry and that I was going to score the winning goal. It was also during this match that I knew that we were going to win our fourth World Cup title. Because, despite such a major blow, the team managed to get back on track. Romário gave me a good pass and I found myself in a one-on-one against Tony Meola. In spite of his size, I managed to find a gap and put the ball into the back of the net."

Völler puts Belgium to the sword

2 JUILLET 1994

GERMANY ⬛ 3-2 🟥 **BELGIUM**

VÖLLER 6e, 40e   GRÜN 8e
KLINSMANN 11e   ALBERT 90e

PROVIDER of the final pass for Jürgen Klinsmann's goal (2-0), Rudi Völler (below) also scored the first German goal by getting in behind the Belgian defence to put the ball past Michel Preud'homme (1–0) and then scored his second with a header from a corner (3–1). It was a great performance by the centre-forward, a finalist in 1986 and then a winner in 1990. "The team played very well, as did I by scoring two goals. It was quite simply my best match in the final stages," acknowledged 34-year-old Völler.

Preud'homme crowned best goalkeeper

With the ban on handling the ball from a deliberate backpass, the goalkeeper's role extended to that of a second sweeper. Already experienced goalkeepers adapted very well to this new rule, like 35-year-old Belgian Michel Preud'homme (below), who played for club side Mechelen. The Belgian only conceded one goal in during the group stages and pulled off several world-class saves in the round of 16 clash Germany (2–3). Preud'homme was crowned the tournament's best goalkeeper by FIFA's Technical Study Group and won the first Lev Yashin Award.

Raí and Sócrates, brothers and captains

Captain of the Brazilian football team for three matches in the group stage before losing his place, Raí was none other than the younger brother of Sócrates. The latter had worn the Brazilian armband during the 1982 tournament. No other siblings have achieved this feat.

"A lack of team spirit"

Lothar Matthäus, German captain

"We should have won, but the main reason for our elimination was the lack of team spirit. We arrived in the United States as favourites with a team that was practically identical to that of 1990, perhaps even a bit stronger, thanks to being bolstered by [East Germans] Stefan Effenberg and Matthias Sammer," explained Lothar Matthäus, the German captain. "However, our team spirit was not as it should have been and the roles were not as well distributed as had been the case four years previously."

◥ Buglaria's Trifon Ivanov shakes hands with Germany's Rudi Völler after the match.

▲ German disappointment. This was the first time Germany had lost in the quarter-finals since 1962.

▶ Swedish goalkeeper Thomas Ravelli saved twice during the penalty shoot-out victory over Romania.

The holders put out in four minutes

10 JULY 1994

BULGARIA	2–1	WEST GERMANY
STOITCHKOV 75, LETCHKOV 78		MATTHÄUS 47 (PEN)

AFTER A QUIET FIRST ROUND (two wins and a draw) and then trouble-free qualification against Belgium in the round of 16 (3–2), Germany started as favourites against Bulgaria on 10 July in New York. But, Bulgaria, who had squeezed past Mexico in the previous round (1–1, 3–1 on penalties), played without inhibition. Just after the break, Yordan Lechkov made slight contact with Jürgen Klinsmann in the penalty area, and Lothar Matthäus made it 1–0 from the spot-kick. Klinsmann thought he had doubled the lead, but the linesman indicated that he was offside. Bulgaria roared back into the match thanks to Stoichkov. His delightful free-kick over the German wall in the 75th minute left Bodo Illgner rooted to the spot (1–1). Three minutes later, Zlatko Yankov crossed for Lechkov, who escaped his marker and scored the winner with a diving header (2–1). In the space of just a few minutes, the Bulgarians had turned it around and qualified for a first-ever semi-final. There was no coming back for Germany, who lined up with nine 1990 World Cup winners and an average of 57 caps per player.

Ravelli, match-winning Swede

10 JULY 1994

ROMANIA	2–2 A.E.T.	SWEDEN
RĂDUCIOIU 88, 101		BROLIN 78, K. ANDERSSON 115

⊕⊕⊕✗⊕✗ 4–5 ✗⊕⊕⊕⊕⊕

In this match between two outsiders (Romania v Sweden), Sweden reached the semi-finals for the first time since 1958. After a brace from Florin Răducioiu, in reply to goals from Tomas Brolin and Kennet Andersson, the decision came down to penalties, and sudden death. Ravelli stopped Belodedici's shot while Larsson showed no nerves, slotting the decisive penalty into the back of the net to send the Swedes through to the last four.

▲ Branco stuns the Netherlands with a powerful free-kick to take Brazil through to the semi-finals.

Branco's show-stopper

9 JULY 1994

NETHERLNDS 2–3 **BRAZIL**

BERGKAMP 64, WINTER 76   ROMÁRIO 53, BEBETO 63, BRANCO 81

▶ Brazilians Mazinho, Bebeto and Romário celebrating Bebeto's goal and the birth of his third son.

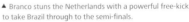

RITICIZED FOR THEIR STYLE OF PLAY, which was less flamboyant than usual, Brazil replied in the best possible way thanks to their strike duo of Romário and Bebeto; the Brazilian team were leading 2–0 against a Netherlands side that was playing good football. However, Dennis Bergkamp broke free on the left-hand side to reduce the lead, before Aron Winter equalized with a header. It mattered little: Carlos-Alberto Parreira's men relaunched their assault on the Dutch goal and, barely ten minutes from the final whistle, Branco scored the winning goal from a magical free-kick.

Rock-a-bye baby...

"It so happens that I had prayed the night before, when I went to bed, that I would have the opportunity to score in honour of my newborn son, the third of my children and the only one for whose birth I had not been present," recalls Bebeto. "During the match, the opportunity presented itself in a way that I could have not thought of as anything other than divine. The ball came to me when Romário had just avoided a tackle. So I controlled the ball, beat a defender and then the goalkeeper and put it calmly into the back of the net," explained Bebeto, the scorer of Brazil's second goal. "When I scored, I thought of my son from the bottom of my heart, celebrating as if cradling him in my arms… Then I noticed that Mazinho and Romário were doing the same thing and then that the whole team was at it… Things happen like that. It may seem incredible, but he's the only one of my children who likes and is gifted at football!"

"Everyone remembers the cannonball."

Branco, the scorer of Brazil's goal.

"That shot, the most crucial of my career, has remained engraved on Brazilians' memory. Wherever I go, everybody remembers that cannonball. It was those three seconds of waiting, between the time I hit the ball and the ball going into the net, which counted the most in my professional and personal career. That goal was a gift from God, considering what I was going through at the time: the Brazilian press had told me

I was in no condition to play and put me under pressure. I went straight to the bench to embrace the doctor and the physio, who had been attending to me until two o'clock that morning. I had told them that the day I set foot again on the pitch I would put the ball in the net for them. I experienced an intensely emotional moment that changed my life, which my children and my grandchildren will remember; that's the most important thing."

▶ Romario tries to break through the Swedish defence, between Håkan Mild and Jonas Thern.

Lacklustre Brazil

13 JULY 1994

SWEDEN ❙❙ 0–1 ◉ BRAZIL

ROMÁRIO 80

D OMINANT BUT INEFFECTIVE, held at bay by the excellent Swedish goalkeeper Thomas Ravelli, Brazil ended up scoring through little Romário, with a header. "When you think about it, that goal was incredible. At 1.67m, I got up to score a header between the Swedes, who were famous for their average height of between 1.83m and 1.84m. It was quite unusual in football, all the more so in the World Cup and especially in the semi-final," chuckled Romário. "Jorginho had the opportunity to pick me out me perfectly and I was able to put my head to the ball: the goalkeeper had no time to react." Twenty-four years after 1970, Dunga's Brazil had at last reached the Final again.

▶ The Brazilians enter the pitch hand in hand before the semi-final against Sweden.

"It's in my nature to be a showman"

Thomas Ravelli, the Swedish goalkeeper, who danced and grimaced a lot during the tournament.

"Having played for so long in the team, **that semi-final was a fine reward.** On our return to Sweden, the welcome was so fantastic that I had only one thing in my mind: not to cry. Very few people have the opportunity to experience something so intense. I love to be demonstrative, but you must always be able to keep your concentration. However, it's in my nature to be a showman."

"Quite the opposite of defensive tactics"

Dunga, defensive midfielder and captain of Brazil.

"Parreira often used to say: 'The Brazilians always know what to do when they have the ball.' Our problem was to organize ourselves when we didn't have it. To take full advantage of our technical repertoire of skills, we had to be able to get the ball back as quickly as possible. At the purely tactical level, everybody believed that the decision to line up with two midfield ball-winners was dictated by defensive considera- tions. It was quite the opposite. The aim was to play as high up the field as possible and to get the ball back into the opposing half to allow Bebeto, Romário and Zinho to find the spaces and to allow Jorginho, Branco and Leonardo to move forward. When our opponents counter-attacked, they unwittingly left themselves exposed. In this type of situation, we could pick up the ball 20 or 30 yards from the opponents' goal."

Stoichkov – Bulgarian icon

▲ Hristo Stoichkov competes for the ball with Italy's Antonio Benarrivo.

HIS CALMLY converted penalty against Italy in the 44th minute (1–2) was not enough: Bulgaria went out in the semi-final. However, Hristo Stoichkov still ended up as the joint top scorer of the World Cup, together with Russian Igor Salenko (six goals). What's more, at the end of the year, the Barcelona striker was awarded the Ballon d'Or. Stoichkov was a talismanic figure for this team. In the United States, under the command of his mentor Dimitar Penev, at 28 years of age, he took full advantage of his first World Cup, lining up in attack in a 4-3-3, alongside Emil Kostadinov and Nasko Sirakov. Stoichkov built on the reputation that had seen him win four titles and a European Cup with Barcelona. After a goalless start against Nigeria (0–3), he converted two penalties against Greece, a match Bulgaria won 4–0. In 16 previous World Cup matches, dating back to 1962, the Bulgarians had failed to win a single one. Success in match number 17 was cause for celebration but there was

more to come. Stoichkov opened the scoring against Argentina, winning his duel with Luis Islas as Bulgaria won 2–0. In the round of 16 against Mexico, it was Stoitchkov who put his team on the right track with a left-footed thunderbolt (1–1, Bulgaria won 3–1 on penalties). Finally, against Germany in the quarter-final, he scored the equalizer from a free kick and Bulgaria won 2–1: "The day before the match, my daughter said to me: 'It's my birthday tomorrow, score a goal for me.' I thought of that when I hit my free kick. As soon as the ball went over the wall I knew I'd scored." The Barça striker had a magical left foot as well as remarkable speed and devastating turns. Despite their semi-final elimination against Italy, Stoichkov was philosophical. "The national team had never won a single match in the World Cup, so we first of all had to change that mentality," stressed the Bulgarian. "I'm proud of our journey, which was the result of great sacrifice, and above all of having shared it with so many people."

Irresistible Italians

13 JULY 1994

BULGARIA	1–2	ITALY
STOITCHKOV 44 (PEN)		R. BAGGIO 20, 25

AS IS OFTEN THE CASE, Italy started to get into top gear during the knockout matches. On 13 July in New York, their pressure caused the Bulgarians serious problems. In the 20th minute, with just one touch of the ball, Roberto Baggio got away from his marker, dribbled past Petar Hubchev and then curled his shot, taking advantage of the position of Trifon Ivanov, who was blocking his own goalkeeper. Five minutes later, Demetrio Albertini fed Baggio, who doubled the lead with an angled right-footed shot. Unstoppable in the first half, Italy conceded a Stoichkov penalty just before half-time after Sirakov was brought down by Alessandro Costacurta. A more balanced second half, contested in suffocating heat, changed nothing, though: Italy reached the Final 12 years from their last.

▼ An emotional Roberto Baggio salutes the fans after Italy beat Bulgaria to secure a place in the Final.

▲ Henrik Larsson scores the third Swedish goal in their 4–0 victory over Bulgaria.

Sweden overpower Bulgaria to take third

16 JULY 1994

SWEDEN	4–0	BULGARIA
BROLIN 8, MILD 30 LARSSON 37 K. ANDERSSON 40		

Thanks to their great success against Bulgaria (4–0, with goals from Tomas Brolin, Håkan Mild, Henrik Larsson and Kennet Andersson), manager Tommy Svensson's Swedish side dominated the third-place playoff. Finalists in 1958, the Swedes had also finished third in 1950.

◤ Italy lose a second World Cup final to Brazil, 24 years after the previous defeat, in the 1970 Final.

▲ Roberto Baggio lifts his attempt over the crossbar and gives Brazil a 3–2 victory in the 1994 FIFA World Cup Final penalty shoot-out.

Brazil's long wait is finally over

17 JULY 1994

BRAZIL 🇧🇷 0–0 🇮🇹 ITALY
A.E.T.
✗✿✿✿ 3–2 ✗✿✿✗✗

T HIS WORLD CUP FINAL, between two three-time winners, was as tight as it was disappointing. Brazil dominated the game on 17 July in Pasadena (recording 18 shots to Italy's four), but could not find the breakthrough. They came close, such as Bebeto's header after the interval and then a strike by Mauro Silva which Italy's goalkeeper Gianluca Pagliuca fumbled against his post. If there were any mitigating circumstances, they were because this match kicked off at 12:30 (to satisfy the demands of European television viewers) and was played in a suffocating heat. However, for the first time in the tournament's history, the Final ended goalless and had to be decided on penalties. For the Italians, Franco Baresi fired over the bar, Daniele Massaro's shot was saved by Taffarel, while Roberto Baggio's went skywards. Only Márcio Santos failed for Brazil.

"What torture!" recalls Branco, the Brazilian defender. "I wouldn't wish it on anyone to play for the trophy by Russian roulette. It's an overwhelming responsibility to take on with the eyes of Brazil and the whole world on you. Márcio Santos's first penalty was saved. Romário's hit the post before going into the net. When my turn came, Pagliuca seemed huge and the net seemed tiny. I planned to strike it hard, but I changed my mind at the last second. I expected Pagliuca to commit himself, which he did, and I put the ball in the other corner. Dunga scored from the next spot-kick, so Bebeto, the fifth penalty-taker, was not called upon. At the end of the day, I believe that we were able to keep our cool better than Italy. The proof is that Baresi, one of the best players in the world, missed with his penalty, as did Massaro and Baggio, who was at the time perhaps the best penalty-taker. Whereas Baggio normally shot low, he hit it very high that day, which clearly showed how stressful these penalty shoot-outs are."

For his part, Brazilian goalkeeper Cláudio Taffarel did not experience any anxiety, convinced that victory would be theirs. "I was certain that we were going to win right from our first match. I knew that the penalty shoot-out would end well for us."

After a 24-year wait, Brazil became the first country to win the World Cup four times. The Brazilian players dedicated their trophy to Brazilian racing driver Ayrton Senna, who had died on 1 May 1994. As well as their tactical discipline, Brazil owed their success to the strike pairing of Romário and Bebeto, who could find each other with their eyes shut. A promising 17-year-old centre forward, Ronaldo, who did not play a single minute, was also a part of their World Cup-winning squad.

Baresi, return in extremis

Injured on 23 June during the match against Norway, Franco Baresi was present for the Final. Heroic against Brazil, the Italian sweeper and captain had undergone a cartilage operation. He returned to action after just 24 days.

▲▲ Penalty shoot-out drama: Brazil's Cláudio Taffarel and Italy's Gianluca Pagliuca take centre-stage.

▲ Brazil huddle for the first penalty shoot-out in a World Cup Final.

▶ Romário, player of the tournament, celebrates Brazil's World Cup victory.

"The worst moment of my career"

Roberto Baggio, whose missed penalty handed the title to Brazil.

THE SCORER OF FIVE out of the previous six Italian goals, Roberto Baggio, who injured his thigh against Bulgaria, still took his place in the Final against Brazil. "At the beginning of the match, I had difficulty loosening up, but I managed to ignore it," explained the Italian number 10. "Neither I nor the team played very well; we were tired." For the penalty shoot-out, Baggio stepped up fourth, knowing that if he missed, Brazil would win the trophy: "I missed only a few penalties in my career, because the goalkeepers saved them; I didn't shoot wide. So I find it hard to explain what happened. I was clear-headed before shooting; I knew that Taffarel always dived, so I decided to shoot down the middle, about halfway up, so that he couldn't touch the ball with his legs. It was the right decision, but unfortunately the ball went over the crossbar. It was the worst moment of my career. I still often dream about it."

"The very happy feeling of having been of some use"

Romário, Brazilian striker, scorer of five goals and winner of Adidas Golden Ball as the tournament's best player.

"1994 was undoubtedly the best year of my life from a professional viewpoint. I had the privilege of playing in all seven matches and I had the very happy feeling of having been of some use. The Brazilian public takes football very seriously and, at that time, 24 years after our last title, we needed to win a World Cup. We did it and we were able to see joy on the faces of our compatriots that was not there before, especially for young people who had never seen Brazil crowned world champions."

1998

Expansion to 32 teams was a giant step towards greater global representation. Host nation France, who played in the first World Cup, took the title at last. In the Final, they beat Brazil, whose star player Ronaldo suffered a pre-match breakdown. Two headed goals by Zinédine Zidane helped France to a 3–0 win, bringing more than a million fans onto the Champs-Élysées in celebration.

France mobilized

◄ Zinédine Zidane celebrates his second goal in the Final against Brazil.

▼ Home fans celebrate the success of a racially diverse French team in the tournament.

HAVING FAILED to qualify for both the 1990 and 1994 tournaments, despite having been semi-finalists in 1982 and 1986, France were chosen to host the World Cup for a second time, having first staged the event in 1938. The Organizing Committee was co-chaired by Michel Platini, triple Ballon d'Or winner and European champion in 1984, while Fernand Sastre, the other co-chair, died at the beginning of the World Cup.

Before the World Cup, there were limited expectations for the host nation, coached by Aimé Jacquet, who had decided not to select certain personalities (Eric Cantona and David Ginola) in favour of the collective approach. Their performances in pre-tournament friendlies had not been very convincing and media criticism intensified, particularly towards Jacquet. Hooliganism was still a major issue and security was tightened after fighting between Tunisia and England fans in Marseille. On 21 June 1998, next to the Félix Bollaert Stadium in Lens, where the Germany vs Yugoslavia game took place, French gendarme Daniel Nivel was attacked by German hooligans. He remained in a coma for six weeks and was permanently disabled. His attackers received a prison sentence.

FRANCE 98

Story of the qualifiers

168 teams, 15 million fans

ALL RECORDS WERE BROKEN during the qualifiers: 168 participants out of 174 registered took part, including 31 new teams; there were 643 matches (compared to 314 for the 1990 tournament), which attracted a staggering 15 million spectators. Having notably beaten the Maldives 17–0, including seven goals from Karim Bagheri, Iran created a surprise during a home-and-away playoff between Asia and Oceania against Australia. After an initial draw in Tehran, Iran found themselves 2–0 down at the Melbourne Cricket Ground, in front of 85,000 spectators. But goals from Bagheri (in the 77th minute) and then Azizi (in the 80th) enabled them to book their tickets to France. In Europe, playoffs were organized for the first time between the groups' second-placed teams, with the exception of the

team with the best record – Scotland, who qualified directly. These playoffs enabled Croatia to qualify, for the first time in their history, as well as Italy, Belgium and Yugoslavia. Sweden, third in 1994, finished third in their group and failed to qualify. Another innovation in South America was the single group of nine teams; Brazil, holders of the title, qualified automatically. The top-four teams (Argentina, Paraguay, Colombia and Chile) also qualified. In the CONCACAF zone, the favourites Mexico and the United States went through un-troubled. The third and final qualifying place went, for the first time, to Jamaica and its "Reggae Boyz". In Africa, South Africa, winner of the Africa Cup of Nations in 1996, were the newcomers. In Asia, Japan also qualified for the finals for the first time.

▲ The Iran team celebrate their surprise victory in the play-offs, over Australia.

Group stage

GROUP A		
BRA	2–1	SCO
MAR	2–2	NOR
NOR	1–1	SCO
BRA	3–0	MAR
NOR	2–1	BRA
MAR	3–0	SCO

	W	D	L	+	–	PTS
BRA	2	0	1	6	3	6
NOR	1	2	0	5	4	5
MAR	1	1	1	5	5	4
SCO	0	1	2	2	6	1

GROUP B		
ITA	2–2	CHI
AUT	1–1	CMR
CHI	1–1	AUT
ITA	3–0	CMR
ITA	2–1	AUT
CHI	1–1	CMR

	W	D	L	+	–	PTS
ITA	2	1	0	7	3	7
CHI	0	3	0	4	4	3
AUT	0	2	1	3	4	2
CMR	0	2	1	2	5	2

GROUP C		
FRA	3–0	RSA
DEN	1–0	KSA
FRA	4–0	KSA
DEN	1–1	RSA
FRA	2–1	DEN
RSA	2–2	KSA

	W	D	L	+	–	PTS
FRA	3	0	0	9	1	9
DEN	1	1	1	3	3	4
RSA	0	2	1	3	6	2
KSA	0	1	2	2	7	1

GROUP D		
PAR	0–0	BUL
NGA	3–2	ESP
PAR	0–0	ESP
NGA	1–0	BUL
ESP	6–1	BUL
NGA	1–3	PAR

	W	D	L	+	–	PTS
NGA	2	0	1	5	5	6
PAR	1	2	0	3	1	5
ESP	1	1	1	8	4	4
BUL	0	1	2	1	7	1

GROUP E		
NED	0–0	BEL
MEX	3–1	KOR
NED	5–0	KOR
MEX	2–2	BEL
NED	2–2	MEX
BEL	1–1	KOR

	W	D	L	+	–	PTS
NED	1	2	0	7	2	5
MEX	1	2	0	7	5	5
BEL	0	3	0	3	3	3
KOR	0	1	2	2	9	1

GROUP F		
YUG	1–0	IRN
GER	2–0	USA
GER	2–2	YUG
IRN	2–1	USA
GER	2–0	IRN
YUG	1–0	USA

	W	D	L	+	–	PTS
GER	2	1	0	6	2	7
YUG	2	1	0	4	2	7
IRN	1	0	2	2	4	3
USA	0	0	3	1	5	0

GROUP G		
ENG	2–0	TUN
ROU	1–0	COL
COL	1–0	TUN
ROU	2–1	ENG
ROU	1–1	TUN
ENG	2–0	COL

	W	D	L	+	–	PTS
ROU	2	1	0	4	2	7
ENG	2	0	1	5	2	6
COL	1	0	2	1	3	3
TUN	0	1	2	1	4	1

GROUP H		
ARG	1–0	JPN
CRO	3–1	JAM
CRO	1–0	JPN
ARG	5–0	JAM
ARG	1–0	CRO
JAM	2–1	JPN

	W	D	L	+	–	PTS
ARG	3	0	0	7	0	9
CRO	2	0	1	4	2	6
JAM	1	0	2	3	9	3
JPN	0	0	3	1	4	0

Knockout stages

ROUND OF 16		
BRA	4–1	CHI
NGA	1–4	DEN

ROUND OF 16		
NED	2–1	YUG
ARG	2–2 / 4–3	ENG

ROUND OF 16		
ITA	1–0	NOR
FRA	1–0 G.G.	PAR

ROUND OF 16		
GER	2–1	MEX
ROU	0–1	CRO

QUARTER-FINAL		
BRA	3–2	DEN

QUARTER-FINAL		
NED	2–1	ARG

QUARTER-FINAL		
ITA	0–0 / 3–4	FRA

QUARTER-FINAL		
GER	0–3	CRO

SEMI-FINAL		
BRA	1–1 / 4–2	NED

SEMI-FINAL		
FRA	2–1	CRO

PLAY-OFF FOR THIRD PLACE		
NED	1–2	CRO

FINAL		
BRA	0–3	FRA

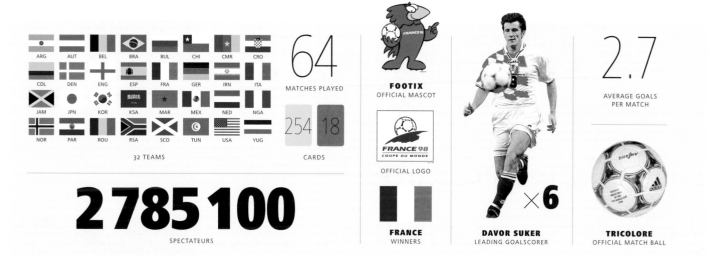

ARG	AUT	BEL	BRA	BUL	CHI	CMR	CRO
COL	DEN	ENG	ESP	FRA	GER	IRN	ITA
JAM	JPN	KOR	KSA	MAR	MEX	NED	NGA
NOR	PAR	ROU	RSA	SCO	TUN	USA	YUG

32 TEAMS

64
MATCHES PLAYED

254 18
CARDS

2785 100
SPECTATEURS

FOOTIX
OFFICIAL MASCOT

FRANCE 98
COUPE DU MONDE
OFFICIAL LOGO

FRANCE
WINNERS

×6

DAVOR SUKER
LEADING GOALSCORER

2.7
AVERAGE GOALS
PER MATCH

TRICOLORE
OFFICIAL MATCH BALL

Host cities and stadiums

A national stadium for France

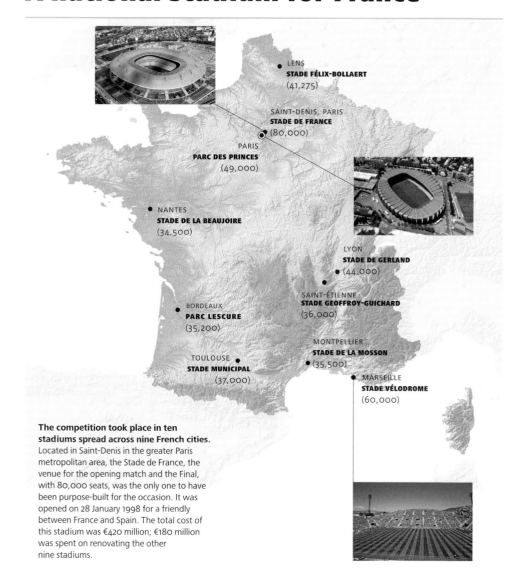

LENS
STADE FÉLIX-BOLLAERT
(41,275)

SAINT-DENIS, PARIS
STADE DE FRANCE
(80,000)

PARIS
PARC DES PRINCES
(49,000)

NANTES
STADE DE LA BEAUJOIRE
(34,500)

LYON
STADE DE GERLAND
(44,000)

SAINT-ÉTIENNE
STADE GEOFFROY-GUICHARD
(36,000)

BORDEAUX
PARC LESCURE
(35,200)

MONTPELLIER
STADE DE LA MOSSON
(35,500)

TOULOUSE
STADE MUNICIPAL
(37,000)

MARSEILLE
STADE VÉLODROME
(60,000)

**The competition took place in ten
stadiums spread across nine French cities.**
Located in Saint-Denis in the greater Paris
metropolitan area, the Stade de France, the
venue for the opening match and the Final,
with 80,000 seats, was the only one to have
been purpose-built for the occasion. It was
opened on 28 January 1998 for a friendly
between France and Spain. The total cost of
this stadium was €420 million; €180 million
was spent on renovating the other
nine stadiums.

Regulations

And then there were 32 …

**In 1970, the FIFA president Sir Stanley Rous
had first proposed that the finals be extended
to 32 teams.** Twenty-eight years later his idea
became a reality. The number of FIFA members
was growing – 100 in 1962, 150 in 1980, while
the 202 mark was reached with six new members
accepted at the Paris Congress at the start of
France '98. From now on, there was no get out
of jail card for third-placed teams, with just the
top two qualifying for the round of 16 from the
eight first round groups. Thanks to the increase
in numbers, Africa's representation went up from
three to five, and Asia's from two to four.

Footix

**Footix was the mascot for the 1998 World
Cup, a cockerel created by graphic designer
Fabrice Pialot.** After the finals, the name "Footix"
became a term for those fans who had recently
discovered the game in the aftermath of the
French triumph and who were accused of
knowing very little about the game!

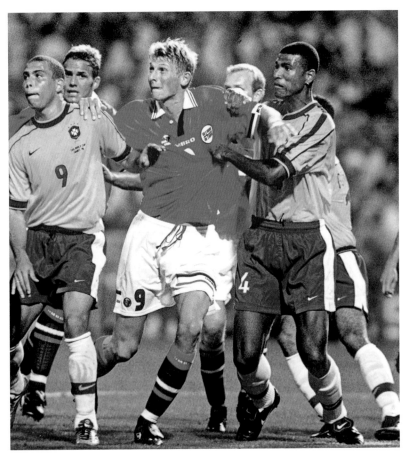

◀ Norway's Tore André Flo, between Ronaldo and Júnior Baiano, won a hotly contested penalty that led to Brazil's first defeat in a first-round group game since 1966.

▶ Argentina's Gabriel Batistuta in action against Jamaica.

▶ *Batigol* celebrates becoming the first player to score a hat-trick at two World Cups.

A penalty to talk about

23 JUNE 1998

BRAZIL 🇧🇷 1–2 🇳🇴 **NORWAY**

BEBETO 78   T.A. FLO 83, REKDAL 89 (PEN)

AVING ALREADY QUALIFIED following opening victories against Scotland (2–1) and then Morocco (3–0), Brazil faced Norway in Marseilles on 23 June. The Norwegian team had opened their campaign with two draws (2–2 against Morocco and 1-1 against Scotland). The titleholders opened the scoring with a 78th-minute header from Bebeto, following a perfect cross by Denílson. However, Tore André Flo equalized with a solo effort in the 83rd minute, before, six minutes later, winning a hotly disputed penalty. Slow motion images, which only showed the end of the action, suggested that the Norwegian centre-forward had dived during his tussle with Júnior Baiano. Kjetil Rekdal calmly converted the penalty and Norway qualified for the second round at the expense of Morocco. "When you realise that there is a penalty for Norway and that the score is 1–1, against Brazil, and that there are only a few minutes left to play, you really focus on your shot," explained the Norwegian number 10. "When I scored, I felt an incredible feeling. We had beaten Brazil and were in the round of 16." American referee Esse Baharmast was criticized by the media, who called for the use of video. A few days later, however, images from a Swedish television camera placed behind the goal showed that Flo's shirt had indeed been pulled. The penalty was justified.

Batistuta takes Argentina through

21 JUNE 1998

ARGENTINA 🇦🇷 5–0 🇯🇲 **JAMAICA**

ORTEGA 31, 55
BATISTUTA 73, 78, 83 (PEN)

AVING SCORED in Argentina's opening match of the tournament against Japan (1–0), Gabriel Batistuta scored a hat-trick against Jamaica on 21 June in the Parc des Princes. Nicknamed "Batigol", he scored Argentina's third and fourth goals with two angled, right-footed drives before converting a penalty won by Ariel Ortega, scorer of the other two goals. It was the 46th hat-trick in the history of the World Cup, but the only one of this tournament. Having scored a hat-trick against Greece in 1994, Batistuta became only the fourth player in World Cup history to claim two – after Kocsis in 1954, Fontaine in 1958 and Müller in 1970 – and he is the only one of the four to achieve this in different World Cups.

◀ Jamaica's Theodore Whitmore in action against Japan.

Theodore Whitmore, Reggae Boy goalscorer

26 JUNE 1998

JAPAN ● 1–2 ✕ **JAMAICA**

NAKAYAMA 74   WHITMORE 39, 54

// A WORLD CUP is the pinnacle of a footballer's life. After having trained for so many years, after having watched the World Cup on TV, this time there we were! Every member of the team wanted to enjoy every moment," recalled Jamaican midfielder Theodore Whitmore. "We had lost our first two matches. However, when I scored the first goal in Lyon against Japan, I knew we couldn't lose, because I knew the quality of my defenders. Then I scored a second. And we had won the match. The Reggae Boyz' first victory in the World Cup!"

Carter sees red

17

In terms of red cards, a record was beaten during this tournament. Mexican referee Arturo Brizio Carter, who refereed three matches in this World Cup and three matches at the 1994 tournament, handed out his seventh World Cup red card. He showed the red card four times in 1998 following the three he had handed out in 1994, not forgetting the 27 yellow cards he had shown in both tournaments. He went ahead of Frenchman Joël Quiniou (five red cards in total). Notably, Carter sent off Zinédine Zidane in the game between France and Saudi Arabia (4–0). Furthermore, during the game between Denmark and South Africa, Colombian referee John Jairo Toro Rendón sent off three players, thereby equalling the existing record.

Cameroonian striker Samuel Eto'o, the youngest player in the competition, made his World Cup debut at 17 years and 99 days. Only Northern Ireland's Norman Whiteside was younger when he made his World Cup debut – 17 years and 41 days.

Prosinečki sees double

14 JUNE 1998

JAMAICA ✕ 1–3 ▦ **CROATIA**

EARLE 45   STANIC 27
PROSINEČKI 53
SUKER 69

◀ Croatia's Robert Prosinečki had previously scored for Yugoslavia at the 1990 World Cup.

W HEN HE SCORED in the 53rd minute against Jamaica in Lens on 14 June (2–1), Croat Robert Prosinečki achieved a rare feat: he became the first player to score for two different countries at the World Cup, following his debut goal in the 1990 tournament for Yugoslavia in their 4–1 victory against the UAE.

▶ Making their World Cup debut, Jamaica have the backing of their enthusiastic fans.

A difficult debut for the new boys

The World Cup draw in December 1997 in Marseille saw three of the four World Cup debutants – Croatia, Jamaica and Japan – end up in Group H. It was Croatia who progressed, alongside Argentina, thanks to victories over the Jamaicans (3–1 with goals from Mario Stanic, Robert Prosinecki and Davor Suker) and the Japanese (1–0 Suker). The other debutant, South Africa, finished third in Group C after losing to France (3–0) and drawing with Denmark (1–1) and Saudi Arabia (2–2).

15

► Spain's Andoni Zubizarreta scores an own goal to let Nigeria back into the match.

Fifteen European teams took part in this tournament (which represented 46 per cent of the 32 countries that qualified). Ten of them qualified for the second stage, six for the quarter-finals (i.e. 75 per cent of the countries that qualified) and three for the semi-finals (again 75 per cent).

"That goal helped me make a name for myself in football."

Sunday Oliseh, Nigerian midfielder, scorer of the winning goal against Spain.

"**My goal against Spain remains my best memory of the competition**. Not only because it was a powerful strike, but also because of what it meant. Our preparation had been very poor and we had lost almost all of our friendlies. So we had seriously doubted ourselves before entering the tournament. In training a day before the match against Spain, Taribo West said to me: 'Do you want to take some shots? I'll go in goal.' And I scored nine out of ten, although Taribo wasn't a goalkeeper (laughter). That's why, during the match, from a header out by a Spanish defender, I didn't think twice," recalled the 23-year-old midfielder. "That goal enabled us to kick-start our competition, have a good World Cup and even begin a long unbeaten run of matches. I believe that goal also helped me make a name for myself in football."

Super Eagles soar as Spain slump

13 JUNE 1998

SPAIN 🇪🇸 2–3 🇳🇬 **NIGERIA**

HIERRO 21, RAUL 47   ADEPOJU 24, ZUBIZARRETA 73 (o.G.), OLISEH 78

DURING THEIR FIRST MATCH on 13 June in Nantes, manager Javier Clemente's Spanish team started favourites, notably thanks to the presence of their stars Fernando Hierro and Raúl, who had just won the Champions League with Real Madrid against Juventus. But they could not underestimate Nigeria, who had been crowned Olympic champions in 1996. The experience of Bora Milutinović and the coming-of-age of an outstanding generation playing in Europe (midfielders Jay Jay Okocha at Fenerbahçe and Sunday Oliseh at Ajax, winger Finidi George at Betis and defender Céléstine Babayaro at Chelsea) made them formidable outsiders. To help motivate the players before the kick-off, Bora Milutinović showed them a video in which their families were giving them messages of encouragement. It was Spain who opened the scoring: Hierro lined up a free-kick that left goalkeeper Peter Rufai rooted to the spot (1–0). However, three minutes later, Mutiu Adepoju, getting his head to a corner, surprised the Spanish defence (1–1). Just after the break, the Real Madrid duo of Hierro and Raúl did what they did best: a perfect pass from the former to the latter, who fired Spain back into the lead with an unstoppable left-footed volley (2–1).

But Nigeria did not give up. In the 73rd minute, Garba Lawal attempted to cross from the goal-line. It was an apparently harmless action but, caught off-guard, goalkeeper Andoni Zubizarreta turned the ball into his own net (2–2). The last word belonged to Nigeria when Sunday Oliseh fired a thunderous half-volley from 30 yards that went in off the inside of the post (2–3). This unexpected victory was a perfect launch pad for Nigeria, who went on to beat Bulgaria (3–1) and qualify for the round of 16 with Paraguay. Weighed down by this difficult start, Spain recorded a draw against Paraguay (0–0) and then crushed Bulgaria (6–1, the highest score in the tournament). They would nevertheless have to content themselves with third place in Group D – and elimination.

◀ Zinédine Zidane leaves the pitch after being sent off against Saudi Arabia.

Zidane's shirt

Shirt worn by French playmaker Zinedine Zidane during their semi-final against Croatia.

◀ FIFA World Football Museum collection.

France lose Zidane

18 JUNE 1998

FRANCE ▮▮ 4–0 ▦▦ **SAUDI ARABIA**

HENRY 37, 78
TREZEGUET 68
LIZARAZU 85

Having beaten South Africa (3–0, thanks to goals from Christophe Dugarry and Thierry Henry plus a Pierre Issa own goal), then Saudi Arabia and finally Denmark with their second string XI (2–1, Youri Djorkaeff with a penalty and Emmanuel Petit), France successfully negotiated the first round. However, Zinédine Zidane was sent off against the Saudis after stamping on Saudi captain Fuad Amin in the 71st minute, while France were already leading 2–0, and picked up a two-match suspension. It would mean that the French playmaker would miss the round of 16.

Bulgarian flop

24 JUNE 1998

SPAIN ▦ 6–1 ▦▦ **BULGARIA**

HIERRO 6 (PEN), LUIS ENRIQUE 18   KOSTADINOV 58
MORIENTES 55, 81
BACHEV 88 (O.G.), KIKO 90+4

Semi-finalists four years earlier, Bulgaria finished bottom of Group D with two defeats and one draw. They finished 29th out of 32 teams. But, above all, Hristo Stoichkov and his teammates collapsed against Spain in their third match. The ageing team, coached by Dimitar Penev, could not rely on its out-of-form playmakers, such as Stoichkov, Krasimir Balakov and Ilian Iliev.

▶ Disappointment for Bulgaria's Hristo Stoitchkov. There was to be no repeat of the heroics of 1994.

▲ Brazil's Ronaldo celebrates after scoring against Chile.

Ronaldo *O Fenômeno* strikes twice

27 JUNE 1998

BRAZIL 🔵 4–1 🟥 CHILE

SAMPAIO 11, 26   SALAS 70
RONALDO 45+3 (PEN), 72

A WORLD CHAMPION FOUR YEARS EARLIER, without having played a single minute, Ronaldo learned a lot in the United States: "It was a very important time. Seeing Romário, Bebeto and players of that calibre in action helped shape the rest of my career. I learned a lot from them in terms of training and concentration," stressed the Brazilian number 9. "A lot of little details as well. Romário sent me to get his boots, or a coffee. As if I was a kid. This took nothing away from my respect, but there was a hierarchy within the team." Four years later, Ronaldo Luís Nazário de Lima became Brazil's number one attacking asset. Having passed through Cruzeiro, PSV Eindhoven and Barcelona, "The Phenomenon", awarded the Ballon d'Or in 1997, was now wearing the colours of Inter Milan. At just 21 years of age, the Brazilian had all the qualities: speed, technique, creativity and calmness in front of goal. In the group stage against Morocco, he scored and provided an assist for Bebeto (3–0). Against Chile, the 1.83m centre-forward confirmed his reputation with two goals, including a penalty that he won himself. The Brazilian also hit the post and crossbar, but, above all, he sowed panic in Brazil's opponents every time he got the ball. "Ronaldo was quite simply the best player in the world," said his teammate, defender Júnior Baiano. "Wearing the Brazilian shirt for a footballer is a bit like a soldier going into battle for his country; it confers a very strong feeling of pride," added Ronaldo. However, despite his four goals and his title as the best passer of the ball, Ronaldo, voted the best player of the tournament, was unable to lead his country to victory in the Final.

Beckham sees red

30 JUNE 1998

ARGENTINA 🇦🇷 2–2 ➕ ENGLAND
A.E.T.

BATISTUTA 5 (PEN)   SHEARER 9 (PEN)
ZANETTI 45+1   OWEN 16

⚽✖⚽⚽⚽ 4–3 ⚽✖⚽⚽✖

TWELVE YEARS after the legendary quarter-final of 1986, the rivalry between Argentina and England was rekindled. After ten minutes of play, the score was already 1–1 following two penalties: David Seaman brought down Diego Simeone and Gabriel Batistuta powerfully converted; then Roberto Ayala impeded Michael Owen and Alan Shearer slammed the ball into the back of the net. In a breathless first half, Owen set off at high speed and finished perfectly after a slaloming run in one of the goals of the tournament. However, Javier Zanetti equalized with his left foot from a cleverly worked Argentinian free-kick. The match turned after the interval: the victim of a bad tackle from behind by Simeone, David Beckham fell and, in a moment of anger, kicked out at his opponent. Danish referee Kim Milton Nielsen took out the yellow card for the Argentinian and the red for the Englishman. Down to ten men, England defended and hung on, but went down on penalties as a result of misses by Paul Ince and David Batty. "To hold on for such a long time against a team like Argentina was some feat. We came very close to an historic victory," Glenn Hoddle, the English manager, consoled himself by saying.

▶ Michael Owen eludes José Chamot and goes on to score one of the best goals of the tournament.

"I know that my teammates and the supporters were very disappointed. However, at 23 years of age, I wasn't ready for everybody to blame me for that defeat."

David Beckham, English attacking midfielder, sent off against Argentina.

◄ Laurent Blanc is about to shoot past José Luis Chilavert and score the first golden goal in World Cup history.

The first Golden Goal

28 JUNE 1998

FRANCE ▮▮ 1–0 G.G. ▭ PARAGUAY

BLANC 114

WITHOUT the suspended Zinédine Zidane, the French pounded the Paraguayan defence for 114 minutes. In the absence of the French number 10, coach Aimé Jacquet brought in Bernard Diomède, and handed him the responsibility of directing the game with Youri Djorkaeff, while youngsters Thierry Henry and David Trezeguet were the attacking duo. At the end of the first period, Henry rapped the Paraguay post, failing in his one-on-one with José Luis Chilavert, the Paraguayan goalkeeper. After the break, Trezeguet missed the goal with his left foot. Despite constant domination, France were severely hampered by the man-to-man marking and discipline of central linchpins Carlos Gamarra and Celso Ayala, one of the best pairings of the tournament. During extra-time, Laurent Blanc went up front and, to the relief of the entire country, scored the first World Cup "golden goal" on the day his teammate Fabien Barthez celebrated his 27th birthday.

"I was no longer playing as a defender."

Laurent Blanc, French defender, scorer of the golden goal against Paraguay.

"My goal came at the right time. I told myself that if we were to go to penalties our chances would really be very slim. The Paraguayans had defended tooth and nail and their goalkeeper was full of confidence. For the last five minutes, I was no longer playing as a defender because, even if it meant losing, it was better to do so during the game than in the penalty shoot-out… I knew it would all end there, because the previous day I had criticized the principle of the golden goal! It must be awful for the team that is beaten like that. During extra-time, the French team wanted to score at any price and Paraguay wanted to wait for penalties. At that moment we were perhaps the most attacking team of the World Cup! Robert (Pires) dribbled into the box, crossed to David (Trezeguet) who headed the ball down to me. David knew that he couldn't finish because he had his back to the goal. He had the stroke of genius to anticipate my movement and find the exact space that would allow me to go one-on-one with Chilavert and score."

Italy, Norway's bogey team

27 JUNE 1998

ITALY ▮▮ 1–0 ▤ NORWAY

VIERI 18

IN EACH OF THE THREE TIMES they have taken part (1938, 1994 and 1998), the Norwegian team has only lost one match. Each time it was by a one-goal margin and each time it was against Italy. Having got through to the round of 16 for the first time in their history, the Norwegians went down to a goal by Christian Vieri, with a right-footed angled shot, put through from deep by Luigi Di Biagio. It was the centre-forward's fifth goal of the tournament. In the second half, Tore André Flo missed a golden chance for Norway and the Italians squeezed through.

► Christian Vieri and Alessandro del Piero celebrate Italy's goal against Norway.

229

◀ Davor Šuker celebrates Croatia's historic win over Germany in unique style.

Šuker's shirt

Shirt worn by Croatian centre-forward Davor Šuker during the finals phase in France.

▶ FIFA World Football Museum collection.

Croatia beat ten-man Germany

4 JULY 1998

GERMANY ▬ 0–3 ▬▬ **CROATIA**

JARNI 45+3, VLAOVIĆ 80, ŠUKER 85

TO FIND AN INSTANCE of Germany being defeated by three clear goals in the World Cup, you had to go back to 28 June 1958, when France won 6–3 in the third-place playoff match. So this quarter-final, played in Lyon, went into the history books. The European Champions under Berti Vogts, who was managing the national team for the 100th time, nevertheless dominated the first half, creating a few chances with headers from Dietmar Hamann and Oliver Bierhoff. However, Christian Wörns committed a serious foul as the last defender in a tackle on Šuker in the 40th minute. "The Germans undoubtedly underestimated us; they thought that their team was superior to ours. But that's the beauty of football; the favourite doesn't always win and a little country can beat a great footballing nation," said Davor Šuker. The Croatian centre-forward believed that "the red card was justified because my leg still hurts today".

With only ten men, Germany suffered. In first-half stoppage time, Robert Jarni found Andreas Köpke's net with his left foot to hand Croatia the lead. After the restart, Croatian goalkeeper Drazen Ladić pulled off a fantastic save from Bierhoff's close-range effort. The Croatians missed several opportunities to score on the counter-

attack, until Goran Vlaović's strike in the 80th minute mirrored the first goal, this time with his right foot, from the right-hand side .

Šuker then narrowly missed at 2–0, but added Croatia's third in the 85th minute, his fourth goal of the competition. "It was like a fairytale… It was a major achievement for Croatian football and one of the best evenings of my career," stressed Šuker. He scored again in the semi-final against France, but could not lead his team into the final: "France played superb football. What upsets me is that Lilian Thuram, who scored two goals against us, did not score in a major tournament after that. But we were very proud of the way in which we played for our country."

In the match for third place against the Netherlands, Šuker scored his sixth goal of the tournament, to end up as the tournament's leading goalscorer and was voted the second-best player (after Ronaldo). Croatia reached the semi-finals in their first appearance at the World Cup. Their manager, Miroslav Blažević, who wore a kepi as a gesture of support for French gendarme Daniel Nivel injured in Lens by German hooligans, called his side's achievements an "historic result".

Laudrup bids farewell

3 JULY 1998

BRAZIL ◉ 3–2 ▬▬ **DENMARK**

| BEBETO 10e | JORGENSEN 2 |
| RIVALDO 25e, 59e | LAUDRUP B. 50 |

DESPITE DANISH goals at the beginning of each half, Brazil qualified for their second successive semi-final thanks to two goals from Rivaldo and one by Bebeto with Ronaldo setting up the first two. It was the last match for legendary Danish captain Michael Laudrup (104 caps, 37 goals): "We had a few problems in the group stages, but we managed to qualify. We found ourselves up against Nigeria, the major surprise of the competition and Spain's executioner. However, we beat them and earned the right to face Brazil. I even dreamed that we beat them, I can tell you. I didn't feel any pressure; I told myself that even if it meant it was the last match of my career it had to be against the Brazilians."

▶ Denmark's Brian Laudrup celebrates his equalizer against Brazil with teammate Søren Colding.

Italian Frenchmen

3 JULY 1998

ITALY ▌▌ 0–0 ▌▌ **FRANCE**
A.E.T.

✪✕✪✪✕ 3–4 ✪✕✪✪✪

FIVE PLAYERS IN AIMÉ JACQUET'S starting line-up played for Italian club sides: Didier Deschamps and Zinedine Zidane at Juventus, Lilian Thuram at Parma, Marcel Desailly at AC Milan and Youri Djorkaeff at Inter. Spending time playing football in Italy enabled them to develop in terms of experience, tactical discipline and defensive culture. "For our World Cup victory we owe a lot to the fact that we had played at major foreign clubs, especially in Italy," recognized French captain Didier Deschamps. "It was not a question of acclimatizing to the training when we got home! As a warning, the *Corriere dello Sport*, on the day before the quarter-final against Italy, wrote: 'We've given birth to monsters.' It's true that I think they helped us grow up, because until then the French team hadn't won very much." During what turned out to be a very tense match, the French team produced an "Italian style" display: their solidity at the back ultimately saw them through against a strong Italy side, even though Roberto Baggio, with a volley, could have scored a golden goal during extra-time. For the third World Cup in a row, Italy went out on penalties following misses by Demetrio Albertini and Luigi Di Biagio, with only Bixente Lizarazu missing for the French. "It was a match against 'the enemy', if I can say that," said French striker David Trezeguet after the match. "A goalless draw, but a match of high quality, even though it might not have been a good spectacle for the public. We nearly lost in extra-time. Baggio didn't generally miss those chances. That time he fortunately put the ball wide. Then, for the penalty shoot-out, the coach once again put his trust in me: I didn't think twice. I was there. I placed my shot well and Pagliuca went the other way."

▶ Dennis Bergkamp shakes off his marker, Roberto Ayala, in the quarter-final between the Netherlands and Argentina.

▼ Christian Vieri in action between Marcel Desailly and Didier Deschamps.

Bergkamp's sublime goal

4 JULY 1998

NETHERLANDS 2–1 **ARGENTINA**

KLUIVERT 12   C. LOPEZ 17
BERGKAMP 90

AFTER OPENING THE SCORING through Patrick Kluivert (1–0, 12th minute), the Dutch conceded an equalizer five minutes later through Claudio Lopez. The Netherlands booked their place in the semi-finals with one of the most sublime goals in the history of the World Cup finals. It was scored by Dennis Bergkamp at the end of the match as extra time loomed. Dutch midfielder Frank De Boer: "My best memory is the winning goal scored by Dennis in the quarter-final against Argentina. My decisive pass was the result of us having played together at Ajax in 1991 and 1992. We got on well on the pitch. So when he saw me, I knew he wanted the long ball. Everything worked out – my long ball from the left, his control and his instantaneous shot with the outside of his left foot… This goal, in the final minute, was a dream."

▲▲ Ronaldo beats keeper Edwin van der Sar to score Brazil's first goal in the semi-final against the Netherlands.

▲ Patrick Kluivert equalizes after winning a one-on-one with Junior Baiano.

▲ Ronaldo returns to the centre circle having scored the first penalty in the shoot-out.

The holders hang on

7 JULY 1998

BRAZIL ◉ 1–1 ▬ NETHERLANDS
A.E.T.

RONALDO 46   KLUIVERT 87

⊛⊛⊛⊛ 4–2 ⊛⊛✗✗

B RAZIL, THE DEFENDING CHAMPIONS, reached their sixth World Cup Final. The cautious Dutch committed multiple fouls against an on-form Ronaldo. However, when they came back out of the dressing room after half-time, the Inter Milan centre-forward shook off Phillip Cocu to score with his left foot between the legs of Van der Sar. Brazil continued to dominate, but were unable to make the game safe, notably when Ronaldo, on a one-on-one with Edwin Van der Sar, was tackled by Edgar Davids running back. With Brazil heading smoothly towards the Final, Ronald de Boer crossed superbly to Patrick Kluivert, who sent the Netherlands into extra-time with a header. Frank de Boer then saved an overhead kick on his line from Ronaldo, who then forced Van der Sar to pull out all the stops from his curling shot. It was again Frank de Boer who ended an incredible overlap by the Brazilian number 9. So it went to penalties: the four Brazilian penalty-takers (Ronaldo, Rivaldo, Émerson and Dunga) held their nerve, while Cocu and Ronald de Boer had their shots saved by penalty expert Cláudio Taffarel.

Cláudio Taffarel, goalkeeping hero in the country of forwards

Having been successful four years earlier in the Final, since he had only let in two of the Italians' five attempts (including one save), Brazilian goalkeeper Cláudio Taffarel went one better against the Netherlands by saving two out the four Dutch penalties. Very comfortable in this position, the Atlético Mineiro player confirmed his status as a national hero in a country that often has the habit of criticizing its goalkeeper, sometimes excessively: "If you mean that too much is expected of the goalkeeper, that's right, but it's nothing new. The proof is that people continue to blame our failures of 1982 and 1986 on the goalkeeper. It's a real tradition," confirmed Taffarel, who was 32 years old at the time. It is an attitude that is explained by the evident taste of Brazilian supporters for the attacking game: "However, for several tournaments, Brazil has been starting to concentrate on its defensive work. We realized that football was not just about attacking and making the net bulge. The Brazil of the 1970s conceded some goals, but scored five or six. Football has changed a lot. Now marking is more difficult. Above all, you must defend. Certain coaches and goalkeepers have played a decisive role in this change of mentality."

Thuram's two incredible goals

After his second goal against Croatia, Lilian Thuram fell to his knees on the turf of the Stade de France, his finger to his lips, having never previously scored for the French team in his 37 matches. "I don't really understand that gesture myself! I did it instinctively. It stays in my memory because it unquestionably reflected my astonishment," admitted the French number 15. "People understood that something was happening that was much bigger than me! When you think about it, you could die laughing, because I never scored, even in training; I don't understand it at all. If I fell to my knees it was not through emotion but through incomprehension. If not for the photos, I wouldn't have remembered anything. Before that match, I never scored goals. That evening I scored two. I didn't score again after that… It must really have been someone else who scored them!"

▲ Lilian Thuram is the hero of France as his two goals take the team to their first World Cup Final.

Fourth time lucky for France

8 JULY 1998

FRANCE ▮▮ 2–1 CROATIA

THURAM 47, 70   SUKER 46

FOLLOWING DEFEATS in the World Cup semi-finals of 1958, 1982 and 1986, France hoped it would be fourth time lucky. Yet, despite dominating in the first half, Didier Deschamps and his teammates were unable to make their superiority count. Worse still, in the 46th minute, Davor Šuker, picked out by Aljosa Asanović, got behind the French defence to slip the ball past Fabien Barthez with his left foot (0–1). It was the Croatian captain's fifth goal of the tournament. At fault for the goal, because he played the Croatian striker onside, Lilian Thuram made amends immediately. Appearing at the other end of the pitch, the French right back took the ball from Zvonimir Boban's feet, passed it to Youri Djorkaeff who returned it with the outside of his foot: Thuram won his duel with

Drazen Ladić and his shot hit the back of the net (1–1). Twenty-three minutes later, in another one-two, this time with Thierry Henry, Thuram doubled the lead with a perfectly curled left-footed shot (2–1). "However, that match could also have been my sporting 'death' because of that goal by Šuker, which I covered instead of playing him offside," admitted Thomas. ælt really would have been a disaster to have been eliminated and, as people always need to find someone to blame, I would have been the one! Sometimes life is left hanging by a thread." France held on to win, but at a price: in the 76th minute, Laurent Blanc pushed the chin of Croatian central defender Slaven Bilić with his hand and picked up a red card that would keep him out of the Final.

"With a bit more experience, we could have been world champions."

Miroslav Blažević, Croatian manager.

"After just six years of independence for Croatia, I made use of the patriotism that pervaded the team because nobody knew about us and our performance put the entire country under the spotlight. My players were highly motivated. The match against Germany was very physical and we were lucky that one of the opposing players was sent off so soon. We were brilliant because very few teams beat Germany 3–0. France beat us in the semi-final, although I believe we would have had our opportunities in the Final against Brazil, but our country was happy and proud to see us finish third. At the same time, I was a bit annoyed, because if we had had more experience, I think that we could have been world champions."

▲ Zinédine Zidane heads home France's first goal following an Emmanuel Petit corner.

Zidane, a national hero

12 JULY 1998

BRAZIL ◉ 0–3 ▮ FRANCE

ZIDANE 27, 45+1, PETIT 90+3

Tickets for the Final

Tickets for the World Cup 1998 final.

▲ FIFA World Football Museum collection.

0.28

The number of goals conceded per match by France. The French back four of Bixente Lizarazu, Laurent Blanc, Marcel Desailly and Lilian Thuram can be regarded as one of the best in World Cup history. Along with Fabien Barthez, who received the Lev Yashin award as the best goalkeeper, the French defence conceded just two goals.

SENT OFF IN THE SECOND MATCH against Saudi Arabia and so suspended for France's matches against Denmark and Paraguay, Zinédine Zidane's introduction to the World Cup had been underwhelming. But the French number 10 put this right in the Final. In the 27th minute he scored with his head at the near post from Emmanuel Petit's inswinging corner. His first goal in the competition. And then he produced a carbon copy just before the break, after Petit and then Stéphane Guivarc'h and missed chances. From a corner on the left-hand side, this time by Youri Djorkaeff, the Juventus playmaker rose again at the near post to deliver a powerful header. "For those set pieces, all six or seven players in the penalty area knew exactly where to position themselves," explained Emmanuel Petit. "If you have a good technique and a good run of the ball, you can put it where you want to seven times out of ten. For the first goal I put it into the near post because I knew that Zizou could get up well. I also noticed that the Brazilians always put a player on the far post for corners but often left their near post uncovered. I needed to hit it both high enough and tight enough to prevent it from being intercepted, by the goalkeeper as well as by the defender."

This brace was a reward for the technical assurance of "Zizou", who tormented the Brazilians throughout with a brilliant display. Brazil pressed in the second half and proved dangerous when Ronaldo's shot at point-blank range was blocked perfectly by Barthez. Despite Marcel Desailly being sent off for a second yellow-card offence in the 68th minute, France widened the gap right at the end of the game. In a final counter-attack, Christophe Dugarry found Patrick Vieira, who put through Petit, who had run from his own penalty area. The Arsenal midfielder put the ball in the back of Cláudio Taffarel's net to make the score 3–0. Despite his illness and the defeat, Ronaldo had proved his status as one of the best in the world during the tournament: "I have very good memories of 1998. It was a spectacular World Cup, where we unfortunately played really badly in the Final against France. I remember the atmosphere. Playing a World Cup Final against the host country is very difficult and it's even more so when you're up against an inspired Zinédine Zidane. Later, when we were teammates, he teased me quite a lot about it."

France won their first world championship title on their home ground. For their part, Brazil lost in the Final for the very first time (even though they had lost against Uruguay in the final match of the 1950 tournament, that had been the last match of a final round-robin stage). Didier Deschamps held the trophy aloft in front of 80,000 delirious spectators. At the end of the year, Zinedine Zidane received the Ballon d'Or.

Laurent Blanc's prophecy

Suspended for the Final, Laurent Blanc went to talk to Zinédine Zidane at about five o'clock on the day of the Final. "I went into his room and I said to him: 'So far you've played well but you haven't won a match for us. So, if you could do that, it would be great for us and for you it would be fantastic.' We had noticed that the Brazilians weren't good on set-pieces, so I asked him to go up a bit further into the penalty area. So, as luck, or fate, would have it, he scored two headed goals from corners. Everything worked out as we had hoped, both individually and collectively!"

▲ Zinédine Zidane – *Zizou* – lifts the FIFA World Cup trophy after the 3–0 French victory over Brazil.

Ronaldo, the mysterious illness

Right up until the last moment, Ronaldo nearly did not play in the Final. Furthermore, the tournament's best player did not appear on the first team sheet, on which Edmundo's name appeared instead. Having suffered convulsions earlier in the day, reported in certain quarters as an epileptic fit or a heart attack, the striker passed tests at the Lilas Clinic and only arrived at the Stade de France 50 minutes before the match. "Without taking anything away from France, who played very good football throughout the tournament, I think that things would have been different if Ronaldo had not had this illness, barely four hours before the final kicked off," explained Brazilian striker Bebeto. "It destabilized the whole team, who were very upset about his alarming health condition. Everybody was running in all directions and Edmundo was crying that Ronaldo was dying. The whole team was totally groggy, which was evident during the match."

◀ Spectacular save by Fabien Barthez against Brazil's Ronaldo.

▲ Davor Šuker and his teammates celebrate a well-earned bronze medal.

Croatia surprise right to the end

11 JULY 1998		
NETHERLANDS	1–2	CROATIA
ZENDEN 22		PROSINEČKI 14, ŠUKER 36

Surprise package Croatia took third place in their first World Cup appearance to cap off a superb tournament. Put through by Robert Jarni, Robert Prosinečki spun and fired in an unstoppable low shot. Shouts of "Hrvatska! Hrvatska!" rang out from the stands of the Parc des Princes. However, Boudewijn Zenden put the teams level following a long run with the ball at his feet. His left-footed, flighted shot deceived Drazen Ladić, who had until then pulled off several match-winning saves. Miroslav Blažević's men regained the advantage with a textbook move: Aljosa Asanović found Zvonimir Boban, who released Davor Šuker, whose shot with the outside of his left foot lodged in Edwin van der Sar's net. Šuker became the tournament's top scorer with six goals. He went ahead of Argentinian Gabriel Batistuta and Italian Christian Vieri (five goals each). Finishing third in their first appearance, Croatia equalled Portugal's performance in 1966 for the best performance by a team making its debut in the competition.

2002

The first FIFA World Cup in Asia was also the first to be staged in separate countries. South Korea went further than Japan, becoming the first country from outside Europe and the Americas to reach the last four. Turkey were the other surprise semi-finalists, but the Final was a first World Cup meeting between superpowers Brazil and Germany. Ronaldo scored both goals in a 2–0 win which gave Brazil a fifth world title.

Destination Asia

◄ Ronaldo and the Brazil team celebrate their country's fifth World Cup title.

▼ Thousands of South Korean fans celebrate on the streets of Seoul after their team's 1–0 victory over Portugal on 14 June.

▼ World Cup fever in Japan as fans get behind their national team and buy replica shirts.

THE WORLD CUP went to Asia for the first time. And for the first time the competition was hosted jointly by two countries: Japan and South Korea. Despite the differences in language and culture, and the large number of sites (ten in each country), this innovation was a great success. And for the first time the supporters in the Far East could watch matches without having to stay up late or get up early! In South Korea, huge crowds took to the streets and squares to watch the national team's matches as fan fests made their World Cup debut in spectacular style. More than seven million people watched broadcasts of the South Korea-Germany semi-final in public screenings. Both hosts drew upon experienced coaches (Frenchman Philippe Troussier for Japan and Dutchman Guus Hiddink for South Korea), and made home advantages count, progressing beyond the group stage for the first time. Asia's other representatives – China and Saudi Arabia – fared less well.

KOREA JAPAN 2002

2002 FIFA WORLD CUP KOREA/JAPAN™

Story of the qualifiers

The return of Turkey

NO FEWER THAN 193 COUNTRIES took part in these qualifiers, playing 777 matches with 2,452 goals scored (an average of 3.16 per match), in front of 17.4 million spectators (22,300 spectators per match). Missing from the list of 15 countries to qualify from Europe were the Netherlands, semi-finalists in 1998, Scotland, Norway, Yugoslavia and the Czech Republic. On the other hand, Slovenia qualified for the World Cup for the first time thanks to its playoff success against Romania. Germany, surprisingly, had to qualify via the playoffs as a result of suffering an historic defeat against England on 1 September 2001 in Munich (1–5), with Michael Owen scoring

a hat-trick. It was only the second qualifier lost by Germany, with the other against Portugal in Stuttgart in 1985. However, after finishing second in their group, the team coached by Rudi Völler beat Ukraine in the playoffs (1–1 away, 4–1 at home). Absent from the tournament since 1954, Turkey returned after demolishing Austria during these same playoffs (1–0 and then 5–0). In South America, Colombia were unable to book their place, while Ecuador made its first appearance. First in its group with six wins from eight matches, China also made the final stages of the tournament for the first time. The fourth newcomer was Senegal.

◄ Turkey's Bülent Korkmaz gets the better of Chinese defender Yang Chen during the group stage of the finals.

Group stage

GROUP A			GROUP B			GROUP C			GROUP D			GROUP E			GROUP F			GROUP G			GROUP H		
SEN	1–0	FRA	PAR	2–2	RSA	BRA	2–1	TUR	KOR	2–0	POL	IRL	1–1	CMR	ARG	1–0	NGA	MEX	1–0	CRO	JPN	2–2	BEL
DEN	2–1	URU	ESP	3–1	SVN	CRC	2–0	CHN	USA	3–2	POR	GER	8–0	KSA	SWE	1–1	ENG	ITA	2–0	ECU	RUS	2–0	TUN
DEN	1–1	SEN	ESP	3–1	PAR	BRA	4–0	CHN	KOR	1–1	USA	GER	1–1	IRL	SWE	2–1	NGA	ITA	1–2	CRO	JPN	1–0	RUS
URU	0–0	FRA	RSA	1–0	SVN	TUR	1–1	CRC	POR	4–0	POL	CMR	1–0	KSA	ENG	1–0	ARG	MEX	2–1	ECU	BEL	1–1	TUN
DEN	2–0	FRA	ESP	3–2	RSA	BRA	5–2	CRC	KOR	1–0	POR	GER	2–0	CMR	SWE	1–1	ARG	MEX	1–1	ITA	JPN	2–0	TUN
SEN	3–3	URU	PAR	3–1	SVN	TUR	3–0	CHN	USA	1–3	POL	IRL	3–0	KSA	ENG	0–0	NGA	CRO	0–1	ECU	BEL	3–2	RUS

	W	D	L	+	–	PTS		W	D	L	+	–	PTS		W	D	L	+	–	PTS		W	D	L	+	–	PTS		W	D	L	+	–	PTS		W	D	L	+	–	PTS		W	D	L	+	–	PTS		W	D	L	+	–	PTS
DEN	2	1	0	5	2	7	ESP	3	0	0	9	4	9	BRA	3	0	0	11	3	9	KOR	2	1	0	4	1	7	GER	2	1	0	11	1	7	SWE	1	2	0	4	3	5	MEX	2	1	0	4	2	7	JPN	2	1	0	5	2	7
SEN	1	2	0	5	4	5	PAR	1	1	1	6	6	4	TUR	1	1	1	5	3	4	USA	1	1	1	5	6	4	IRL	1	2	0	5	2	5	ENG	1	2	0	2	1	5	ITA	1	1	1	4	3	4	BEL	1	2	0	6	5	5
URU	0	2	1	4	5	2	RSA	1	1	1	5	5	4	CRC	1	1	1	5	6	4	POR	1	0	2	6	4	3	CMR	1	1	1	2	3	4	ARG	1	1	1	2	2	4	CRO	1	0	2	2	3	3	RUS	1	0	2	4	4	3
FRA	0	1	2	0	3	1	SVN	0	0	3	2	7	0	CHN	0	0	3	0	9	0	POL	1	0	2	3	7	3	KSA	0	0	3	0	12	0	NGA	0	1	2	1	3	1	ECU	1	0	2	2	4	3	TUN	0	1	2	1	5	1

Knockout stages

ROUND OF 16			ROUND OF 16			ROUND OF 16			ROUND OF 16		
GER	1–0	PAR	ESP	1–1 3–2	IRL	DEN	0–3	ENG	SWE	1–2 G.G.	SEN
MEX	0–2	USA	KOR	2–1 G.G.	ITA	BRA	2–0	BEL	JPN	0–1	TUR

QUARTER-FINAL			QUARTER-FINAL			QUARTER-FINAL			QUARTER-FINAL1		
GER	1–0	USA	ESP	0–0 3–5	KOR	ENG	1–2	BRA	SEN	0–1 G.G.	TUR

SEMI-FINAL			SEMI-FINAL		
GER	1–0	KOR	BRA	1–0	TUR

PLAY-OFF FOR THIRD PLACE		
KOR	2–3	TUR

FINAL		
GER	0–2	BRA

64
MATCHES PLAYED

272   17
CARDS

32 TEAMS

2 705 197
SPECTATORS

THE SPHÉRIKS
OFFICIAL MASCOT

2002
FIFA WORLD CUP
KOREA JAPAN

OFFICIAL LOGO

BRAZIL
WINNERS

×8

RONALDO
LEADING GOALSCORER

2.5
AVERAGE GOALS
PER MATCH

FEVERNOVA
OFFICIAL MATCH BALL

Host cities and stadiums

Twenty stadiums – a record

Object

Fans for the fans

With ten stadiums in each of the two host countries, no World Cup has ever had more venues. Groups A to D were held in Korea, E to H in Japan. The only movement between the two was in the round of 16, when eight teams switched countries and for the play-off for third place and for the Final.

A symbol of Japanese and South Korean culture, the fan is particularly used in the theatre (*noh* and *kabuki* in Japan), traditional dance and martial arts. It was an ideal souvenir for supporters from around the world.

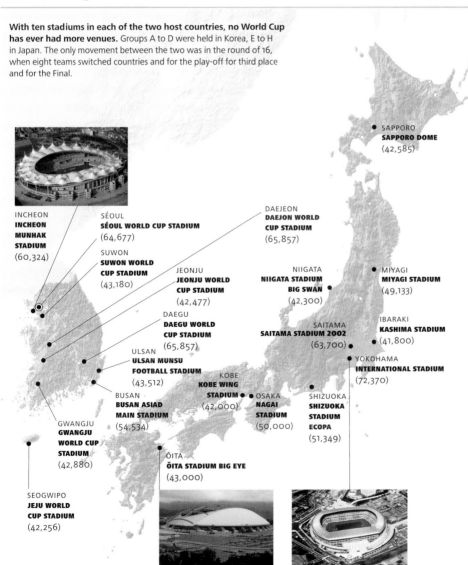

INCHEON
INCHEON MUNHAK STADIUM
(60,324)

SÉOUL
SÉOUL WORLD CUP STADIUM
(64,677)

SUWON
SUWON WORLD CUP STADIUM
(43,180)

JEONJU
JEONJU WORLD CUP STADIUM
(42,477)

DAEGU
DAEGU WORLD CUP STADIUM
(65,857)

ULSAN
ULSAN MUNSU FOOTBALL STADIUM
(43,512)

BUSAN
BUSAN ASIAD MAIN STADIUM
(54,534)

GWANGJU
GWANGJU WORLD CUP STADIUM
(42,880)

SEOGWIPO
JEJU WORLD CUP STADIUM
(42,256)

ÕITA
ÕITA STADIUM BIG EYE
(43,000)

KOBE
KOBE WING STADIUM
(42,000)

OSAKA
NAGAI STADIUM
(50,000)

SHIZUOKA
SHIZUOKA STADIUM ECOPA
(51,349)

DAEJEON
DAEJON WORLD CUP STADIUM
(65,857)

NIIGATA
NIIGATA STADIUM BIG SWAN
(42,300)

SAITAMA
SAITAMA STADIUM 2002
(63,700)

SAPPORO
SAPPORO DOME
(42,585)

MIYAGI
MIYAGI STADIUM
(49,133)

IBARAKI
KASHIMA STADIUM
(41,800)

YOKOHAMA
INTERNATIONAL STADIUM
(72,370)

▲ **FIFA World Football Museum collection.**

▲ Sylvain Wiltord, Alain Boghossian and Zinédine Zidane on the bench during the game against Senegal.

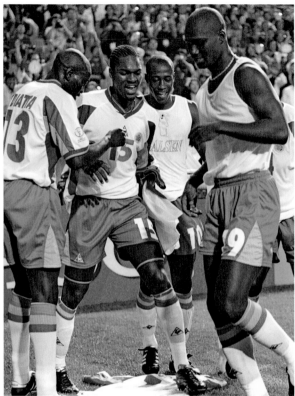

▲ Senegal's players celebrate their win over defending champions France in the opening match of the 2002 FIFA World Cup.

Bolt from the blue in Seoul

31 MAY 2002

FRANCE ❚❚ 0–1 ❚●❚ **SENEGAL**

BOUBA DIOP 30

PERHAPS FRANCE, the defending champions and reigning European champions (in 2000), were over-confident when they arrived in Asia. However, they lost Zinedine Zidane, with an injury to his left thigh, in a friendly against South Korea just before the finals. Against Senegal, during the opening match in Seoul, France, lacking ideas and inspiration, went down 1–0 to a goal from Pape Bouba Diop scored in the 30th minute, following a cross by El Hadji Diouf. In their first-ever World Cup match, Senegal had caused a huge suprise, because, on paper, the French team, coached by Roger Lemerre, looked to be even stronger than that of 1998. Their new faces included the top goalscorer in the French championship (Djibril Cissé, AJ Auxerre), the English championship (Thierry Henry, Arsenal) and the Italian championship (David Trezeguet, Juventus). In their second match, France – without Henry, who was sent off in the 25th minute for a badly timed tackle – drew with Uruguay (0–0). Finally, despite the

return of Zidane, who was still not at his best, the holders went down to Denmark in the third match (2–0, with goals from Dennis Rommedahl and Jon Dahl Tomasson) and finished up bottom of Group A with just one point having failed to score a single goal in three matches.

"After our victories in the World Cup and the European Championship, we turned up with a sense of euphoria," admitted French defender Lilian Thuram. "We didn't have our feet on the ground and thought that the results would come. We'd forgotten that to have luck on our side we needed to create it. And I remember that after the defeat to Denmark we had the feeling that we hadn't turned up at the World Cup. I just don't believe we were there – as simple as that."

The tournament was indeed a disaster for the French. They were the first defending champions not to score a goal; the first to fall at the first stage since 1966; and the first to finish bottom of their first round group.

"I'd known for a long time who to put up against the major threats of the French team."

Bruno Metsu,
Senegal's French coach.

"The French weren't really up for that opening match. I'm not saying that they took us lightly but they weren't as focused as if we had been Brazil. However, we set ourselves up as an exceptional collective unit against them. I'd begun to prepare for that match in my head from the Final of the Africa Cup of Nations, in February 2002. And I'd never been worried. In my game plan, I knew who to put up against the major threats of the French team and how to counter them. Because I had the players that I needed. Against Lizarazu I had Moussa Ndiaye; I had Bouba Diop and Salif Diao against Vieira and Petit; Fadiga against Thuram. The key to this match was that the French strikers should not receive the ball closer than 20 yards from our goal. To do that, we had to put numbers in the middle of the park and cut off all through balls. My idea was as follows: to put Aliou Cissé in the gap between our two midfielders, Bouba Diop and Diao. The other priority of our organization against France was not to get sucked in. We wanted to retrieve the ball in the middle of the field because my players were good at long runs. If you had Frank Lebœuf and Marcel Desailly 20 yards from their goal, they were not easy to pass. But if you took them on with long runs, 40 yards from their goal, they had problems. You only had to look at how Diouf exposed Lebœuf."

Italy scrape through to last 16

8 JUNE 2002

ITALY ▮▮ 1–2 CROATIA

VIERI 55   OLIĆ 73, RAPAIĆ 76

I T WAS BECOMING A TRADITION. Italy had got into the habit of starting slowly. After a win against Ecuador (2–0, thanks to a brace from Christian Vieri), Giovanni Trapattoni's team were caught out at the end of the match by Croatia (1–2), before snatching a draw in desperate circumstances against Mexico, thanks to a goal from Alessandro Del Piero with a diving header in the 85th minute (1–1). Second in Group G, well behind the Mexicans, Italy nevertheless qualified for the round of 16, taking advantage of Ecuador's first World Cup victory in its third and final match against Croatia (1–0), with a goal by Édison Méndez from a low left-footed half-volley. A semi-finalist four years earlier, Croatia missed a golden opportunity to qualify at Italy's expense.

▲ Croatia's Ivica Olić tussles with Damiano Tommasi of Italy.

5

For China's manager, the Serbian Bora Milutinović, it was his fifth experience of reaching the final stages of the World Cup (1986, 1990, 1994, 1998 and 2002) – a record broken by Carlos Alberto Parreira in 2010. This time, having enabled China to qualify for its first World Cup, "the sorcerer" did not create a miracle: the Chinese lost their three group matches and left the tournament with nine goals conceded and none scored.

Argentina fall at first hurdle

7 JUNE 2002

ENGLAND ✚ 1–0 ARGENTINA

BECKHAM (PEN) 41

D ESPITE BIG NAMES like Javier Zanetti (Inter Milan), Gabriel Batistuta (AS Rome), Pablo Aimar (FC Valencia) and Juan Sebastián Verón (Manchester United), Marcelo Bielsa's Argentina went out in the first round. The 3-4-3 formation that they set up did not work well and the individual qualities of the Argentinians were not enough to make the difference. Argentina were the big-name casualties of a particularly difficult group, one some people dubbed the "group of death". In their first match, the Argentinians beat Nigeria, thanks to a headed goal by Batistuta from a corner (1–0). However,

Argentina then went down to England (0–1): Michael Owen first of all hit the post from an angled strike, before winning a penalty that was forcefully converted by David Beckham in the 44th minute. After the restart, English goalkeeper David Seaman brought out a superb reflex stop from a header by Mauricio Pochettino. Finally, in their third match, Sweden opened the scoring thanks to a free-kick by Anders Svensson before Hernán Crespo equalized right at the end of the game (1–1). Third in Group F, behind Sweden and England, it was the first time Argentina had fallen at the first hurdle since 1962.

▲ England's goalkeeper, David Seaman, saved the day for England on an Argentine attack.

"When I saw the ball's trajectory, I was so happy."

Anders Svensson, striker for Sweden, who qualified for the round of 16.

"In the final match against Argentina, about an hour into the game, when the score was still 0–0, I won a free-kick in a good position by accelerating with the ball at my feet. Henrik Larsson, who had taken two or three free-kicks up until that point, asked me if I 'felt' it. I said 'yes'. He said to me: 'Go on'. When I saw the ball's trajectory, I was so happy, for myself and for the team (1–0). Because we just needed a draw to get through and get out of this very difficult group. It was my first World Cup and I shall remember it all my life," explained the Swedish number 7.

◀ Coach Marcelo Bielsa barks out orders during Argentina's final group match, against Sweden.

▲ Japan's coach, Philippe Troussier, celebrates his side's victory.

▲ A first win at the World Cup for Japan thanks to a goal from Junichi Inamoto (number 5).

Civil war in Ireland

As soon as the Republic of Ireland arrived in Japan, they lost their one world-class player, Manchester United's Roy Keane, who argued with coach Mick McCarthy over the training facilities. "I've come over here to do well and I want people around me to want to do well," Keane said. "If I feel we're not all wanting the same things, there's no point." He was sent home. "I cannot and will not tolerate being spoken to with that level of abuse being thrown at me, so I sent him home," McCarthy replied.

An historic first victory for Japan

9 JUNE 2002

JAPAN ● 1-0 ▬ **RUSSIA**

INAMOTO 51

AT THEIR OWN WORLD CUP, Japan took advantage of the experience of its midfielders Junichi Inamoto (Arsenal), Hidetoshi Nakata (Parma) and Shinji Ono (Feyenoord). Disciplined and in perfect physical condition, the Japanese drew their opening match against Belgium. In their second game against Russia, on 9 June in Yokohama, Nakata missed a goal when a cross was pushed out of the danger area by Russian goalkeeper Ruslan Nigmatullin. After the interval, Inamoto, just onside, took advantage of a clever defection by Atsushi Yanagisawa to beat Nigmatullin at point-blank range. Despite a few scares, when Vladimir Beschastnykh dribbled past Japanese goalkeeper Seiko Narazaki, but only found the side netting,

Japan remained in front. Near the end of the game, Nakata, with a strike from more than 20 yards, smashed the Russian crossbar. At the final whistle, the stadium was delirious. It was Japan's first win at the World Cup, following on from their first point, won in the Belgium game. In the third match against Tunisia, Philippe Troussier's men again made the difference in the second half (2–0, with goals from Hiroaki Morishima and then Nakata) and did not let the opportunity to reach the round of 16 pass them by. Having finished 31st out of 32 four years earlier, during their first tournament appearance, the Japanese finished first in Group H, ahead of Belgium, with Russia and Tunisia going out of the competition.

▲ Ireland's Roy Keane was sent home after a training ground bust-up with manager Mick McCarthy

Germany with six goalscorers

1 JUNE 2002

GERMANY 8-0 **SAUDI ARABIA**

KLOSE 20, 25, 70, BALLACK 40
JANCKER 45+1, LINKE 73
BIERHOFF 84, SCHNEIDER 90+1

ON 1 JUNE IN SAPPORO, Germany won 8–0 against Saudi Arabia. Beaten three times in three matches (12 goals conceded, 0 scored), the team coached by Nasser Al Johar had the worst record in this tournament. For its part, the German team had six different goalscorers. Besides Klose's hat-trick, Ballack, Jancker, Linke, Bierhoff and Schneider all found the back of the net. It was nevertheless not a World Cup record since Hungary (10–1 against El Salvador in 1982 and 9–0 against the Republic of Korea in 1954) and Yugoslavia (9–0 against Zaire in 1974) had done better. One record Germany did help to set, however, was the total of 16 yellow cards shown in their 2–0 victory over Cameroon, eight of them German!

◤ Park Ji-sung scored the only goal of the match in the victory over Portugal.

Raul and Morientes inspire Spanish clean sweep

▲ Fernando Morientes (left) and Raúl (middle) scored five goals between them for Spain in the group stage.

Spain were one of just two teams to emerge from the group stage with a 100 per cent record. The attacking partnership of Real Madrid duo Raúl and Fernando Morientes played a large part in their success. In three Spanish wins (3–1 against Slovenia and Paraguay, then 3–2 against South Africa), Raul scored three times in total whilst Morientes found the back of the net twice.

Home advantage pays off

14 JUNE 2002

PORTUGAL 0-1 **SOUTH KOREA**

PARK JI SUNG 70ᵉ

AFTER BEATING POLAND (2-0) and then a draw against the United States (1-1), South Korea then beat Portugal on 14 June in Incheon to finish top of Group D. In the 27th minute, João Pinto picked up a straight red card for a two-footed tackle from behind on Park Ji Sung. Then Beto left just nine of his teammates on the pitch when he received his second yellow card (66'). In a match that was for a long time low in clearcut opportunities and relatively disjointed, South Korea ended up making the difference count after a superb trap on his chest, dummy and left-footed half-volley by Park Ji Sung, which went through Vítor Baía's legs. Near the end of the game, Luis Figo failed to equalize from a free kick. Portugal pressed forward but left huge gaps, whilst South Korea played on the counter-attack, not taking advantage of their numerical superiority. However, on their sixth appearance in the finals, Guus Hiddink's men at last qualified for the round of 16. In those six finals, the Koreans had played 14 matches without ever seriously threatening to win a match. So to win two of their Group games was an incredible achievement. Uncompromising in one-on-ones, prowling as a collective unit, sometimes technically brilliant, their campaign was about to hit top gear. As for Portugal, it was a resounding failure. All the more so because the team included in its ranks Luís Figo, winner of the Ballon d'Or in 2000.

▲ First Portugal, now Italy. Seol Ki-hyeon equalizes against Italy with just two minutes remaining. South Korea scored the winner in extra-time.

◣ Christian Vieri and Angelo di Livio contest the devision of referee Byron Moreno to send off Francesco Totti.

Achievement and controversy

18 JUNE 2002

SOUTH KOREA ◉ **2–1** ▐▌ **ITALY**
G.G.

K.H. SEOL 88, J.H. AHN 117   VIERI 18

ABOURED IN THE FIRST ROUND, the Italian team faced a host country, which had toppled Poland and Portugal in the first round to finish top of their group. After five minutes of play, Christian Panucci brought down Seol Ki Hyeon in the penalty area: Ahn Jung Hwan stepped up to take the penalty, but his low shot was brilliantly pushed away by Gianluigi Buffon. Italy opened the scoring in the 18th minute when Christian Vieri jumped higher than everyone to head in a corner taken by Francesco Totti (0–1). An hour into the game, South Korea's manager Guus Hiddink brought on two additional strikers. The move paid off, after Seol picked up on a sloppy clearance by Panucci and, with an instant left-footed shot, slid the ball into the opposite corner of the goal with just two minutes remaining (1–1). During extra-time, in the 113th minute, Totti tumbled in South Korea's penalty area and appealed for a penalty; instead, Ecuadorian referee Byron Moreno showed a second yellow card for simulation: it was a controversial moment. As was Damiano Tommasi's disallowed goal for offside a few moments later. With numerical superiority, South Korea snatched the win with a golden goal, when Ahn headed in a cross from left-back Lee Young Pyo in the 117th minute. The Daejeon stadium went wild, while the Italians left the tournament with a huge feeling of injustice. Italian manager Giovanni Trapattoni accepted the result with grace: "We could have and should have won that match but we didn't have what it took."

"One goal will be enough to beat the Koreans."

Francesco Totti, Italy's forward

Maldini family records

256

Aged 70 years and 131 days, Cesare Maldini, Paraguay's Italian coach (beaten in the round of 16 by Germany 0–1, with a goal from Oliver Neuville), was the oldest manager in the final stages of this World Cup . His son Paolo Maldini ended his World Cup career with a total of 13 matches as captain – the joint third highest behind Diego Maradona (16) and Dino Zoff (14).

Two hundred and fifty-six urine and blood samples were taken during the World Cup – from two players per team for each of the 64 matches. All proved negative and no banned substances were identified. For the first time in a FIFA competition, blood samples were taken in order to detect doping, particularly the use of erythropoi-etin (EPO) and darbepoetin (DPO).

▶ Henri Camara's golden goal against Sweden earns Senegal a place in the quarter-finals, the first African nation since Cameroon in 1990 to reach that stage..

◀ American keeper Brad Friedel punches the ball away safely during the USA's 2–0 win over Mexico.

Americans' perfect shot

17 JUNE 2002

MEXICO ▮•▮ 0–2 ▦ **USA**

MCBRIDE 8, DONOVAN 65

AT THE BEGINNING of the game on 17 June in Jeonju, Claudio Reyna broke loose down the right-hand side; his cross from the goal-line was flicked back by Josh Wolff for Brian McBride, who steered it past Oscar Pérez. Mexico pushed for an equalizer, but the United States goalkeeper, Brad Friedel, remained vigilant. After half-time, Friedel pushed a Mexican free-kick onto his crossbar. It was another fine performance from him, following his two penalty saves in the group stages (against South Korea and Poland). After the interval, the United States staged the perfect counter-attack: a cross from the left by Eddie Lewis straight onto the head of Landon Donovan, who made it 2–0. The duel between the North American neighbours therefore turned in favour of Bruce Arena's team, who reached the quarter-finals for the first time in the post-war period and kept their first clean sheet at the finals since beating England in 1950.

Camara's big day

16 JUNE 2002

SWEDEN ▦ 1–2 ▮•▮ **SENEGAL**
G.G.

LARSSON 11   H. CAMARA 37, 104

THE SURPRISE TEAM of the first round, Senegal continued to astonish in their first World Cup appearance. However, on 16 June in Oita, it was not the team's big-name stars El Hadji Diouf (RC Lens) and Khalilou Fadiga (Auxerre) who took centre stage. It was Henri Camara (Sedan), a substitute in the first two matches. After Henrik Larsson opened the scoring for Sweden with a header from a corner, Camara equalized from a delightful move: trapping it with his chest, taking it away from the defender and striking the ball low. In extra-time, Pape Thiaw back-heeled the ball to Camara, who went past the defender and sent the Senegalese into the quarter-final with a golden goal.

Host country go out despite Nakata

18 JUNE 2002

JAPAN ● 0–1 ▣ **TURKEY**

UMIT DAVALA 12

THE FINAL DAY of the round of 16 matches saw the two host nations in action. First up was Japan against Turkey in Rifu. However, in the rain, Japan were caught cold when a corner from Ergün Penbe was headed in by Ümit Davala. Again in the first half, a free-kick by Alex, a Japanese player of Brazilian origin, hit the crossbar. After the break, Philippe Troussier's men pushed forward with Hidetoshi Nakata leading the charge. However, the Parma midfielder was unable to break down the Turks, who defended intelligently and, in their first World Cup finals appearance since 1954, hung on to reach the quarter-finals. For Japan, a first round of 16 appearance, cemented their reputation as a fast-improving football nation.

◀ Turkey's Ümit Davala and Japan's Hidetoshi Nakata during the round of 16 match..

"It wasn't just down to luck."

Philippe Troussier, Japan's French coach.

"I had the feeling of having brought to maturity a process that began in 1998. I had at the time been managing the Under-20s, with whom I had been a World Cup finalist in 1999, losing against Xavi's Spain. I was also in charge of the Olympic team that finished fifth at Sydney in 2000. In short, it was teamwork that involved several categories of youth players and, of course, the senior team. It wasn't just down to luck."

Lacklustre Germany

21 JUNE 2002

GERMANY ▬ 1–0 ▬ USA

BALLACK 39

OFTEN UNDER PRESSURE DURING THE GAME, Germany owed a huge debt of thanks to their goalkeeper Oliver Kahn. But, thanks to a header by playmaker Michael Ballack in the 39th minute, they won this quarter-final against the USA. Just before the break, Miroslav Klose missed a gilt-edged chance when he smashed his header against Brad Friedel's goalpost. It was a far from vintage performance, but Germany were in the last four for the first time since 1990.

▶ Captains Oliver Kahn and Claudio Reyna before the Germany-USA quarter-final.

Kahn's gloves

Gloves worn by the German keeper Oliver Kahn during the finals in South Korea and Japan.

▲ FIFA World Football Museum collection.

"We deserved to win."

Claudio Reyna, United States playmaker.

"We had reached the quarter-finals for the first time. We had lost to Germany, who then went on to play in the Final, although we deserved to win after a superb performance on our part. However, we were unsuccessful and came up against an excellent goalkeeper. It was a really special experience: we spent around six weeks together, including the preparation. I was proud to be the captain of the team that had knocked out our historic rivals Mexico in the round of 16."

Oliver Kahn, the German wall

CRUCIAL IN EVERY MATCH, Oliver Kahn only conceded one goal in Germany's first six matches. In the round of 16 against the United States, the German captain again pulled off several world-class saves: in a lone foray by Landon Donovan, the Bayern Munich goalkeeper got down at lightning speed to deflect the American striker's shot. In another move started from deep by Donovan, Kahn remained upright and gave him no clues before authoritatively winning his one-on-one. After the break, from a Gregg Berhalter shot at point-blank range, Kahn responded with an astonishing reflex save. These three stops showed once again his talent and especially the breadth of his range. An imposing figure at 1.88m and with a strong character, Kahn never thought twice about facing down his opponents and delivering some well chosen words, such as "Every opponent's goal is an insult to me" or "I don't need anything or anybody to win on the pitch".

A modern goalkeeper who was comfortable on the ball and brilliant in the air, he was an unusual squad member of the 1994 and 1998 World Cups, as well as at the 1996 European Championships won by Germany. He was a late starter, his time finally coming at the 2002 World Cup: "I was never a great player, even in the lower age categories. I didn't go through the youth teams as was the case for others. In my day there was no real training. I used my abilities to the full," stressed Kahn. With such a safe pair of hands behind them, the German team only conceded three goals in eight matches, including two in the Final against Ronaldo's Brazil. Thanks to his outstanding performances, the German captain was the first goalkeeper to receive the Adidas Golden Ball as the best player of the tournament. "That title is close to my heart. No goalkeeper had picked it up before me. I was particularly proud of it." He also received the Lev Yashin Award for the best goalkeeper. "I also remember that we only qualified through the playoffs and didn't play well in our warm-up matches, but it didn't stop us from getting to the Final." Already a winner of the 2001 Champions League, the 1996 UEFA Cup, a four-time winner of the German championship with Bayern Munich, and a two-time winner of the German cup, Kahn ended his career as one of the most decorated goalkeepers in football history.

Ronaldinho, hero sent off

▶ Brazil's Ronaldinho is sent off during the quarter-final against England.

21 JUNE 2002

ENGLAND ✚ 1–2 ◉ BRAZIL

OWEN 11   RIVALDO 45+2, RONALDINHO 50

ON 21 JUNE IN SHIZUOKA, Michael Owen took advantage of a mistake by Lúcio to open the scoring with a delightful chip. However, just before half-time, Ronaldinho, full of running and with the ball at his feet, took Ashley Cole out of the game and then released Rivaldo, who hit it with his left foot past David Seaman. Back out of the dressing room, Ronaldinho succeeded with another stroke of genius: from a free-kick on the right-hand side, some 40 yards out, the Paris-Saint-Germain number 10 surprised David Seaman with a masterful lob. "When the foul was given, Cafú told me to try a direct shot because the goalkeeper, Seaman, was a bit off his line. This is what I did and the ball went into the top corner of the net. Not exactly where I wanted, but it was a goal all the same," joked the player nicknamed "Ronnie". Just seven minutes after scoring the goal, though, the Brazilian picked up a red card for stamping on Danny Mills. "The transition was difficult because, at that moment, I was determined to do everything to help the team. I was amazed because I had not even received a yellow card. I picked up a straight red for one bad action. I was in a bit of a state of shock because I really hadn't expected that," recalled Ronaldinho. But ten-man Brazil still managed to hold on to their advantage and progressed to the semi-finals.

End of the journey for the Senegal

22 JUNE 2002

SENEGAL ▮ 0–1 ☾ TURKEY
G.G.
ILHAN MANSIZ 94

THIS DUEL between outsiders ran away from Senegal in spite of several chances, including a disallowed goal by Henri Camara for offside in the first half. In extra-time, Turkey got through with a golden goal scored by substitute İlhan Mansız, who met Ümit Davala's cross perfectly. Senol Günes's men were in the semi-final for the first time. However, Senegal, newcomers to the competition, lit up this tournament with their enthusiasm and their talent.

South Korea make history

▲ Hong Myung-bo beats Iker Casillas in the penalty shootout against Spain to send South Korea through to the semi-final.

22 JUNE 2002

SPAIN ▮ 0–0 ☷ SOUTH KOREA
A.E.T.
⊕⊕⊕✗ 3–5 ⊕⊕⊕⊕⊕

THIS intense match could have gone either way and it was thanks to penalties that the Koreans became the first team from outside Europe and the Americas to make it through to the semi-finals. The match turned on a controversial incident in the second minute of extra time. Spain's Joaquín picked up the ball on the right wing, ran to the goal line to cross for Fernando Morientes to head home what would have been a golden goal. The linesman flagged that the ball had crossed the line although replays appear to show that it hadn't.

"It was not a question of going there to be ridiculed."

Bruno Metsu, Senegal's coach.

"To get a taste of the World Cup is magic. You're on another planet. As the matches progressed, we saw that people were falling in love with Senegal and its game. And then it was our first appearance, with young players. I often said to my players that Cameroon was the example to follow. The Cameroonians had power, personalities and huge confidence when they went onto the pitch. The first thing I did when I took over Senegal was to bring them together so that they believed in their team. Ferdinand Coly, Salif Diao and Tony Sylva were no longer playing for Senegal. El Hadji Diouf was dragging his feet. I said to them: 'But do you realize that it's our chance to play in a World Cup?' For me it was not just a question of going there as the Jamaicans had done four years previously… to be ridiculed. I wanted to go there to show everyone what we were capable of."

Hiddink's enormous challenge

WHO WOULD HAVE bet that South Korea would end up fourth in the World Cup? Basically nobody. As a result, manager Guus Hiddink's stock was at an all-time high. Coach of many clubs (PSV Eindhoven, with whom he won the European Cup in 1988, Fenerbahçe, Valencia, Real Madrid and Betis) as well as of the Dutch team that reached the semi-finals in 1998, Hiddink agreed to lead a team that had never won a match in the final stages. After starting the job in 2001, the Dutchman increased the number of friendlies, sometimes with very heavy defeats, tried out numerous systems, accepted no compromises and ousted some well-known players in favour of younger ones. The 55-year-old technician also brought his good humour and outspokenness to the job. He owed his success in particular to flawless physical preparation: "When I took over the team, the challenge was enormous. I knew that it would take me a lot of time to prepare the players. Almost nobody saw us getting through the group stages. However, we used that long period of preparation to build solid links within the team and develop a feeling of confidence. The most important thing was to reach perfect physical fitness, such that each player built up genuine confidence in himself." The manager also showed that he could be very close to his troops: "The real turning point in my career was Guus Hiddink," explained midfielder Park Ji Sung. "By believing in me, he helped me to believe in me. That's extremely important for a young footballer…" "

I'm very impressed by his natural authority. He never lose loses sight of the general balance of the team and does so without neglecting the individuals who make it up. I learned a lot during that tournament and I hope to be able to be like him one day," added Hwang Sun-Hong. Despite the defeat to Germany, Hiddink became a national hero in South Korea.

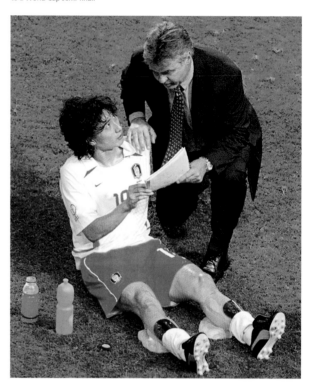

▼ South Korean coach Guus Hiddink proved to be an inspired choice. Thanks to the Dutchman, the Koreans were the first team from outside Europe or the Americas to make it to a World Cup semi-final.

Hero Ballack kept out of the final

25 JUNE 2002		
GERMANY 1–0 SOUTH KOREA		
BALLACK 75		

I N SEOUL ON 25 JUNE, the whole country believed the seemingly impossible was about to happen. However, in this intense first semi-final, the Koreans created few chances and the German goalkeeper, Oliver Kahn, was alert to a strike by Lee Chun Soo from a superb volley. In the second period, Lee Chun Soo sowed panic in the German defence: in the 71st minute, just outside his penalty area, Michael Ballack could only scythe down the Korean number 14 and he justifiably received a yellow card that kept him out of the Final (he had already been booked against Cameroon and Paraguay). Fortunately for the Germans, the resulting free-kick led to nothing. A few minutes later, Oliver Neuville broke loose down the right-hand side and crossed the ball back for Ballack, who, at the second attempt, first with his right foot and then his left, beat Lee Woon Jae at point-blank range (1–0). This earned him a kiss from manager Rudi Völler. Right at the end of the game, Park Ji Sung, although well placed, failed to equalize when he fired wide and, despite their constant competitiveness, the Koreans' fairytale was over. It was, nevertheless, the best-ever performance by an Asian team at the World Cup, and a reward for South Korea's fifth consecutive appearance since 1986. Solid but unexceptional, Germany had qualified for a seventh World Cup Final.

► Germany's Michael Ballack celebrates his winning goal against South Korea.

2

Two out of the four semi-finalists were newcomers to this level of the competition. The first time since 1934.

▲ Ronaldo scores Brazil's winning goal to send his team through to their seventh World Cup Final.

Rüstü's war paint

With rugged features bearing the scars of a serious road accident, a ponytail, sometimes black lines under his eyes like an American footballer, and an imposing size (1.87m and 76 kilos), Turkish goalkeeper Rüstü Reçber never went unnoticed, even though his make-up was intended to prevent reflection from electric lighting in the stadiums.

Excellent throughout the tournament, the 29-year-old Fenerbahçe goalkeeper epitomized this golden generation of Turkish football: "When I started out in the team, Turkey was not used to playing the leading roles. Until then, our results had been quite mediocre. Our generation changed the destiny of Turkish football. It was a wonderful feeling, something of which I'm very proud."

Third consecutive final for the Brazilians

26 JUNE 2002

BRAZIL 🔵 1–0 🇹🇷 **TURKEY**

RONALDO 49

HAVING ALREADY faced each other in their first match (which Brazil won 2–1), the two teams found themselves in an unprecedented semi-final. In the first period, Brazil dominated without making it count. Turkish goalkeeper Rüstü Reçber saved from Cafú. Then he pushed out a shot from Roberto Carlos and then the rebound from Ronaldo. In the 49th minute, fed by Gilberto Silva, Ronaldo broke the deadlock thanks to an unexpected toe-poke that took Rüstü by surprise. "It was an astonishing goal, wasn't it? A Romário-type goal. It wasn't very pretty, but it was so important. In fact, I scored with my toe. In the situation I was in, I couldn't have done anything else," said Ronaldo about his sixth goal of the tournament. Kléberson missed a late chance following a Brazil counter-attack, but it mattered not. Always in control, Brazil qualified for their third consecutive final, the seventh in their history.

PLAY-OFF FOR THIRD PLACE

Super-quick Şükür

▲ Turkey finished third at only their second World Cup finals appearance.

29 JUNE 2002

SOUTH KOREA 🇰🇷 2-3 🇹🇷 **TURKEY**

E.Y. LEE 9, C.G. SONG 90+3   HAKAN ŞÜKÜR 1, ILHAN MANSIZ 13, 32

From the Korean kick-off, the Turks pressed forward and recovered the ball. This allowed Hakan Şükür to open the scoring after just 11 seconds of play. The record, which went back to 1962 and Czech player Václav Mašek, scorer after 14 seconds against Mexico, was beaten. "I didn't score as many goals as I should have liked during that World Cup, but I recorded the fastest goal of the competition in the third-place match," the Turkish captain and number 9 was proud to say. "That historic goal relieved me of some of the pressure that was weighing on my shoulders. I hope that we shall again have the good fortune to contest a World Cup semi-final, or to do even better." Thanks to that super-quick opening score, the Turks won (3–2) and took third place. The tournament was one for quick goals since Uruguayan substitute Richard Morales scored 16 seconds after coming on against Senegal during the group stage, thereby breaking the record of Dane Ebbe Sand (who 21 seconds after coming on in 1998).

▲ Brazil's Ronaldo celebrates his first goal against Germany in the 2002 FIFA World Cup Final.

▲ Brazilian captain Cafu lifts the cup as his team-mates celebrate a fifth World Cup for the country.

The Three Rs
inspire Brazil to a fifth title

30 JUNE 2002

GERMANY ▬ 0-2 ◆ BRAZIL

RONALDO 67, 79

"Ronaldo is quite simply a genius because of his speed, his physical capabilities and his ability to score in all positions."

Oliver Kahn

WITH SEVEN WORLD TITLES BETWEEN THEM, from the 16 World Cups played before this one, the two most successful nations met for the first time in a World Cup match. Germany went into the Final without their playmaker Michael Ballack, while the Brazilians could boast the three best players in the world – Ronaldo, Rivaldo and Ronaldhino (The Three Rs). In the 19th minute, Ronaldinho put through Ronaldo, who lost his one-on-one with Oliver Kahn. The two created a carbon copy ten minutes later, but Ronaldo's control left him too stretched to finish. Then, in the 42nd minute, Kléberson, put through from deep, could not find the goal with his left foot, just before he struck the German crossbar, this time with his right. Finally, in stoppage time, a cross-shot from Roberto Carlos landed at the feet of Ronaldo, who turned quickly and forced Kahn to pull off a great save. In the second half, Germany started to create chances of their own: from a corner by Oliver Neuville, Jens Jeremies' header was blocked in desperate circumstances by Edmílson. Two minutes later, Neuville caused excitement among the 69,000 spectators when his 30-yard free-kick was tipped onto his post by Marcos, the Brazilian goal-keeper. The Brazilian team regained its pose: in the 67th minute, Ronaldo picked up the ball and passed it

to Rivaldo, who immediately fired in a low shot. Kahn made a rare mistake by pushing the ball out to Ronaldo, who followed up the rebound and fired home. Twelve minutes later, Kléberson broke through on the right-hand side and crossed for Rivaldo, who dummied and let the ball run for Ronaldo. The Brazilian number 9 controlled the ball and side-footed it past Kahn. A brace for Ronaldo, taking his tally to eight for the tournament. At the end of the game, Torsten Frings found Oliver Bierhoff in the penalty area. The AC Milan centre-forward shot immediately, but Marcos was at full stretch to tip it round the post. Brazil had won their fifth World Cup and they owed this title not only to the talents of its attacking trio but also to its two wide attacking full-backs (Cafú and Roberto Carlos) and its back three (Lúcio, Edmílson and Roque Junior).

"I'd never known a Brazilian team as calm before a World Cup Final," explained Brazilian captain Cafú, who won two Gold and a Silver in his record three World Cup Final appearances. "We all knew precisely what we had to do. We were aware of everything that was happening around the Brazilian team, but at the same time it didn't affect us, we felt really good. We were relaxed and, as if to prove it, we made it into football history!"

▲ The two Ronnies: Ronaldinho and Ronaldo shed tears of joy after the Final.

Pierluigi Collina's medal

Medal for the finals' referees. Italy's Perluigi Collina (below) was this match's main referee.

▲ **FIFA World Football Museum collection.**

Ronaldo's fairytale

"You never make up for such a loss."

Michael Ballack,
German midfielder, suspended for the Final.

SCINTILLATING throughout the entire tournament and the scorer of eight goals, including two in the Final, Ronaldo, who was an unused substitute in 1994 and who was ill before the 1998 Final against France, finally got the winners medal he deserved. "That victory was all the more pleasing for me because I'd experienced four difficult years after the 1998 World Cup. I'd suffered two serious knee injuries from which it took me a long time to recover and which kept me off the pitch for two years," explained the Brazilian number 9. "Many people then doubted my ability to get back to my former level. Through the grace of God, I recovered just in time to regain my level and my physical condition and then take part in the final stages."

Already a winner in 1994, but without having played a single minute, the Inter Milan centre-forward was crowned the top goal scorer at the 2002 tournament, but only the second best player, behind Oliver Kahn. It was a ranking that did not affect the Brazilian in any way: "The best moment was when I put my hands on the trophy, when I lifted it and kissed it. My only regret is that there isn't a photo of that moment," pointed out Ronaldo, who, at 26 years of age, was at the top of his game. "That trophy represents the greatest reward that a footballer can receive. It's a collective title, a global title that every country dreams of winning.

"At the time I picked up my yellow card against South Korea, I found myself in the thick of the action and I didn't fully realize. I was disappointed, but at those moments you're gripped by the game and I hoped that the team would assert itself in the final," explained the Bayer Leverkusen midfielder. "It's only a few weeks or even a few months later that you get things into perspective. You then realize how difficult and extraordinary it is to play in a World Cup Final. You never make up for such a loss. I was really unlucky, but that's football. I'm professional enough to accept things as they are, but at the time it was another matter."

▸ Germany's Michael Ballack sits out the 2002 FIFA World Cup Final following his yellow card in the semi-final.

2006

At the 2006 finals, not even defeat by Italy in a dramatic semi-final could completely dampen the celebratory mood and pride of the German people. Ronaldo scored a record 15th finals goal for Brazil, but Europe provided all four semi-finalists for the first time since 1982. In the Final, Italy beat France on penalties after a 1–1 draw – it was Italy's first shoot-out win in any World Cup.

From Merkel to the Kaiser, Germany was ready

◀ Fabio Cannavaro and his Italian team-mates celebrate their victory over France in the Final.

▼ Angela Merkel, the German chancellor, and Franz Beckenbauer, president of the World Cup Organizing Committee.

FOR THREE DECADES the Berlin Wall had been a symbolic divide, not only between East and West Germany, but also between communist Eastern Europe and the West. In 1989, that symbol was torn down, a pivotal moment in the history of Europe. The 2006 FIFA World Cup was always intended to be a celebration of the reunification of the two German nations. It was chosen as hosts by the FIFA Executive Committee on 6 July 2000, albeit in controversial circumstances. South Africa had hoped to be the first African nation chosen, in what would be a celebration of the post-Apartheid era in the country. But the Germans won by 12 votes to 11 after New Zealander Charles Dempsey abstained in the third round of voting. South Africa would have to wait four years to get its chance. Many expected a home win for Germany. This was the tenth World Cup played in Europe, and between them West Germany and Italy had won six of the previous nine contests. It was the Italians who were to bring Germany's hopes to a premature end in the semi-finals and they went on to claim a fourth title, having triumped in Rome in 1934, Paris in 1938, and Madrid in 1982. Berlin was added to that impressive list of European capitals.

GERMANY 2006

2006 FIFA WORLD CUP GERMANY™

Story of the qualifiers

Uruguay wide of the mark

6

TWO-TIME WORLD CHAMPIONS URUGUAY, ranked fifth among the South American teams during the qualifying stages, had to get through a playoff to secure the last World Cup place in Germany. They faced Australia, whom they had knocked out of the previous World Cup. In the first leg, in Montevideo, Uruguay won by the smallest of margins (1–0) after a goal from Darío Rodríguez. Four days later, on 16 November 2005, in front of a crowd of 82,600 in Sydney, Australia – under Dutch manager Guus Hiddink (who had taken over only four months previously) – won the game by the same score thanks to a goal from Mark Bresciano. A penalty shoot-out would decide the result. The Aussie captain Mark Viduka missed, but the four others scored, while both Rodríguez and Marcelo Zalayeta had their shots batted away by Aussie keeper Mark Schwarzer. Thirty-two years after their last appearance, after failing to qualify in seven straight campaigns, Australia were back in the World Cup.

▶ Mark Schwarzer was the hero for Australia as they beat Uruguay in a penalty shoot-out in the play-off.

This was the first World Cup since 1982 to feature teams from all six confederations (14 from Europe, one from Oceania, four from Asia, five from Africa, four from South America, and four from North and Central America and the Caribbean).

Group stage

GROUP A	GROUP B	GROUP C	GROUP D	GROUP E	GROUP F	GROUP G	GROUP H
GER 4–2 CRC	ENG 1–0 PAR	ARG 2–1 CIV	MEX 3–1 IRN	ITA 2–0 GHA	BRA 1–0 CRO	FRA 0–0 SUI	ESP 4–0 UKR
POL 0–2 ECU	TRI 0–0 SWE	SCG 0–1 NED	ANG 0–1 POR	USA 0–3 CZE	AUS 3–1 JPN	KOR 2–1 TOG	TUN 2–2 KSA
GER 1–0 POL	ENG 2–0 TRI	ARG 6–0 SCG	MEX 0–0 ANG	ITA 1–1 USA	BRA 2–0 AUS	FRA 1–1 KOR	ESP 3–1 TUN
ECU 3–0 CRC	SWE 1–0 PAR	NED 2–1 CIV	POR 2–0 IRN	CZE 0–2 GHA	JPN 0–0 CRO	TOG 0–2 SUI	KSA 0–4 UKR
ECU 0–3 GER	SWE 2–2 ENG	NED 0–0 ARG	POR 2–1 MEX	CZE 0–2 ITA	JPN 1–4 BRA	TOG 0–2 FRA	KSA 0–1 ESP
CRC 1–2 POL	PAR 2–0 TRI	CIV 3–2 SCG	IRN 1–1 ANG	GHA 2–1 USA	CRO 2–2 AUS	SUI 2–0 KOR	UKR 1–0 TUN

	W	D	L	+	–	PTS		W	D	L	+	–	PTS		W	D	L	+	–	PTS		W	D	L	+	–	PTS		W	D	L	+	–	PTS		W	D	L	+	–	PTS		W	D	L	+	–	PTS		W	D	L	+	–	PTS
GER	3	0	0	8	2	9	ENG	2	1	0	5	2	7	ARG	2	1	0	8	1	7	POR	3	0	0	5	1	9	ITA	2	1	0	5	1	7	BRA	3	0	0	7	1	9	SUI	2	1	0	4	0	7	ESP	3	0	0	8	1	9
ECU	2	0	1	5	3	6	SWE	1	2	0	3	2	5	NED	2	1	0	3	1	7	MEX	1	1	1	4	3	4	GHA	2	0	1	4	3	6	AUS	1	1	1	5	5	4	FRA	1	2	0	3	1	5	UKR	2	0	1	5	4	6
POL	1	0	2	2	4	3	PAR	1	0	2	2	2	3	CIV	1	0	2	5	6	3	ANG	0	2	1	1	2	2	CZE	1	0	2	3	4	3	CRO	0	2	1	2	3	2	KOR	1	1	1	3	4	4	TUN	0	1	2	3	6	1
CRC	0	0	3	3	9	0	TRI	0	1	2	0	4	1	SCG	0	0	3	2	10	0	IRN	0	1	2	2	6	1	USA	0	1	2	2	6	1	JPN	0	1	2	2	7	1	TOG	0	0	3	1	6	0	KSA	0	1	2	2	7	1

Knockout stages

ROUND OF 16	ROUND OF 16	ROUND OF 16	ROUND OF 16
GER 2–0 SWE	ITA 1–0 AUS	ENG 1–0 ECU	GHA 0–3 BRA
ARG 2–1 A.E.T. MEX	SUI 0–0 / 0–3 UKR	POR 1–0 NED	ESP 1–3 FRA

QUARTER-FINAL	QUARTER-FINAL	QUARTER-FINAL	QUARTER-FINAL
GER 1–1 / 4–2 ARG	ITA 3–0 UKR	ENG 0–0 / 1–3 POR	BRA 0–1 FRA

SEMI-FINAL		SEMI-FINAL	
GER 0–2 A.E.T. ITA		POR 0–1 FRA	

THIRD-PLACE PLAYOFF

GER 3–1 POR

FINAL

ITA 1–1 / 5–3 FRA

ANG	ARG	AUS	BRA	CIV	CRC	CRO	CZE
ECU	ENG	ESP	FRA	GER	GHA	IRN	ITA
JPN	KOR	KSA	MEX	NED	PAR	POL	POR
SCG	SUI	SWE	TOG	TRI	TUN	UKR	USA

32 TEAMS

64
MATCHES PLAYED

345 28

CARDS

3 359 439
SPECTATORS

GOLEO VI AND PILLE
OFFICIAL MASCOT

OFFICIAL LOGO

ITALY
WINNERS

MIROSLAV KLOSE
LEADING GOALSCORER ×5

2.3
AVERAGE GOALS
PER MATCH

TEAMGEIST
OFFICIAL MATCH BALL

Host cities and stadiums

A stadium revolution

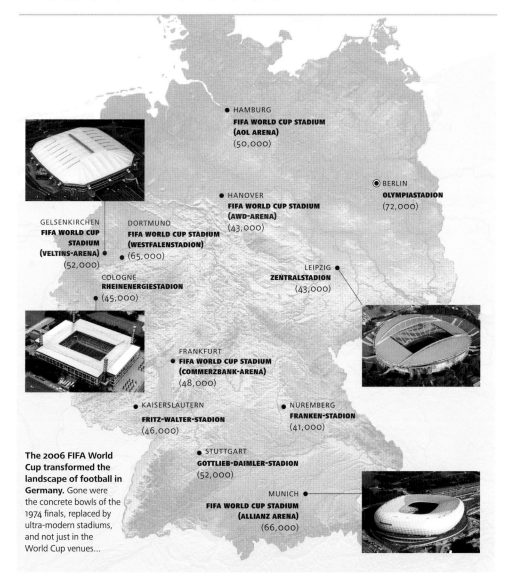

- HAMBURG
  **FIFA WORLD CUP STADIUM
  (AOL ARENA)**
  (50,000)

- BERLIN
  OLYMPIASTADION
  (72,000)

- HANOVER
  **FIFA WORLD CUP STADIUM
  (AWD-ARENA)**
  (43,000)

GELSENKIRCHEN
**FIFA WORLD CUP
STADIUM
(VELTINS-ARENA)**
(52,000)

DORTMUND
**FIFA WORLD CUP STADIUM
(WESTFALENSTADION)**
(65,000)

COLOGNE
RHEINENERGIESTADION
(45,000)

LEIPZIG
ZENTRALSTADION
(43,000)

FRANKFURT
**FIFA WORLD CUP STADIUM
(COMMERZBANK-ARENA)**
(48,000)

KAISERSLAUTERN
FRITZ-WALTER-STADION
(46,000)

NUREMBERG
FRANKEN-STADION
(41,000)

STUTTGART
GOTTLIEB-DAIMLER-STADION
(52,000)

MUNICH
**FIFA WORLD CUP STADIUM
(ALLIANZ ARENA)**
(66,000)

The 2006 FIFA World Cup transformed the landscape of football in Germany. Gone were the concrete bowls of the 1974 finals, replaced by ultra-modern stadiums, and not just in the World Cup venues...

Regulations

The end of the golden goal

The golden goal rule only lasted for two World Cup campaigns. On 28 February 2004, the International Football Association Board (IFAB), the body governing the Laws of the Game, decided to return to the previous arrangement, whereby a match that was drawn after extra-time would be decided by a penalty shootout. For David Taylor, general chief executive of the Scottish FA and a member of IFAB, "The important thing was to have a single method to determine the outcome of a match. There was concern expressed that we already had the golden goal and the silver goal, and when were we going to get a bronze goal? FIFA has consulted national associations worldwide and it is clear that the favoured method is a return to extra-time and penalty kicks when a game is tied."

Fan fests

Twelve cities – Berlin, Cologne, Dortmund, Frankfurt, Gelsenkirchen, Hamburg, Hanover, Kaiserslautern, Leipzig, Munich, Nuremberg and Stuttgart – hosted matches at the 2006 FIFA World Cup. But a major innovation was the concept of official fan fests, building on the success of 2002 when the large public gatherings to watch games on giant screens had contributed enormously to the tournament. The idea behind the fan fests, in addition to showing the matches on a big screen, was to organize concerts and involve more fans in the World Cup experience. Leipzig was the only venue in what had been East Germany. Four first-round matches and a round of 16 match were scheduled at the city's venerable Zentralstadion, opened in 1956, which originally had a capacity of 100,000. It was rebuilt in 2003 and converted to a 44,000-seater stadium with a curved roof. Three of the other stadiums were brand new and designed exclusively for football: Munich, Cologne and Gelsenkirchen. In 1974 the final had been held in Munich's Olympiastadion. In 2006 it was the turn of Berlin's Olympiastadion, venue for the 1936 Olympics.

▲ The World Cup was just six minutes old when Philipp Lahm scored the opening goal, a powerful shot against Costa Rica and one of the goals of the tournament.

Lahm's missile

9 JUNE 2006

GERMANY 🇩🇪 4–2 🇨🇷 **COSTA RICA**

LAHM 6	WANCHOPE 12, 73
KLOSE 17, 61	
FRINGS 87	

THE PREVIOUS TEN World Cup opening matches had produced just nine goals. This one alone saw six as hosts Germany beat Costa Rica 4–2 in a thriller. In Munich, in front of 66,000 spectators, the first player to stand out was 22-year-old German defender Philipp Lahm. After cutting inside the defender, he struck a right-footed curled shot from the edge of the box, driving the ball into the top corner on the far side of José Porras's net. In a post-match interview, the ever-modest Lahm said: "If I knew how to score a goal like that I'd do it in every match; I have to admit that I was extremely lucky there." Lahm would conclude his international career eight years later by lifting the World Cup.

Klose's player pass

Player pass belonging to Germany's Miroslav Klose for the 2006 tournament.

▲ **FIFA World Football Museum collection.**

A major first for Trinidad and Tobago

10 JUNE 2006

TRINIDAD AND TOBAGO 🇹🇹 0–0 🇸🇪 **SWEDEN**

▼ Dwight Yorke led Trinidad and Tobago to their first appearance at the World Cup finals.

WITH A POPULATION OF AROUND 1.3 MILLION, Trinidad and Tobago was the smallest country taking part in the World Cup. *The Soca Warriors* had qualified in December 2005 by eliminating Bahrain, semi-finalists in the AFC Asian Cup a year before, in an intercontinental head-to-head between CONCACAF and AFC (triumphing 2–1 on aggregate). In their first-ever World Cup match, Trinidad, headed up by the experienced Dutch manager and former Real Madrid coach Leo Beenhakker, pulled off a major coup with a 0–0 draw against Sweden. Their star players were goalkeeper Shaka Hislop of West Ham and, above all, the 34-year-old forward Dwight Yorke, who had played at Manchester United from 1998 to 2002, during which time, in 1999, he had won the Champions League, the Premier League (in which he was the league's top scorer), the FA Cup and Intercontinental Cup. "I was three when my country almost qualified for the 1974 World Cup, but we let our chance slip away. In 1989 we needed just one point to go to Italy, but were beaten at home by the United States. This time we just had to make it," confided Yorke, who had stepped down as captain in 2002. Trinidad lost their final two matches, against England and Paraguay.

◀ The Côte d'Ivoire's Bakary Koné is surrounded by Dutch players André Ooijer, Ruud van Nistelrooij and John Heitinga.

Drogba is not enough

16 JUNE 2006

NETHERLANDS 2–1 **CÔTE D'IVOIRE**

V. PERSIE 23, V. NISTELROOY 27   KONÉ 38

HENRI MICHEL'S CÔTE D'IVOIRE were taking part in their first World Cup and had not been lucky in the draw. Six days after losing 2–1 to Argentina in their opening match, with Didier Drogba reducing the deficit in the 82nd minute, they faced the Netherlands in Stuttgart. The Ivorians battled valiantly against Van der Saar, Van Bommel, Robben and their teammates, but they were beaten by the methodical play of the men in orange. Robin van Persie curled his free-kick beautifully, placing the ball in the top corner of the net in the 23rd minute, and six minutes later Ruud van Nistelrooy doubled the lead from inside the area. Bakary Koné's score in the top corner before half-time gave the Côte d'Ivoire hope, and they went on to lay siege to the Dutch goal. But Drogba and his teammates could not find an equalizing goal, despite putting up a brave fight. "Côte d'Ivoire has a great future, I'm convinced of that," said the captain. "Against the Netherlands we lacked realism up front – I take responsibility for that – and experience. It's a shame."

A stroll in the park for Argentina

16 JUNE 2006

ARGENTINA 6–0 **SERBIA-MONTENEGRO**

RODRIGUEZ 6, 41
CAMBIASSO 31, CRESPO 78
TÉVEZ 84, MESSI 88

SERBIA-MONTENEGRO HAD POSTED THE BEST DEFENSIVE RECORD in the qualifiers, conceding just one goal. In Gelsenkirchen, however, Ilija Petković's men suffered nothing less than a thrashing at the hands of José Pekerman's squad. Three goals in each half saw the South Americans completely dominate the game. The scorers were Maxi Rodríguez (twice), Cambiasso (his goal came after 24 passes and 55 seconds of uninterrupted possession), Crespo, Tévez and lastly Messi. To make matters worse for Serbia-Montenegro, they also had Mateja Kežman sent off in the 64th minute.

◀ Didier Drogba and Bakary Koné were two of the stars of an Ivorian team making its debut at the World Cup.

2 000

FC Copenhagen forward Marcus Allbäck, who had previously played in Italy, England, the Netherlands and Germany, was taking part in his second World Cup. When he equalized for Sweden against England in the 51st minute in Cologne on 20 June (his 24th goal in 59 internationals), he scored the 2,000th goal in the history of the World Cup finals, Lucien Laurent having got the first, Rob Rensenbrink the 1,000th.

▶▶ Lionel Messi made his World Cup debut at the 2006 tournament in the match against Serbia-Montenegro.

▶ Argentina's Maxi Rodriguez celebrates his team's first goal against Serbia-Montenegro.

Three yellow cards for Šimunić

	22 JUNE 2006	
CROATIA 🇭🇷	2–2	🇦🇺 AUSTRALIA
SRNA 2		MOORE 38 (PEN)
N. KOVAC 56		KEWELL 79

E NGLISH REFEREE Graham Poll, who had already officiated in the South Korea–Togo (2–1) and Ukraine–Saudi Arabia (4–0) games, will no doubt have wished he could forget all about the Australia–Croatia match (2–2). The 22 June tie in Stuttgart would decide the runner-up spot in Group F, dominated by Brazil. During a stop-and-start game the referee dished out no fewer than three yellow cards to Australia-born Croatian defender Josip Šimunić! Poll, who had previously refereed in the 2002 World Cup and Euro 2000, gave Šimunić his first caution in the 62nd minute. In the 85th minute he sent off the Croat Dario Šimić, with the Australian Brett Emerton following two minutes later. In stoppage time, he showed Šimunić another yellow card for a harsh tackle, but heard Šimunić's Australian accent and wrote "Australia number 3" in his book by mistake. It was not until after the final whistle that Poll then showed a third yellow to the Hertha Berlin defender, who had trotted over to tell Poll exactly what he thought of his officiating. Šimunić was, therefore, the first player in history to be shown three yellow cards and a red. Poll's tally in just three matches in this World Cup was 24 cards: 20 yellows and 4 reds.

◀ English referee Graham Poll pulls out the red card for Josip Šimunić after three yellows.

◀ Stephen Appiah celebrates after scoring from the penalty spot which won the game for Ghana against the USA.

▲ Ghanaian Haminu Draman opens the scoring in the victory over the USA.

Pride of the Black Stars

	22 JUNE 2006	
GHANA 🇬🇭	2–1	🇺🇸 USA
DRAMAN 22, S. APPIAH 45+2 (PEN)		DEMPSEY 43

A FTER LOSING TO ITALY (0–2) and then beating the Czech Republic by the same score, Ghana, the four-time winners of the Africa Cup of Nations, kicked off their all-important match against the United States without both the goal scorers from their previous match, Sulley Muntari and Asamoah Gyan, who had been suspended. Before the game, the Cameroonian player Samuel Eto'o had come by to rally them. In Nuremburg, in front of a 41,000-strong crowd, Michael Essien was shown a yellow card in the sixth minute. His teammate Haminu Dramani opened the scoring in the 22nd minute with a cross-shot with the inside of his foot into the side of the net after USA captain Claudio Reyna lost control of the ball. Just before half-time, Clint Dempsey equalized for the United States with a powerful strike, but in stoppage time at the end of the first half Ghana were awarded a penalty when Razak Pimpong took a tumble after contact from defender Oguchi Onyewu inside the area. Captain Stephen Appiah, previously at Juventus but playing for Turkish side Fenerbahçe at the time, slammed the ball into the back of the net after wrong-footing keeper Kasey Keller. In the second half, Ghana held on to their lead and qualified for the round of 16, in which they would take on Brazil in Dortmund. Ghana's Serbian manager Ratomir Dujković, former goalkeeper for Red Star Belgrade, was clearly delighted. "I'm over the moon and above all so incredibly proud," he confessed. "We have just made millions of Ghanaians incredibly happy." Gyan underlined the importance of the win: "We're playing for Africa and our country. That is an honour for us. This is the first time we have qualified for the World Cup and we've shown just what we're capable of."

Theo Walcott, born in London on 16 March 1989, was picked for England's World Cup squad by manager Sven-Göran Eriksson, to everyone's surprise. The Arsenal winger, who had joined the Gunners in January 2006 from Southampton, had yet to play in the Premier League. Aged just 17, Eriksson's wild card was the youngest player in the competition. "It's a big gamble; I know it's a gamble," admitted Eriksson. Walcott failed to make it off the bench.

Celebrations all round for France

23 JUNE 2006

TOGO 0–2 **FRANCE**

VIEIRA 55, HENRY 61

ON 23 JUNE IN COLOGNE, it was a day of celebrations. Lilian Thuram was about to win his 117th cap (to become France's most-capped player) and Zinédine Zidane, who was suspended for the Togo game, was celebrating his 34th birthday. France's stand-in captain for the day, Patrick Vieira, was also celebrating his birthday that day – his 30th. And the midfielder marked the occasion in style, opening the scoring in the 55th minute, when he wrong-footed Kossi Agassa with his right foot. Six minutes later, Vieira, again, headed the ball to Thierry Henry, who scored to make it 2–0. France, second in the group, had qualified for the round of 16.

▲ Captain for the day Patrick Vieira opens the scoring for France against Togo on his 30th birthday.

Henry's shirt

Shirt worn by French striker Thierry Henry in their quarter-final against Brazil.

◀ **FIFA World Football Museum collection.**

◀ Thierry Henry outpaces Massamesso Tchangai to score the second French goal in their 2–0 victory over Togo.

◀ Ronaldo celebrates
his record-breaking goal
against Ghana.

Prediction time

On the day before the France–Spain round of 16 match on 27 June in Hanover, the Spanish sports daily *Marca* ran the headline: "*Vamos a jubilar a Zidane*," which means, "We are going to retire Zidane." Luis Aragones's men began the tie as favourites. They had dominated Group H, racking up nine points in three victories, including a 4–0 win over Ukraine. As the match began, it looked as though *Marca* was going to be right. David Villa opened the scoring from the penalty spot. But Franck Ribéry equalized and Patrick Vieira then put France ahead. Zidane himself scored in stoppage time, wrong-footing his Real Madrid teammate Iker Casillas. The France playmaker wasn't ready for retirement just yet. To its credit, the next day *Marca* published: "He gave us the *coup de grâce*, and it's fair to say it was a beautiful death…"

Ronaldo eclipses Gerd Müller's record

27 JUNE 2006

BRAZIL 3–0 GHANA

RONALDO 5
ADRIANO 45+1
ZÉ ROBERTO 84

N 1994, RONALDO HAD BECOME A WORLD CUP WINNER at the age of 17. Except that in the USA World Cup the young prodigy did not play in a single minute of the competition. Four years later, in France, the holder of the Ballon d'Or scored against Morocco, Chile (twice) and the Netherlands. In South Korea and Japan he again played a decisive role, hitting goals against Turkey, China, Costa Rica (twice), Belgium and Turkey again in the semi-final, and scoring twice more in the final against Germany. And it was in Germany in 2006, in his fourth World Cup finals, that he managed to beat Gerd Müller's 32-year-old record as the World Cup's all-time top scorer. He had, however, begun the campaign racked with self-doubt. The media criticized him for his weight; he was eight kilos heavier than he had been in 2002. And he was also returning from injury, having not played for Real Madrid since April. But the World Cup inspired him. In the third game of the first round, against Japan on 22 June, he scored twice, with a header at the far post and with the inside of his right foot. With a total of 14 goals, he had equalled Müller's record (Müller's combined total from the 1970 and 1974 competitions). In Brazil's round of 16 match against Ghana, he went one better. In the fifth minute of play in Dortmund, he deftly sidestepped keeper Richard Kingston and pushed the ball into an empty net – his 15th World Cup goal and 62nd in 96 internationals. Adriano (45th minute), scoring Brazil's 200th World Cup finals goal, and Zé Roberto (84th minute) added extra gloss to the victory over Ghana, but the man of the hour was Ronaldo, newly crowned the top scorer of all time in the competition. "I would love to be in Brazil celebrating with the Brazilian supporters, who are incredible," he commented.

▶ Ashley Cole (right)
congratulates David
Beckham, whose goal
from one of his trademark
free-kicks was enough to
beat Ecuador.

Beckham saves the day for England

25 JUNE 2006

ENGLAND 1–0 ECUADOR

BECKHAM 60

OR THE FIRST round of 16 game in their history, plucky Ecuador, surprise qualifiers from Group A along with hosts Germany, were out to add a victory over England to those over Poland and Costa Rica. But in the 60th minute the referee awarded England a free-kick and captain David Beckham took charge. Kicking from the left 25 yards out, he curled the ball beautifully, beating the Ecuadorian keeper Cristian Mora. In the 87th minute, manager Sven-Göran Eriksson substituted his scorer for Lennon, earning Beckham a burst of well-deserved applause, the first Englishman to score at three World Cup finals. England had made it to the quarter-finals of the World Cup for the eighth time.

◄ Dutchman Wesley Sneijder is held back by the Portuguese after pushing Petit to the ground during the infamous "Battle of Nuremberg".

The "Battle of Nuremberg"

25 JUNE 2006

PORTUGAL 1–0 **NETHERLANDS**

MANICHE 23

THE EAGERLY ANTICIPATED clash at Nuremberg's Frankenstadion, a rematch of the Euro 2004 semi-final, was more a rowdy squabble, with six yellow cards being awarded in a three-minute spell at one point! The atmosphere was electric, so much so that the Russian referee Valentin Ivanov was forced to bring out his cards 20 times, four of which were red (Costinha and Deco for Portugal; Khalid Boulahrouz and Giovanni van Bronckhorst for the Netherlands). It was a regrettable record. In the end the only goal, scored by Maniche from a set-up by Pauleta with his back to the goal, seemed almost a footnote. Portugal were deprived of Cristiano Ronaldo, who went off injured after 33 minutes, the victim of some nasty challenges by a Dutch team who bore the major responsibility for the horror on show in Nuremberg.

An amazing goal from Maxi Rodríguez

24 JUNE 2006

ARGENTINA 2–1 **MEXICO**
A.E.T.

CRESPO 10, RODRIGUEZ 98   R. MARQUEZ 6

THE MEXICANS were getting used to it: they were eliminated at this stage of the competition for the fourth time in a row. But it had, again, been a close call. Captain Rafael Márquez opened the scoring for Mexico from the far post, latching on to Mario Mendez's wayward header. But Argentina were not behind for long. Five minutes later, they equalized from a corner thanks to a combination of Jared Borgetti's head and Hernan Crespo's leg. After that, the game became tactical. Mexico's manager Ricardo La Volpe knew his opponents like the back of his hand: he had been Argentina's third-string goalkeeper in the 1978 World Cup. At the end of regulation time, Lionel Messi thought he had won the match for his team, but his goal was ruled offside. This meant, however, that Argentina started extra-time on the front foot. In the 98th minute, Atlético Madrid forward Maxi Rodríguez scored a superb goal from Juan Pablo Sorín's cross, powering the ball into Oswaldo Sánchez's net with a left-footed volley after controlling it with his chest. He joined a growing list of scorers of spectacular goals at the World Cup called Rodríguez. "Mexico have always been a tough opponent, but we are Argentina. Football is a game of many facets, and there are lots of reasons why this match was a difficult one: tactics, the emotional state of the players. We showed clarity at the key moments," summed up Argentina coach José Pekerman.

Australia put up a fight

26 JUNE 2006

ITALY 1–0 **AUSTRALIA**

TOTTI 90+5 (PEN)

AS MANAGER OF SOUTH KOREA four years earlier, Guus Hiddink had pulled off the major coup of knocking out Italy. This time heading up the Australian squad, he narrowly failed to repeat the exploit. In their first World Cup round of 16 match, the *Socceroos*, even without Brett Emerton (suspended) and the injured Harry Kewell, were beaten only in stoppage time after a questionable penalty scored by Francesco Totti. Marcello Lippi could breathe a sigh of relief, having had to do without the injured Alessandro Nesta. He brought in Marco Materazzi to his defensive line to support captain Fabio Cannavaro. But Materazzi had a funny way of repaying the favour: in the 51st minute in Kaiserslautern he was shown a red card for a tackle on Mark Bresciano. But the Australians failed to capitalize on their numerical superiority, despite testing Gianluigi Buffon. They seemed to have settled for extra-time when defender Fabio Grosso was blocked by Lucas Neill in the box. Totti, who had been brought on 20 minutes earlier, beat Mark Schwarzer from the spot.

► Italy's Francesco Totti scores a controversial penalty in stoppage time to knock out Australia.

Luca Toni makes his mark

30 JUNE 2006

ITALY ▌▌ 3–0 ▬ **UKRAINE**

ZAMBROTTA 6, TONI 59, 69

T HE UKRAINIAN PRESIDENT Viktor Yushchenko did not turn out to be the good-luck charm the national team had hoped for when they wrote to him asking him to come along to give them inspiration. In Hamburg, Andriy Shevchenko's teammates went down 0–3 to Italy. Gianluca Zambrotta found a gap in the first half, and after the break 29-year-old Luca Toni scored twice (a header in the 59th minute and in the 69th minute after being set-up by Zambrotta). The much-maligned Toni, who had not played well until then, finally showed the form that had made him that season's leading goalscorer in Serie A with Fiorentina (31 goals, the most prolific tally in the Italian championship since 1959). Italy's manager Marcello Lippi spoke of how he had told the forward that this would be his day at that morning's warm-up. "I told him: 'You're going to score.' An inch or two the other way and it would have missed!"

▲ Luca Toni scored twice for Italy against Ukraine.

Lehmann the hero

▼ German keeper Jens Lehmann checks his pre-match notes before the penalty shoot-out against Argentina.

30 JUNE 2006

GERMANY ▬ 1–1 A.E.T. ▬ ARGENTINA

KLOSE 80   AYALA 49

Ⓖ Ⓖ Ⓖ Ⓖ 4–2 Ⓖ ✗ Ⓖ ✗

I N THIS MATCH-UP between the two most impressive teams in the tournament so far (each with ten goals scored and two conceded), the key role would come down to a goalkeeper: Jens Lehmann, fast approaching his 37th birthday. But the keeper for the three-time world champions could do nothing when, in the 49th minute, Roberto Ayala inched Argentina towards the semi-finals by powering in a diving header from the penalty spot from Juan Román Riquelme's corner. Ayala's goal was a just reward for Argentina's domination and the growing unease of the 66,000-strong crowd in Berlin's Olympiastadion was barely quelled when Argentina's keeper Roberto Abbondanzieri was forced to give up his place to Leo Franco in the 72nd minute after he was injured in a mid-air clash. Eight minutes later, the ever-reliable Miroslav Klose equalized with a close-range header after Tim Borowski glanced on a Michael Ballack cross from the left. Both teams were flagging and extra-time was played at a more sedate pace. Lehmann did, however, get a nasty fright when, in the 115th minute, an unexpected mishit cross from Fabricio Coloccini struck the crossbar. But in the penalty shoot-out the Arsenal keeper was on fire, batting away both Ayala's and Esteban Cambiasso's efforts. He had carefully read the notes on the opponents' penalty-takers slipped to him on a piece of paper by goalkeeper coach Andreas Köpke. And just before it began, Oliver Kahn, who had lost his place as starting keeper not long before, went over to Lehmann to shake his hand and murmur: "Good luck. You're up now. You can do it." And do it he did. Oliver Neuville, Michael Ballack, Lukas Podolski and Borowski held their nerve as the Germans won the shoot-out 4–2. This defeat signalled the end of the road for the Argentine manager Pekerman. "It's the end of an era. I can't see myself carrying on after that," he conceded. There were ugly scenes at the end when Germany's coaching staff were attacked, after which Leandro Cuffre, an unused substitute, was sent off for assaulting Per Mertesacker.

▲ Zinédine Zidane was the star player as France beat Brazil in the quarter-finals..

▲ France goalkeeper Fabien Barthez makes a decisive save against Brazil.

◀ Thierry Henry thanks Zidane for the pass which led to his winning goal against Brazil.

▼ Wayne Rooney is sent off in the quarter-final against Portugal as England lose a third penalty shoot-out at a World Cup finals.

Zidane's masterclass

1 JULY 2006

BRAZIL 0–1 ▌FRANCE

HENRY 57

T HE NOTABLE THING about this quarter-final in Frankfurt was that it featured Zinédine Zidane's first and only pass in a France game for Thierry Henry to score from. It was the only goal of the game. This match, in which France knocked out the reigning world champions, was Zidane's best match at the finals since the 1998 Final against the same opponents. Roberto Carlos and Ronaldo, his teammates at Real Madrid, were given the run-around by Zidane's consummate skill in this match. His show began in the very first minute, when he effortlessly avoided two tackles by executing his trademark stepover before sidestepping Zé Roberto. The rest of the game continued in the same vein. His gift to Henry in the 57th minute – the forward was waiting for the ball at the far post from Zidane's free-kick and side-footed a volley under Dida's crossbar – was the perfect illustration. After the game, Éric Abidal went as far as to claim: "You could say Zizou played like a Brazilian in this match." But the greatest tributes came from two legends. Pelé said: "Zidane was the magician of the match." And Franz Beckenbauer questioned Zidane's intention to retire after the finals: "I'm baffled he wants to stop when he is as good as he was four years ago. If he is playing well, he should continue!" High praise indeed!

Rooney sees red

1 JULY 2006

ENGLAND ✚ 0–0 A.E.T. ◉ PORTUGAL

✗⊘✗✗ 1–3 ⊘✗✗⊘⊘

T HIS GAME WENT TO PENALTIES, with Portugal winning 3–1 thanks to a solid performance by the Portuguese keeper Ricardo, who batted away attempts by Frank Lampard, Steven Gerrard and Jamie Carragher. But the key moment of the match took place in the 62nd minute. The English forward Wayne Rooney was shown a red card for stamping in between defender Ricardo Carvalho's legs while wrestling for the ball. Several England players were unhappy about the way the Portuguese, Cristiano Ronaldo chief among them, demanded that the referee send him off, especially since Ronaldo and Rooney were team-mates at Manchester United.

▲ France celebrate as they reach their second World Cup Final, just eight years after the first.

▲ Lilian Thuram gets the better of Cristiano Ronaldo during the semi-final between France and Portugal.

Thuram's fountain of youth

5 JULY 2006

PORTUGAL 0 0-1 **FRANCE**

ZIDANE 33 (PEN)

10

The number of World Cup finals matches after France's 1–0 victory in the semi-final against Portugal in which Fabien Barthez did not let in a goal. France's goalkeeper also played in the 1998 and 2002 campaigns. With ten clean sheets, he equalled England's Peter Shilton's record (set at the 1982, 1986 and 1990 World Cups).

AFTER FUMBLING their way through the first round, Raymond Domenech's France opted for the same starting line-up that had faced Spain in the last 16 and Brazil in the quarter-finals. Fabien Barthez was in goal, with a no-nonsense defensive line-up in front of him (Willy Sagnol, Lilian Thuram, William Gallas and Éric Abidal), Claude Makélélé and Patrick Vieira in the holding position, Franck Ribéry and Florent Malouda out wide, and Zinédine Zidane positioned up front supporting Thierry Henry as the lone striker. The match was held in Munich in front of 66,000 spectators, with the Portuguese team strengthened by the inclusion of Deco and Costinha, both of whom had been suspended for the England game. Cristiano Ronaldo and Luis Figo, who had been looking doubtful, were also on the pitch. The Portuguese got off to a strong start and nearly scored after just four minutes. Ronaldo passed to Deco from the left wing, but his shot flew past Barthez. This was the French keeper's 16th match for his country at the finals, overtaking the previous record, held by Maxime Bossis. Figo, Pauleta and Maniche were proving a threat for Portugal, while Costinha seemed to have the upper hand in containing Zidane. But it was the French who took the lead. In the 32nd minute, Ricardo Carvalho fell over in the penalty area and looked to have clipped Henry's leg. The Frenchman made the most of it and the Uruguayan referee Jorge Larrionda awarded a penalty. Having already scored a golden goal against Portugal in exactly the same way during the Euro 2000 semi-final, Zidane pulled it off once again. With almost no run-up, and despite Ricardo guessing his dive correctly, he scored. It was Zidane's 30th international goal. In the second half the Portuguese stepped up their attacks. Helder Postiga and Simão were brought on as fresh legs but Barthez was impenetrable, protected by a solid defensive line exemplified by the fearless 34-year-old Thuram. Despite seven more attempts on goal than the French, Portugal were were knocked out, the second time they had fallen just shy of the Final, following on from 1966. Their Brazilian coach Luis Felipe Scolari missed out on the opportunity to become the first man to coach two different sides in a Final, having taken Brazil there in 2002. His twelve World Cup victories was a new record for a coach. France found themselves in their second Final, eight years on from 1998. Thuram couldn't hold back the tears. "It was better than in 1998," he said. "I've just been so incredibly lucky." And to think that he hadn't wanted to return to the French team, having grudgingly coming out of his international retirement just one year earlier.

◄ An emotional Michael Ballack applauds the German supporters after their semi-final defeat.

▲ After a counter-attack, Alessandro del Piero finds a way past Jens Lehmann to score the second Italian goal.

PLAY-OFF FOR THIRD PLACE

▲ Miroslav Klose and Bastian Schweinsteiger celebrate Germany's third-place finish at the own World Cup.

Grosso changes everything

4 JULY 2006

GERMANY ▬ 0–2 ▮▮ ITALY
A.E.T.

GROSSO 119, DEL PIERO 120+1

THE ATMOSPHERE at Dortmund's Westfalenstadion was electric. Germany had never been beaten on Borussia Dortmund's home turf, with 13 victories and a draw in the 14 matches. But Italy had strength in depth and were gaining momentum. And they had never lost a competitive game to the Germans. Everyone may have been talking about captain Ballack's Germany, but Gianluigi Buffon put up a solid wall. No one was able to find a way through in regulation time, forcing the host nation to play their second extra-time game in five days. The additional 30 minutes began with a flourish when Alberto Gilardino's strike hit Lehmann's post. In the 104th minute, Marcello Lippi sent on Alessandro Del Piero. With just two minutes remaining, Andrea Pirlo's pass of the tournament found Fabio Grosso, who curled a strike with his left foot to put Italy 1–0 up. And only a minute and a half later, in a counter-attack continued by Gilardino, Del Piero made the win even more emphatic. "It was a fantastic and difficult match. We were facing a very strong team who were capable of scoring first, but we showed that our desire to fight and win was greater than theirs," commented Del Piero with relish. German chancellor Angela Merkel sportingly congratulated Italian European Commission president Romano Prodi. Ballack struggled to hide his misery: with tears streaming down his face, he saluted the crowd on a lap of honour.

Schweinsteiger puts on a show

8 JULY 2006

GERMANY ▬ 3–1 ▮▯ PORTUGAL

SCHWEINSTEIGER 56, 78, PETIT 60 (o.g.)   NUNO GOMES 88

Germany manager Jürgen Klinsmann certainly had a sense of occasion. He gave the captain's armband to goalkeeper Oliver Kahn, who was to retire from international competition after this game, his 66th cap. On the other side of the pitch, Luís Figo, starting the match on the bench, was set to do the same. There were various things at stake in this "minor final": Luiz Felipe Scolari's boys were vying for the chance to finish on the podium for only the second time (the first being in 1966), while Germany, playing in their fourth third-place play-off, were keen to make up for the disappointment of failing to go all the way in front of their own fans. In any event, the fans at the Gottlieb-Daimler Stadion in Stuttgart gave the Germans a tremendous welcome. The game was fast-paced, good-natured and spirited. At half-time, despite a number of opportunities, neither side had scored. But after the break, Bastian Schweinsteiger swung into action. In the 56th minute he ran past three players and released a fierce shot from 25 yards out that wrong-footed Ricardo. Four minutes later, his powerful free-kick straight at the Portuguese goal was sliced into his own net by Petit. In the 78th minute, the 21-year-old Bayern Munich midfielder scored his second goal with another rocket from distance after cutting to the right to line up his shot. Portugal did, however save face in the 88th minute when Luis Figo, who had come in to the game 11 minutes earlier in captain Pauleta's place, right-footed a cross to Nuno Gomes, whose header duped Oliver Kahn. This was not enough to dampen Kahn's spirits. "The atmosphere was extraordinary. It makes you wonder what would have happened if we'd actually won the world title! This has been one of the most emotionally charged games I've ever played in, if not the most emotional one in my entire career. You can't wish for a better end to an international career."

▲ This aerial battle between Fabio Cannavaro and Zinédine Zidane is won by the Italian.

▶ Marco Materazzi was a key figure in the 2006 FIFA World Cup Final. Here team-mates congratulate him after scoring the equalizer.

Materazzi makes the difference

9 JULY 2006

ITALY ▌▌ **1–1** ▌▌ **FRANCE**
A.E.T.

MATERAZZI 19   ZIDANE 7 (PEN)

⦿⦿⦿⦿⦿ 5-3 ⦸✗⦿⦿

"I started to panic."

Italy goalkeeper Gianluigi Buffon looks back at the penalty shootout.

"I don't have fond memories of it. In my career, I've always done quite well in penalty shootouts. So I was pretty sure I would save at least one or two. But I didn't touch the ball once! The French scored every time, except Trezeguet, who hit the crossbar. I remember that Pirlo went first, but I couldn't watch. Each time we took a penalty, I focused on two French supporters and said to myself: 'If they stay sitting down, it means we've scored.' But when Grosso stepped up to take his, I couldn't see the two French fans anywhere! They must have moved. I started to panic. I needed them, and they had disappeared. They had moved to different seats. I did manage to find them again. A second later, I saw they were still sitting down. I turned around to see my team-mates running all over the place. I joined them and we all hugged each other. We had just pulled off a historic win, something we would never had thought we were capable of."

IN HIS SECOND WORLD CUP FINAL, Zinedine Zidane scored and was sent off. And Italy were crowned World Champions for the fourth time in their history. The match had barely begun when a stunned Thierry Henry was momentarily sidelined after a clash with Italian captain Fabio Cannavaro's shoulder. And then, in the fifth minute, Gianluca Zambrotta was shown a yellow card for downing Pàtrick Vieira. Soon afterwards, Marco Materazzi clashed with Florent Malouda in the box. Stepping up to take the penalty against a goalkeeper who knew his game intimately, Zidane scored a "Panenka", sending the ball up to bounce off the crossbar and into the goal. In the 19th minute, Materazzi made amends by heading the equalizer past Fabien Barthez from an Andrea Pirlo corner. The game was fast-paced and slightly dominated by the Italians, with Luca Toni heading against the bar. At the start of the second half, France were the more dominant side. In the 56th minute, Vieira, who had been pushing the pace in midfield, suffered a thigh strain, forcing a substitution with Alou Diarra. Henry thought he was the hero after winning his duel against Cannavaro, but Buffon palmed it away. Zidane was floored after being hit in the back. His right shoulder was hurting but he stood firm. In the 86th minute, Marcello Lippi, in the knowledge that his team often came up with the goods at the last minute, substituted Alessandro del Piero for Mauro Camoranesi. Extra-time was only nine minutes old when Franck Ribéry's right-footed strike skimmed past the post. Sixty seconds later, Ribéry was replaced by David Trezeguet. Raymond Domenech's men were starting to gain the upper hand. Willy Sagnol's well-placed centre ball fed Zidane with a magnificent header which Buffon, yet again, converted into a corner. Henry came off with cramp and was replaced by Sylvain Wiltord. Zidane's head-butt into Materazzi's chest was punished with a red card, echoing Marcel Desailly's expulsion in the 1998 Final and leaving the crowd open-mouthed. For the second time in the history of the World Cup, the result of the Final was to be decided by a penalty shoot-out. When this last happened in 1994, Italy had lost to Brazil. Pirlo was the first to go, wrong-footing Barthez. Taking his turn, Wiltord sent Buffon the wrong way. Then Materazzi made sure his went in. But Trezeguet failed to follow suit: his high shot hit the crossbar and didn't go in. Daniele De Rossi put the Italians further ahead, but Éric Abidal reduced the deficit by beating Buffon. Del Piero held his nerve and then Willy Sagnol kept France's hopes alive. If Palermo left back Fabio Grosso, who had scored in the semi-final against Germany, converted his penalty, Italy were world champions. The rest, as they say, is history.

Cannavaro, a hundredth cap for the World Cup winner

◤ Cannavaro becomes the fourth Italian captain to receive the World Cup after Combi, Giuseppe Meazza and Dino Zoff

▲ Zinédine Zidane loses his head and possibly the Final for France. He was sent off for this incident in extra time.

THE MAN OF THE HOUR ON 9 JULY 2006, watched by a worldwide television audience and the 69,000 supporters at Berlin's Olympiastadion, may have been 32-year-old Marco Materazzi – he had been responsible for Italy conceding the penalty in the seventh minute (he clipped Florent Malouda in the penalty area), but had scored the equalizer in the 19th minute from a Pirlo corner. He had then been instrumental in Zidane's sending-off in extra-time and had safely scored from the penalty spot in the shootout. But the man holding the World Cup high above his head was also deserving of high praise. Central defender Fabio Cannavaro had celebrated his 100th cap in style. In all of Italy's international outings in which he had participated since 1998, the Naples-born 32-year-old had never played as well as in this tournament. In the semi-final against Germany he had shone, earning the praise of midfielder Gennaro Gattuso: "The reason we are in the Final is because of Fabio. Apart from playing exceptionally well, has always given us the strength to keep going. He is not just a terrific defensive player, he is also a truly great captain, a real leader." Against France, squaring up to Thierry Henry, Franck Ribéry et al, Italy's captain again played a faultless game. Italy had conceded only two goals in seven games. His rigorous positioning, determination, decisive interventions and undeniable charisma kept the team riding high. Neither a very tall (1.76m) nor a big player (under 75 kilos), it was his experience and energy that made the difference. 2006 was an *annus mirabilis* for Cannavaro: that autumn he would go on join his Juventus manager Fabio Capello at Real Madrid and earn the *France Football* Ballon d'Or. Only two other defensive players have won that honour: Franz Beckenbauer and Matthias Sammer. His game-winning performance in Berlin had a lot to do with it. "Any footballer who wins the World Cup becomes a legend. I think that's a good way of summing up how a player's life changes after a world title," he said.

Lippi and his glasses

Fabio Grosso's winning penalty in the shoot-out meant that Italy were world champions for the fourth time: all the Italian players, substitutes, officials and technical staff rushed on to the pitch to celebrate. Only manager Marcello Lippi stayed where he was. He turned his back on the jubilation, took off his glasses and put them on the bench. Only then did he join the team to celebrate the title. Why this uncharacteristic moment of calm? Ten years earlier, when in charge at Juventus, he had experienced a similar situation in the 1995–96 Champions League Final against Ajax, but in all the excitement he had lost his glasses, returning later to find them mangled on the turf. Not the sort of man to make the same mistake twice, Lippi had preferred to take the time to make sure his specs were safe before joining in the celebrations with his players. Those same glasses he looked after carefully in 2006 are now on show in the FIFA World Football Museum.

2010

Thousands of vuvuzelas provided the soundtrack for the first World Cup held in Africa, and the volume remained undimmed even after South Africa became the first hosts to be eliminated at the group stage. Spain lost their first match but won the next six to lift the Cup. In the Final, they beat the Netherlands 1–0 in Johannesburg's Soccer City. Andrés Iniesta scored near the end of extra-time.

A first for Africa

◀ Andrés Iniesta kisses the trophy after Spain became the eighth nation to win the World Cup.

▼ Archbishop Desmond Tutu and Nelson Mandela show their delight as South Africa is named as host of the 2010 FIFA World Cup on 15 May 2004.

EVER SINCE 15 MAY 2004, when its nomination was confirmed (by 14 votes ahead of Morocco with ten), South Africa had been doing its utmost to ensure the success of what would be the first FIFA World Cup on its continent's soil. Present at FIFA headquarters in Zurich for this announcement, Nelson Mandela was unable to hold back his tears. The country's delegation was completed by two other Nobel Peace Prize winners: Frederik De Klerk and Desmond Tutu. Despite financial difficulties and certain lingering doubts concerning the stadiums, motorways and the ability of the South African authorities to guarantee visitors' safety, the "Rainbow Nation" that had emerged from the ashes of the Apartheid regime since its demise in 1991 was determined to welcome the rest of the planet . Played in South Africa's winter, the finals were unaffected by the usual summer heat. Although many of the first-round games lacked excitement and drama, the tournament got better as it went on, culminating in Spain's historic first title as they became the eighth nation to be crowned world champions and the first Europeans to do so in another continent.

SOUTH AFRICA 2010

2010 FIFA WORLD CUP SOUTH AFRICA™

Story of the qualifiers

The hand of scandal

THE FINAL PHASE was to be contested by 32 nations from all continents. Europe was allotted 13 places (Germany, England, Denmark, Spain, France, Greece, Italy, the Netherlands, Portugal, Serbia, Slovenia, Switzerland and Slovakia, who were FIFA World Cup debutants) and Africa six (the host country, Ghana, Cameroon, Algeria, the Côte d'Ivoire and Nigeria). France, however, had come within a whisker of missing out altogether, and the manner of their qualification via a playoff with the Republic of Ireland provoked widespread controversy. Having emerged from Croke Park, Dublin, with a slender lead (1–0), France appeared overawed by the pressure of the occasion in the return match four days later. But then during extra-time at the Stade de France, triggered by a Robbie Keane strike that levelled the tie over two legs, French captain Thierry Henry used his hand to divert the ball to William Gallas, who promptly netted the deciding goal in the 103rd minute (1–1). The referee had completely missed it. The subsequent debate on fair play was intense, with even the Irish Prime Minister, Brian Cowen, demanding that the match be replayed. FIFA, on appeal, ruled that the result would stand. "As the rules of the game clearly state, decisions taken by the referee during the match are final."

Group stage

GROUP A		
RSA	1–1	MEX
URU	0–0	FRA
RSA	0–3	URU
FRA	0–2	MEX
MEX	0–1	URU
FRA	1–2	RSA

	W	D	L	+	–	PTS
URU	2	1	0	4	0	7
MEX	1	1	1	3	2	4
RSA	1	1	1	3	5	4
FRA	0	1	2	1	4	1

GROUP B		
KOR	2–0	GRE
ARG	1–0	NGA
ARG	4–1	KOR
GRE	2–1	NGA
NGA	2–2	KOR
GRE	0–2	ARG

	W	D	L	+	–	PTS
ARG	3	0	0	7	1	9
KOR	1	1	1	5	6	4
GRE	1	0	2	2	5	3
NGA	0	1	2	3	5	1

GROUP C		
ENG	1–1	USA
ALG	0–1	SVN
SVN	2–2	USA
ENG	0–0	ALG
USA	1–0	ALG
SVN	0–1	ENG

	W	D	L	+	–	PTS
USA	1	2	0	4	3	5
ENG	1	2	0	2	1	5
SVN	1	1	1	3	3	4
ALG	0	1	2	0	2	1

GROUP D		
SRB	0–1	GHA
GER	4–0	AUS
GER	0–1	SRB
GHA	1–1	AUS
AUS	2–1	SRB
GHA	0–1	GER

	W	D	L	+	–	PTS
GER	2	0	1	5	1	6
GHA	1	1	1	2	2	4
AUS	1	1	1	3	6	4
SRB	1	0	2	2	3	3

GROUP E		
NED	2–0	DEN
JPN	1–0	CMR
NED	1–0	JPN
CMR	1–2	DEN
DEN	1–3	JPN
CMR	1–2	NED

	W	D	L	+	–	PTS
NED	3	0	0	5	1	9
JPN	2	0	1	4	2	6
DEN	1	0	2	3	6	3
CMR	0	0	3	2	5	0

GROUP F		
ITA	1–1	PAR
NZL	1–1	SVK
SVK	0–2	PAR
ITA	1–1	NZL
PAR	0–0	NZL
SVK	3–2	ITA

	W	D	L	+	–	PTS
PAR	1	2	0	3	1	5
SVK	1	1	1	4	5	4
NZL	0	3	0	2	2	3
ITA	0	2	1	4	5	2

GROUP G		
CIV	0–0	POR
BRA	2–1	PRK
BRA	3–1	CIV
POR	7–0	PRK
PRK	0–3	CIV
POR	0–0	BRA

	W	D	L	+	–	PTS
BRA	2	1	0	5	2	7
POR	1	2	0	7	0	5
CIV	1	1	1	4	3	4
PRK	0	0	3	1	12	0

GROUP H		
HON	0–1	CHI
ESP	0–1	SUI
CHI	1–0	SUI
ESP	2–0	HON
SUI	0–0	HON
CHI	1–2	ESP

	W	D	L	+	–	PTS
ESP	2	0	1	4	2	6
CHI	2	0	1	3	2	6
SUI	1	1	1	1	1	4
HON	0	1	2	0	3	1

Knockout stages

ROUND OF 16		
NED	2–1	SVK
BRA	3–0	CHI

ROUND OF 16		
URU	2–1	KOR
USA	1–2 A.E.T.	GHA

ROUND OF 16		
ARG	3–1	MEX
GER	4–1	ENG

ROUND OF 16		
PAR	0–0 5–3	JPN
ESP	1–0	POR

QUARTER-FINAL		
NED	2–1	BRA

QUARTER-FINAL		
URU	1–1 4–2	GHA

QUARTER-FINAL		
ARG	0–4	GER

QUARTER-FINAL		
PAR	0–1	ESP

SEMI-FINAL		
URU	2–3	NED

SEMI-FINAL		
GER	0–1	ESP

PLAY-OFF FOR THIRD PLACE		
URU	2–3	GER

FINAL		
NED	0–1 A.E.T.	ESP

ALG ARG AUS BRA CHI CIV CMR DEN
ENG ESP FRA GER GHA GRE HON ITA
JPN KOR MEX NED NGA NZL PAR POR
PRK RSA SRB SUI SVK SVN URU USA

32 TEAMS

64
MATCHES PLAYED

253 9
CARDS

3 517 856
SPECTATORS

ZAKUMI
OFFICIAL MASCOT

SOUTH AFRICA 2010 FIFA WORLD CUP
OFFICIAL LOGO

SPAIN
WINNERS

2.3
AVERAGE GOALS
PER MATCH

×5
**FORLAN, MÜLLER,
VILLA, SNEIJDER**
LEADING GOALSCORERS

JABULANI
OFFICIAL BALL

Host cities and stadiums

Six stadiums refurbished, four newly built

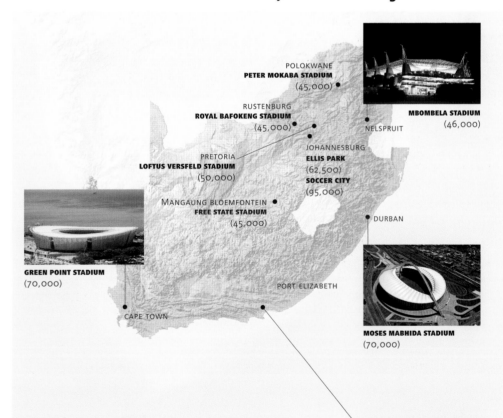

POLOKWANE
PETER MOKABA STADIUM
(45,000)

RUSTENBURG
ROYAL BAFOKENG STADIUM
(45,000)

NELSPRUIT

MBOMBELA STADIUM
(46,000)

PRETORIA
LOFTUS VERSFELD STADIUM
(50,000)

JOHANNESBURG
ELLIS PARK
(62,500)
SOCCER CITY
(95,000)

MANGAUNG BLOEMFONTEIN
FREE STATE STADIUM
(45,000)

DURBAN

GREEN POINT STADIUM
(70,000)

PORT ELIZABETH

CAPE TOWN

MOSES MABHIDA STADIUM
(70,000)

**NELSON MANDELA
BAY STADIUM**
(48,000)

Ten stadiums were selected to host the event. Six of them were renovated (Royal Bafokeng in Rustenburg, Loftus Versfeld in Pretoria, Peter Mokaba in Polokwane, Ellis Park Stadium and Soccer City in Johannesburg, and Free State in Bloemfontein). Four were newly constructed, and just in the nick of time (Mbombela in Nelspruit, Moses Mabhida in Durban, Green Point in Cape Town and Nelson Mandela Bay in Port Elizabeth). Among the most attractive was Green Point, with its capacity of 70,000 and state-of-the-art solar water-heating system. Moreover, 95 per cent of the old stadium which had stood on the site had been recycled or reused, while 93 per cent of the seats were fully sheltered from the midday sun. Stadium costs came to $1.1 billion but the biggest spend was the $1.3 billion on road, rail and air links.

Regulations

Clubs get compensated

At an Executive Committee meeting held in December 2009 on Robben Island in South Africa, it was decided that the total prize money at the 2010 finals would be $420 million – an increase of 61% from 2006. The winners would receive $30 million, the losing finalists $24 milion, the losing semi-finalists $20 million and the losing quarter-finalists $18 million. There was $9 million for those knocked out in the round of 16 and $8 million for teams eliminated at the group stage. Each team also received $1 million preparation costs. A further $40 million fund was set up to compensate clubs which had players at the finals – $1,600 per day per player.

The Draw

"Be happy." That's the translation of the Zulu word *jabulani*, the name given to the official match ball (made by sports equipment manufacturer Adidas) for the World Cup. The groups were drawn on 4 December 2009 in Cape Town by South African actress Charlize Theron (above), flanked by sporting icons such as David Beckham and the Ethiopian long-distance runner Haile Gebreselassie.

▲ Brazil's Luis Fabiano celebrates the second of his two goals against the Côte d'Ivoire.

▶ Didier Drogba gets the better of Gilberto Silva.

Brazil too good for Côte d'Ivoire

20 JUNE 2010

BRAZIL 3–1 **CÔTE D'IVOIRE**

LUIS FABIANO 25, 50, ELANO 62   DROGBA 79

6

The Brazilian Carlos Alberto Parreira, coach of South Africa, had won the World Cup with Brazil back in 1994. In 2010, he was managing a team at football's showpiece event for the sixth time: Kuwait (1982), the United Arab Emirates (1990), Brazil (1994 and 2006), Saudi Arabia (1998) and now South Africa. Having suffered three defeats at the hands of France (in 1982, 1998 and 2006), he exacted his revenge on 22 June in Bloemfontein, after which France's coach Raymond Domenech controversially refused to shake his hand.

IT CAME AS SCANT CONSOLATION, but when he netted with an angled header in the 79th minute from a cross by Yaya Touré, Didier Drogba, who had been playing with his arm in a splint (having broken the bone in his forearm at the start of June), became the first African to score against Brazil at a World Cup. At Johannesburg's Soccer City, the Chelsea striker and Côte d'Ivoire captain had made his sole attempt on goal count, but his side were soundly beaten and the result left them at serious risk of elimination. In what was a particularly tight group, also featuring North Korea and Portugal, the Ivorians had managed a draw (0–0) five days earlier against Cristiano Ronaldo's Portugal. Brazil had laboured somewhat in their opener against North Korea (2–1), but were now approaching top form. Kaká, *Ballon d'Or* winner in 2007, set the tone in the 25th minute when he wriggled past two defenders before playing in Luís Fabiano on the edge of the box. Homing in on goal, Fabiano produced a fierce strike from a tight angle which goalkeeper Barry could only watch sail past his near post and into the roof of the net. Later, in the 62nd minute, Kaká would cut the ball back invitingly for the unmarked Elano after a mazy run down the left (3–0). But before that, Luís Fabiano bagged his brace when, in a bewildering bout of flicking and juggling, he guided a high bouncing ball through a posse of perplexed Ivorian

defenders, before emphatically firing home. Despite the fact the Sevilla forward appeared to touch the ball twice with his arm in the process, French referee Stéphane Lannoy failed to blow his whistle, triggering anger among the Africans. "It was handball twice, and that did us a lot of damage: 1–0 and 2–0 are not the same thing. We simply couldn't recover," lamented Drogba. For Luís Fabiano, however, it marked the end of a six-match drought with Brazil dating back to 5 September 2009, when he'd netted against Argentina. Kaká, meanwhile, became the first player at this World Cup to provide two goal assists in the same game. But not quite everything went perfectly for the Real Madrid midfielder, as he was sent off for two yellow cards in three minutes (85th and 88th), the second somewhat harshly for a slight push on Kader Keita. Sven-Goran Eriksson's Ivorian charges had battled bravely, but now their destiny was out of their hands, whereas Brazil were through to the knockout stage. "We had to stay focused at all times in this match, because the Côte d'Ivoire have a fast and very direct style," observed Dunga, Brazil's coach. Kolo Touré, the Côte d'Ivoire defender, himself bemoaned a "lack of composure in the final third… Brazil were able to keep things tight after opening the score, and that's what made the difference."

Soccer City in Johannesburg was the venue for both the opening game and the Final of the 2010 FIFA World Cup.

Waka Waka, the international hit

The official song of the World Cup was "Waka Waka (This Time for Africa)", sung by the Colombian pop star Shakira, accompanied by the South African group Freshlyground. The song was performed during the tournament's opening ceremony at Orlando Stadium in Soweto, and again at the final in Johannesburg. "The FIFA World Cup is a miracle of global excitement, connecting every country, race, religion and condition around a single passion. It represents an event that has the power to unite and integrate, and that's what this song is about," enthused the singer after she was chosen. Shakira met Spanish international Gerard Piqué while filming the video for the song.

Bafana Bafana's rainbow nation

11 JUNE 2010

SOUTH AFRICA 🇿🇦 1–1 🇲🇽 **MEXICO**

TSHABALALA 55   MÁRQUEZ 79

THE NOISE from the vuvuzelas was deafening as the 2010 FIFA World Cup kicked off for the first finals game played on African soil. A total of 84,490 fans packed the redesigned Soccer City stadium in Johannesburg for the opening ceremony and a game that lived up to all expectations. Carlos Vela had a goal disallowed for offside in a first half dominated by the Mexican, but South Africa fought back in the second half. Ten minutes in and the stadium erupted when Siphiwe Tshabalala scored a goal that would have graced any World Cup. Kagisho Dikgacoi's pass from midfield out to the left was picked up by Tshabalala who ran on and scored with a beautiful shot with his left foot which ended up in the top right corner of the Mexican goal. But Rafael Márquez dampened South African spirits with just over ten minutes to play and there was further agony to be suffered by the host nation when Katlego Mphela ran on to a long clearance and hit the outside of the left post. It would cost his side dear as it was Mexico who went on to beat South Africa into third place in the group – on goal difference.

Lippi takes the blame

24 JUNE 2010

SLOVAKIA 🇸🇰 3–2 🇮🇹 **ITALY**

VITTEK 25, 73, KOPUNEK 89   DI NATALE 81, QUAGLIARELLA 90+2

DESPITE BEING REIGNING WORLD CHAMPIONS, Italy exited the competition in the very first round, without winning a game. They even finished bottom of a Group F that was arguably the weakest of the tournament. Eliminated after registering two draws (1–1 against Paraguay and New Zealand) and a defeat (3–2 against Slovakia), the Italians failed to reach the second round for the first time since 1974. It was the fourth time such a fate had befallen the title holders, after Italy again in 1950, Brazil in 1966 and France in 2002. Their coach Marcello Lippi, the World Cup-winning coach four years earlier, immediately took responsibility for the failure. "What's happened is entirely down to me," he said right at the start of his post-match press conference in the bowels of Ellis Park. "If a team such as ours fails to perform or express itself in such an important game, then the coach simply hasn't done his job properly, either tactically, physically or psychologically. I'm extremely disappointed for our fans and for the football association, but I've failed. This team was capable of doing better, but we didn't manage it, so it's of course my fault." Lippi then quit his post with immediate effect and took a two-year sabbatical from the game.

Italy coach Marcello Lippi saw his side finish bottom of Group F.

Knysna and the French psychodrama

◀ Raymond Domenech reads the players' press release announcing that they were on strike.

◀ The French team stay on the bus and refuse to attend a training session.

A FTER FINISHING RUNNERS-UP at the previous tournament, France slunk out of this World Cup by the back door. First came a draw against Uruguay (0–0), swiftly followed by two defeats, against Mexico (2–0) and against hosts South Africa (2–1). But apart from their on-field shortcomings, France drew most attention for certain off-the-field events. Even before the tournament began, the mood among the squad was scarcely chipper: they'd qualified by the skin of their teeth, thanks to Thierry Henry's hand-ball against the Republic of Ireland, while Franck Ribéry and Karim Benzema were mired in a court case involving underage prostitution. They'd also badly underperformed in their pre-tournament friendly games, including a defeat to China in La Réunion just before flying to South Africa. Holed up at their base camp in Knysna, the French squad then chose to boycott a training session and, even worse, one that was open to the public, forcing Raymond Domenech to read out a press release explaining their actions. It was the players' way of showing their support for Nicolas Anelka, who'd been axed from the squad after the front page of the sports daily L'Équipe quoted insults aimed by the striker at his coach during half-time in the Mexico match. This strike was a sad first and even led the French president, Nicolas Sarkozy, to call a meeting on the general state of governance of French football. The football association's chairman, Jean-Pierre Escalettes, resigned as a result on 28 June.

The vuvuzela's deafening drone

This quirky musical instrument was one of the unexpected stars of the 2010 World Cup. Having been popularized during the 1990s by fans of the two Soweto clubs (Kaizer Chiefs and Orlando Pirates), the vuvuzela – derived from the Zulu words for "produces" (*vuvu*) and "noise" (*zela*) – had made its debut on the international stage during the 2009 Confederations Cup, also staged in South Africa. It raised a few concerns even then. "They should be banned. They make it hard for the players to concentrate and communicate,"

warned the Spanish midfielder Xabi Alonso. At around 70 centimetres long, the vuvuzela delivers a simply thunderous buzzing sound reminiscent of a swarm of bees. A part of local folklore, it can reach up to 130 decibels, causing an incessant racket in the stands and a constant backdrop to the TV broadcasts of matches. Mindful of the problem, FIFA requested that spectators refrain from using their vuvuzelas during the ceremonies, hymns and speeches, but people were still allowed to use them during matches.

▶ Green Point Stadium in Cape Town hosted eight matches during the finals.

◀ Milan Jovanović scores the only goal of the game, past Manuel Neuer, in Serbia's 1–0 win over Germany.

▼ Goalkeeper Vladimir Stojković celebrates Serbia's win over Germany.

Serbia surprise Germany

18 JUNE 2010

GERMANY 0–1 **SERBIA**

JOVANOVIĆ 38

▶ New Zealand line up before their second group match, against Italy.

THERE ARE SOME MATCHES where luck just isn't on your side. Impressive in their opener against Australia (4–0), Germany then came unstuck against Serbia, at the Nelson Mandela Bay Stadium in Port Elizabeth. The first body blow for Germany came in the 37th minute, when they were reduced to ten men after goal-poacher supreme Miroslav Klose was shown two yellow cards. One minute later, the Serbs opened the scoring through their striker Milan Jovanović, just signed by Liverpool, who found himself with only Manuel Neuer to beat after the towering Nikola Zigić (202 cm) headed down a Miloš Krasić cross. The breakthrough inspired Radomir Antić's men, who had tasted defeat in their opening game against Ghana (1–0). In the second half, after Nemanja Vidić had handballed in the penalty box, Lukas Podolski, scorer of the opening goal against Australia, missed the 60th-minute spot-kick. The miss came as a shock: the Germans generally excelled when it came to penalty kicks, not having missed one at a World Cup since 1982. But Vladimir Stojković pushed away the Cologne winger's attempt, before seeing Thomas Müller's follow-up fly over the bar. Joachim Löw's players were down and just about out, as they watched another Jovanović shot strike the post (67th) and then a Zigić header come back off the bar (74th). There were no further goals in this fiercely contested match, which produced nine yellow cards (two of them adding up to red) and ended in a first defeat for Germany in the group stage since a 2–0 loss to Denmark back in 1986.

Kiwis unconquered

In what was their second appearance at a FIFA World Cup final phase after their appearance in 1982, New Zealand, coached by Ricki Herbert, who had been in their side 28 years earlier, were once again eliminated in the first round. But bizarrely, they were the only country at the tournament not to lose a game. Viewed as the minnows of the competition, New Zealand drew all three of their games: against Slovakia (1–1), against Italy (1–1) and against Paraguay (0–0). This respectable three-point tally took them to within a hair's breadth of qualification for the knockout phase. "This team has been incredible," enthused the coach. "The players are torn between delight at performing so well and disappointment at going out of the competition." Just one goal in their game against Paraguay would have been enough to take the *All Whites* through to the round of 16.

275

▲ England's Matthew Upson pulls a goal back against Germany.

▲ Shades of 1966. Frank Lampard's shot in the England-Germany round of 16 match hits the crossbar and lands clearly over the goal-line, but a goal is not given.

Bielsa's nightmare

28 JUNE 2010

BRAZIL 3–0 **CHILE**

JUAN 35
L. FABIANO 38
ROBINHO 59

BRAZIL LIVED UP TO their reputation as Chile's bogey team. Already, during the qualifiers, the Chileans had conceded three goals against them at home in Santiago and four away in Salvador de Bahia. Then, on 28 June, at Johannesburg's Ellis Park Stadium, goalkeeper and captain Claudio Bravo and co. let in three more. Juan headed home the first from a Maicon corner. Three minutes later, following a counter-attack prompted by Robinho, Luís Fabiano collected the ball from Kaká before dribbling round Chile's keeper and slotting the ball into an unguarded net. The *coup de grâce* came just before the hour, when Robinho unleashed a low shot that found the corner of the net after a piercing run from Ramires. Marcelo Bielsa, the beaten coach, was very candid in his assessment. "We got through to this round because we deserved it and we were beaten today by the Brazilians also because we deserved it. The margin of defeat could have been narrower, although they were undoubtedly better than us. They are very difficult to stop, but we've showed that with one of the youngest sides at the tournament, we could achieve good things. And with a bit more experience, we can do great things."

The case for goal line technology

27 JUNE 2010

GERMANY 4–1 **ENGLAND**

KLOSE 20, PODOLSKI 32, MÜLLER 67, 70   UPSON 37

WHEN ASKED TO ANALYSE the crushing defeat suffered by England in their very lively clash against Germany in Bloemfontein, England captain Steven Gerrard was the consummate gentleman, not seeking to make any excuses. "Germany are a fantastic team and deserved to win. We're going to go home and analyse what went wrong for us. There's a reason why we couldn't go any further. We paid the price for our lack of concentration," the midfielder opined. He could have added to that the refereeing error which proved to be the game's turning point. The Germans had opened the scoring early on through Miroslav Klose (20th minute, his 12th goal at three FIFA World Cups and his 50th in 99 international appearances), who produced a smart finish under pressure from the onrushing David James. Germany doubled their advantage 12 minutes later when Lukas Podolski capped a flowing move involving Klose and Thomas Müller. But Fabio Capello's men reacted rapidly by reducing the deficit through a Matthew Upson header from a Gerrard cross. Then just a few seconds later, an astute lob from Frank Lampard struck the underside of the crossbar before bouncing down into the goal and then spinning out. Although the ball had clearly crossed the line by some margin, the referee's assistant didn't spot it. It was a poor decision which led directly to the introduction of goal line technology at the 2014 finals. Still trailing when they should by rights have been level, England kept fighting and struck the bar again with a powerful 35-yard free-kick from the battling Lampard (51st minute), but it was not to be for England, a fact underlined when Thomas Müller, aged just 20, seized two golden opportunities in the space of three minutes (67th and 70th) to add gloss to Germany's victory. Joachim Löw's players had reached the last eight for the 16th time in 17 attempts. "We produced an exceptional performance against a highly experienced England team," the German coach purred. "I think the public enjoyed the spectacle. We were in confident mood and the first two goals gave us control of the game." Their opponents, conversely, were understandably disappointed, not least the unfortunate Lampard. "I'm in favour of goal line technology, especially tonight. The ball crossed the line, it was in. And it was such a key moment... If we'd got back to 2–2 then, things would have been different. It's a massive disappointment." German midfielder Bastian Schweinsteiger, meanwhile, was over the moon. "I'm so proud to be part of this team and of what we achieved during 90 minutes. In terms of tactics, we were spot on. There's so much talent in this side."

◀ The Paraguay players celebrate their penalty shoot-out victory over Japan in Pretoria.

Cardozo clinches it for Paraguay

29 JUNE 2010

PARAGUAY 0–0 ● JAPAN
A.E.T.

⦾⦾⦾⦾⦾ 5-3 ⦸✗⦾⦾

POOR YUICHI KOMANO. The third Japanese player to step up in the penalty shoot-out saw his attempt come back off the crossbar, but Oscar Cardozo, Paraguay's last penalty-taker, didn't falter, just like his teammates. And so the South Americans were through to the FIFA World Cup quarter-finals for the first time in their history, after a tie unlikely to linger long in the minds of the 37,000 spectators in attendance at Pretoria's Loftus Versfeld. After all, neither normal nor extra-time had produced a single goal. But in a penalty shoot-out, there always has to be a hero, and in this case it was Paraguay's Benfica striker who, at the end of extra-time, had specifically asked his coach Gerardo Martino if he could take the fifth penalty. Japan's goalkeeper Eiji Kawashima was promptly sent the wrong way. "I managed to clear my head completely and block out any pressure," explained the jubilant Cardozo later. "It was as if I was taking a penalty on the playing field back in my neighbourhood."

"I've showed I'm not finished yet."

Carlos Tévez, the Argentinian striker after scoring twice against Mexico (3–1).

"We struggled to play our usual game as they were monopolizing possession. But I was lucky enough to be presented with two clear chances and score two vital goals. Diego Maradona had told me that he preferred me in an out-and-out attacking role. He asked me not to drop so deep like a midfielder, but I couldn't stop myself dropping back to help with our pressing game, it's in my blood. We will savour this win over Mexico, as it wasn't easy.

Portugal submit to Villa's law

▼ David Villa scores the only goal of the game in Spain's win over Portugal.

29 JUNE 2010

SPAIN 1–0 PORTUGAL

VILLA 63

SPAIN coach Vincente del Bosque replaced David Villa with Pedro in the 88th minute, but the striker from Valencia, who had just signed for Barcelona, had already earned tumultuous applause from the public at Cape Town's Green Point Stadium. Eclipsing a disappointing Fernando Torres, Villa had come to Spain's rescue again in the 63rd minute with the only goal of the game. Andrés Iniesta fed Xavi, who played in Villa with a back-heel. His first shot was parried by Eduardo's outstretched boot, but Spain's all-time leading goalscorer showed his customary sharpness to produce a second strike that sailed over the Portuguese keeper and in off the crossbar. Coming against a keeper previously unbeaten for 333 minutes, his fourth goal of the competition was just reward for Spain's domination of Carlos Queiroz's men, who had created little in the game. The Portuguese were reduced to ten men at the end of the game, when the defender Costa, his side's best performer on the night , was dismissed in the 89th minute for barely touching Joan Capdevila. Xavi was ecstatic: "It was us that played the most complete football, especially in the second half. We had more of the ball and played the football we love. The goal did us the world of good, as it helped us relax and play our game." Spain's coach Vicente del Bosque added, "When we play like that, we're very hard to stop."

▲ Dutchman Wesley Sneijder scores his second goal with a header to knock out Brazil.

Brazil depart without glory

2 JULY 2010

NETHERLANDS 2–1 BRAZIL

SNEIJDER 53, 68   ROBINHO 10

Klose to the record

Miroslav Klose will long remember his 100th appearance for the German national side.
By scoring two goals against an Argentinian side coached by Diego Maradona, the first in the 68th minute from a Lukas Podolski pass and the second from a Mesut Özil cross, he had brought himself within touching distance of Brazil's Ronaldo, who then held the mantle of the World Cup's all-time leading goalscorer with 15 goals. Now with 14 goals, the Bayern Munich striker had drawn level with his countryman Gerd Müller and outstripped both Pelé (12) and Just Fontaine (13, in a single tournament). But rather than lap up the plaudits, he preferred to place the emphasis on his team's collective performance. "Playing like we did, so soon after the match we had against England, is quite simply amazing," he said. "I'm proud of the team that was out there on the pitch, but also those on the bench. Everyone has a role to play in this squad. We've achieved the objectives we set ourselves at the start and I'm delighted. Now anything more will be a bonus."

BRAZIL'S QUARTER-FINAL DEFEAT was bitterly disappointing for their star player Kaká. For the second tournament running the winners in 2002 had fallen just short of the semi-finals. "It's extremely painful after all the effort we put in," the playmaker underlined, before adding: "This is a difficult moment for me. I have a very strong bond with the national team, but I'm currently going through my worst time as a professional footballer and I'm going to have to think long and hard about quite a few things." Felipe Melo too cut a despondent figure. Suspended for the round of 16, he had looked sharp early in the game, most notably providing a defence-splitting assist for Robinho's tenth-minute strike. Brazil seemed firmly in control, but the next significant action was less enjoyable for midfielder Melo, at the time plying his trade for Juventus. When Wesley Sneijder lifted in an angled cross in the 53rd minute, Melo and his keeper Cesar both jumped for the ball, which brushed lightly off the midfielder's head and sailed past Brazil's stranded keeper into the net. The Netherlands had their equalizer and it proved to be the turning point of the match, as Robben later confirmed: "You only had to see the sheer joy on the bench to know that the whole group then thought it was going to be 'our day'. We hadn't lost faith, as we knew they were beatable, but drawing level so early [in the second half] was the key." Twenty minutes later, matters went from bad to worse for Melo, when he made a dreadful tackle from behind on Arjen Robben, compounding it by stamping on the Dutch player's left thigh. The Juve player was rightly dismissed for his cynical act. Five minutes earlier Sneijder had conjured up another goal when, from a corner, he stooped to send a bullet header into the net. Brazil's sixth world title was going to have to wait for another tournament.

◄ Luis Suárez stops a
certain injury-time winner
for Ghana with his hand.

Forlan's headband

In 2010, Diego Forlán
set tongues wagging
with both his talent,
winning the Golden
Ball for best player, and
his haircut. To hold his
abundant locks out of
the way, he used this
headband.

▲ **FIFA World Football
Museum collection.**

Uruguay wreck Ghana's dream

2 JULY 2010

URUGUAY 🇺🇾 **1-1** 🇬🇭 **GHANA**
A.E.T.

FORLAN 55   MUNTARI 45+2

⊗✕⊛⊛⊛ **4-2** ✕✕⊛⊛

RARELY HAS A MATCH provided as many thrills, twists and turns as this encounter between Ghana and two-time world champions Uruguay. First, the South Americans lost their captain Diego Lugano to injury before the break, replacing him with Andrés Scotti. In the aftermath, Kevin-Prince Boateng executed a sublime bicycle kick from a cross from the right, but Uruguay's keeper Fernando Muslera was not unduly troubled. Then, just before half-time, the deadlock was broken courtesy of a 35-yard scorcher from the left boot of Sulley Muntari, the same player who had threatened to leave the Ghana camp the week before after falling out with his coach! It was the first time Uruguay had been behind in the tournament, and they were swift to react. In the 55th minute, Diego Forlán powered home a free-kick from the left-hand edge of the box, catching out a poorly positioned Richard Kingson to level the score. There followed a frenetic spell of end-to-end football, but remarkably, the end of normal time arrived without any further goals. During extra-time, the pace waned slightly, although Nicolás Lodeiro and Diego Forlán for the Uruguayans, and Stephen Appiah and Asamoah Gyan for Ghana, all spurned gilt-edged opportunities to settle the tie.

Then, in the 120th minute, from an angled free-kick 30 yards from Uruguay's goal, six Ghanaian players went up for John Paintsil's cross. As a bout of head tennis ensued, the under-pressure Muslera struggled to clear the ball, until 20-year-old Dominic Adiyiah knocked a header goalwards that looked sure to offer victory to Ghana. Luis Suárez, however, had dropped back onto his goal-line and flung himself at the ball, blatantly keeping it out with his hand. The referee showed him the red card and Suárez duly left the fray, later crowing: "It was the save of the tournament!" John Mensah, Ghana's captain, was jubilant, as were his teammates. All that remained was to convert the penalty. Up stepped Asamoah Gyan, Ghana's hero against the United States… only to see his shot strike the crossbar! And so it came down to a penalty shoot-out. Undaunted by his miss minutes earlier, Gyan duly converted the first, but Mensah and Adiyiah both proceeded to miss theirs, as did Uruguay's Maxi Pereira. It was now up to Sebastián Abreu. If he scored, Uruguay were through. He did so with a daring "Panenka". So Ghana would not be bettering Cameroon in 1990 and Senegal in 2002 by becoming the first African side to reach the final four. Their sorrow seemed to know no bounds, while Uruguay's coach Oscar Tabárez struggled to analyse the miracle he had just witnessed. "People who believe in fate will no doubt have an explanation for what happened today, but not me. We weren't really at our best, but we came through by virtue of sheer guts." And thanks to one of the most outrageous acts in the history of the World Cup, he might have added.

0

With Argentina having been swept aside by Germany (4–0) in the quarter-finals, Lionel Messi exited the tournament with just one assist and no goals in five matches, despite having 29 shots in all. He'd been heralded as the star of the tournament, after lifting the *Ballon d'Or* in 2009 and clocking up an incredible 47 goals in 53 games in all competitions with Barcelona that season. But deployed behind Gonzalo Higuaín and Carlos Tévez, the 23-year-old number 10 struggled to reproduce his form with the Catalan club in a blue & white shirt.

▲ A diving header from
Carles Puyol sends Spain
through to the Final.

▶ Sergio Ramos, Gerard
Piqué, Andrés Iniesta and
Xavi Hernández
congratulate Carles Puyol.

Puyol the surprise package

7 JULY 2010

GERMANY 🇩🇪 0–1 🇪🇸 **SPAIN**

PUYOL 73

THE RE-RUN OF THE EURO 2008 final between Spain and Germany produced the same winner and the same score. In Durban, the only goal of the encounter was a bullet header in the 73rd minute from defender Carles Puyol following a Xavi corner. Rarely on the scoresheet, the Barcelona captain was lauded by his teammates. "Today is officially 'Puyi' day," enthused Xavi, his colleague for club and country. "He got a great goal and he deserves it, not least for the fine job he does in defence." Sergio Busquets was singing from the same hymn sheet: "If anyone deserved to get the winner, he did. He was all over the field, in defence, midfield and attack… He's one of the world's top defenders and it might be his last World Cup, so he has well and truly earned his night of glory."

▶ Spain's Xavi Hernández
surges past Germany's
Bastian Schweinsteiger.

▲ Giovanni van Bronckhorst celebrates his goal with his team-mates.

Van Bronckhorst's pearler

---
6 JULY 2010

URUGUAY 2–3 NETHERLANDS

FORLAN 41	V. BRONCKHORST 18
M. PEREIRA 90+2	SNEIJDER 70
	ROBBEN 73

W HAT AN ABSOLUTE GEM! The opening goal in the semi-final between the Netherlands and Uruguay on 6 July in Cape Town in the 18th minute. Unmarked on the left-hand side, the Dutch defender Giovanni van Bronckhorst unleashed a ballistic missile from nearly 25 metres out, its coordinates firmly locked onto the top right-hand corner of the goal. Wesley Sneijder, who netted the Netherlands' second in their eventual 3–2 win, may have been named man of the match, but this goal from Gio, timed at 109 kilometres an hour, was one of the tournament's finest. Closing in on retirement at the age of 35, Van Bronckhorst was earning his 105th cap.

PLAY-OFF FOR THIRD PLACE

Forlán forlorn

▲ Germany finish third for the second tournament running with a play-off victory over Uruguay.

---
10 JULY 2010

URUGUAY 2–3 GERMANY

CAVANI 28, FORLAN 51	MÜLLER 19, JANSEN 56, KHEDIRA 82

Germany's fifth third-place play-off match at a World Cup brought their fourth bronze medal success. So the Germans left South Africa with a sense of having performed well, courtesy of the most prolific attack at the tournament (16 goals), and the young revelation: Thomas Müller (aged 20), scorer of five goals from as many shots on target! Against Uruguay, he got on the scoresheet again, putting his side in front when a shot from Bastian Schweinsteiger was poorly dealt with by Fernando Muslera, a strike which took him level with Wesley Sneijder and David Villa atop the scorers' chart. Nine minutes later, Luis Suárez played in Edinson Cavani, who beat 36-year-old Hans-Jörg Butt with a right-footed toe-poke. Then, in the 51st minute, Diego Forlán, named player of the tournament, conjured up a lovely volley to beat Butt and join the other two players on five goals for the tournament. But the Germans are renowned for never knowing when they're beaten and, five minutes later, Marcelle Jansen pipped Muslera to a Jérôme Boateng cross to equalize. Then, with just eight minutes remaining, Sami Khedira sealed victory with his header from a Mesut Özil corner. The irrepressible Forlán again came close in added time, but his free-kick came back off the crossbar. As in 1970, the *Celeste* were to be denied third place by the Germans.

▲ Spain celebrate their
first world title.

Iniesta to
the rescue

11 JULY 2010

NETHERLANDS 0–1 SPAIN
A.E.T.

INIESTA 116

14

The number of yellow
cards issued by the
Englishman Howard
Webb, a former police
sergeant, in the Final.
There were nine cautions
for the Netherlands: Van
Persie on 15 minutes, Van
Bommel on 22, De Jong
on 29, Van Bronckhorst
on 54, Heitinga on 56,
Robben on 84, Van der
Wiel on 111 and Mathijsen
on 118. Heitinga was
shown a second yellow in
the 109th minute for a
professional foul, resulting
in his expulsion. Spain,
meanwhile, collected five
yellow cards: Puyol on 16
minutes, Ramos on 23,
Capdevila on 67, Iniesta
on 118 and Xavi on 120. In
total, the Netherlands
clocked up 24 yellow
cards during the
competition, equalling
Argentina's unenviable
record from 1990.

SPAIN BECAME THE FIRST European nation to be crowned world champions at a tournament played outisde Europe. But they found it very tough going against a stubborn Netherlands side coached by Bert van Marwijk, who deployed a highly effective 4-2-3-1 formation. Marred by numerous fouls, this encounter went all the way to the end of extra-time, when it was finally settled by an Andres Iniesta goal (116th minute) as penalties loomed. It was the third time in five finals that added time had been required.

Spain had been the first to display their attacking intent when, from a 35-yard Xavi free-kick in the fifth minute, Sergio Ramos powered in a header that was turned away by Maarten Stekelenburg. Six minutes later, the Real Madrid defender was again in the thick of the attacking action, outsmarting Dirk Kuijt and crossing low and hard in front of goal. John Heitinga put it out for a corner, from which David Villa ended up firing a left-footed volley into the side netting. On 22 minutes, Mark van Bommel committed a bad foul on Iniesta; then seven minutes later, Nigel de Jong went in wildly with his studs high on Xabi Alonso, catching the Spanish midfielder on his torso. In both cases, referee Howard Webb issued only yellow cards where reds would have been justified. Shortly after the half-hour mark, Heitinga almost caught Casillas out with a shot from inside his own half, but the Spanish keeper was more alert when Arjen Robben fired in a low shot in

first-half added time. A key moment came in the 62nd minute, when Robben found himself one-on-one with the goalkeeper, but the diving Casillas blocked the flying winger's attempt. Robben was very much at the heart of the action and, with seven minutes of normal time remaining, he burst through the middle again. Despite being held by Carlos Puyol, he battled through on goal, only to be thwarted once again by the outstretched body of Casillas.

Extra-time was more evenly balanced and in the 95th minute, having been played through by Iniesta, Cesc Fàbregas was presented with a golden opportunity, but it was Stekelenburg's turn to win the one-on-one duel. Six minutes later, a cross-shot from Jesús Navas was deflected by Giovanni van Bronckhorst into the side netting. Then, in the second period of extra-time, Heitinga was shown a second yellow card for holding back Iniesta. Spain's deliverance came seven minutes later, from a move sparked by Fernando Torres. Unmarked on the left, his attempted cross for Iniesta was cut out on the edge of the box. The loose ball fell to Fàbregas, who fed it through to Iniesta on the right side of the area. The Barça midfielder controlled the ball adeptly and then volleyed firmly with his right to beat Stekelenburg at the far post. The relief was immense… Vincente del Bosque's men were on top of the world, despite having managed just eight goals all tournament, the lowest ever total for a winning team.

◄ Iker Casillas saves the day for Spain with this crucial save from Arjen Robben on the hour mark.

Tiki-taka to the top

W AS this Spain side the best in the history of international football? Perhaps of any team in the history of football? Their World Cup triumph in 2010 was the second leg of an historic treble, sandwiched between European Championship wins of 2008 and 2012. Based on the best talent that Barcelona and Real Madrid had to offer, these were players who were used to winning. Playing a style of football known as tiki-taka, developed at Barcelona under Pep Guardiola but having its origins in Johan Cruijff's time there as coach, they dominated games with short, fluid passing movements. And their record bears comparison with the very best.

Before this Spanish team, three other international teams had stood out for their consistency: Hungary had an extraordinary record from 1951 to 1955. They played 45, won 37, drew 6 and lost 2. From 1968 to 1973, Pelé's famous Brazil team played 43, won 32, drew 10 and lost 1; and the France of Zinedine Zidane from 1998 to 2001 played 44, won 31, drew 11 and lost 2.

Compare that with Spain's record from the beginning of 2007 until the World Cup Final… played 55, won 50, drew 3 and lost 2. Simply sensational.

Robben's misery

In the 1978 World Cup Final, Rob Rensenbrink was the width of the post away from winning the game in the final minute. Arjen Robben will know how he felt. In a one-on-one with Iker Casillas on the hour mark, Robben had his shot tipped past the post by the Spanish keeper. And then, with seven minutes left, Casillas stole the ball from his feet. "I should have scored, there's no excuse," acknowledged the Bayern wide man. "Casillas made an exceptional stop with the tip of his toe. Otherwise, the ball would have been in the net."

Sneijder's World Cup Final boots

Boots worn by Dutch striker Wesley Sneijder (left) during the finals phase. He scored five goals in seven matches in South Africa.

▲ **FIFA World Football Museum collection.**

◄ Andrès Iniesta scores Spain's World Cup Final-winning goal.

2014

Brazil hosted the World Cup for the second time, but suffered a shock as traumatic as in 1950. Their 7–1 semi-final defeat by Germany was one of several extraordinary results in a remarkable tournament. Germany were the first Europeans to win the trophy in the Americas and, as in 1990, they won it by beating Argentina 1–0 in the Final. Mario Götze became the first substitute to score the winner in a Final.

A South American World Cup

◄ Bastian Schweinsteiger holds the FIFA World Cup trophy aloft.

▼ Demonstrators in Brazil argued that the money spent on the World Cup would have been better spent elsewhere.

THE FIFA WORLD CUP returned to South America after an absence of 36 years and came to Brazil for the first time since 1950. But it didn't go ahead without controversy. For two years the focus of world sport was to be on this giant South American nation, with the Rio Olympics being held two years later. The host status for both had been awarded when the country had been riding high on economic success and optimism, but when the time came to pay the bills there was less money around. With civil servants going unpaid, the $4 billion spent on stadiums and facilities began to seem like a callous excess and, before the 2013 Confederations Cup, more than a million people took to the streets voicing their displeasure. But football is football and once the tournament was in full swing, the troubles were largely forgotten.

At the first World Cup, the Uruguayans had built the Torre del Homenaje in the Estadio Centenario, which celebrated in its design the ways people travelled to the tournament – by plane, train and ship. And travel to the tournament was the story of these finals too. Thousands of Americans turning up by ship, transatlantic flights arrived from Europe, and who can forget the convoys of fans in their camper vans making the journey over the Andes from Chile. This was their tournament and the attendance figure of 3,386,810 was the second highest in history.

And the tournament itself? It was full of surprises. Brazil 2014 refused to stick to the script. Defending champions Spain were humiliated by the Netherlands, Italy were knocked out by Costa Rica and Brazil suffered a shock as big, if not bigger, than the Maracanzo of 1950. And who would have bet on a European nation winning the World Cup in South America?

Brasil 2014

2014 FIFA WORLD CUP BRAZIL™

Story of the qualifiers

Bosnia the only new boys

A RECORD 202 countries took part in the various regional qualifying tournaments for the 2014 World Cup, playing 820 matches, with an average of 2.87 goals scored. In Europe, Belgium, Italy, Germany, the Netherlands, Switzerland, England and Spain came through the qualifiers unbeaten. Meanwhile, Bosnia-Herzegovina were the only new team to make it to the next stage. They were also the only European team to qualify on goal difference (+24 as opposed to +8 for the Greeks), thanks to Edin Džeko (ten goals) and Vedad Ibišević (eight goals), the most prolific attacking duo on the European scene. France, Greece,

Portugal and Croatia qualified as a result of playoffs. Regular participants such as Denmark (lowest-scoring second-ranking team in the nine groups, so not admitted to the playoffs), Sweden and Romania failed to win their tickets for Brazil. In South America, Colombia were making a comeback after 16 years' absence, while Paraguay, last in a pool of nine nations, did not qualify. Mexico, who dominated New Zealand (5–1 away , 4–2 at home), and Uruguay (5–0 and 0–0 against Jordan) were involved in intercontinental playoffs. In Africa and Asia the line-ups were almost identical to 2010, with Iran qualifying instead of North Korea.

▶ Bosnians Edin Džeko and Miralem Pjanić in a qualifying match against Lithuania in October 2013.

Group stage

GROUP A		GROUP B		GROUP C		GROUP D		GROUP E		GROUP F		GROUP G		GROUP H	
BRA	3–1 CRO	ESP	1–5 NED	COL	3–0 GRE	URU	1–3 CRC	SUI	2–1 ECU	ARG	2–1 BIH	GER	4–0 POR	BEL	2–1 ALG
MEX	1–0 CMR	CHI	3–1 AUS	CIV	2–1 JPN	ENG	1–2 ITA	FRA	3–0 HON	IRN	0–0 NGA	GHA	1–2 USA	RUS	1–1 KOR
BRA	0–0 MEX	AUS	2–3 NED	COL	2–1 CIV	URU	2–1 ENG	SUI	2–5 FRA	ARG	1–0 IRN	GER	2–2 GHA	BEL	1–0 RUS
CMR	0–4 CRO	ESP	0–2 CHI	JPN	0–0 GRE	ITA	0–1 CRC	HON	1–2 ECU	NGA	1–0 BIH	USA	2–2 POR	KOR	2–4 ALG
CMR	1–4 BRA	AUS	0–3 ESP	JPN	1–4 COL	ITA	0–1 URU	HON	0–3 SUI	NGA	2–3 ARG	USA	0–1 GER	KOR	0–1 BEL
CRO	1–3 MEX	NED	2–0 CHI	GRE	2–1 CIV	CRC	0–0 ENG	ECU	0–0 FRA	BIH	3–1 IRN	POR	2–1 GHA	ALG	1–1 RUS

	W D L + – PTS		W D L + – PTS		W D L + – PTS		W D L + – PTS		W D L + – PTS		W D L + – PTS		W D L + – PTS		W D L + – PTS
BRA	2 1 0 7 2 7	NED	3 0 0 10 3 9	COL	3 0 0 9 2 9	CRC	2 1 0 4 1 7	FRA	2 1 0 8 2 7	ARG	3 0 0 6 3 9	GER	2 1 0 7 2 7	BEL	3 0 0 4 1 9
MEX	2 1 0 4 1 7	CHI	2 0 1 5 3 6	GRE	1 1 1 2 4 4	URU	2 0 1 4 4 6	SUI	2 0 1 7 6 6	NGA	1 1 1 3 3 4	USA	1 1 1 4 4 4	ALG	1 1 1 6 5 4
CRO	1 0 2 6 6 3	ESP	1 0 2 4 7 3	CIV	1 0 2 4 5 3	ITA	1 0 2 2 3 3	ECU	1 1 1 3 3 4	BIH	1 0 2 4 4 3	POR	1 1 1 4 7 4	RUS	0 2 1 2 3 2
CMR	0 0 3 1 9 0	AUS	0 0 3 3 9 0	JPN	0 1 2 2 6 1	ENG	0 1 2 2 4 1	HON	0 0 3 1 8 0	IRN	0 1 2 1 4 1	GHA	0 1 2 4 6 1	KOR	0 1 2 3 6 1

Knockout stages

ROUND OF 16		ROUND OF 16		ROUND OF 16		ROUND OF 16	
BRA	1–1 / 3–2 CHI	FRA	2–0 NGA	NED	2–1 MEX	ARG	1–0 A.E.T. SUI
COL	2–0 URU	GER	2–1 A.E.T. ALG	CRC	1–1 / 5–3 GRE	BEL	2–1 A.E.T. USA

QUARTER-FINAL		QUARTER-FINAL		QUARTER-FINAL		QUARTER-FINAL	
BRA	2–1 COL	FRA	0–1 GER	NED	0–0 / 4–3 CRC	ARG	1–0 BEL

SEMI-FINAL		SEMI-FINAL	
BRA	1–7 GER	NED	0–0 / 2–4 ARG

PLAY-OFF FOR THIRD PLACE

BRA	0–3 NED

FINAL

GER	1–0 A.E.T. ARG

ALG	ARG	AUS	BEL	BIH	BRA	CHI	CIV
CMR	COL	CRC	CRO	ECU	ENG	ESP	FRA
GER	GHA	GRE	HON	IRN	ITA	JPN	KOR
MEX	NED	NGA	POR	RUS	SUI	URU	USA

32 TEAMS

64
MATCHES PLAYED

178 10
CARDS

3429873
SPECTATORS

FULECO
OFFICIAL MASCOT

FIFA WORLD CUP
Brasil
OFFICIAL LOGO

GERMANY
WINNERS

×6

JAMES RODRIGUEZ
LEADING GOALSCORER

2.7
AVERAGE GOALS
PER MATCH

BRAZUCA
OFFICIAL BALL

Host cities and stadiums

From the Atlantic to the Amazon

MANAUS
ARENA AMAZÔNIA
(40,549)

FORTALEZA
ESTÁDIO CASTELÃO
(60,342)

NATAL
ESTÁDIO DAS DUNAS
(39,471)

RECIFE
ARENA PERNAMBUCO
(42,610)

SALVADOR
ARENA FONTE NOVA
(51,400)

CUIABÁ
ARENA PANTANAL
(41,112)

BRASÍLIA
ESTÁDIO NACIONAL
(69,349)

BELO HORIZONTE
ESTÁDIO MINEIRÃO
(58,170)

RIO DE JANEIRO
MARACANÃ
(74,738)

SÃO PAULO
ARENA DE SÃO PAULO
(62,601)

CURITIBA
ARENA DA BAIXADA
(39,631)

PORTO ALEGRE
ESTÁDIO BEIRA-RIO
(43,394)

Twelve stadiums in 12 cities were used. Their capacities ranged from 39,631 to 74,738. The Maracanã, the venue for the Final, had been completely refurbished for the tournament and was now an all-seater stadium.

Regulations

First appearance of spray cans and goal line technology

THE FORMAT of the competition remained unchanged for a record-breaking fifth tournament. The major new developments were to do with refereeing. To ensure that the "wall" was placed at the regulation distance for free-kicks (9.15m/10 yards), referees were equipped with a can of white spray so they could draw a white line on the pitch which the players must not cross, a simple innovation but a surprisingly effective one. The spray dissolved rapidly after the kick was taken. Secondly, goal line technology was used for the first time. The system relied on 14 high-speed cameras, seven for each goal-mouth, linked up to a computer, to determine whether or not the ball had completely crossed the line. One further innovation: the referee could grant three-minute refreshment breaks if the temperature exceeded 32 degrees.

▲ Robin van Persie scores an extraordinary headed goal to put the Dutch back on level terms against defending champions Spain.

The holders crash out

13 JUNE 2014

SPAIN 1–5 **NETHERLANDS**

ALONSO 27 (PEN)   V. PERSIE 44, 72, ROBBEN 53, 80, DE VRIJ 65

"A stunning blow."

Andrés Iniesta, Spanish playmaker, speaking after his team had been eliminated at the group stage

"Getting eliminated in the first round, when we were expecting to go much further, is a stunning blow. But in this sort of competition, when you don't get things right, you pay dearly for your mistakes," reflected the Spain and Barcelona midfielder. "That's what we have found. Spain – or rather we – were just not up to it. That has been very painful, considering our recent record and the make-up of our team."

ON 13 JUNE fans in Salvador were witness to a truly extrtaordinary game, in a rematch of the 2010 Final. The game began well for the defending champions Spain, who two years earlier had won the European Championship. Running into the Dutch penalty area, Diego Costa had the beating of Stefan de Vrij, who brought down the Atletico Madrid centre-forward with a late tackle. The ensuing penalty was converted by Xabi Alonso (1–0). Then David Silva, with only Jasper Cillessen to beat, just failed to make it 2–0 with a chip over the goalkeeper's head. But the Dutch had other ideas: Daley Blind lofted a 50-metre pass up the field, which Robin van Persie, diving forward, headed spectacularly over Iker Casillas (1–1). It was a truly sublime goal. After the break Arjen Robben put in a virtuoso performance. The Bayern Munich striker put the Dutch ahead after weaving round Gerard Piqué and beating Casillas (1–2). Then, from a free-kick whipped in by Wesley Sneijder, De Vrij headed the ball in at the far post (1–3). There was little hope of a Spanish comeback. When their goalkeeper mismanaged the ball after a back-pass, Van Persie sniffed a chance and rushed in to score his second (1–4). The Spanish nightmare was complete when Robben broke forward at speed, left Sergio Ramos standing and made his way round Casillas to close the scoring (1–5). Spain did not know what had hit them.

Unusually, manager Vicente del Bosque tried to comfort each of his substitutes. The two greatest causes of concern for Spain were the fragility of their defence and the physical fitness of their squad, who looked worn down at the end of a long season. "Things are not going well, but I have the strength of character to accept this defeat without losing my grip. How we let in five goals is impossible to explain. We are not a defensive team, that's certain, but we have always been solid at the back. In the first half, we created some space, despite the pressure they applied, but they were able to take control by getting in behind our defenders," explained Del Bosque. "It would be wrong to point the finger at Casillas. If we lost, the whole team is to blame. You can't compare this defeat with the one we suffered against the Swiss four years ago. Nowadays, we have the experience required to deal with the fact that we have lost three points. We have to lift our heads and look forward, like any athlete wanting to achieve their next objective." Even so, after this initial defeat, the Spaniards lost to Chile (0–2), only saving face by beating Australia (3–0), and finished third in Group B. Their 5–1 debacle was the heaviest defeat ever suffered by a title-holder. It was also the first time Spain had conceded more than four goals since their home defeat to Scotland in 1963 (2–6). An extraordinary start to what would turn out to be an extraordinary tournament.

Neymar carries Brazil

12 JUNE 2014

BRAZIL  3–1 **CROATIA**

NEYMAR JR 29, 71 (PEN)   MARCELLO 11 (O.G.)
OSCAR 90+1

IN a difficult group, Brazil played their opening match against a Croatian team featuring Luka Modrić (Real Madrid) and Ivan Rakitić (Sevilla). Though under pressure, the hosts claimed victory, thanks to a double by Neymar. The Brazilian no. 10 equalized with a left-footed shot that went in off the Croatian post, then put his team ahead from a penalty given away by Stipe Pletikosa. Oscar completed the scoring. More laboured in their second match against Mexico (0–0), Brazil topped the group with a dominant display against Cameroon (4–1), with Neymar scoring another double.

▼ Georgios Samaras of Greece battles with the Côte d'Ivoire's Giovanni Sio.

▲ Brazil's Neymar scored twice in the 3–1 victory over Croatia in the opening match of the 2014 finals.

For the eighth tournament in a row, the World Cup welcomed a new European nation: Bosnia-Herzegovina. The team fronted by Emir Spahić (Bayer Leverkusen), Miralem Pjanić (Roma) and Edin Džeko (Manchester City) was following in the footsteps of Denmark (1986), the Republic of Ireland (1990), Greece (1994), Croatia (1998), Slovenia (2002), Ukraine (2006) and Slovakia (2010). The only debutants in this World Cup, Bosnia-Herzegovina finished third in Group F, following defeats by Argentina (1–2) and Nigeria (0–1) and a win over Iran (3–1).

Samaras puts Greece through

24 JUNE 2014

GREECE 2–1 **CÔTE D'IVOIRE**

SAMARIS 42, SAMARIS 90+3 (PEN)   B. WILFRIED 74

AFTER a defeat to Colombia (3–0) and a draw with Japan (0–0), Greece had to beat Côte d'Ivoire to reach the round of 16. Following a shot that hit the bar from José Holebas, assisted by Georgios Samaras, the Greeks opened the scoring when they picked up a poor pass by Cheick Tioté. Samaras found Andreas Samaris, who put the ball past goalkeeper Boubacar Barry (1–0). The Ivoirians piled on the pressure, but it was Greece who threatened to score next, when Georgios Karagounis rattled Barry's crossbar. Côte d'Ivoire then equalized with a text-book goal: Gervinho crossed back to Wilfried Bony, who fired past Panagiotis Glykos (1–1). As things stood, the Ivory Coast were on course to qualify for the next stage, but in stoppage time the referee awarded a penalty to Greece for a foul on Samaras by Giovanni Sio. The Greek giant did not hesitate for a moment, shooting with the side of his foot to ensure his team's qualification (2–1). "What did I feel when taking the penalty? Nothing, absolutely nothing," Samaras recalled. "I took the ball, placed it on the spot. It was all between me and the goalkeeper. I emptied my mind, concentrated and tried to hit the back of the net. I had done so thousands of times in training, sometimes in matches. Whether there is just one person at the end of a training session or thousands in a stadium makes no difference. Before I began my run, I knew where I was going to place it. I had a clear picture in my mind. I only had to put my plan into effect. We never lost hope and fought until the last second. We have all heard stories about matches which were decided by the very last sequence of play." Taking part for the third time in the final stages of the World Cup, the 2004 European champions had made it to the round of 16 for the first time in their history.

Mondragón overtakes the "Old Lion"

24 JUNE 2014

JAPAN ● 1–4 ▬ **COLOMBIA**

OKAZAKI 45 +1   CUADRADO 17 (PEN), JACKSON M. 55, 82, JAMES 90

▶ A red card for Alex Song during Cameroon's 4–0 defeat at the hands of Croatia. Cameroon lost all three of their group-stage matches.

WITH his country winning Group C after victories against Greece (3–0) and the Ivory Coast (2–1), Faryd Mondragón, at the ripe old age of 43 years and 3 days, became the oldest-ever player to take part in the World Cup. On 14 June, he beat the record of the Cameroon's "Old Lion" Roger Milla (42 years and 39 days in 1994). Mondragón was brought on in the 85th minute of Colombia's third match, against Japan, in place of David Ospina, when the Colombians were leading 3–1. The Deportivo Cali goalkeeper, who in the course of his career had also played for Argentinos Juniors, Independiente, Real Zaragoza, Metz, Galatasaray and 1. FC Köln, had made his previous appearance in the tournament in 1998, 16 years earlier – a record gap. "It is an honour for me to be here. By setting this record, I become the embodiment of Colombian football and the history of Colombian football," enthused the new record-holder. As he approached the touchline and the fourth official brandished his number, the whole stadium rose up with appreciation. Mondragón even parried a goal-bound shot, restricting the score to 4–1, "It was amazing. I think everyone was anticipating that moment. I would like to say a big thank you to José Pekerman (Colombia's coach), the whole team and my friends. Thanks to them, my dream has come true. By the way we are playing, and our results, we are already writing history. The nine points with which we are ending this group phase enable us to go on in complete confidence. The advantage we have is that 95 per cent of our present team play for European clubs. They therefore have the individual experience and maturity to compete at the highest level. In the 1994 World Cup, 95 per cent of the squad were playing in Colombia." It was to be Faryd Mondragón's last match, marking the end of his career. He had won 51 caps and had been in three World Cup squads (1994, 1998 and 2014).

Cameroon tamed by Croatia

18 JUNE 2014

CAMEROON 🟦 0–4 ▬ **CROATIA**

OLIĆ 11
PERIŠIĆ 48
MANDŽUKIĆ 61, 73

◀ Colombian keeper Faryd Mondragón celebrates his team's qualification for the round of 16.

THOUGH they came with a strong squad of players, Cameroon finished 32nd and last in the overall tournament rankings. The team nicknamed the "Lions" lost their opening match to Mexico in a hard-fought encounter (0–1). And things for the team coached by the German Volker Finke got worse. Reduced to ten men after Alexandre Song was sent off, they were overwhelmed by Croatia (0–4). "The result is really painful. It is always difficult to play ten against 11, but that does not justify our performance," admitted Finke. "Croatia were undoubtedly more effective in attack, but Cameroon also had opportunities to get the ball in the net. We must now look to the future, because we have some good young players." In their third and final match, with no hopes of proceeding further, Cameroon were beaten by Brazil (4–1), even though Joël Matip equalized in the first half, scoring Cameroon's only goal of the tournament.

◀ The headlines of Italian daily newspaper *La Gazzetta dello Sport*: "Italy out: A failure. A shambles".

▼ Steven Gerrard and Wayne Rooney can't stop England crashing out at the group stage for the first time since 1958.

Italy and England disappoint

I N Group D, Italy and England, two of the giants of world football, were eliminated at the first hurdle. After winning against Roy Hodgson's men (2–1, with goals by Claudio Marchisio and Mario Balotelli, and one in reply by Daniel Sturridge), Italy lost 1–0 to both Costa Rica and Uruguay, a match during which Luis Suárez took a bite out of Giorgio Chiellini. The outcome: a poor third place for the Italians. England, meanwhile, were defeated by Uruguay (2–1), then could only manage a draw against Costa Rica (0–0), thus finishing fourth and last. It was an astonishing result for a team that included star players such as Steven Gerrard (Liverpool) and Wayne Rooney (Manchester United). Taking every-one by surprise, Costa Rica finished top of the group, thanks to some fine saves by their goalkeeper, Keylor Navas.

Video proves its worth

15 JUNE 2014		
FRANCE	3–0	HONDURAS

BENZEMA 45 (PEN), 72, VALLADARES 48 (O.G.)

F ANS IN THE ESTÁDIO Beira-Rio in Porto Alegre on 15 June were witness to World Cup history. For the first time, referees had access to goal line technology following a decision taken by the International Football Association Board (IFAB) on 5 July 2012 authorizing its use in official competitions. The GoalControl-4D system uses 14 high-speed cameras installed around the pitch (seven for each goalmouth). With special recognition software, the ball is isolated from the sequences of images and its three-dimensional position is plotted in real time. This provides a faithful virtual reconstruction in "four dimensions". If the ball crosses the goal line completely between the posts and beneath the crossbar, the monitoring computer sends an encrypted signal in less than a second to the referee's watch, which vibrates and displays the word "GOAL", to confirm that a goal has been scored.

In the 48th minute of the France–Honduras match, Karim Benzema fired in a left-footed shot. The ball struck the post and rebounded off the Honduran goalkeeper, Noel Valladares, in such a way that its position was hidden from the match officials. Goal line technology revealed that the ball had gone over the line, giving the French their second goal, recorded as an own goal by Valladares. Benzema scored again towards the end of the game. Officials also awarded a goal on this basis in the Costa Rica–Italy match (1–0, a header by Bryan Ruiz which struck the bar before going in), and turned one down in the game between the Netherlands and Argentina (when Sergio Romero blocked a shot by Ron Vlaar, and the ball rebounded onto – but not across – the goal line). In total, the new technology, providing special slow-motion replays, was used seven times to validate refereeing decisions.

◀ Karim Benzema scores his second goal against Honduras to put France 3–0 ahead.

▼ Goal-line technology confirms that Benzema's second goal is valid.

▲ Abdelmoumene Djabou, who scored for Algeria, applauds the crowd after the defeat to Germany.

▶ Aerial battle between Germany's Thomas Müller and Algeria's Mehdi Mostefa.

A heroic display by the Desert Foxes

30 JUNE 2014

GERMANY ▬ 2–1 🇩🇿 **ALGERIA**
A.E.T.

SCHÜRRLE 92, ÖZIL 120   DJABOU 120+1

THANKS to some spirited performances in the group stage – an initial defeat by Belgium (2–1), followed by a victory over South Korea (4–2) and a draw with Russia (1–1), Algeria progressed to the knockout stage for the first time. Facing Germany in the round of 16, Vahid Halilhodžić's men fought bravely. They even came close to opening the scoring in the 17th minute, when Faouzi Ghoulam fired in a left-footed shot. Rais Mbolhi, the Algerian goalkeeper and man of the match, then had to keep out Toni Kroos and Mario Götze (in the 40th minute), save a shot from Philipp Lahm (in the 55th minute) and a point-blank header from Thomas Müller (in the 80th minute). In extra-time, Müller centred for André Schürrle, who squeezed the ball in off his heel (1–0). Medhi Mostefa, countering on the right, just failed to equalize. Then Mesut Özil put the Germans two up, scoring from close range after an initial shot by Schürrle (2–0). In the final seconds, Algeria got one back, thanks to Abdelmoumene Djabou (1–2). With surprising skill and energy, the Algerians had tested the German team to their limits, effectively dominating the first half.

Dutchmen take on water (AND INSTRUCTIONS)

29 JUNE 2014

NETHERLANDS ▬ 2–1 🇲🇽 **MEXICO**

SNEIJDER 88, HUNTELAAR 90+4 (PEN)   G. DOS SANTOS 48

THE great novelty of this stage of the tournament was the introduction of the refreshment break, permitted by FIFA in the event of high temperatures. It was the medical officer's job to measure the temperature with a Wet Globe Bulb Temperature (WBGT) device before the match and note any changes. Should the temperature exceed 32° C, the referee could allow a three-minute break 30 minutes into each half. The Dutch cleverly used this break as a tactical time-out in the second half of their round of 16 match against Mexico: Van Gaal gathered his players in the middle of the pitch and instructed them to send long balls up to Klaas-Jan Huntelaar, whom he brought on in the 76th minute, when Mexico were 1–0 up thanks to a 48th-minute volley from Giovanni Dos Santos: "I switched to my plan B during the refreshment break, which was an intelligent way of using it. And I make no secret of it," admitted the Dutch manager. His strategy was effective, as Sneijder first equalized (in the 88th minute) and then Huntelaar scored the winning goal from a penalty (in the fourth minute of added-on time). An informal refreshment break had previously been held in the United States–Portugal match in Group F.

▶ Dutch coach Louis van Gaal takes advantage of a water break in the round of 16 match against Mexico to instruct his players.

"We are now part of Algerian football history."

Rais Mbolhi, Algeria's goalkeeper, speaking after the defeat by Germany

"We had to deal with a great German side. We are very disappointed because we felt we might get to the next stage. It wasn't the physical aspect that decided it. We are now part of Algerian football history, as we are the first team to have progressed so far. It's a foundation for the future. The fact that we reached the knock out stage, we owe to our coach. We want to thank him for all the work he has done with and for this team."

▲ Germany goalkeeper Manuel Neuer as a defender against Islam Slimani.

Neuer, goalkeeper or sweeper?

MORE than anyone else, Germany's Manuel Neuer was outstanding in his ability to extend the role of the goalkeeper beyond shot stopping. Against Algeria, the Bayern Munich keeper impressed with his heading of the ball, speed off the mark and sense of anticipation, as he made a large number of forays up field, including a successful tackle on Islam Slimani, who was through and advancing towards goal. A goalkeeping sweeper, Neuer covered 5,517 metres in this round of 16 match against Algeria and made 42 passes. "This is exactly what we were expecting of him. He clearly enjoys playing in this way. No one is concerned when he comes out of his penalty area, as he always gives the impression he knows exactly what he is doing," commented Andreas Köpke, the German goalkeeping coach. Neuer added, "As I see it, I'm playing as I have been doing for years. I haven't changed my style of play in any fundamental way, but it has come under the spotlight here in the World Cup. People especially remember the match against Algeria, when I often came out of my area and joined the rest of the team. "I had to take those risks

because the situation required me to, with our team playing high up the field and our opponents making rapid counter-attacks. This was something new for people not familiar with my style of play, but in the Bundesliga everyone knows how I play."

The leader – and often the saviour – of his team, Neuer nevertheless took a very collective view of his role: "I see myself above all as a team player. I depend on those around me on the pitch, on their positioning, the way they attack. This means I may well have to come out of my goal and take part in the game. It is a team effort, a joint endeavour that I can't manage on my own and, fortunately, we are almost always a well-oiled team." With Neuer as keeper, Germany conceded only four goals in seven matches. Like Oliver Kahn in 2002, Neuer (aged 28) won the Lev Yashin award for best goalkeeper and enabled his team to win their fourth world title: "Obviously, I am very pleased with my performance. I know I have had a good tournament. But individual performances are only one side of the coin. What matters is us winning as a team."

4

Rafael Márquez, the Mexican defender, was the first player to compete in four World Cup finals as captain of his team (2002, 2006, 2010 and 2014). The Barcelona defender also scored in three World Cups, including the 2014 game against Croatia.

8/8

This was the first time since 32 nations had been admitted to the final stages of the World Cup that every one of the eight teams that finished on top of their groups in the group stage (Germany, France, Brazil, Colombia, Argentina, Belgium, the Netherlands and Costa Rica) won their round of 16 matches to qualify for the quarter-finals.

▶ A tense Brazil team in the penalty shoot-out against Chile in the round of 16.

Neymar's shirt

Shirt worn by Brazil's Neymar during the finals of the 2014 tournament.

▲ FIFA World Football Museum collection.

A close shave for Brazil

28 JUNE 2014

BRAZIL 🔵 **1–1** 🔴 **CHILE**
A.E.T.

DAVID LUIZ 18   ALEXIS 32

⊗✗⊗✗⊗ **3–2** ✗✗⊗⊗✗

AFTER comfortably winning their first round group, Brazil came up against tough Chilean opponents, led by two star players: Alexis Sánchez (Barcelona) and Arturo Vidal (Juventus). But the host country quickly asserted themselves: from a corner taken by Neymar and flicked on by Thiago Silva, David Luiz beat Claudio Bravo at point-blank range in the 18th minute (1–0). A lapse of concentration enabled Chile to equalize: following a loose throw-in by Hulk, Sánchez took possession of the ball and beat Júlio Cesar with a low shot (1–1). Brazil quickly resumed their dominance: in the 35th minute, a header by Neymar was kept out by Francisco Silva; then, in the 39th minute, Fred, six metres from goal, shot over the bar after a foray by Neymar.

After the break, Hulk was denied a goal, not very convincingly, on the grounds of hand ball. But as the game went on, Luiz Felipe Scolari's men started to struggle. Júlio César did well to save a 64th-minute shot from Charles Aránguiz. Although Brazil dominated in extra-time, it was Mauricio Pinilla who missed the chance of the match by hitting the crossbar in the 120th minute. In the shoot-out, Júlio Cesar was his nation's saviour, blocking the attempts of Pinilla and Sánchez.

Thiago Silva, the Brazilian captain, was a key player for the host nation. But he had been unusually tense since the beginning of the competition. Bizarrely, the central defender had burst into tears before the penalty shoot-out, which he spent lying down in the centre circle. Thiago had asked not to be included in the list of penalty-takers. Questions were asked later in the Brazilian press. Was he shirking his responsibilities? "I am an emotional person. I'm easily moved. Emotion is natural for a human being," replied the man known as "The Monster". "But I don't let it get to me on the pitch. There was a lot of pressure during the match. Had we lost, we would have been on our way home."

Pogba makes the difference

30 JUNE 2014

FRANCE ▌▌ 2–0 ▌▌ **NIGERIA**

POGBA 79, YOBO 90+2 (O.G.)

WITH his amazing hairstyles (mohican dyed blond), height (1.91m) and incredible technique, Frenchman Paul Pogba is a noticeable presence on the pitch. In France's round of 16 match against Nigeria, the Juventus midfielder scored the opening goal. In the 79th minute, from a Mathieu Valbuena corner, Pogba took advantage of a mistimed intervention by the Nigerian keeper to head the ball into the net (1–0). Earlier Vincent Enyeama had kept out his superb volley in the 22nd minute. The second French goal was an own goal by Joseph Yobo from a Valbuena cross in the 90th minute (2–0).

Powerful, creative, effective in both attack and defence, 21-year-old Pogba was awarded the title of Best Young Player of the tournament. "To play in the World Cup was a childhood dream. I am well aware of my faults. I sometimes take risks. I also need to learn to pace myself over 90 minutes. I should not play solely by instinct. These are things I need to be careful about in my position, because it is in midfield that you control the game, you touch the ball a lot and you can change the rhythm of a match. You are in the engine room and you can't afford to make mistakes." Despite having Pogba, France went down in the quarter-final (0–1), but were clearly a team making progress: "Our defeat at the hands of Germany has made me even more determined to win a title with my country. I feel I am maturing and I now have other objectives and greater ambition."

Keshi, always the first

Stephen Keshi, the Nigeria manager, was the first African coach to take a team beyond the group stage. As a player, Keshi had reached the round of 16 in 1994. "Every defeat is painful, especially when the team follow your instructions and play as they did against France (0–2). We did not deserve to lose, but this is football and you have to accept it," observed the Nigerian.

◄ France's Paul Pogba in a one-on-one against Nigerian John Obi Mikel.

▼ Romelu Lukaku and Kevin de Bruyne set up a goal for each other in Belgium's 2–1 win over the USA.

Dominance rewarded

1 JULY 2014

BELGIUM ▌▌ 2–1 ⬛ **USA**
A.E.T.

DE BRUYNE 93, LUKAKU 105   GREEN 107

DESPITE dominating possession, Belgium, buoyed by a second "golden generation" of players – Thibaut Courtois and Eden Hazard (Chelsea), Vincent Kompany (Manchester City), Axel Witsel (Zenith Saint-Petersburg), Kevin De Bruyne (Wolfsburg) – found it difficult to convert their chances on 1 July in Salvador. Tim Howard, the American goalkeeper, was on top form, stopping a total of 16 shots. After countless attempts, De Bruyne put the Red Devils ahead at the start of extra-time, following a run by Romelu Lukaku, who had just come on as 93rd-minute substitute (1–0). Then it was De Bruyne's turn to assist Lukaku, who unleashed a powerful shot in the 105th minute to make it 2–0. Such had been the dominance of Marc Wilmots's players, it was a well-deserved lead. But out of the blue, receiving the ball from Michael Bradley, substitute Julian Green (aged 19) revived the Americans' hopes by scoring a goal (1–2). It was all in vain. Having failed to qualify in 2006 and 2010, the Belgians were back in the quarter-finals for the first time since 1986. "We had 27 shots on goal, the first in the second minute, and we kept up the barrage until the end of extra-time. I want to congratulate Jürgen Klinsmann and his team," commented Belgian manager Marc Wilmots. "Tim Howard, in particular, had a fantastic match, though I think our victory was well deserved. We played the game, we showed courage, and we pushed ourselves beyond our limits. Sometimes the result is not as clear as you might hope, especially when you miss so many opportunities. But we never let up."

◄ James Rodríguez scores from the penalty spot against Brazil. It was his sixth goal, making him the tournament's top scorer.

◄ Neymar was badly injured against Colombia and would miss the rest of the tournament.

James Rodríguez, Colombian goal machine

Brazil win again but lose Neymar

4 JUNE 2014

BRAZIL 🇧🇷 2–1 ▬ COLOMBIA

T. SILVA 7, DAVID LUIZ 69 | JAMES 80 (PEN)

AFTER THEIR STRUGGLES in the previous match against Chile, Brazil soon found their rhythm against Colombia. Barely six minutes had elapsed when Thiago Silva kneed in a corner from Neymar (1–0). Colombia almost equalized in the 11th minute with a left-footed shot by Juan Cuadrado, which went wide. Then, in the 20th minute, both Hulk and Oscar were denied by David Ospina. A few minutes later, Hulk received the ball from Marcelo on the left of the penalty area, but again his shot was stopped by the Colombian goalkeeper. In the 69th minute, David Luiz relieved the pressure on Brazil with a magnificent, dipping free-kick that curled into the top corner (2–0). But Colombia were not daunted and pulled a goal back in the 80th minute thanks to a James Rodríguez penalty. Brazil held on to qualify for the semi-finals, but they had two serious problems to contend with: Neymar (four goals and one assist in five matches) went off injured in the 88th minute, having fractured his third lumbar vertebra; and Thiago Silva would also be absent from the semi-final, having been booked in the second half, his third yellow card of the tournament.

IN THE ABSENCE OF RADAMEL FALCAO, their top goalscorer in the qualifiers with a tally of nine, Colombia found an effective new striker in James Rodríguez. Aged 22, the AS Monaco midfielder scored six goals in Brazil, each very different in character: a roll-in against Greece (3–0 final score), a powerful header from a corner against Côte d'Ivoire (2–1) and a dribble followed by a chip over the goalkeeper against Japan (4–1). In the round of 16 match with Uruguay, James got a pair: a beautifully controlled volley into the top corner of the net – a strong contender for the best goal of the tournament – and a right-footed flick into the empty goal from a Juan Cuadrado headed cross. Not to mention his penalty in the quarter-finals against Brazil (1–2). "I scored six goals. All were important in the sense that they helped the team to win. My volleyed shot against Uruguay is a strike I practise a lot in training. I put it in the net roughly two times out of five. I attempted it here and it went in under the bar. But personally I prefer my goal against Japan. It had more class, more magic," explained the Colombian No. 10 with the silky left-foot. His six goals, plus two assists, won him the adidas Golden Boot Award. They also marked a transition for Rodríguez, who was for a long time seen as a traditional playmaker, laying on creative passes: "But I'm also drawn to goal-scoring. Just passing is not enough." Finally, James was symbolic of the Colombian revival, after a 16-year absence from the World Cup, alongside such talented players as Juan Cuadrado (Fiorentina) and Carlos Bacca (Sevilla): "Yes, we did well. I'm happy I was able to help Colombia reach the quarter-finals. We would have liked to go further, but Brazil have some great players. The dream ended there." It continued, though, for Rodríguez: immediately afterwards, he signed for Spanish giants Real Madrid.

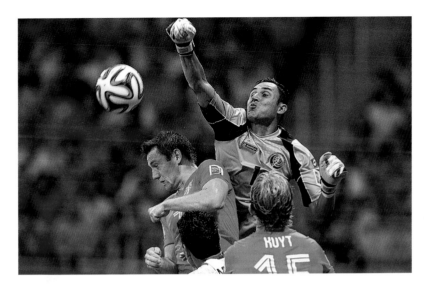

◄ Costa Rican keeper Keylor Navas had a great game against the Netherlands, but his luck ran out in the penalty shoot-out defeat.

Dutch win in spite of Navas

5 JULY 2014

NETHERLANDS ▬ 0–0 ▬ COSTA RICA
A.E.T.

⦿⦿⦿⦿ 4–3 ⦻×⦿⦿×

KEYLOR NAVAS, the Costa Rican goal-keeper, performed magnificently for the full 120 minutes, coming out to save a ball from the feet of Robin van Persie, stopping a shot from Memphis Depay with his foot, diving brilliantly to save a free-kick by Wesley Sneijder. But the Dutch sprung a surprise with the penalties looming: Jasper Cillessen was replaced by Tim Krul for the shoot-out and his saves

from Bryan Ruiz and Michael Umaña proved crucial as the Dutch qualified for the semi-finals. "This World Cup has nevertheless been a great experience. We can leave with our heads held high. Everyone has worked hard. We excelled ourselves on the pitch," commented Keylor Navas. "No one likes losing. It's tough. But we were never beaten. Going out in a penalty shoot-out is not a defeat".

Belgium fall short against Argentina

5 JULY 2014

ARGENTINA ▬ 1–0 ▮▮ BELGIUM

HIGUAIN 8

THANKS to an eighth-minute goal by Gonzalo Higuaín, who pounced on a blocked pass by Ángel Di María, Argentina qualified for the semi-finals for the first time since 1990. But the Belgians, led by Kevin De Bruyne, showed great quality at times. They relied, in particular, on the skills of their goalkeeper, Thibaut Courtois, who intervened decisively against Lionel Messi in injury time. They went on to top the FIFA/Coca-Cola World Ranking in the spring of 2016.

◄ Belgian keeper Thibaut Courtois gives the crowd a thumbs up after losing to Argentina.

History repeats itself

4 JULY 2014

FRANCE ▮▮ 0–1 ▬ GERMANY

HUMMELS 13

HAVING BEATEN FRANCE in their previous two World Cup encounters, in 1982 and 1986, Germany made it three in a row with a 1-0 victory in this quarter-final. In the 13th minute, a free-kick by Toni Kroos found the head of Mats Hummels, who got the better of Raphaël Varane and directed the ball into the top corner of Hugo Lloris's goal (1–0). Then Manuel Neuer came to the fore for Germany. The Bayern goalkeeper first parried a shot from Mathieu Valbuena (36') then a header from Varane (59'). He was even more solid in stopping a volley from Blaise Matuidi (77') and a strike by Benzema after a one-two with Olivier Giroud (90+2'). Towards the end of the game, Germany failed to put the result beyond doubt. Chances were missed by Thomas Müller (81') and André Schürrle, who from six metres had only Lloris to beat (84'). "We are disappointed, sad and frustrated, but life goes on. I hope this squad will stay together for a long time. I still have lot of work to do with this team, but the initial results are promising. We must not forget that a lot of good things have come out of this tournament. It was very close today. We are less experienced than the Germans, who are accustomed to these big occasions," was the analysis of Didier Deschamps, the French manager.

"We shall learn our lesson."

Marc Wilmots, the Belgian manager, speaking after his team's elimination by Argentina

"Argentina had the advantage of experience. They were the favourites, they scored early on, and they kept their lead by breaking up the rhythm. We shall learn our lesson: in these competitions, even minor mistakes are costly, and you sometimes have to be more intelligent than the opposing team. We tried everything, but fortune did not smile on us. There is no disgrace in losing to Argentina. You have to look on the bright side: Belgium played well and they got the recognition they deserved. For us, it has been a good competition."

2000

In the game against Brazil, Thomas Müller scored the 2000th goal for Germany's national team. 106 years before, on 5 April 1908, Fritz Becker had chalked up the first goal for the Germans in a match against Switzerland (which they lost 5–3).

◀ Dejected Brazilian players look on as Miroslav Klose (out of shot) scores the second German goal.

Nightmare for Brazil

8 JULY 2014

BRAZIL 1–7 **GERMANY**

OSCAR 90   MÜLLER 11, KLOSE 23, KROOS 24, 26, KHEDIRA 29, SCHÜRRLE 69, 79

BRAZIL NOW HAD a *Mineirazo* to add to the *Maracanazo* of 1950. This was an historic rout. A day of national mourning. The semi-final, played on 8 July in Belo Horizonte, was one of the most remarkable World Cup matches ever played. Brazil were simply humiliated by Germany before 58,000 dumbfounded supporters. The nightmare began when Thomas Müller, unmarked, swept in a corner from Toni Kroos (11'). Between the 23rd and 29th minutes, the Germans added four more goals in just 400 seconds: Miroslav Klose scored after his first shot had rebounded off the goalkeeper, then Kroos scored twice, with a low left-foot shot and after one-two with Sami Khedira, then Khedira himself scored, assisted by Mesut Özil. The score had progressed to 5–0 in just six minutes! Staggering! The Brazilians were in a state of total shock; their central defenders Dante and David Luiz overwhelmed. Things improved marginally for the hosts after the break, but then, in the 69th minute, André Schürrle tapped in a cross from Philipp Lahm, and ten minutes later he scored Germany's seventh with a left-footed bullet into the top corner. Not until the 90th minute did Oscar pull one back with a nice body-swerve to beat Neuer.

A few figures to give a better idea of the scale of this debacle: it was only the second time in history that Brazil had lost a match by six goals (following their 6–0 defeat by Uruguay in 1920); it was the first time Brazil had lost a competitive match at home for 39 years (when they suffered a 3–1 defeat to Peru in the semi-final of the 1975 Copa América at Belo Horizonte). This 7–1 victory equalled Germany's second-highest score in the World Cup, matching their 6–0 win over Mexico in 1978 and just short of their 8–0 thrashing of Saudi Arabia in 2002. Further evidence of Germany's dominance: no team had previously scored seven goals at this stage of the tournament. Without Neymar and their captain, Thiago Silva, Brazil were all at sea, totally overwhelmed by the pressure of the situation, with an ill-balanced, disjointed team in which the forwards contributed little to the defence. "The score does not reflect the difference in quality between the two teams," concluded Dante, the Brazilian. "On the other hand, it perfectly reflects the way in which, psychologically, we approached this World Cup. There was such pressure that we were not prepared to face a serious setback."

Müller's tracksuit top

Tracksuit top worn by German striker Thomas Müller before the semi-final against Brazil.

▲ **FIFA World Football Museum collection.**

"The worst moment in my footballing career."

Luiz Felipe Scolari, the Brazilian manager, after his team's disastrous defeat by Germany

"This evening, I have experienced the worst moment in my footballing career. But life goes on. Who is responsible for this result? I am, of course. We have all played our part in this catastrophe but, in the final analysis, I was the one who decided who should be in the team and what strategy we should adopt. I take responsibility for my decisions," explained the Brazilian manager, Luiz Felipe Scolari, who had led the team to the title in 2002. "We did what we could. We gave our all, but we had to contend with a great German side. We didn't know how to react, once they had opened the scoring. We were disorganized and we panicked. Then it all fell to pieces. Even the Germans cannot really explain what happened. We shall need to come to terms with this result. To the Brazilian people, I just want to say: forgive us for this ignominious performance."

Klose makes history

By scoring in the 23rd minute against Brazil, Miroslav Klose became the top scorer in the history of the World Cup. With 16 goals to his credit, the German centre-forward pulled ahead of Ronaldo (15), Gerd Müller (14) and Just Fontaine (13). Klose set this record over four competitions, in all of which Germany reached at least the semi-finals. He scored five goals in 2002, five in 2006 and four in 2010, the Lazio striker scored a further two in Brazil, against Ghana at the group stage (2–2), with his first touch of the ball as a substitute, and in this semi-final. Having featured in 24 World Cup matches, including the 2014 Final, he was also the second most capped player in this competition, after Lothar Matthäus (25). Following the 2014 World Cup, he retired from international football, having scored a total of 71 goals in 137 appearances during the 13 years he was part of the national team. A final amazing statistic: Germany never lost a match in which Klose scored (49 games in all). "Of course, it's a very special moment for me," explained Klose, aged 36. "There's no doubt about it, especially as we have won the world title, which is really the cherry on the cake. But the main thing is to have helped the team."

Dutch out on penalties

9 JULY 2014

NETHERLANDS **0–0** ARGENTINA
A.E.T.

✗⊙✗⊙ 2–4 ⊙⊙⊙⊙

A FREE-KICK by Lionel Messi, safely dealt with by Jasper Cillessen (15'), and a strike by Arjen Robben in the closing seconds, kept out by Javier Mascherano... the 90 minutes of normal time offered little in the way of excitement. In the 115th minute, Rodrigo Palacio, receiving an overhead pass from Maxi Rodríguez, headed the ball but could not get enough power on it. During the penalty shoot-out, Sergio Romero managed to block Ron Vlaar's shot, then made a perfect dive to keep out the strike of Wesley Sneijder, the third Dutch penalty-taker. For their part, all four of the Argentinians (Messi, Ezequiel Garay, Sergio Agüero and Maxi Rodríguez) found the net.

▶ Lionel Messi sneaks past Nigel de Jong and Ron Vlaar in the semi-final between Argentina and the Netherlands.

▶ Arjen Robben battles Argentina's Pablo Zabaleta and Lucas Biglia.

▲ Germany's Mario Götze scores the winning goal of the 2014 FIFA World Cup Final against Argentina.

Götze wins it for Germany

13 JULY 2014

GERMANY ▬ **1-0** ▬ **ARGENTINA**
A.E.T

GÖTZE 113

THIS WAS A RECORD THIRD meeting of these two teams in a World Cup Final, following on from 1986 (3–2 for Argentina) and 1990 (1–0 in favour of Germany). Since their display of fireworks against Brazil in the semi-final, Joachim Löw's men had been the favourites for the game at the Maracanã. But, even with Ángel Di María out injured, Alejandro Sabella could count on the individual talents of Lionel Messi and Gonzalo Higuaín and a robust defence (only three goals conceded in six matches). The first real opportunity fell to Argentina, following a risky back-header by Toni Kroos: Higuaín was through on Manuel Neuer but shot wide (20'). The Germans responded with a strike by André Schürrle, causing Sergio Romero to make a flying save (37'). In the 40th minute, Messi found some space in the German penalty area, but Jérôme Boateng saved on the line. Finally, in stoppage time at the end of the first half, following a corner, Benedikt Höwedes rattled Romero's post. In the second-half, Messi just failed to open the scoring: having found a way behind the German defence,

Messi pulled his shot across the face of goal (47'). Subsequent German attacks lacked precision, Kroos in particular missing the target (81').

In extra-time, Rodrigo Palacio failed to deliver the knockout blow, after Mats Hummels had misjudged an overhead cross. Palacio only had Neuer to beat, but lifted his lob wide of the goal. The day was finally won for Germany when Mario Götze, coming on in the 88th minute, controlled the ball with his chest and volleyed the ball into the net with his left foot (1-0, 113'). The Bayern Munich centre-forward had scored the biggest goal of his career to hand Germany a fourth world title. "We played attractive football. In all seven matches, we performed best. The boys have developed an amazing team spirit. They have fantastic technical qualities, and the determination to do all it takes," enthused Joachim Löw, who had built his team around a number of players (Neuer, Höwedes, Boateng, Khedira, Özil and Hummels) who had been in his 2009 European Under-21 Championship side.

Lahm retires on a high note

The World Cup Final marked the end of Philipp Lahm's career with the national team. The 30-year old Germany captain played his 113th and final game for his country. Only Lothar Matthäus (150), Miroslav Klose (137) and Lukas Podolski (116) had earned more caps. The Bayern Munich right-back thus became the fourth German captain to lift the World Cup trophy, after Fritz Walter (1954), Franz Beckenbauer (1974) and Matthäus (1990). "When the referee blew the final whistle, I felt tremendous relief, as if all the German defeats of previous years had suddenly been wiped out," explained Lahm, who had played in the 2006 and 2010 tournaments. "The two hours which followed were unforgettable."

◀ Bastian Schweinsteiger tries to console Lionel Messi.

Lahm's armband

Captain's armband worn by German defender Philipp Lahm in the final.

▲ **FIFA World Football Museum collection.**

18

Germany's 18 goals in these finals were the most by any team since Brazil's 19 in 1970.

▲ Lionel Messi and Manuel Neuer receive their prizes: best player for Messi, and best keeper for Neuer.

Messi, the uncrowned king

BRILLIANT for much of the tournament (four goals, one assist), Lionel Messi was unable to swing it for Argentina in the final. In the first half, the Barcelona player got in behind the German defence and controlled the ball with his head to get round Hummels, but Boateng saved on the line. Just after the break, in his favourite position, breaking through on the left, he failed to find the target, his cross-goal shot grazing Neuer's far post. Finally, 15 minutes from the end, he rolled another shot wide. Closely marked by the Germans, who put several players on him, the Argentinian captain was a constant threat. But in the absence of Di María, he bore the entire responsibility for the Argentinian attack. It came as scant consolation for his disappointment, but the Barcelona star was awarded the adidas Golden Ball trophy for best player of the tournament: "At such times, nothing else matters. The only thing we wanted was to lift the Cup and bring it back to Argentina to celebrate with our people. We deserved a bit more after the way we played. It's painful to lose like that. Maybe Germany had more possession," he added, "but we created the most dangerous situations. The fault lies with us, the forwards, as we had three clear opportunities: me, Gonzalo Higuaín and Rodrigo Palacio. But we didn't convert any of them. We shall regret it all our lives." Messi had started the tournament well, scoring four goals in the three group matches. But he was not as effective in the knockout rounds. Argentina scored just twice in four games, neither of which came from Messi. There were positives, however: "It has been a long time since Argentina got beyond the quarter-finals. On this occasion, we reached the Final, and that is a considerable achievement, but it does not mitigate the disappointment of not winning."

PLAY-OFF FOR THIRD PLACE

The nightmare continues

12 JULY 2014

BRAZIL 0–3 NETHERLANDS

V. PERSIE 3 (PEN)
BLIND 17
WIJNALDUM 90+1

Not yet recovered from their semi-final defeat, the Brazilians conceded a goal in the third minute, following a foul by Thiago Silva on Arjen Robben, who was through on goal. Although last defender in this instance, the captain of the *Seleçao* was shown only a yellow card. Robin van Persie converted the penalty. In the 17th minute, Daley Blind doubled the scoreline with a right-footed shot. The Dutch added a third from a counter-attack that ended with Georginio Wijnaldum scoring what was the tenth goal Brazil had conceded in just five days.

2018

The first World Cup to be held in Eastern Europe was won by a Western European country for an unprecedented fourth consecutive tournament. The winner's curse struck again with Germany's first-round elimination, while Croatia played three periods of extra time en route to their first appearance in the Final. There they lost 4-2 to France, who won the trophy for the second time in 20 years.

A World Cup to remember

◀ France celebrate after beating Croatia in the 2018 FIFA World Cup Final.

▼ Russian fans in Moscow celebrate after their team's victory over Spain.

RUSSIA 2018 was hailed as the best World Cup for a generation – a festival of football marked by some outstanding matches and enjoyed by fans who had descended on Russia from all over the world. The colour, atmosphere and positive impact of the finals was a welcome contrast to the build up to the event, which was rarely out of the headlines from December 2010 when Russia was named as hosts. It wasn't just the FIFA investigation into the voting process which provided a focus for the international media. There were also fears that Russia's notorious hooligans would blight the tournament, especially after the trouble they had been involved with at the Euro 2016 finals in France. There was also the continuing saga of state-sponsored doping that had seen Russian athletes banned from the 2016 Olympics in Rio. And just before the finals, frosty diplomatic relations between Russia and a number of countries in the West, following a case of poisoning in the English city of Salisbury, briefly raised the spectre of a boycott. None of these fears materialised and the Russian people proved to be the perfect hosts.

RUSSIA 2018

Story of the qualifiers

Buffon's tears

GIANLUIGI BUFFON was one match away from becoming the first player to be selected for six World Cups, but in a turn-up for the books the Italians were knocked out by Sweden in the play-offs. They had been drawn in the same qualifying group as Spain and had finished as runners-up and in the first leg of the play-off lost 1-0 to a Jakob Johansson goal in Stockholm, but try as they might they could not break down a stubborn Swedish defence in Milan and were out – the first time they had not reached the finals since 1958. There were debut qualifications for Iceland and Panama, taking the number of nations to have qualified since 1930 to 79. Iceland topped a group that included eventual Finalists Croatia. There were dramatic scenes in Panama City where a Román Torres goal saw Panama upset the odds, helped by Trinidad & Tobago's victory over the USA, who failed to qualify for the finals for the first time since 1986. In Asia, Syria almost made it to Russia, despite the devastating effects of the civil war tearing the country apart, but their dream was brought to an end in a play-off against Australia.

▶ A dejected Gianluigi Buffon after Italy's play-off defeat against Sweden.

Group stage

GROUP A		GROUP B		GROUP C		GROUP D		GROUP E		GROUP F		GROUP G		GROUP H	
RUS 5-0 KSA		POR 3-3 ESP		FRA 2-1 AUS		ARG 1-1 ISL		BRA 1-1 SUI		GER 0-1 MEX		BEL 3-0 PAN		POL 1-2 SEN	
EGY 0-1 URU		MAR 0-1 IRN		PER 0-1 DEN		CRO 2-0 NGA		CRC 0-1 SRB		SWE 1-0 KOR		TUN 1-2 ENG		COL 1-2 JPN	
RUS 3-1 EGY		POR 1-0 MAR		FRA 1-0 PER		ARG 0-3 CRO		BRA 2-0 CRC		GER 2-1 SWE		BEL 5-2 TUN		POL 0-3 COL	
URU 1-0 KSA		IRN 0-1 ESP		DEN 1-1 AUS		NGA 2-0 ISL		SRB 1-2 SUI		KOR 1-2 MEX		ENG 6-1 PAN		JPN 2-2 SEN	
URU 3-0 RUS		IRN 1-1 POR		DEN 0-0 FRA		NGA 1-2 ARG		SRB 0-2 BRA		KOR 2-0 GER		ENG 0-1 BEL		JPN 0-1 POL	
KSA 2-1 EGY		ESP 2-2 MAR		AUS 0-2 PER		ISL 1-2 CRO		SUI 2-2 CRC		MEX 0-3 SWE		PAN 1-2 TUN		SEN 0-1 COL	

	W	D	L	+	–	PTS
URU	3	0	0	5	0	9
RUS	2	0	1	8	4	6
KSA	1	0	2	2	7	3
EGY	0	0	3	2	6	0

	W	D	L	+	–	PTS
ESP	1	2	0	6	5	5
POR	1	2	0	5	4	5
IRN	1	1	1	2	2	4
MAR	0	1	2	2	4	1

	W	D	L	+	–	PTS
FRA	2	1	0	3	1	7
DEN	1	2	0	2	1	5
PER	1	0	2	2	2	3
AUS	0	1	2	2	5	1

	W	D	L	+	–	PTS
CRO	3	0	0	7	1	9
ARG	1	1	1	3	5	4
NGA	1	0	2	3	4	3
ISL	0	1	2	2	5	1

	W	D	L	+	–	PTS
BRA	2	1	0	5	1	7
SUI	1	2	0	5	4	5
SRB	1	0	2	2	4	3
CRC	0	1	2	2	5	1

	W	D	L	+	–	PTS
SWE	2	0	1	5	2	6
MEX	2	0	1	3	4	6
KOR	1	0	2	3	3	3
GER	1	0	2	2	4	3

	W	D	L	+	–	PTS
BEL	3	0	0	9	2	9
ENG	2	0	1	8	3	6
TUN	1	0	2	5	8	3
PAN	0	0	3	2	11	0

	W	D	L	+	–	PTS
COL	2	0	1	5	2	6
JPN	1	1	1	4	4	4
SEN	1	1	1	4	4	4
POL	1	0	2	2	5	3

Fair play points: Japan -4, Senegal -6

Knockout stages

ROUND OF 16	
URU 2-1 POR	
FRA 4-3 ARG	

ROUND OF 16	
ESP 1-1 (3-4) RUS	
CRO 1-1 (3-2) DEN	

ROUND OF 16	
BRA 2-0 MEX	
BEL 3-2 JPN	

ROUND OF 16	
SWE 1-0 SUI	
COL 1-1 (3-4) ENG	

QUARTER-FINAL	
URU 0-2 FRA	

QUARTER-FINAL	
RUS 2-2 (3-4) CRO	

QUARTER-FINAL	
BRA 1-2 BEL	

QUARTER-FINAL	
SWE 0-2 ENG	

SEMI-FINAL	
FRA 1-0 BEL	

SEMI-FINAL	
CRO 2-1 A.E.T. ENG	

PLAY-OFF FOR THIRD PLACE

BEL 2-0 ENG

FINAL

FRA 4-2 CRO

ARG AUS BEL BRA COL CRC CRO DEN
EGY ENG ESP FRA GER ISL IRN JPN
KOR KSA MEX MAR NGA PAN PER POL
POR RUS SEN SRB SWE SUI TUN URU

32 TEAMS

64
MATCHES PLAYED

219   4
CARDS

3 031 768
SPECTATORS

ZABIVAKA
OFFICIAL MASCOT

FIFA WORLD CUP RUSSIA 2018
OFFICIAL LOGO

FRANCE
WINNERS

×6

HARRY KANE
LEADING GOALSCORER

2.64
AVERAGE GOALS
PER MATCH

TELSTAR 18
OFFICIAL BALL

Host cities and stadiums

Russia's stadium transformation

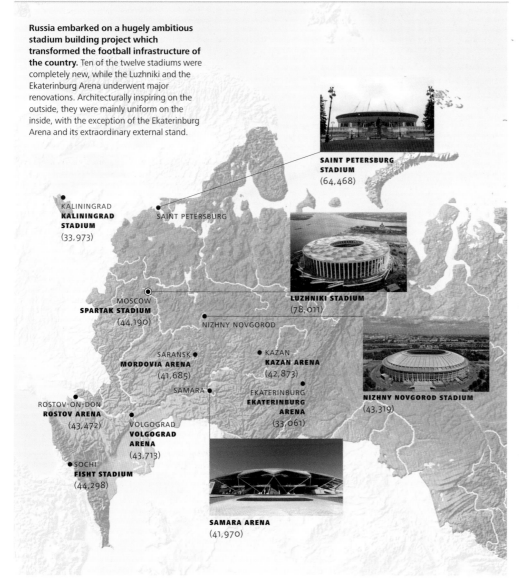

Russia embarked on a hugely ambitious stadium building project which transformed the football infrastructure of the country. Ten of the twelve stadiums were completely new, while the Luzhniki and the Ekaterinburg Arena underwent major renovations. Architecturally inspiring on the outside, they were mainly uniform on the inside, with the exception of the Ekaterinburg Arena and its extraordinary external stand.

SAINT PETERSBURG
SAINT PETERSBURG STADIUM
(64,468)

KALININGRAD
KALININGRAD STADIUM
(33,973)

MOSCOW
SPARTAK STADIUM
(44,190)

LUZHNIKI STADIUM
(78,011)

NIZHNY NOVGOROD

SARANSK
MORDOVIA ARENA
(41,685)

KAZAN
KAZAN ARENA
(42,873)

SAMARA

ROSTOV-ON-DON
ROSTOV ARENA
(43,472)

EKATERINBURG
EKATERINBURG ARENA
(33,061)

NIZHNY NOVGOROD STADIUM
(43,319)

VOLGOGRAD
VOLGOGRAD ARENA
(43,713)

SOCHI
FISHT STADIUM
(44,298)

SAMARA ARENA
(41,970)

Regulations

Innovations - VAR

Russia 2018 was a tournament of innovations. The world was introduced to the video assistant referee (VAR). The referee on the pitch retained the final decision on all matters but he could receive advice where there was a "clear and obvious error" or a "serious missed incident" in the following key areas: goals, penalties, direct red cards and in cases of mistaken identity. The historic decision to use VAR at the 2018 FIFA World Cup Russia was taken by the FIFA Council at its meeting in Bogotá in March 2018 following the approval to include VAR in the Laws of the Game at the 132nd Annual General Meeting of The IFAB a few weeks earlier. The success and acceptance of VAR represented a new era for football, with video assistance for referees helping to increase integrity and fairness in the game. The VAR team in Russia was based at the International Broadcast Centre in Moscow where they had full access to the camera footage being recorded by the outside broadcast units in the all the stadiums.

▲ VAR operation room at the International Broadcasting Centre in Moscow.

Cheryshev on fire!

14 JUNE 2018

RUSSIA 5-0 **SAUDI ARABIA**

GAZINSKY 12, CHERYSHEV 43, 90+1,
DZYUBA 71, GOLOVIN 90+4

THERE WERE MANY around the world – including many of the Russians in the stadium, who thought Saudi Arabia could well beat a Russian team that was three places below them in the FIFA/Coca-Cola World Ranking. But the Russians rose splendidly to the occasion. Iury Gazinsky headed home on 12 minutes to set the tone for the afternoon (1-0) and Denis Cheryshev played the game of his life, scoring twice in a 5-0 win. It was the biggest win in an opening game since Italy beat the USA 7-1 in 1934 and it matched Brazil's 5-0 win over Mexico in 1954. It was a sensational start to the tournament.

A World Cup epic

15 JUNE 2018

PORTUGAL 3–3 **SPAIN**

CRISTIANO RONALDO 4 (PEN), 44, 88   DIEGO COSTA 24, 55, NACHO 58

JUST TWICE IN HISTORY had the European champions gone on to win the World Cup two years later – Germany in 1974 and Spain in 2010 – but after a dazzling display by Cristiano Ronaldo in this match, the Portuguese seemed determined to join them. This was a riveting game that ebbed and flowed, right from Ronaldo's early penalty just four minutes in (1-0). Diego Costa was a constant thorn in Portugal's side, twice equalising for Spain, and Portugal rode their luck at times. It's not often that David De Gea gifts a goal to you, in what was the first of a number of goalkeeping howlers in this World Cup, but Ronaldo was a grateful recipient just before half-time (2-1). Spain had five World Cup winners on the pitch and they took the lead early in the second half, Nacho's superb effort worthy of any World Cup (2-3). With the Spanish heading for a win, Ronaldo stepped up to the mark. Whisper it quietly, his record at free kicks is rather hit and miss, but he nailed this one with style and a World Cup epic finished 3-3.

▶ Yury Zhirkov's corner led to the opening goal of Russia 2018.

◀ Cristiano Ronaldo prepares to take an 88th-minute free-kick against Spain. He scored to make it 3-3 and complete his hat-trick.

"I always believe in myself."

Cristiano Ronaldo

Spain in crisis

The sensational start to the World Cup on the pitch was matched by events off it. Before a ball had even been kicked, the Spanish camp was plunged into crisis when Real Madrid announced that Spain coach Julen Lopetegui would replace Zinédine Zidane after the World Cup. The Spanish FA were incensed at the timing and the fact that they had not been consulted, and on the day the finals kicked off, Lopetegui was sacked and replaced by Fernando Hierro.

◀ Fernando Hierro (right) stepped in as Spain coach after Julen Lopetegui (left) was sacked the day before the tournament.

▲ More than 40,000 Peruvian fans travelled to Russia for the tournament.

Fans from the Americas

The sheer number of fans from the Americas was impressive. They came from Peru, Argentina, Uruguay, Brazil, Colombia, Costa Rica, Panama and Mexico, and they came in their thousands. It had been a similar story four years earlier in Brazil, but this was unique. In the stadiums they heavily outnumbered their European counterparts, and they transformed the streets of the cities in which they were playing into an oasis of colour and song.

Mbappé's shirt

Shirt worn by French player Kylian Mbappé during
his World Cup debut against Australia.

▲ **FIFA World Football Museum collection.**

VAR takes off

**There were 20 VAR reviews at Russia 2018, while 455 incidents in
total were checked in the background. This led to 17 match-chang-
ing decisions being corrected, and the consensus was that this big
leap forward in the Laws of the Game was a success.** The number of
penalties awarded in Russia increased to 29 from the 13 given in Brazil as a
result of the closer scrutiny, with there also being an increase also in the
number of the goals coming from set pieces.

A game-changer

16 JUNE 2018

FRANCE ▌▌ 2-1 🇦🇺 **AUSTRALIA**

GRIEZMANN 58 (PEN), BEHICH (O.G.) 81   JEDINAK 62 (PEN)

AS A GAME it wasn't much to write
home about, but this match
launched a new technological age
at the World Cup. In Brazil four years
earlier, the French had been the first to
benefit from goal-line technology (GLT),
and here they were the first to benefit from
the video assistant referee (VAR). N'Golo
Kanté found Paul Pogba in the centre circle,
who threaded a beautiful long pass into
the path of Antoine Griezmann on the
edge of the penalty area. A challenge by
Joshua Risdon saw Griezmann claim a
penalty, but Uruguayan referee Andrés
Cunha waved play on for 24 seconds
before stopping the game. It was the first
of 20 visits by a referee at this World Cup
to the VAR booth on the touch line, and
a minute later Cunha gave the penalty,
allowing Griezmann to score the first goal
awarded by VAR past Aussie keeper Maty
Ryan (1-0). Cunha didn't need any help
four minutes later when Samuel Umtiti
inexplicably handled an Aaron Mooy free
kick which went over his head and was on
its way out of play. Mile Jedinak, the first
player to captain Australia at two World
Cups, scored the second penalty of the
match (1-1). France eventually won the
match thanks to a combination of tech-
nologies, their second goal confirmed by
GLT after a deflected shot from Pogba hit
the underside of the bar and came down
just behind the line (2-1).

▶ Referee Andrés Cunha
makes the first visit to the
VAR booth in World Cup
history.

◣ One of six yellow cards
shown to Senegal. It led
to their elimination.

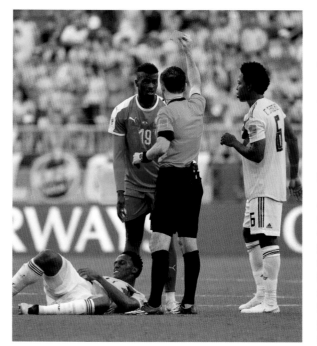

Senegal out on yellow cards

28 JUNE 2018

SENEGAL 🇸🇳 0-1 🇨🇴 **COLOMBIA**

MINA 74

SENEGAL PLAYED some adventurous
football in Russia, and after winning
their opening match against Poland
(1-2) and drawing with Japan in their second
(2-2), they were in a strong position going
into their final match against Colombia. They
were awarded a penalty after 16 minutes,
but following a review by VAR, referee Milo-
rad Mažić deemed it a fair challenge by
Dávinson Sánchez. With 16 minutes of the
game left, Yerry Mina scored a goal that
changed the whole dynamic of the group
(0-1). With Japan losing 1-0 to Poland, both
the Japanese and Senegalese now had identical records. Crucially, however, Japan had
picked up two fewer bookings, a new
system introduced at this World Cup to
separate teams with identical records. While
Senegal pushed for a goal, the Japanese
concentrated on not conceding, either a
goal or any more bookings. It paid off and
Senegal's exit meant there were no African
representatives in the round of 16 since the
current format was adopted in 1986.

Halldórsson saves the day

16 JUNE 2018

ARGENTINA 1-1 **ICELAND**

AGÜERO 19 FINNBOGASON 23

THIS WAS ARGENTINA'S 78TH MATCH at the World Cup and Iceland's first, but the debutants more than held their own. Sergio Agüero gave Argentina the lead (1-0) but that lasted just four minutes, Gylfi Sigurðsson's ball into the crowded box finding Alfreð Finnbogason, who scored Iceland's first-ever World Cup goal (1-1). The match will be remembered for a penalty in the second half. Iceland goalkeeper Hannes Halldórsson is a film producer by trade and can count writing his country's Eurovision Song Contest entry in 2012 amongst his list of achievements, but saving Lionel Messi's penalty will rank at the top of that list. Iceland defended deep but held on for an historic draw.

The gloves that saved a Messi penalty

Iceland goalkeeper Hannes Halldórsson wore these gloves against Argentina. His penalty save earned Iceland a draw.

▲ **FIFA World Football Museum collection.**

▲ Hannes Halldórsson saves a penalty from Lionel Messi during Iceland's World Cup debut.

▶ Tunisia's Fakhreddine Ben Youssef scores the 2,500th goal in the history of the World Cup.

123

The number of players under contract with English clubs to appear at Russia 2018. Spain provided the second highest number with 81, while Germany was third with 67. Manchester City was the most represented club among the 32 squads in Russia with 16 players.

◀ Rafael Márquez has captained Mexico in five World Cups.

▼ The fastest booking in World Cup history. Against Sweden, Mexico's Jesús Gallardo was shown the yellow card after just 27 seconds.

2,500

Fakhreddine Ben Youssef's equalising goal for Tunisia against Panama was the 2,500th goal in the history of the World Cup finals. Other landmark goals include the first, scored by Lucien Laurent in 1930, and the 1,000th, a penalty scored by Rob Rensenbrink in 1978.

Osorio, the master tactician

Mexico travelled to Russia with the Colombian Juan Carlos Osorio as their coach, one of the most astute tactical students of recent years. It was his thorough planning – and constant reference to his notebooks – that enabled Mexico to pull off their stunning 1-0 victory over defending champions Germany in their opening match. In the 74th minute of that game, Osorio sent on Rafael Márquez who thus joined an exclusive club of three players to have appeared in five World Cups, alongside compatriot Antonio Carbajal, and Lothar Matthäus. Remarkably, he also captained the Mexicans in all five tournaments.

The Love Train

This was the World Cup of set pieces. 37% of the goals originated from a set piece and the English were the masters at it. Nine of their 12 goals came this way, a deliberate tactical ploy by England coach Gareth Southgate. He realised that as his team were rather lacking in the creative midfield department, they would need to maximise set play opportunities when they arose. The "Love Train", a term popularised by former England coach Glenn Hoddle in his TV commentaries during the finals, proved particularly effective at corners and free kicks.

◄ Down and out. Germany contemplate their shock World Cup exit after their 2-0 defeat by South Korea.

◄ Former England manager Glenn Hoddle baptised this set-piece formation the "Love Train".

◄ At 45, Essam El Hadary set a new record for the oldest player to take part in a World Cup. He also saved a penalty against Saudi Arabia.

Egypt, Salah and El Hadary

It had been a season like no other for Egyptian forward Mohamed Salah. He was the top scorer in African qualifying for the World Cup and had scored an astonishing 44 goals for Liverpool in a season that had seen them reach the UEFA Champions League Final, a match in which a Sergio Ramos challenge had left him nursing a shoulder injury. The whole of Egypt was on tenterhooks in the following days, but although he did make the Egyptian World Cup squad, he missed the first game against Uruguay and was well below par in the defeats at the hands of Russia and Saudi Arabia – despite scoring twice. But there was one thing for Egyptians to celebrate: goalkeeper Essam El Hadary became the oldest player ever to play at a World Cup. The 45-year-old even saved a penalty.

Löw's long-term view

"Until quite recently we have been consistent, always among the final four. Now we are out which is an absolute sadness and disappointment but we have young players who are very talented. This has happened to nations before."

The winner's curse strikes again!

27 JUNE 2018

SOUTH KOREA ⊙ 2–0 ▬ **GERMANY**

KIM YOUNG GWON 90+3, SON HEUNG MIN 90+6

ACTUALLY, GERMANY COULD COUNT THEMSELVES UNLUCKY. They had more possession and passing success than everyone bar Spain at this World Cup and they topped the charts for breaking into their opponent's penalty area as well as for the number of crosses per match. But they scored just two goals in three matches, one of them a dramatic free-kick winner deep into injury time against Sweden, a veritable Kroos missile. That goal looked as if it might rescue their campaign after their opening game defeat at the hands of Mexico, but they didn't count on the South Koreans playing the match of their lives. The permutations to progress from the group were endless but when Sweden took a commanding second-half lead against Mexico, Germany simply had to win. They threw everything at the Koreans, but Jo Hyeon Woo had a great game in goal, brilliantly saving Leon Goretzka's header just after half-time. Mario Gómez, Marco Reus, Timo Werner and Mats Hummels all had chances that they should have put away. Then three minutes into injury time, the Koreans had a goal disallowed for offside, a decision that was correctly overturned by VAR (1-0). And with Germany desperately pushing forward and goalkeeper Manuel Neuer almost playing in midfield, Son Heung Min put a long ball forward by Ju Se Jong into an empty net to seal an historic victory for South Korea (2-0). Both teams were out but Germany followed in the footsteps of Italy in 1950, Brazil in 1966, France in 2002, Italy in 2010 and Spain in 2014 as defending champions knocked out in the first round. This was only Germany's second first-round exit, and their first since 1938. As 1938 was played purely as a knockout tournament, remarkably, it meant that Russia 2018 was the first time that they had failed to get past the group stage at a World Cup.

19

The age of French teenager Kylian Mbappé. His two goals against Argentina saw him become the first teenager since Pelé in 1958 to score twice in a World Cup match. At these finals, Mbappé also became the youngest player to appear for France at the World Cup.

Adios Leo

30 JUNE 2018

FRANCE ▮ **4–3** ▭ **ARGENTINA**

GRIEZMANN 13 (PEN), PAVARD 57, MBAPPÉ 64, 68   DI MARÍA 41, MERCADO 48, AGÜERO 90+3

◤ Benjamin Pavard scores a spectacular goal for France against Argentina.

▲ Lionel Messi bows out of the World Cup.

THIS WAS ONE OF THE GREAT WORLD CUP GAMES which seemed to mark a changing of the guard. Lionel Messi had cut an unhappy figure for much of the tournament and up against him was the irrepressible French teenager Kylian Mbappé. Didier Deschamps was rewriting the modern football coaching rule book with the French sitting deep and maintaining their shape. There was no reliance on possession and pressing – tiki-taka this was not. Instead, the French were effective at set pieces and broke from defence quickly and effectively. As Deschamps pointed out, "teams who were in control of the game, and in possession of the ball, were punished on quick counter-attacks". And that's exactly what happened to Argentina for Benjamin Pavard's goal (2-2) and Mbappé's second (4-2). Pavard's took a mere ten touches and 19 seconds from goalkeeper to goal; Mbappé's just nine touches and 12 seconds. Argentina were simply blown away when it mattered most. They scored twice, either side of half-time, but the French were behind for just nine minutes – the only time they trailed in the tournament. This was Mbappé's day. His burst of speed had won the penalty after 13 minutes, while his first goal came from a sensational dribble (3-2).

Adeus Cristiano

30 JUNE 2018

URUGUAY ▬ **2–1** ▮ **PORTUGAL**

CAVANI 7, 62   PEPE 55

▲ Cristiano Ronaldo helps an injured Edinson Cavani during the match between Uruguay and Portugal.

IT WASN'T A GOOD DAY for the two great stars of world football. Earlier, Lionel Messi had said goodbye to the World Cup in Kazan. Later that evening it was the turn of Cristiano Ronaldo in Sochi, and gone, perhaps, was the last realistic chance for either to win the one major trophy that has eluded them. This match turned into the Edinson Cavani – Luis Suárez show. After seven minutes, Cavani switched the play to the left wing to find Suárez, who took three touches before finding Cavani unmarked at the far post to head in (1-0). Portugal equalised from a short corner taken by João Mário to Raphaël Guerreiro, who swung the ball in to Pepe, unmarked on the edge of the six-yard box, to head past Fernando Muslera (1-1). Parity lasted just seven minutes before Muslera launched a long ball upfield towards Rodrigo Bentancur. He passed to Cavani, whose first-time effort beat Rui Patrício (2-1). European champions Portugal were out.

223 secs

That's how long it took for Denmark and Croatia to score the fastest two goals from the start of a game in World Cup history. The Danes went ahead after 55 seconds through Mathias Jørgensen, but Mario Mandžukić equalised for Croatia after three minutes and 43 seconds. And that's how the match finished. The time was 9 seconds quicker than the two goals scored in the Argentina - Nigeria match in 2014, and it also beat Austria - Czechoslovakia in 1954 and Soviet Union - Hungary in 1986.

The death knell for tiki-taka?

1 JULY 2018

SPAIN 🇪🇸 1–1 🇷🇺 RUSSIA
A.E.T.

IGNASHEVICH (O.G.) 12   DZYUBA 41 (PEN)

⊘⊘✕⊘✕ 3–4 ⊘⊘⊘⊘

Russia 2018 was not the best advert for possession football. Sitting in front of a massed defence while trying to unpick it had little success at this World Cup. In a tense game at the Luzhniki, Spain succumbed to a determined Russian side for whom goalkeeper Igor Akinfeev was the hero with two saves in the penalty shoot-out – the captain writing himself into Russian footballing folklore in their long tradition of heroic goalkeepers such as Lev Yashin.

1,031

The number of passes completed by Spain out of 1,137 attempted during their match against hosts Russia. And still they lost the match! In comparison, Russia completed just 204. Spain also had 74% possession of the ball, but all to no avail. The Russians were certainly more active on the pitch, running 145,786 metres in total, compared to the 137,009 metres of the Spanish. In the end it all came down to penalties.

▼ Nacer Chadli scores an injury-time winner for Belgium against Japan.

◥ England celebrate their first-ever penalty shoot-out win at a World Cup.

England win a shoot-out at last!

3 JULY 2018

COLOMBIA ▬ 1–1 ✚ ENGLAND
A.E.T.

MINA 90+3   KANE 57 (PEN)

⊘⊘⊘✕✕ 3–4 ⊘⊘✕⊘⊘

It was fourth time lucky for England as they put an end to their World Cup penalty shoot-out hoodoo after losing on spot kicks in 1990, 1998 and 2006. In a tempestuous game, the English took the lead from a penalty after 57 minutes, Harry Kane's sixth goal of a tournament in which he finished as the leading scorer (0-1). It was a game of few chances and England looked to have secured only their fifth win in the knockout phase since an Englishman last won the Golden Boot – Gary Lineker in 1986 – but they were denied by a Yerry Mina goal deep into injury time (1-1). In the shoot-out, it looked as if England would fail again when Jordan Henderson's effort was saved by David Ospina, the latest in the line of England number eights to miss a penalty, but first Mateus Uribe and then Carlos Bacca failed from the spot, leaving Eric Dier to win it and spark wild celebrations both on the pitch and back in England.

Belgium stun Japan

2 JULY 2018

BELGIUM ▮▮ 3–2 ● JAPAN

VERTONGHEN 69, FELLAINI 74, CHADLI 90+4   HARAGUCHI 48, INUI 52

A MATCH THAT WILL BE REMEMBERED for a long time thanks to a sensational second half. Japan surged into a comfortable two-goal lead, only for Belgium to stage possibly the greatest comeback in the knockout rounds since Portugal against North Korea in 1966. Eden Hazard and Kevin De Bruyne were key to this drama, but only after Belgium were caught by two sucker punches within seven minutes of the restart, the first from Genki Haraguchi (1-0), the second a 25-yard belter from Takashi Inui (2-0). Belgium were in trouble. Then, with 21 minutes left on the clock, the first of two corners in four minutes which led to goals – a looping header by Jan Vertonghen (1-2) and a second from Marouane Fellaini (2-2). There were just 33 seconds of injury time left when Belgium scored a contender for goal of the tournament. Thibaut Courtois rolled the ball to De Bruyne, who advanced into the Japan half and sent a perfectly timed pass to Thomas Meunier on the right. His first-time pass across the penalty area found Nacer Chadli, who scored with 20 seconds to spare (3-2). Although he didn't touch the ball, Romelu Lukaku made the goal possible, his clever running pulling the Japanese out of position.

7

Mexico fell in the last 16 for the seventh successive World Cup, a record unlikely ever to be beaten, unless the Mexicans themselves extend the record at future World Cups. In that time they have lost to Bulgaria (on penalties), Germany, the USA, Argentina (twice), the Netherlands and now Brazil.

Tie worn by Roberto Martínez

The Spaniard Roberto Martínez took Belgium to their best ever finish at a World Cup.

▲ **FIFA World Football Museum collection.**

0

With Germany bowing out in the group stage and Argentina in the round of 16, the quarter-finals had no representative from the Final of the previous World Cup for only the second time since 1966. The other occasion had been in 2010 when both Italy and France had been knocked out at the group stage.

◀ Danijel Subašić saves his fourth penalty of the World Cup against Russia. He had earlier saved three against Denmark.

▼ Brazil's Fernandinho (17) scores an own goal against Belgium.

A thriller in Sochi

7 JULY 2018		
RUSSIA	2–2 A.E.T.	CROATIA
CHERYSHEV 31, MÁRIO FERNANDES 115		KRAMARIĆ 39, VIDA 101

✗⦿✗⦿⦿ 3–4 ⦿✗⦿⦿⦿

I N A PULSATING QUARTER-FINAL IN SOCHI, the never-say-die attitude of both Russia and Croatia was illustrated once again as both were forced to endure extra time and penalties for the second game in a row. It had been Denis Cheryshev who had first set alight Russian hopes in this tournament in their opening match against Saudi Arabia. Here, he had the hosts dreaming of a place in the semi-finals with an opening goal of supreme quality, unleashing a perfectly placed effort from 25 yards out that gave Danijel Subašić in the Croatian goal no chance (1-0). But as they proved time and again at these finals, this was a Croatia team that just didn't know when it was beaten. From a goal kick, they broke down the left and when Mario Mandžukić on the edge of the six-yard box pulled the ball back and across the goal, Andrej Kramarić was there to head home (1-1). Russia had been in the lead for just eight minutes.

In the second half, Ivan Perišić hit the inside of the post but no-one was there to finish it off as the rebound ran invitingly across the face of goal. In extra time, set pieces were always likely to make the

difference and after 11 minutes the Croatians took the lead from a Luka Modrić corner. Domagoj Vida's header didn't seem to have much power but it evaded Mário Fernandes and Fedor Smolov while Igor Akinfeev remained rooted to the spot in the Russian goal (1-2). It would have been a disappointing way for the hosts to exit the tournament but they too were saved by a set piece after Josip Pivarić handled the ball on the corner of the penalty area. Alan Dzagoev's free kick found Fernandes, who headed home unopposed to bring the scores level with his first goal for his adopted nation (2-2).

So another penalty shoot-out for both teams. Smolov got the Russians off to the worst possible start with a weak effort down the middle which left Subašić with the time to readjust his dive to save. Both keepers had been heroes in their previous shoot-outs and when Akinfeev tipped Mateo Kovačić's effort past the post, Russian hopes were revived. But with the very next kick Mário Fernandes pulled the ball wide of the left post and for the second game running Ivan Rakitić scored the winner.

Belgium dazzle in Kazan

6 JULY 2018		
BRAZIL	1–2	BELGIUM
RENATO AUGUSTO 76		FERNANDINHO (O.G.) 13, DE BRUYNE 31

Brazil were blown away by Belgium in one of the great first-half performances at any World Cup. Thirteen minutes in, a superb pass by Kevin De Bruyne put Marouane Fellaini through but his shot was deflected by Miranda for a corner. It was from the corner that Belgium took the lead. Nacer Chadli's right-foot in-swinger caught Fernandinho on the bicep at the near post, giving Alisson in goal no chance (0-1). If the first goal had an element of luck about it, Belgium's second was pure class. From a Neymar corner, Fellaini headed clear at the near post. The ball was picked up by Romelu Lukaku, who turned and ran with the ball midway into the Brazil half before feeding the onrushing De Bruyne, who took it to the edge of the penalty area before firing home (0-2). It had taken 16 seconds and 14 touches after the corner to score.

The flow of the match changed in the second half as Brazil took the game to Belgium, but it wasn't until 73 minutes, when Renato Augusto reduced the deficit, that Brazil looked as if they could salvage the game (1-2). But in the end, Belgium hung on for a famous victory.

Uruguay at a loss without Cavani

6 JULY 2018

URUGUAY 0–2 **FRANCE**

VARANE 40, GRIEZMANN 61

THE SOUTH AMERICANS STRUGGLED without the injured Edinson Cavani, their two-goal hero from the previous round, and the game turned on a foul by Uruguay's Rodrigo Bentancur on Corentin Tolisso just outside the penalty area – fertile territory for an Antoine Griezmann free kick. When Griezmann cleverly checked his run before taking the kick, the Uruguay defence failed to respond to the delay and the ball found the onrushing Raphaël Varane in space (0-1). His glanced header crept just inside the far post. Then on the hour France doubled their lead with a goal that will haunt Fernando Muslera forever. Griezmann's shot, which was straight at Muslera, bounced off the keeper's arm and into the net (0-2).

▲ The Nizhny Novgorod Stadium during the quarter-final between Uruguay and France.

Grizou's Uruguay connections

France became the first team to beat four Southern Hemisphere teams at the same World Cup – Australia, Peru, Argentina and Uruguay.

Antoine Griezmann was conflicted after scoring against Uruguay. "I didn't celebrate because when I started out in football I was taught by someone from Uruguay (Chory Castro at Real Sociedad) who taught me the good and bad of football. I have respect for Uruguay. I love the Uruguayan culture and people." Griezmann has also formed a close friendship with his Atlético Madrid team-mate Diego Godín, the Uruguay captain, who is godfather to Griezmann's daughter.

◥ Antoine Griezmann enjoying *mate*, a traditional South American drink.

▼ Another set-piece goal for England: Harry Maguire opens the scoring against Sweden.

Harry to the rescue

7 JULY 2018

SWEDEN 0–2 **ENGLAND**

MAGUIRE 30, ALLI 59

NOT UNTIL THE 18TH MINUTE did the English attack get the better of the massed Swedish defensive ranks, with Harry Kane shooting just wide from outside the box. Kane wasn't able to add to his six goals in this match, but as one English commentator said "If one Harry doesn't get you, the other will". And that's what happened on the half-hour when Harry Maguire scored his first goal for England, climbing above Emil Forsberg to head home from a corner (0-1). Raheem Sterling should have made it 2-0 when clean through just before half-time but there was a vital touch by Robin Olsen in the Swedish goal.

Then in the second half, something of a rarity at this World Cup – an England goal from open play. With the ball circling around the penalty area, Kieran Trippier found Jesse Lingard, who with his first touch sent the ball over to the far post, where Dele Alli headed home having got ahead of Emil Krafth (0-2). In the end it looked rather easy for England but Jordan Pickford had been in outstanding form again, making three vital saves – one from Viktor Claesson and twice from Marcus Berg. For England, it meant a first semi-final since Italia '90.

Umtiti wins it

5

The number of World Cups in which all four semi-finalists have come from Europe – 1934, 1966, 1982, 2006 and 2018. In recent years, the balance of power in world football has shifted markedly to Europe. Of the 16 semi-final places at stake from 2006 to 2018, Europe claimed 13 of them with just Uruguay in 2010, and Argentina and Brazil in 2014, getting in on the act.

▲ Samuel Umtiti scores the goal that sends France into the Final.

▼ Former French international Thierry Henry was Belgium's assistant coach during the finals.

10 JULY 2018

FRANCE ▮ ▮ 1–0 ▮ ▮ BELGIUM

UMTITI 51

I N THE END IT CAME DOWN TO game management. A goal from a corner was all that separated the two teams in a tight and tense encounter. Belgium started the better, and for the first half an hour were in control. Eden Hazard continued to probe and test the French defence, and on 19 minutes his goal-bound shot was steered over the crossbar by Raphaël Varane. Two minutes later, Hugo Lloris saved well to deny Toby Alderweireld. But France edged their way back into the game in the last 15 minutes of the half. Olivier Giroud shot wide and then, having been put through by Kylian Mbappé, Benjamin Pavard's shot was deflected across the face of the goal by the leg of Thibaut Courtois.

Belgium went on the attack from the restart. Lukaku had a chance but moments later a Giroud shot was deflected wide for a corner by Vincent Kompany. Antoine Griezmann's left-foot inswinger was met by Samuel Umtiti, who got his head to the ball before Marouane Fellaini (1-0). There was nothing Courtois could do except fall backwards. The French were beginning to match the English as masters of the set piece.

That was pretty much the end of the

game as a spectacle. Game management kicked in. The French were content to sit deep and exploit their undoubted prowess on the break. But there was little for Mbappé to feed on. A nice backheel put Giroud through, but his shot was blocked by Mousa Dembélé. And there was little the Belgians could do to break down the barriers. A rasping shot by Axel Witsel was parried by Lloris and that was about it.

Courtois was dejected in defeat. "The team in front of us has defended well with 11 players 35 metres in front of their goal. And they've done that the whole tournament. Against Uruguay, they scored with a free kick. Today, a goal from a corner. A pity, but that's football." The Belgians missed the suspended Thomas Meunier and the balance he brought to the team, and too often Kevin De Bruyne found himself in areas of the pitch where his influence was less effective. He had had a superb tournament and was more forgiving than Courtois. "At Manchester City I play against teams that play so defensively 90 per cent of the time. That is football. What France do, they do well. Both teams had opportunities. That one goal makes the difference."

1st

Russia 2018 was the first World Cup in which the semi-finals did not feature at least one of Brazil, Argentina or Germany.

Thierry Henry

There were mixed emotions for Thierry Henry during the semi-final between France and Belgium. As part of the Belgian coaching staff in Russia, Henry had played with Didier Deschamps in the 1998 World Cup team. "It's bizarre" said Deschamps. "He's French but he will be on the opponent's bench!"

Croatia surpass their class of '98

11 JULY 2018

CROATIA 🇭🇷 2–1 A.E.T ➕ **ENGLAND**

PERIŠIĆ 68, MANDŽUKIĆ 109   TRIPPIER 5

THIS WAS A GAME OF TWO HALVES with England in control in the first, but after that it was almost one-way traffic for Croatia. After just five minutes, Dele Alli was brought down by Luka Modrić on the edge of the penalty arc and Kieran Trippier curled the resulting free kick over the wall and past Danijel Subašić (0-1). England had chances to extend their lead in the first half but failed to capitalise.

In the second half, Croatia pegged back Trippier and Ashley Young, England's wing backs, forcing England into a back five, allowing them to take control of midfield. Modrić and Ivan Rakitić rarely let the English out of their own half, recovering every loose ball and feeding both Ivan Perišić and Ante Rebić out wide. It was from the right wing that Croatia equalised after 69 minutes. Šime Vrsaljko's cross was met by Perišić, who twisted to score with an acrobatic volley past Jordan Pickford (1-1). England were now clinging on and twice Croatia came close to clinching the match in normal time.

In the first period of extra time, Vrsaljko cleared a John Stones header off the line, but with Croatia contemplating a third penalty shoot-out, Perišić found Mandžukić to score the winner (2-1).

▲ Mario Mandžukić scores Croatia's winning goal against England.

⌐ While celebrating the goal, the Croatia players fall on Mexican photographer Yuri Cortez.

◀ Cortez managed to take photos before being swamped.

▶ Belgium celebrate their historic third-place finish.

PLAY-OFF FOR THIRD PLACE

A first third place for Belgium

14 JULY 2014

BELGIUM 🇧🇪 2–0 ➕ **ENGLAND**

MEUNIER 4, E HAZARD 82

Just three minutes in, a trademark Belgium move started with Courtois. Five touches and 11 seconds later, the ball was nestling in the back of the England net. Chadli headed on the keeper's clearance and received the ball back from Lukaku before crossing for Meunier to slide the ball home – the tenth different scorer at this World Cup for the Belgians (1-0). Kane shot wide when it seemed easier to score and Dier had a shot cleared off the line, but this was Belgium's day. Eden Hazard's goal shortly before the end and took his side's tally to 16 (2-0). Only Brazil in 2002 and Germany in 2014 with 18 goals had scored more since 1970.

Boots worn by Ivan Perišić

Perišić scored Croatia's equaliser in the semi-final against England while wearing these boots.

▲ FIFA World Football Museum collection.

France reign supreme in Moscow

15 JULY 2018

FRANCE 🇫🇷 4–2 🇭🇷 **CROATIA**

MANDŽUKIĆ (O.G.) 18, GRIEZMANN 38 (PEN), POGBA 59, MBAPPE 65   PERIŠIĆ 28, MANDŽUKIĆ 69

ONCE AGAIN, France had Antoine Griezmann to thank for getting them into a match. Sensing a challenge from Marcelo Brozović in a dangerous position, he won a soft free-kick. Croatia were unhappy at the decision, but they defended far too deep and when Griezmann floated the ball in, it came off the top of Mandžukić's head, leaving Subašić with neither the time nor the space to react (1-0). Totally against the run of play, France suddenly found themselves a goal ahead after 18 minutes.

It took a great saving tackle from Vida to stop Mbappé shortly after, but ten minutes after going behind Croatia were level, the omnipresent Perišić controlling the ball with his right foot and firing home with his left (1-1). And then came the moment that changed the game. From a France corner, Blaise Matuidi got in front of Perišić and the ball went from head to hand in a split-second. The French appealed and after consulting with VAR, referee Néstor Pitana gave a controversial penalty. Was it deliberate? Was there movement of the hand to the ball? Griezmann duly scored from the spot and the French went into the break 2-1 ahead.

Not since the first Final in 1930 had a team losing at half-time fought back to win, and the spirit of the Croatians appeared to have been dimmed. A fine save by Lloris prevented an equaliser, but on the hour Pogba started and finished one of the moves of the tournament. Deep in his own half, he unleashed a pinpoint 55-metre first-time pass into the path of Mbappé. Via Griezmann the ball came back to Pogba, who had sprinted to the edge of the penalty area to score – the first goal in a Final from outside the penalty area since Marco Tardelli's in 1982 (3-1).

Six minutes later, France were 4-1 up and cruising to the title. Pogba found Lucas Hernández on the left touchline who squared the ball to Mbappé 25 metres out. His shot was perfectly placed, with Subašić unsighted by Vida as the Frenchman became the first teenager to score in a Final since Pelé in 1958. There was some consolation for Croatia when Mandžukić was the beneficiary of yet another goalkeeping howler, this time from Lloris, but it was too little, too late (4-2).

And then there were three...

At Russia 2018, Didier Deschamps became the third member of an exclusive club of people to have won the World Cup as both a player and a coach, joining Mário Zagallo and Franz Beckenbauer. With Beckenbauer, he is part of an even more exclusive club – both have won it as a captain and a coach.

◤ Mario Mandžukić scores the first ever own goal in a World Cup Final, giving France a 1-0 lead.

Mbappé and the academy boys

THERE CAN BE LITTLE DOUBT that the seeds of victory for the 1998 and 2018 World Cups were sown on the playing fields of Clairefontaine and the 13 other elite academies spread across France. Since the 1970s, they have produced player after player, with Kylian Mbappé just the latest. It is a system much imitated around the world, but the French have had 40 years to refine and perfect the workings of it and the results are certainly impressive. From 1974 to 2018, Brazil appeared in three of the 12 Finals played. In 2018, however, France reached their third Final in the last six tournaments. But there was a word of warning for Mbappé from Deschamps. "When I won the World Cup as a player in 1998, I had two 19-year-old team-mates, Thierry Henry and David Trezeguet. We also thought they would win more World Cups. But no. We must take the opportunity when it comes."

Kick-off ball for the Final

The Telstar 18 used during the group stage of the 2018 FIFA World Cup was replaced by the Telstar Mechta for the knockout rounds.

▼ FIFA World Football Museum collection.

▲ Kylian Mbappé – the first teenager to score in a Final since Pelé in 1958.

◢ Paul Pogba celebrates scoring his side's third goal in the Final.

4

Only four teenagers have played in a World Cup Final – Rubén Morán in 1950 for Uruguay; Pelé in 1958 for Brazil; Giuseppe Bergomi for Italy in 1982; and Kylian Mbappé for France in 2018. And all four won.

Luka Modrić

Modrić was appearing in his eleventh major Final and he had won all previous ten of them. All good runs have to come to an end at some point, but there was consolation for the Croatia captain when he was later named as The Best FIFA Men's Player as well as *France Football*'s Ballon d'Or for 2018. In his acceptance speech for The Best, he paid tribute to the Croatia team that reached the semi-finals of France '98. "That team gave us belief that we could achieve something great in Russia. Hopefully we can be the same for next generations."

6

The number of appearances in the Final of the World Cup for countries with a population of under ten million. In 2018, Croatia were the first to do so since Sweden in 1958, and only they and Uruguay have achieved that feat with less than five million inhabitants.

Uruguay	1930	1.7m
Uruguay	1950	2.2m
Croatia	2018	4.2m
Sweden	1958	7.4m
Hungary	1938	9.1m
Hungary	1954	9.7m

Pogba the orator

Paul Pogba was a vocal member of the French team, noted for giving pep talks to encourage his team-mates. Usually they were delivered in flamboyant fashion. But before the Final he changed his tone. In a measured and calm voice, he gave the speech of a lifetime. "We have played I don't know how many games in our lives, but this is the match, it changes everything. It changes the whole story. I want this evening to remain in the memories of all the French people watching us. Their children, their grandchildren, and their grandchildren too. Today, there are 90 minutes for us to make history for life. For life, guys. Now I'm looking at you, I'm not going to scream, I want us to go onto the pitch as leaders, as warriors, and then I want to see tears; not tears of sadness, but tears of joy."

FIFA WORLD
FOOTBALL MUSEUM

www.fifamuseum.com

O PENED IN FEBRUARY 2016, the FIFA World Football Museum sits in the heart of Zurich, opposite Zürich Enge railway station and five minutes walk from the lake. With a mission to preserve and celebrate the rich heritage of association football, it has over 1000 exhibits across three floors. The museum is divided into four main halls which in total equate to the size of a football pitch. **Planet Football** celebrates the 211 member associations of FIFA through our *Rainbow of National Team Shirts* and our *Timeline of World Football*. The second gallery is called **The Foundations**, which describes the early years of the game and how it established itself across the world. In **The FIFA World Cup Gallery**, every World Cup is showcased – men's and women's – with historic artefacts and state of the art interactive displays. This gallery is the new home of the *FIFA World Cup Trophy* and the *FIFA Women's World Cup Trophy*, both of which are on permanent display at the entrance to the gallery. After watching an eight-minute film in our 180° **Cinema**, glass lifts take you to the final gallery, called **Fields of Play**, an area dedicated to football's influence on people around the world, revealing how the game inspires and entertains in equal measure.

The FIFA World Cup Gallery is the historic heart of the museum and pride of place goes to the *FIFA World Cup trophy* at the entrance to the gallery. From 1974 until 2016, Gazzanigga's masterpiece was kept securely locked in a Zürich bank vault in-between World Cups, but is now on permanent display while not on World Cup duty. It sits opposite the *FIFA Women's World Cup Trophy* in a gallery which also features the *FIFA Wall of Champions*, a display where World Champions can sign their name. Each World Cup is marked with a showcase displaying a newly commissioned poster telling the story of the tournament and featuring unique artefacts from each tournament. From the 1930 showcase displaying the silver medal awarded to Guillermo Stabile, the top scorer in the first finals; to the tracksuit top worn by Thomas Müller before Germany's semi-final against Brazil in 2014, the story of every World Cup is told through objects, words, images and film. Interactive stations let you explore the history of the balls, the posters, and the shirts that have featured in the World Cup since 1930. And there are games to play such as testing your refereeing skills as well as seeing if you can master some of the more famous goal celebrations in the Soccer Dance area. At the end of the gallery is a 180° **Cinema** in which visitors can watch a film called *The Final*, featuring highlights of World Cup Finals.

The FIFA World Football Museum features a number of priceless exhibits from football's past including all that remains of the Jules Rimet Cup, created by Abel Lafleur for the first World Cup in 1930. A bigger Lapis Lazuli base, with room for more names, replaced the original in 1958. And now, the original lapis lazuli base can be seen in **The Foundations**, along with the first minute book of the International Football Association Board from 1886, and the draft Laws of the Game, handwritten by Sir Stanley Rous in 1934. The museum also contains one of the largest collections of football books with over 10,000 items, many of them housed on site in **The Library** situated on the second floor, where researchers can also book access to view the publicly available documents within the **FIFA Archive**. In the **Fields of Play** Gallery, are housed a number of unique objects, from the smallest trophy ever made in world football to the oldest football artefact of the Museum – a 2000 year old sculpture of a mesoamerican figure holding a ball. Throughout the museum there are 60 screens showing over 500 videos, including the giant ten by eight metre screen in **Planet Football**.

1. The Rainbow of national team shirts
2. The Foundations
3. The Jules Rimet Trophy with the original Abel Lafleur base
4. The FIFA World Cup Gallery
5. The FIFA Women's World Cup Trophy
6. The FIFA World Cup Gallery
7. Fields of Play

Picture Credits

The publishers would like to thank the following sources for their kind permission to reproduce the pictures in this book. Location indicator: t=top, b=bottom, l=left, r=right, c=centre.

A Bola: /Nuno Ferrari: 102bl. **Action Images:** 210tl; /Carlos Barria/Reuters: 277br; /Andrew Boyers: 268; /Michæl Craig/Sporting Pictures: 234t; /Scott Heavey: 281t; /Yves Herman/Reuters: 275tl; /Gary Hershorn/Reuters: 214r; /Nick Kidd/Sporting Pictures: 198tl, 202tr; /Chris Lobina/Sporting Pictures: 230tl; /Tony Marshall/Sporting Pictures: 177tr; /Dylan Martinez/Reuters: 240tr, 290bl; /Jeff Mitchell/Reuters: 210r; /Alex Morton: 263tl; /Sergio Perez/Reuters: 243bl; /Kai Pfaffenbach/Reuters: 265tl, 266tr, 276l, 279tl, 299bl; /Stefano Rellandini/Reuters: 292c; /Murad Sezer/Reuters: 290tr, 291tr; /John Sibley: 244tl; /Sporting Pictures: 147tr; /Paulo Whitaker/Reuters: 260tl. **ANSA:** /DPA: 169br; /EPA/STR: 116r. **British Newspaper Archive:** 9. **FIFA Archive:** 2, 5, 10, 12, 17tl, 27tl, 39tl, 51tl, 61tl, 61l, 61bl, 61bc, 73tl, 73l, 73r, 73b, 84r, 85tc (logo), 85c (Estadio Carlos Dittborn), 85b (Estadio Braden Cooper Co.), 97tl (mascot & logo), 102c, 111tl (mascot & logo), 125tl (mascot & logo), 139tl (mascot & logo), 155tl (mascot & logo), 173tl (mascot & logo), 173l, 173r, 173bl, 173br, 189tl (mascot & logo), 207tl (mascot & logo), 223tl (mascot & logo), 223l, 223c, 239tl (mascot & logo), 239l, 239bc, 255tl (mascot & logo), 271tl (mascot & logo), 287tl (mascot & logo), 305tl (mascot & logo). **FIFA Museum:** 15, 16bl, 17tr, 21r, 23tr, 27tr, 30tr, 32l, 39tr, 44tr, 47r, 48, 51tr, 51r, 55tl, 57tr, 60bl, 61tr, 61r, 65tr, 69t, 73tr, 78tl, 81bl, 84l, 85tr, 85r, 88l, 91tr, 96, 97tr, 97br, 100r, 111tr, 111c, 115tl, 117r, 117br, 119tr, 125tr, 127l, 135tl, 138, 139tr, 139br, 141bl, 150l, 155tr, 159tr, 160br, 166br, 168bl, 173tr, 177tl, 179bc, 185tc, 189tr, 195tr, 197tl, 199tr, 207tr, 210bl, 223tr, 227tr, 230tr, 234bl, 239tr, 239br, 246l, 251tr, 255tr, 256bl, 259bl, 267r, 271tr, 274c, 279tr, 283r, 287tr, 294bl, 298br, 301tr, 305tr, 307tl, 308l, 311br, 315bc, 317tr, 318, 319tl, 319tr, 319l, 319c, 319r, 319bl, 319br; /Leonidas Collection: 39tc; / Faouzi Mahjoub Archive: 140bl; /Pozzo Collection: 24, 25, 26, 27l, 27c, 27bl, 28tl, 29tr, 30tl, 31, 32tl, 32tr, 34, 35tr, 35c, 35bl, 35br, 36, 39b, 40tr, 42tl, 42tr, 42bc, 42br, 45tr, 46, 47tr, 47bl, 47br, 49, 50bl, 51l, 52tr, 52bl, 54bl, 77tr; /Sport Archive: 23r, 54tr, 55r, 55bl, 58, 68tl, 68tr, 85tc (Albert & Sánchez), 85c (Estadio Sausalito), 93br, 97bl, 97bc, 107tr, 111r, 130br, 155r, 155bl. **Gazzetta dello Sport:** 291tl. **Getty Images:** 17bl, 237bc; /AFP: 45bl, 45br, 51tc, 64tr, 129tl, 155bc, 172r, 182r, 184r, 194tr, 200t, 267tr; /AMA/Corbis: 271br; /Allsport: 151br, 191tr, 198bl; / Nelson Almeida/AFP: 285; /Vincent Amalvy/AFP: 209r; /Odd Andersen/AFP: 267br; /The Asahi Shimbun: 247l; /Nicolas Asfouri/AFP: 264bl, 264tr; /Brian Bahr: 248br; /Lars Baron/FIFA: 287r, 296l, 301br, 309tr, 311l, 312tl, 314br, 315r, 316t; /Remi Benali/Gamma-Rapho: 206; /Gunnar Berning/Bongarts: 242tl, 245tr; /Bettmann: 83; /Bongarts: 189br, 190br; /Lutz Bongarts/Bongarts: 213tc, 255l, 255c, 255bc; /Shaun Botterill: 244tr, 260r; /Shaun Botterill/Allsport: 207l; / Shaun Botterill/FIFA: 273tr, 284, 299r, 300t, 300br; /Marcus Brandt/AFP: 263r; /Paul Buck/AFP: 212br; /David Cannon: 207c, 239tc, 241bl, 241br; /David Cannon/Allsport: 212tl; /Central Press: 30br; /Central Press/Hulton Archive: 99tl, 100br; /Derrick Ceyrac/AFP: 171; /Robert Cianflone: 261br, 271tc (Müller), 298tl; /Robert Cianflone/FIFA: 316r; /Timothy A Clary/AFP: 258c; /Phil Cole: 257bc; /Max Colin/Onze/Icon Sport: 163bl; /contrast/Behrendt/ullstein bild: 266tl; /Yuri Cortez/AFP: 315bl; /Kevin C Cox: 314t; /Carl de Souza/AFP: 271tc (Forlan); /Jacques Demarthon/ AFP: 248tr; /Adrian Dennis/AFP: 259tl; /Stephen Dunn/Allsport: 207tc (Salenko); /Fairfax Media: 254; /Tony Feder/Allsport: 222; /Jonathan Ferrey: 258tr; /FIFA: 305c, 305bl, 305br; /Franck Fife/ AFP: 269, 274l, 291br; /Julian Finney: 297bl; /Fox Photos/Hulton Archive: 107tl; /Stuart Franklin/FIFA: 287tc, 287c, 305bc; /Daniel Garcia/AFP: 199tl, 217br, 219tl, 221; /Jack Garofalo/Patrick Jarnoux/Paris Match: 158t, 158bl, 167bl; /Paul Gilham/FIFA: 272tr, 277tr; /Laurence Griffiths: 241tr, 259r, 289bl; /Alex Grimm/FIFA: 294t, 295tr; /Jorge Guerrero/AFP: 308bl; /Pascal Guyot/AFP: 238; /Haynes Archive/Popperfoto: 16r, 63; /Alexander Heimann/Bongarts: 256br; /Patrick Hertzog/AFP: 208l, 209l, 235bl; /Mike Hewitt: 4; /Mike Hewitt/FIFA: 271tc (Sneijder), 271c (Mbombela Stadium), 271l, 274br, 292tl, 293tl, 297br, 306bl, 308tr, 308br, 311tr, 313br; / Maja Hitij/FIFA: 306br; /Simon Hofmann/FIFA: 306r, 306bc; /Horstmüller/ullstein bild: 128tl; /Philippe Huguen/AFP: 247tr; /Hulton Archive: 97tc, 97l; /Imagno: 37; /Tom Jenkins: 263br; / Keystone: 153; /Keystone-France/Gamma-Keystone: 44tl; /Mike King/Allsport: 183tr; /Ross Kinnaird: 241r; /Christof Kœpsel: 271tc (Villa); /Christof Kœpsel/Bongarts: 259br; /Patrick Kovarik/ AFP: 230br; /Philippe Le Tellier/Paris Match: 70, 80tr, 95; /Streeter Lecka: 275br; /Christopher Lee: 296r; /Alex Livesey: 249tl, 252; /Alex Livesey/FIFA: 298tl, 299tl, 301c; /Dimitri Lundt/Corbis/VCG: 232tl; /Jœl Mabanglo/AFP: 209bl, 213l; /John MacDougall/AFP: 278bl; /Joosep Martinson/FIFA: 305l, 312r, 315tl; /Jamie McDonald: 278t; /Damien Meyer/AFP: 245br, 251br; /Ryan Pierse/FIFA: 283tl; /Jan Pitman/Bongarts: 261tl; /Mikhail Pochuyev/TASS: 303; /Jœrn Pollex: 276tr; /Paul Popper/Popperfoto: 224tl; /Popperfoto: 11, 14, 17tc, 19tl, 21tl, 23tl, 23bl, 50r, 56tl, 75tl, 76tr, 77r, 82, 85tc (Vavá), 85br, 86tl, 89tl, 90tr, 91tl, 93bl, 105tl, 115tr, 116tl, 116tr, 119tl, 120l, 136, 151tl, 228r, 232br; /Mike Powell: 207bl, 216tr; /Jerome Prevost/TempSport/Corbis/ VCG: 227tl, 233tl; /Alfredo Quant/AFP: 110; /Ben Radford/Allsport: 219bl, 231tr, 239bl; /David Ramos/FIFA: 305tc, 317bl; /Michæl Regan/FIFA: 7, 302, 306tl, 307r, 308r, 310tr, 313tr, 315l, 317tl, 317br; /Andreas Rentz/Bongarts: 240tl, 246tr, 251bc; /David Rogers: 271c (Moses Mabhida Stadium); /Rolls Press/Popperfoto: 98tr, 100tl, 106t, 115bl, 117tl, 142tl; /Emilio Ronchini/Mondadori Portfolio: 71; /Quinn Rooney: 288bl; /Clive Rose: 301tl; /Martin Rose/Bongarts: 253; / Vladimir Rys/Bongarts: 265r; /STF/AFP: 271b; /STR/AFP: 28tr; /Mark Sandten/Bongarts: 229br; /Issouf Sanogo/AFP: 257l; /Jürgen Schwarz/AFP: 255bl; /Patrick Smith/FIFA: 313L; /Jamie Squire/ FIFA: 277tl, 310br; /Michæl Steele: 257tl, 276tl; /Billy Stickland/Allsport: 196tl, 201tl; /Patrik Stollarz/AFP: 262tl, 265tr; /Henri Szwarc/Bongarts: 194tl, 219l, 226l; /Team 2/Sportphoto/ullstein bild: 262br; /Bob Thomas: 154, 155tc, 157tl, 161tl, 161br, 162t, 165tl, 167br, 168l, 169t, 173tc, 176br, 177bl ,179br, 180tl, 181br, 192br, 193tl, 193bl, 195tl, 197tr, 203l, 208tr, 208r, 208bl, 210tr, 211t, 214c, 215bc, 219tr, 245bl, 251tl, 266l; /Bob Thomas/Popperfoto: 6, 13, 17br, 18tl, 18br, 19tr, 20tl, 20tr, 23br, 29r, 56tr, 57b, 64tl; /Omar Torres/AFP: 211bl, 217bc; /Tony Triolo/Sports Illustrated: 107br; /Pedro Ugarte/AFP: 224r; /ullstein bild: 53r, 59, 60tr, 67r, 69r; /View Pictures/ UIG: 189b; /Jeff Vinnick: 176bl; /Friedemann Vogel/FIFA: 287l, 287b; /Chris Wilkins/AFP: 218tr. **IOC Museum:** 8. **Iconsport:** /Michel Barrault: 155l; /Aldo Liverani: 195br. **Imago:** /ActionPictures: 288t; /AFLOSPORT: 187, 201br, 249br; /Alternate: 207br; /Edu Andrade/Urbanandsport/ Cordon Press: 291r; /Oliver Behrendt: 223tc, 232r; /Buzzi: 180tr, 218tl, 244r; /CTK Photo: 27tc, 33tl; /Camera 4: 223br, 228br, 231bl, 241r, 245tl, 246bl; /Chen Cheng/Xinhua: 307bl; /Paul Chesterton/Focus Images: 309tl; /Matteo Ciambelli/ZUMA Press: 304; /Colorsport: 126bl, 147tl, 147l, 159l, 164l, 168br, 175tr, 177bc, 213br, 224tr; /Aleksander Djorovic: 286; /Eissner/Kicker: 188; /Bruno Fahy: 295bl; /Fotoarena: 283bl; /Frinke: 125bc, 156bl; /HJS: 216bl; /Ferdi Hartung: 61tc, 126tr, 185bl, 189c (Giuseppe Meazza, San Siro); /Frank Hœrmann/Sven Simon: 309bl; / Horstmüller: 73tc, 75bl, 79tl, 85tc (Ivanov), 85b (Estadio Nacional), 92tr, 125bl, 133l, 139l, 139c, 156t; /ImagePhoto/Gribaudi: 283br; /Kyodo News: 250tl, 310tl; /Liedel/Kicker: 173l, 174tr, 174r, 174bl, 179tl; /Uwe Kraft: 227br; /Marcelo Machado de Melo: 299br; /Magic: 128l; /Roberto Maya: 297tl; /Metelmann/Kicker: 103br, 113tr; /Werner Otto: 125l; /PanoramiC: 134tl, 242tr, 243tr, 274tl; /Laci Perenyi: 184tl, 184tr, 185br, 202tl, 214tr, 214l, 280br; /Pressefoto Baumann: 104tl, 104tr, 107r, 126tl, 131bl, 132tr, 133tl, 134tr, 140tl, 140tr, 140l, 142r, 143tl, 144tl, 144tr, 146tl, 148tl, 148tr, 149br, 150tl, 191tl, 257br; /Norbert Schmidt: 190r, 200br, 214tl, 218br; /Sven Simon: 85tc (Garrincha), 102t, 111l, 117tr, 118t, 120tr, 121tr, 121bc, 137, 139bc, 142tr, 143b, 146tr, 163br, 165tr, 167tr, 174c, 178tr, 192t, 195bl, 225tr, 232tr, 243tl, 249tr, 280t; /Sportfoto Rudel: 145bl, 150tr, 160t, 163tl, 166tl; /Team 2: 256tl; /Ulmer/PUX: 272tl, 275tr; /United Archives International: 81tr, 87, 106bl; /VI Images: 172tl; /Werek: 111tc, 114l, 119br, 120tl, 125tc, 125c, 127bl, 128tr, 130tr, 130r, 131tl, 132tl, 132l, 133tr, 135r, 139r, 143c, 145tr, 149tl, 157tr, 159br, 166l, 174l, 175b, 178bl, 179r, 182t, 183tl, 189tc, 189c (Olimpico), 189l, 196br, 197l, 203bl, 205, 207tc (Stoichkov), 211br, 213r, 215t, 216r, 216br, 225bl, 226tr, 229c, 233tr, 233br; /Xinhua: 280r, 282, 292br; /Thomas Zimmermann: 139tc; /ZUMA Press/Keystone: 129tr. **Keystone:** /Interfoto/Lookback: 126bc; /Walter Scheiwiller: 62. **Mirrorpix:** 109, 114tl, 159bc; /Daily Mirror: 94, 101t; /Monte Fresco: 98tl, 129br; /Irish Daily Mirror: 270; /John Varley: 113tl. **Newsweek Media Group:** 208tl. **Offside Sports Photography:** /Archivi Farabola: 69c, 89tr; /Best Photo Agency: 57tl; /Bildbyran/Witters: 81l; /Sebastien Boue/Presse Sports: 289t, 295c, 296tl; /Patrick Boutroux/André Lecoq/ Jean-Claude Pichon/Presse Sports: 170, 176tl; /Patrick Boutroux/Robert Legros/Jean-Claude Pichon/Presse Sports: 184bl, 185l; /Patrick Boutroux/Jean-Claude Pichon/Presse Sports: 181tl; /Gerry Cranham: 103tr, 112tl; /Alain de Martignac/Presse Sports: 217tl, 235tr, 247br; /Didier Fevre/Presse Sports: 258bl; /Fonds Excelsior/Presse Sports: 38, 39r, 40tl, 41, 43tr, 45tl; /Hans Dietrich Kaiser/Witters: 77bl, 88tr, 90l, 114tr, 121tl, 121r; /Pierre Lahalle/Presse Sports: 255tc; / Alain Landrain/Presse Sports: 186, 196tr, 203r; /Richard Le Moël/Presse Sports: 181tr; /André Lecoq/Presse Sports: 85tc (Jerković), 86tr, 90tl, 92tl, 93tr, 203t; /Mark Leech: 203br, 212tr, 215r, 223bc, 228tl; /Robert Legros/Presse Sports: 191br; /Marca: 260tc, 260c; /Richard Martin/Presse Sports: 293tr; /Jean-Claude Pichon/Presse Sports: 180br, 202r, 229t; /Presse Sports: 19c, 22, 39l, 39c, 43tl, 51c, 64r, 65tl, 66, 67bl, 72, 74tr, 76tl, 78tr, 78l, 79tr, 80tl, 81tl, 103tl, 103r, 118bl, 127t, 141tr, 144br, 156l, 162br, 164t, 165l, 166tr, 168tr, 168c, 183br, 236, 250bl; /Richiardi Foto/ Presse Sports: 264tl; /John Varley: 135tc, 135bl; /Witters: 123, 149tr, 225tl. **PA Images:** 105r; / Istvan Bajzat/DPA: 133tc; /DPA: 93tl, 122, 152, 167tl; /EMPICS Sport: 99tr, 101br; /Natascha Haupt/Werek/DPA: 125r; /Ross Kinnaird/EMPICS Sport: 198bc, 198br; /Peter Robinson/EMPICS Sport: 2c; /S&G and Barratts/EMPICS Sport: 99r; /Schirner Sportfoto Archive/DPA: 47tl, 86b; /Werner Schulze/DPA: 135l; /Sven Simon/DPA: 108; /Kirsty Wigglesworth: 242br. **Picture Alliance:** /Masao Goto Filho/Estadao Conteudo: 204; /Volkmar Hoffmann/DPA: 112r. **REX/Shutterstock:**/AP/REX: 225br, 250tr; /Luca Bruno/AP/REX: 283l; /Shizuo Kambayashi/AP/REX: 237br; /Alessandra Tarantino/AP/REX: 273br **silviogazzaniga.com:** 124. **Sony Music Entertainment**: /Epic Records: 273tl. **Topfoto:** /AP: 53tl; /Keystone/Imagno: 33r; /Roger Viollet: 29bl. **Ullstein bild:** 65br; /bpk/Hubmann: 69bl; /Camera 4: 263tr; /Ferdi Hartung: 74tl; /Firo: 220, 267tl; /Horstmüller: 129r; /Nagel/Sportbild: 235br; /Sven Simon: 148r, 281br; /Bernd Wende: 190tl, 190tr. **Wikimedia Commons:** 17c, 51bc

Every effort has been made to acknowledge correctly and contact the source and/or copyright holder of each picture and Welbeck Non-fiction Limited apologises for any unintentional errors or omissions that will be corrected in future editions of this book.